Communications
in Computer and Information Science   394

Editorial Board

Simone Diniz Junqueira Barbosa
Pontifical Catholic University of Rio de Janeiro (PUC-Rio),
Rio de Janeiro, Brazil

Phoebe Chen
La Trobe University, Melbourne, Australia

Alfredo Cuzzocrea
ICAR-CNR and University of Calabria, Italy

Xiaoyong Du
Renmin University of China, Beijing, China

Joaquim Filipe
Polytechnic Institute of Setúbal, Portugal

Orhun Kara
TÜBİTAK BİLGEM and Middle East Technical University, Turkey

Igor Kotenko
St. Petersburg Institute for Informatics and Automation
of the Russian Academy of Sciences, Russia

Krishna M. Sivalingam
Indian Institute of Technology Madras, India

Dominik Ślęzak
University of Warsaw and Infobright, Poland

Takashi Washio
Osaka University, Japan

Xiaokang Yang
Shanghai Jiao Tong University, China

Pavel Klinov   Dmitry Mouromtsev (Eds.)

Knowledge Engineering and the Semantic Web

4th International Conference, KESW 2013
St. Petersburg, Russia, October 7-9, 2013
Proceedings

 Springer

Volume Editors

Pavel Klinov
University of Ulm
Institute of Artificial Intelligence
89069 Ulm, Germany
E-mail: pavel.klinov@uni-ulm.de

Dmitry Mouromtsev
Saint Petersburg National Research University
of Information Technologies, Mechanics and Optics
Intelligence Systems Laboratory
197101 St. Petersburg, Russia
E-mail: d.muromtsev@gmail.com

ISSN 1865-0929   e-ISSN 1865-0937
ISBN 978-3-642-41359-9   e-ISBN 978-3-642-41360-5
DOI 10.1007/978-3-642-41360-5
Springer Heidelberg New York Dordrecht London

Library of Congress Control Number: Applied for

CR Subject Classification (1998): H.3, H.2, I.2, H.5

© Springer-Verlag Berlin Heidelberg 2013
This work is subject to copyright. All rights are reserved by the Publisher, whether the whole or part of the material is concerned, specifically the rights of translation, reprinting, reuse of illustrations, recitation, broadcasting, reproduction on microfilms or in any other physical way, and transmission or information storage and retrieval, electronic adaptation, computer software, or by similar or dissimilar methodology now known or hereafter developed. Exempted from this legal reservation are brief excerpts in connection with reviews or scholarly analysis or material supplied specifically for the purpose of being entered and executed on a computer system, for exclusive use by the purchaser of the work. Duplication of this publication or parts thereof is permitted only under the provisions of the Copyright Law of the Publisher's location, in ist current version, and permission for use must always be obtained from Springer. Permissions for use may be obtained through RightsLink at the Copyright Clearance Center. Violations are liable to prosecution under the respective Copyright Law.
The use of general descriptive names, registered names, trademarks, service marks, etc. in this publication does not imply, even in the absence of a specific statement, that such names are exempt from the relevant protective laws and regulations and therefore free for general use.
While the advice and information in this book are believed to be true and accurate at the date of publication, neither the authors nor the editors nor the publisher can accept any legal responsibility for any errors or omissions that may be made. The publisher makes no warranty, express or implied, with respect to the material contained herein.

Typesetting: Camera-ready by author, data conversion by Scientific Publishing Services, Chennai, India

Printed on acid-free paper

Springer is part of Springer Science+Business Media (www.springer.com)

Preface

These proceedings contain the papers accepted for oral presentation at the 4th Conference on Knowledge Engineering and Semantic Web (KESW 2013). The conference was held in St. Petersburg, Russia, October 7–9, 2013.

A large part of KESW's mission is integrating Russian researchers' in the areas related to the Semantic Web into the international research community. To this end, KESW 2013 made a giant leap towards the international standards for academic conferences. First, it was the first in the series that was held entirely in English. Second, all submissions were formally reviewed by at least two (three for the research track papers) PC members. The PC was truly international this year with many members having served on the PC for major conferences in the area. KESW 2013 featured a balanced trio of established academic and industrial keynote speakers. Last but not least, these proceedings have been published in Springer's CCIS series, which is unprecedented for Semantic Web conferences in Russia.

Of course, the aforementioned efforts would have had a lesser impact without a broad international participation. Fortunately, KESW 2013 enjoyed quite a lot of the latter: the authors of the accepted papers represented 11 different countries (with Russia and Germany contributing most papers). We are confident that the resulting dialogue will foster all sorts of exciting collaboration between Russian and foreign researchers to their mutual benefit.

It deserves to be mentioned that the movement towards international standards has not been entirely painless. In particular, less than 50% of all submitted contributions (25 out of 52) were accepted for the proceedings (which does not even account for incomplete submissions). Many authors, especially younger researchers, had their very first experience of writing a paper for such an event. We do hope that lessons will be learned and there will be more high-quality submissions in the next years.

18 papers out of the 25 accepted ones are full research or industry-focused publications. The other 7 are short system descriptions, which were specifically selected for publication since the Semantic Web is an application-oriented field. Some system description papers also explain how a particular system can be demonstrated to the attendees of the event.

Finally, we would like to express our gratitude to various people who made KESW 2013 possible. First, our thanks go to the authors of all submissions as well as to the PC members and the secondary reviewers for their efforts. Second, we thank our keynote speakers: Birte Glimm, Kendall Clark, and Peter Haase. Next, we are grateful to our sponsors whose support cannot be overestimated. Special thanks are extended to our Web designer Maxim Kolchin, the adminis-

tration of St. Petersburg, and the St. Petersburg State University of Information
Technologies, Mechanics and Optics for their support in organizing the event.

July 2013   Pavel Klinov
                                                          Dmitry Mouromtsev

Organization

Organizing Committee

General Chair

Dmitry Mouromtsev

St. Petersburg National Research University of Information Technologies, Mechanics and Optics, Russia

Program Chair

Pavel Klinov

University of Ulm, Germany

Program Committee

Sören Auer	University of Leipzig, Germany
Samantha Bail	University of Manchester, UK
Sergey Balandin	Finnish-Russian University Cooperation in Telecommunications, Finland
Igor Bessmertny	St. Petersburg National Research University of Information Technologies, Mechanics and Optics, Russia
Anastasia Bonch-Osmolovskaia	Moscow State University, Russia
Alexander Boukhanovsky	St. Petersburg National Research University of Information Technologies, Mechanics and Optics, Russia
Josep Maria Brunetti	University of Lleida, Spain
Kendall Clark	Clark & Parsia, USA
Chiara Del Vescovo	University of Manchester, UK
Ivan Ermilov	University of Leipzig, Germany
Timofey Ermilov	University of Leipzig, Germany
Rafael S. Gonçalves	University of Manchester, UK
Vladimir Gorovoy	St. Petersburg State University, Russia
Daniel Hladky	W3C Russia Office, Russia
Matthew Horridge	Stanford University, USA
Dmitry Ignatov	Higher School of Economics, Russia
Natalya Keberle	Zaporizhzhya National University, Ukraine
Ali Khalili	University of Leipzig, Germany
Evgeny Kharlamov	University of Oxford, UK
Jakub Klímek	Charles University in Prague, Czech Republic
Boris Konev	University of Liverpool, UK
Roman Kontchakov	Birkbeck College, UK
Markus Krötzsch	University of Oxford, UK

Dmitry Kudryavtsev   Business Engineering Group, Russia
Jose Emilio Labra Gayo   University of Oviedo, Spain
Thorsten Liebig   derivo GmbH, Germany
Natasha Noy   Stanford University, USA
Michail Panteleev   St. Petersburg State Electrotechnical
                            University, Russia
Bijan Parsia   University of Manchester, UK
Rafael Peñaloza   Dresden University of Technology, Germany
Svetlana Popova   St. Petersburg State University, and
                            St. Petersburg State Polytechnic University,
                            Russia
Olexandr Pospishniy   Kyiv Polytechnic Institute, Ukraine
Héctor Pérez-Urbina   Clark & Parsia, USA
Irina Radchenko   Higher School of Economics, Russia
Mariano Rodriguez-Muro   Free University of Bolzano, Italy
Valery Rubashkin   St. Petersburg State University, Russia
Felix Sasaki   DFKI / W3C Fellow, Germany
Thomas Scharrenbach   University of Zurich, Switzerland
Daria Stepanova   Vienna University of Technology, Austria
Darya Tarasowa   University of Leipzig, Germany
Julia Taylor   Purdue University, USA
Ioan Toma   STI Innsbruck, Austria
Dmitry Tsarkov   University of Manchester, UK
Jörg Unbehauen   University of Leipzig, Germany
Serge Yablonsky   St. Petersburg State University, Russia
Dmitriy Zheleznyakov   University of Oxford, Uk

Additional Reviewers

Ruslan Fayzrakhmanov   Hans-Gert Graebe
Alireza Khoshkbariha   Thomas Schneider
Mantas Šimkus

Sponsors

Platinum Sponsors

Russian Foundation for
Basic Research
STI Innsbruck

Gold Sponsors

Eventos

Silver Sponsors

LOD2

Table of Contents

Research and Industry Publications

System Description and Demo Publications

Experiments on Using LOD Cloud Datasets to Enrich the Content of a Scientific Knowledge Base

Zinaida Apanovich and Alexander Marchuk

A.P. Ershov Institute of Informatics Systems
Russian Academy of Sciences, Siberian Branch
6, Acad. Lavrentiev pr., Novosibirsk 630090, Russia
apanovich_09@mail.ru, mag@iis.nsk.su

Abstract. This paper describes the issues arising when employing the Linked Open Data (LOD) cloud datasets to enrich the content of a scientific knowledge base as well as the approaches to solving them. The experiments are carried out with the help of a toolkit intended to simplify the analysis and integration of data from different datasets. The toolkit comprises several tools for application-specific visualization. The dataset of the Open Archive of the Russian Academy of Sciences and several bibliographic datasets are used as test examples.

Keywords: linked open data, visualization, knowledge enrichment, Open Archive knowledge base.

1 Introduction

Due to the fast progress of Semantic Web and its rapidly developing branch, Linked Open Data, large amounts of structured information from various fields are becoming available on the Web. Nowadays the Web of Data contains more than 28 billion RDF triples. New applications arise that are trying to use information from different data sources.

One of the projects carried out at the A.P. Ershov Institute of Informatics Systems of the Siberian Branch of the Russian Academy of Sciences (IIS SB RAS) is aimed at enriching the Open Archive of the Siberian Branch of the Russian Academy of Sciences (SB RAS Open Archive, Open Archive)[1] [1, 2] with the data of the Open Linked Data cloud (LOD) [3]. A fragment of the Open Archive page devoted to Academician A.P. Ershov is shown in Fig. 1.

The structure of the Open Archive knowledge base is organized with the so-called Basic Ontology for Non-specific Entities (BONE). We are working on the enrichment of the Open Archive content with the data of various datasets of

---

[1] http://duh.iis.nsk.su/turgunda/Home

P. Klinov and D. Mouromtsev (Eds.): KESW 2013, CCIS 394, pp. 1–14, 2013.
© Springer-Verlag Berlin Heidelberg 2013

RKBExplorer[2] such as DBLP dataset[3], ACM dataset [4], CiteSeer dataset[5], etc. Their data sets are structured by the AKT reference ontology[6]

A four-step strategy for the integration of Linked Data into an application is proposed in [4]. This strategy consists of access to linked data, vocabularies (schema, ontology) normalization, identity resolution, and data filtering. There exist specialized tools for solving separate problems [5-8]. However, the greatest part of problems can be solved using a suitable set of SPARQL 1.1 queries. For these reasons, we use in our experiments a toolkit containing the previously developed ontology visualization program [9, 10]. This program is extended by various facilities for SPARQL queries processing. Several application specific tools such as citation networks visualization are also used in our experiments.

Fig. 1. A fragment of the Open Archive page devoted to Academician A.P. Ershov

1.1   Related Work

The three main areas of related work concern expressive properties of different ontologies, visual interfaces simplifying the task of integration of data from different data sets, and identity resolution.

The lack of relation attributes in the RDF model is a familiar problem. In particular, it is addressed in [11] with respect to temporal and spatial attributes of relations: "...it is crucial to capture the time periods during which facts happen". To handle this problem, an "SPO + Time + Location" model is proposed.

---

[2] http://www.rkbexplorer.com/

[3] http://dblp.rkbexplorer.com/

[4] http://acm.rkbexplorer.com/

[5] http://citeseer.rkbexplorer.com/

[6] http://www.aktors.org/ontology

In our point of view, the SPOTL model can be considered using additional classes for describing temporal and spatial aspects of facts implicitly whereas the BONE ontology uses additional classes with all the needed attributes explicitly.

The key problem faced by researchers working with ontology-based data sets integration is ontology understanding. A common way to facilitate ontology understanding is provided by graph visualization methods. There exist a huge number of publications devoted to this subject [12-14]. Most of them are summarized in the survey [15]. Our approach to ontology visualization addresses the problem mentioned in [15]: "The visualization of relation links is also problematic and the display becomes cluttered very quickly". Besides, the relation links visualization is becoming even more important in the Linked Open Data context since the *owl:ObjectProperty* links correspond to the RDF predicates used in the LOD data sets descriptions.

Another related issue is establishing correspondence between the entities of two ontologies. Matching algorithms are used to discover correspondences automatically. The process of refining these correspondences is facilitated by graphical mapping interfaces. A great number of papers is devoted to the ontology matching problem. For a comprehensive overview on ontology matching, we refer to a recent survey [16]. Some examples of tools with visual matching interfaces are: (Alviz [17], CogZ [18], AgreementMaker [19], OPTIMA [20]. A survey devoted to visual interfaces for ontology alignement is [21]. Nevertheless, according to [22] "...most ontology alignment systems are limited to detect simple equivalence or subsumption correspondences between single entities and research concentrates on improving their quality on various datasets more than on finding more complex matches. However, simple correspondences often are not sufficient to correctly represent the relation between the aligned entities". Due to the constructive features of the BONE ontology, a new correspondence pattern has been suggested making possible automatic generation of SPARQL queries.

As for the identity resolution problem, there exist several well-known link-discovering frameworks such as SILK [6] and LIMES [7] using different similarity measures. But our experiments with the datasets of RKBExplorer have shown that equivalence of strings that identify two person cannot guarantee the identity of these persons and additional methods should be developed.

1.2 Structure of the Paper

Section 2 demonstrates specific features of the BONE ontology and AKT Reference ontology. Their structures are compared and a strategy of links creation between the data sets based on these two ontologies is discussed. A SPARQL-query template for establishing correspondence between groups of classes and relations of the two ontologies is presented. Generation of SPARQL-queries based on the two ontologies visualization is demonstrated. The problem of identity resolution is discussed in Section 3. Section 4 demonstrates a tool for SPARQL-queries creation and visualization.

2   Comparison of BONE and AKT Reference Ontologies

The content of the SB RAS Open Archive provides various documents (photo documents mainly) reflecting information about people, research organizations and major events that have taken place in the SB RAS since 1957. The Open Archive contains information about the employments, research achievements, state awards, titles, and participation in conferences, academic and social events for each person mentioned in the Archive. The Open Archive has 20 505 photo documents, facts about 10 917 persons and 1519 organizations and events. The data sets of the Open Archive are available as an RDF triple store, as well as a Virtuoso endpoint[7] for the SB RAS Archive. Its RDF triple store comprises about 600 000 RDF triples.

The structure of the Open Archive knowledge base is organized with the so-called BONE Ontology, described in OWL and comprising 44 classes. Classes and relations of the BONE ontology are shown in Fig. 2.

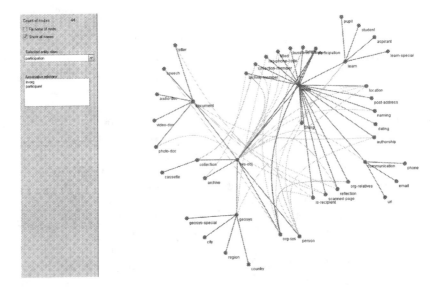

Fig. 2. Classes and relations of the BONE ontology

This figure demonstrates some specific features of the BONE ontology, as well as specific features of our approach to ontology visualization. The ontology visualization is constructed by the hierarchical edge bundles method [22]. Nodes correspond to ontology classes and edges correspond to ontology relations. Tree edges represent the *rdfs:subClassOf* links. They can be drawn either by a radial or circular tree drawing algorithm or by a layered drawing algorithm for directed graphs. Curvilinear edges represent the *owl:ObjectProperty* relationships and are laid out above the taxonomy drawing.

---

[7] http://duh.iis.nsk.su/VirtuosoEndpoint/Home/Samples

As the edge bundles method reduces the clutter, it is very well suited for the representation of the relation links. Moreover, different shape of edges depending on their type improves ontology comprehensibility. Additionally, we have significantly reduced the number of nodes in the ontology view by displaying only the class nodes. Visualization of the instances of classes is delegated completely to the SPARQL visualization component, since it is possible to obtain all the instances of any class with a simple query like this:

```
SELECT ?instance
WHERE { ?instance a Class-name }.
```

There exists a "Select class" list-box and an "Associative relations" drop-down list in the left part of the ontology visualization panel intended for the investigation of edges corresponding to the *owl: objectProperty*. When a user selects an item in the "Select class" list box, all the edges connecting the chosen class with other classes are displayed on the visualization panel. Simultaneously, the names of links incident to the selected class node are displayed in the "Associative relations" drop-down list. For example, the *bone:participation* class node selected in Fig. 2 has links connecting this node to the *bone:person* and *bone:org-sys* classes.

This visualization shows a specific feature of the BONE ontology: many entities usually described by means of relationships in other ontologies are described as instances of classes in the BONE ontology. This feature compensates the lack of attributes of the RDF predicates. For example, using the "from-date" and "to-date" properties of the *bone:participation* class, we are able to specify facts such as "Academician A.P. Ershov was the head of a department at the Institute of Mathematics SB AS from 1959 to 1964 and the head of a department at the Computing Center SB USSR AS from 1964 to 1988"[8]

For the same reasons, such classes as *bone:dating, bone:naming, bone:authorship* are used in the BONE ontology instead of predicates such as *akt:has-author akt:has-date* or *akts:has-pretty-name*, used in the AKT Reference ontology.

The Portal Ontology which is a part of the AKT reference ontology is shown in Fig. 3. This ontology is used for the description of bibliographic datasets of the LOD Cloud such as DBLP, CiteSeer, ACM, etc. We intend to use these datasets as a source of additional data for the Open Archive.

For example, we would like to extend the Open Archive knowledge base with information about the publications by the people who have previously worked at the A.P. Ershov Institute of Informatics Systems. For these purposes we need to establish mappings just between several classes and relations of the BONE ontology and the AKT Reference ontology.

For our experiments we do not need such a powerful ontology alignment tool as the Agreement Maker or a SPARQL query generation tool like the TopBraid Composer [9] . We have a tool of our own which can generate SPARQL-queries on the basis of the visualization of two ontologies.

---

[8] http://duh.iis.nsk.su/turgunda/home/ our own portrait?id=piu_200809051791
[9] http://www.topquadrant.com/products/TB_Composer.html

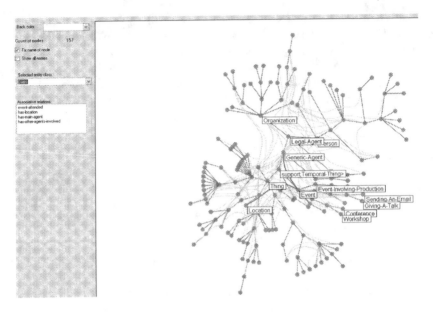

Fig. 3. Links of the "AKT-Event" class

There is an obvious correspondence between the *bone:person* and the *akt:Person* classes. Other correspondences are much less straightforward. To illustrate the problem, let us consider the *bone:participation* class which is used to specify the facts of someone's participation in various events like academic symposia or his/her affiliation to some organizations.

As shown in Fig. 2, this class is connected by the *bone:participant* links to the *bone:person* class and by the *bone:in-org* links to the *bone:org-sys* class. But in the AKT Reference ontology the same facts can be represented by several relationships. These can be the *akt:works-for* link between the *akt:Employee* and *akt:Organization* classes, the *akt:has-affiliation* link between the *akt:Person* and *akt:Organization* classes,the *akt:has-main-agent*, *akt:has-other-agents-involved* links between the *akt:Event* class and the *akt:Generic-Agent* class.

This means that there is no exact matching for the *bone:participation* class in the AKT Reference ontology. If, for example, it is necessary to translate information about people's jobs from the data sets of the RKBExplorer to the Open Archive, an instance of the *bone:participation* class should be generated for every "*akt:has-affiliation*" link between instances of the *akt:Person* and *akt:Organization* classes. The same rule should be applied to other BONE classes such as *bone:authorship*.

This implies that it is necessary to establish systematically correspondence between different groups of classes and relations of these two ontologies. More precisely, a correspondence between one or several groups of the form "Class1 - relation1 - Class2" of the AKT Reference ontology and one or several groups of the form "Class3 - relation2 - Class4 -relation3 - Class5" of the BONE ontology should be created. In particular, a new instance of the Class4 for every triple

<Class1:instance1, relation 1, Class2:instance2> should be created. This kind of translation can be carried out by an appropriate SPARQL-query.

A simplified template of a SPARQL query that generates instances of the Class4 is as follows:

```
PREFIX iis: <http://iis.nsk.su#>
PREFIX akt: <http://www.aktors.org/ontology/portal#>
PREFIX akts: <http://www.aktors.org/ontology/support#>
PREFIX rdfs: <http://www.w3.org/2000/01/rdf-schema#>
CONSTRUCT {
_:p a iis:Class4.
_:p iis:relation2 ?instance1.
_:p iis:relation3 ?instance2.
}
WHERE {
    ?instance1 akt:relation1 ?instance2.
    ?instance1 a akt:Class1.
    ?instance2 a akt:Class2.
}
```

In this template such elements as Class1, relation1 are empty positions which should be filled with the names of real classes and relations. Since the needed SPARQL-queries are rather tedious, we have created a program that can generate this kind of queries using the visualization of two ontologies. An example generating instances of the *bone:participation* class with respect to the *akt:has-affiliation* relation is shown in Fig. 4 The two ontologies are drawn side-by-side and several additional buttons are used to control the alignment process. When the "Fix matching" check box is activated we can choose groups of classes and relations for alignment in both visualization panels. The group "<Person> has-affiliation <Organization>" of the AKT Reference ontology is selected in the left panel and the group "<sys-obj> participant <participation> in-org <org-sys>" of the BONE ontology is selected in the right panel. A SPARQL query, that generates the instances of the *bone:participation* class is as follows:

```
PREFIX iis: <http://iis.nsk.su#>
PREFIX akt: <http://www.aktors.org/ontology/portal#>
PREFIX akts: <http://www.aktors.org/ontology/support#>
PREFIX rdfs: <http://www.w3.org/2000/01/rdf-schema#>
CONSTRUCT {
_:p a iis:participation.
_:p iis:participant ?instance1.
_:p iis:in-org ?instance2.
}
WHERE {
    ?instance1 akt:has-affiliation ?instance2.
    ?instance1 a akt:Person.
    ?instance2 a akt:Organization. }
```

A generic SPARQL endpoint[10] accepting SPARQL 1.1 queries has been used.

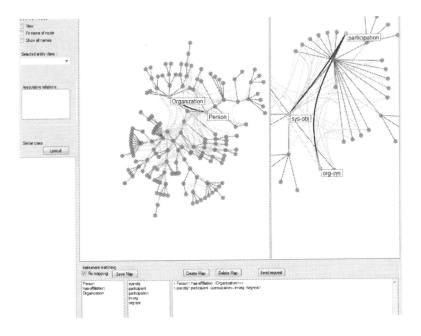

Fig. 4. Interactive matching between two groups of classes and relations

However, in order to use these queries effectively, we must select people described in the Open Archive from the RKBExplorer list. In other words, the identity resolution problem should be solved.

3   Identity Resolution Problem

The step of identity resolution is very important for enriching the Open Archive content. In the Open Archive all persons are specified by means of the *bone:name* attribute. The format of this attribute is <Last Name, First Name Middle Name>. This attribute has two options: the Russian-language version and the English-language version. The English version is a transliteration of the Russian version.

The datasets of RKBExplorer use the *akt:full-name* attribute, and there are many variants of the *akt:full-name* attribute for every instance of the Open Archive, for example, <First Name Last Name>, <First Name First letter of the Middle Name Last Name> <First letter of the First Name First letter of the Middle Name Last Name> , etc.

For every person mentioned in the Open Archive all possible variants of the *akt:full-name* can be easily generated. Regrettably, the problem of personal identification has not been solved yet. In other words, if an *akt:full-name* attribute

---

[10] http://demo.openlinksw.com/sparql

is similar to a *bone:name* attribute, it does not necessarily mean that they are the same person.

Let us consider the following example. There exists an instance of the *bone: person* class describing "Kotov Vadim Evgenievich", the former director of the IIS SB RAS, in the SB RAS Open Archives. We can find two distinct persons whose *akt:full-name* is "Vadim Kotov" at the http://citeseer.rkbexplorer.com address. The first person has the following list of Equivalent URIs:

- http://citeseer.rkbexplorer.com/id/resource-CSP168322-edfa4d57ca35c11ccbce8e7551242dce
- http://kisti.rkbexplorer.com/id/PER_00000000000000146828

There are four publications corresponding to this person on the RKBExplorer site. The second person has the following list of Equivalent URIs:

- http://acm.rkbexplorer.com/id/person-289779-4255d8bbbcb9d678ad18fc77dfb0417d
- http://citeseer.rkbexplorer.com/id/resource-CSP168328-a3b1b1337798d4fb1e6cbeb53d779d0e
- http://dblp.rkbexplorer.com/id/people-d32852eb011dfc13e96887308c2f2ca7-0bcd588a7cc1face18d201042b25fb76
- http://dblp.rkbexplorer.com/id/people-d32852eb011dfc13e96887308c2f2ca7-b32d490fa9c88856f4726444caf33829

There is a list of another 19 publications corresponding to the latter person on the RKBExplorer site. The two lists of publications do not intersect while all of them belong to "Kotov" from the SB RAS Open Archive.

In addition, it is possible to find several other people with distinct identifiers and the "Vadim E. Kotov" *akt:full-name* at the acm.rkbexplorer.com. Each person has a single publication which does not intersect with the previous lists. They have no equivalent URIs lists.

On the other hand, it is possible to find a list of 32 publications by "Vadim E. Kotov" on the http://dblp.l3s.de address. All these publications belong to "Kotov" from the Open Archive. However, there exists another list of 2 publications belonging to "Vadim Kotov", and only one publication in this list belongs to "Kotov" from the Open Archive.

In other words, it is necessary to collect publications from different lists and check if they belong to people from the Open Archive and not to their homonyms.

The Open Archive provides a list of jobs with related periods for every person. Basically, these data can be used to identify people from RKBExplorer. However, RKBExplorer does not provide job periods, and information about jobs is also rare.

Our experiments with full-text versions of publications have demonstrated that authors usually cite their earlier publications. This allows several people with distinct identifiers to be considered as a single person.

The citation information is represented by the *akt:cites-publication-reference* relation on RKBExplorer, but , regrettably, it is also incomplete. There is little or almost no information about affiliations and job periods are not specified at all. The information about citation is also incomplete.

Therefore, the citation network generated on the basis of the *akt:cites-publi-cation-reference* relationship between publications of a single author is sparse with many isolated nodes. An example of the citation network generated for publications by "V. E. Kotov" is shown in Fig. 5. A program extracting this information from the full-text versions of publications is under development.

Fig. 5. An example of a citation network for publications by one author

To include the publications of researchers into the Open Archive content, more sophisticated transformations are needed. First, an instance of the *bone: docu-ment* class should be created for each individual of the *akt:publication-reference* class; then for each *akt:has-author* relationship, it is necessary to generate an in-stance of the *bone: authorship* class along with the *bone: adoc* and *bone: author* relationships linking the instances of the *bone:authorship* class with relevant in-stances of the *bone:person* and *bone:document* classes. All these transformations can be carried out with a SPARQL- query similar to the one described above.

4   Visualization of SPARQL-Queries for Data Set Analysis

The main tools for the investigation of the content of a semantic system are the creation of application-specific SPARQL-queries and query results visualization. This visualization can be generated by either a standard or specialized visual-ization algorithm. A window for SPARQL-query input is shown in Fig. 6. It consists of three panels. The left panel shows a list of the main classes and rela-tions of the semantic system under investigation; the top right panel is used for SPARQL-query input. In this panel a SPARQL-query is displayed. This query generates a graph whose nodes are persons and edges are "colleague" relations between these persons.

The "colleague" relation corresponds to the fact that people are affiliated to the same organization or take part in the same event. Note that SPARQL-queries are closely related to the RDF file structure. SPARQL inquires RDF graphs, and RDF graph is a set of triples or "statements". Each triple has three parts: a subject , a predicate and an object. Each predicate is described in a corresponding ontology by means of the *owl:objectProperty* clause. This is the reason why ontology visualization is so helpful at the stage of the creation of a SPARQL-query.

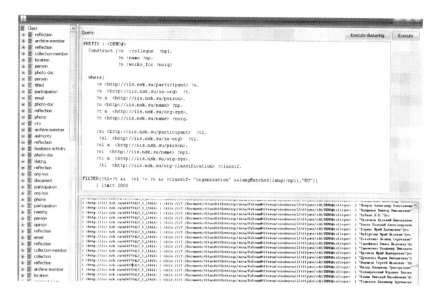

Fig. 6. The window for SPARQL-query input

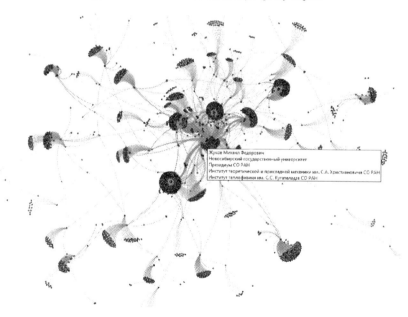

Fig. 7. A "colleagues" graph generated by the SPARQL query from Fig. 6

The bottom right panel displays the query results in a text form. There is an "Execute" button and an "Execute clustering" button in the top right corner of the visualization panel. The first button starts generation of the query results as a graph, and the second one creates clustering of the resulting graph.

The query result in the graph form is shown in Fig. 7. A graph consists of several connected components. People are grouped around the organizations in which they have worked previously or are working now. As we do not use filtration by date, some people are assigned to several organizations. There is a high-density component in the center of the drawing which corresponds to the teachers of Novosibirsk State University. In this way, they are colleagues of other people working at the institutes of the SB RAS.

After a number of experiments, we have found that the dataset of the Open Archive is rather complete and clustering is not quite important for it since it is possible to extract any part of the corresponding graph by SPARQL-queries with appropriate attributes. The clustering algorithm is needed in the case when the structure of the resulting graph is not as obvious. This kind of dense graphs arises, for example, during extraction of a co-authorship network from the DBLP dataset or a citation network from the CiteSeer dataset.

5   Conclusion

The first experiments on the enrichment of the SB RAS Open Archive with the data of the LOD cloud have been described. The structure of the BONE ontology has been compared to that of the AKT Reference Ontology, and one regular source of their structural difference has been identified. A template for SPARQL queries that establish correspondence between groups of classes and relations of the two ontologies has been developed. This template makes possible automatic generation of SPARQL queries based on the two ontologies visualization. The problem of identity resolution is discussed and approaches to its solution are proposed. All the experiments have been conducted with a toolkit developed at the IIS SB RAS. The experiments have shown that the data sets of the LOD cloud can be really useful for the enrichment of the SB RAS Open Archive. In its turn, the content of the SB RAS Open Archive can be a useful source of information about famous researchers.

Acknowledgements. This work has been supported by the RFBR grant №11-07-00388-a and the SBRAS grant 15/10.

References

1. Marchuk, A.G., Marchuk, P.A.: Specific features of digital libraries construction with linked content. In: Proceedings of the RCDL 2010 Conference, pp. 19–23 (2010) (in Russian)
2. SBRAS Open Archive, http://duh.iis.nsk.su/turgunda/Home
3. Bizer, C., Heath, T., Berners-Lee, T.: Linked Data – The Story So Far. Int. J. Semantic Web Inf. Syst. 5(3), 1–22 (2009)
4. Schultz, A., Matteini, A., Isele, R., Mendes, P.N., Becker, C., Bizer, C.: How to integrate LINKED DATA into your application. In: Semantic Technology & Business Conference, San Francisco (June 5, 2012), http://mes-semantics.com/wp-content/uploads/2012/09/Becker-etal-LDIF-SemTechSanFrancisco.pdf

5. Tramp, S., Williams, H., Eck, K.: Creating Knowledge out of Interlinked Data: The LOD2 Tool Stack, http://lod2.eu/Event/ESWC2012-Tutorial.html

6. Isele, R., Jentzsch, A., Bizer, C.: Silk Server - Adding missing Links while consuming Linked Data. In: 1st International Workshop on Consuming Linked Data (COLD 2010), Shanghai (November 2010)

7. Ngomo, A.-C.N., Auer, S.: LIMES - A Time-Efficient Approach for Large-Scale Link Discovery on the Web of Data. In: IJCAI 2011: Proceedings of the 22nd International Joint Conference on Artificial Intelligence, Barcelona, Catalonia, Spain, July 16–22, pp. 2312–2317 (2011)

8. Oren, E., Delbru, R., Catasta, M., Cyganiak, R., Stenzhorn, H., Tummarello, G.: Sindice.com: A document-oriented lookup index for open linked data. Int. J. Metadata, Semantics and Ontologies 3(1), 37–52 (2008)

9. Apanovich, Z.V., Vinokurov, P.S.: Ontology based portals and visual analysis of scientific communities. In: First Russia and Pacific Conference on Computer Technology and Applications, Vladivostok, Russia, September 6-9, pp. 7–11 (2010)

10. Apanovich, Z.V., Kislicina, T.A.: Ontology and content of large science portals visualization with hierarchical edge bundles. In: Proceedings of the Third Knowledge and Ontologies Workshop *ELSEWHERE*2011, pp. 29–34 (2011) (in Russian), http://psi.nsc.ru/psi11/elsewhere/index

11. Hoffart, J., Suchanek, F.M., Berberich, K., Lewis-Kelham, E., de Melo, G., Gerhard Weikum, G.: YAGO2: A Spatially and Temporally Enhanced Knowledge Base from Wikipedia. In: WWW 2011Proceedings of the 20th International Conference Companion on World Wide Web, pp. 229–232 (2011)

12. Storey, M.A., Musen, M.A., Silva, J., Best, C., Ernst, N., Fergerson, R., Noy, N.F.: Jambalaya: Interactive visualization to enhance ontology authoring and knowledge acquisition in Protege. In: Workshop on Interactive Tools for Knowledge Capture, K-CAP-2001, Victoria, B.C., Canada (2001)

13. Alani, H.: TGVizTab: An Ontology Visualization Extension for Protege. In: Proceedings of Knowledge Capture (K-Cap 2003),Workshop on Visualization Information in Knowledge Engineering, Sanibel Island, Florida, USA (2003)

14. Sintek, M.: Ontoviz tab: Visualizing Protégé ontologies (2003), http://protegewiki.stanford.edu/wiki/OntoViz

15. Katifori, A., Halatsis, C., Lepouras, G., Vassilakis, C., Giannopoulou, E.: Ontology Visualization Methods - A Survey. ACM Computing Surveys 39(4) (2007)

16. Shvaiko, P., Euzenat, J.: Ontology matching: State of the art and future challenges. IEEE Transactions on Knowledge and Data Engineering 25(1), 158–176 (2013)

17. Lanzenberger, M., Sampson, J.: AlViz—A Tool for Visual Ontology Alignment. In: Proceedings of the 10th International Conference on Information Visualization, London, UK, pp. 430–440 (2006)

18. Falconer, S.M., Storey, M.- A.: A cognitive support framework for ontology mapping. In: Aberer, K., Choi, K.-S., Noy, N., Allemang, D., Lee, K.-I., Nixon, L.J.B., Golbeck, J., Mika, P., Maynard, D., Mizoguchi, R., Schreiber, G., Cudré-Mauroux, P. (eds.) ASWC 2007 and ISWC 2007. LNCS, vol. 4825, pp. 114–127. Springer, Heidelberg (2007)

19. Cruz, I.F., Stroe, C., Caimi, F., Fabiani, A., Pesquita, C., Couto, F.M., Palmonari, M.: Using AgreementMaker to Align Ontologies for OAEI 2011 (2011)

20. Kolli, R., Doshi, P.: OPTIMA: Tool for Ontology alignment with Application to Semantic Reconciliation of Sensor Metadata for Publication in Sensor Map. In: Proceedings of 2008 IEEE International Conference on Semantic Computing, pp. 484–485 (2008)

21. Granitzer, M., Sabol, V., Weng Onn, K., Lukose, D., Tochtermann, K.: Ontology Alignment: A Survey with Focus on Visually Supported Semi-Automatic Techniques. Future Internet 2, 238–258 (2010)
22. Scharffe, F., Ding, Y., Fensel, D.: Towards Correspondence Patterns for Ontology Mediation. In: Ontology Matching Workshop (2007)
23. Holten, D.: Hierarchical edge bundles: Visualization of adjacency relations in hierarchical data. IEEE Transactions on Visualization and Computer Graphics 12(5), 741–748 (2006)

Ontology-Based Content Trust Support of Expert Information Resources in Quantitative Spectroscopy

Alexander Fazliev[1], Alexey Privezentsev[1],
Dmitry Tsarkov[2], and Jonathan Tennyson[3]

[1] V.E.Zuev Institute of Atmospheric Optics SB RAS,
Zuev Square 1, 634021, Tomsk, Russia
{faz,remake}@iao.ru
[2] School of Computer Science, University of Manchester,
Oxford Road, Manchester M13 9PL, UK
tsarkov@cs.man.ac.uk
[3] Department of Physics and Astronomy, University College London,
London WC1E 6BU, UK
jtennyson@ucl.ac.uk

Abstract. An approach to assessing the content trust of information resources based on a publishing criterion has been developed and applied to several tens of spectroscopic expert datasets. The results represented as an OWL-ontology are shown to be accessible to programmable agents. The assessments enable the amount of measured and calculated trusted and distrusted data for spectroscopic quantities and ranges of their change in expert datasets to be determined. Building knowledge bases of this kind at virtual data centers intended for data intensive science will provide realization of an automatic selection of spectroscopic information resources exhibiting a high degree of trust.

Keywords: Trust, OWL Ontology, Quantitative Spectroscopy.

1 Introduction

Spectral line parameters are used in different subject domains: remote sensing, climate studies, astronomy, etc. Data of this type are in great demand, and the number of expert data providers is increasing progressively [10, 5, 7, 4, 18, 17, 26]. More stringent requirements are imposed on data quality, including data accuracy, completeness, validity, trust and resource consistency. For a wide range of applied tasks, currently available expert data are shown to be inadequate to meet the requirements, because they contain outdated, distrusted and incomplete information [14].

Quantitative spectroscopy is a data-intensive science dealing with information collected over the course of ninety years, but it is in the last six years when semantic technologies have been used in this domain. Processing of the long-term

P. Klinov and D. Mouromtsev (Eds.): KESW 2013, CCIS 394, pp. 15–28, 2013.
© Springer-Verlag Berlin Heidelberg 2013

data, linking together results of investigations retrieved from different publications and aligning these data provide an adequate valid data exchange and access to trusted information resources. In quantitative spectroscopy, this implies a low threshold of the spectral knowledge transfer to applied sciences. The low threshold has its practical benefits because investigators engaged in applied sciences lack sufficient knowledge to understand all the relevant aspects of expert data. The choice of researchers is most often based on trust rather than on checks of data for validity. This is why investigators need information on validity and trust criteria to be satisfied by expert data.

We have assessed the expert data content trust and presented the results obtained as an OWL ontology. The ontology is intended for two types of users 1) researchers using the ontology to assess trust in expert resources for certain purposes and 2) programmable agents making decisions on the selection of the parts of similar expert data that deserve the highest degree of trust in this ontology. The assessment of trust is part of a solution to the task of assessment of trust in the content of expert information resources. This task is broken down into four subtasks: (1) building multisets of values of physical quantities available in primary data sources, (2) alignment of values of physical quantities, (3) definition of quantitative restrictions found in a publishing criterion in different ranges of change of physical quantities and (4) decomposition of expert data. Solutions to these subtasks are presented in W@DIS[1] in the form of trusted consistent information resources for programmable agents. A publishing criterion specifies ranges of change of the physical quantity under study and permissible difference in the values of this quantity between published primary and expert data in these ranges.

A rigorous solution to the task of assessment of trust in expert resources of an information system will take a complete set of valid aligned published values of physical quantities. As of now, datasets of this type have been published solely for the ground electron state of isotopologues of the water molecule [23–25], hydrogen sulfide [16] and carbon monoxide [22].

The ontology under consideration has been built using a standard methodological approach wherein existing models for data and metadata for the subject domains being studied are assimilated into newly developed ontologies. The models are examined and extended (or reduced) to provide the required granulation level inherent to the subject domain in question.

2   A Simplified Data Model for Quantitative Spectroscopy

Before proceeding to a data model for quantitative spectroscopy, we emphasize the fact that the proposed model does not include all facts relating to this subject domain. However, this is a major part of data applied in different disciplines of interest. The data of this type were obtained both theoretically and experimentally. This division into theory and experiment makes it possible to classify data measurements and predictions.

---

[1] Information system W@DIS, http://wadis.saga.iao.ru

The data associated with measurements or computations from one publication are referred to as a primary data source. The primary experimental and theoretical data are interrelated. This is due to the fact that the values of properties of transitions and states are not all measured. Among these are quantum numbers whose values are found only in the framework of mathematical models of molecules. Composite data are also used in spectroscopy in addition to primary data. Two types of composite data are of importance from the standpoint of applications: reference and expert data. The former are calculated by means of a multiset of measured data, whereas the latter are a set of consistent calculated, measured and reference data. The data layer includes three types of datasets. Arrows pointing from applications to datasets indicate data-producing applications, whereas arrows pointing from datasets to applications imply applications using the data.

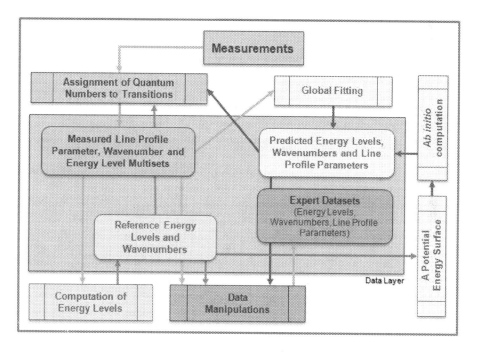

Fig. 1. Schematic representation of the relationship between applications and their associated input and output data

Figure 1 demonstrates four groups of data and their association with experiment and calculations. These groups are related to six tasks of quantitative spectroscopy and a task of building expert datasets. The quality of data included in three datasets (a multiset of measured transitions and predicted and reference transitions) can be assessed by formal criteria alone (validity), whereas expert datasets should be tested according to trust criteria, because formal methods for building such datasets remain to be developed. The computational method used to formalize data manipulation for construction of expert datasets was described in [13]. Since spectral information resources in the form of expert datasets are in great demand, it is the expert data which are the focus of attention in this paper. There are two reasons for that. First, expert data are acquired for applied subject domains the number of which is over several tens. Notably, the data intended for one or another subject domain must satisfy certain requirements on their quality. Second, expert data are acquired from informal manipulations in which case professional skills and preferences of experts play an important role. This is why different forms of publishing criteria appear to be a useful tool for assessing the expert data quality.

3   Content Quality of Information Resources for Quantitative Spectroscopy

According to the Semantic Web (SW) approach, the content of information resources involves data, information and knowledge. These terms are treated in the literature in an apparently contradictory way. We will follow the terminology being created within the SW approach and employ the terms "data", "linked data" and "ontology" to mean data, information and knowledge, respectively. In the SW approach, the terminological interpretation of data, information and knowledge is closely related to the semantics of formal languages (XML, RDF and OWL). Moreover, the terms "data layer", "information layer" and "knowledge layer" were introduced in e-Science [20] to describe the infrastructure of information resources. In particular, W@DIS whose information resources are dealt with in this work has a three-layer architecture of this type [1].

The object of this paper is to assess the data extension quality. The emphasis is on the data extension trust and validity. Validity is taken to mean that the data satisfy formal constraints derived from mathematical molecular models and conditions for consistency of identical canonical parts of spectral data sources. The publishing criterion is applied to canonical parts of data sources to identify distrusted values of physical quantities. These may be unpublished data or data unaligned with primary data. Students of applied subject domains using expert spectral data would have to check distrusted data according to criteria employed in the relevant subject domain.

There are different interpretations of trust in the literature [6, 3, 15, 21, 2, 9] and, accordingly, a rich variety of trust criteria are suggested. Common to the majority of interpretations is the fact that trust criteria are partially formalized constraints. The publishing criterion formulated in [14] refers to a set of criteria for assessing the content trust of information resources [2, 9]. The publishing criterion enables the distributed part of the content to be identified. The use of the publishing criterion assumes that a check is made of values of identical spectral line parameters in the expert dataset for a fit to published primary data within a specified accuracy.

Early in the development of the SW approach, the notion of trust has come to occupy the central place. Trust implies that Internet users will get access to valid information sources characterized by a high degree of trust. Dealing with information resources, researchers can check the resources of interest for validity within their competence. Moreover, their professional skills and experience allow for making decisions in the case where partially formalized trust criteria are available, whereas the trust assessment is based on resources characterized by an uncertainty. The SW approach is intended not only for a scientific community but for programmable agents capable of solving tasks of this type as well. "In a Semantic Web where content will be reflected in ontologies and axioms, how will a computer decide what sources to trust when they offer contradictory information?" [2]. The question refers to programmable agents.

Along with papers on methods of assessing trust in information resources on the basis of knowledge about providers, developers of agents and relevant technologies, there have been recent publications pertaining to the content trust of resources [2, 9], where 19 factors influencing the content trust were described. The factors can be divided into two groups. One group includes factors independent of social relations or outlook of the researcher: topic (resource trusted within certain domains may be distrusted within others), content trust, alternative resources available, provenance, limited or biased resources, specificity, likelihood, age, deception and regency. The other group includes popularity, authority, recommendations, direct experience, user expertise and ability to make decisions.

Expert data in quantitative spectroscopy satisfy a number of trust factors. These are popularity, authority, recommendations for applied subject domains, several expert groups of providers and absence of deceptive intentions. However, there are factors that cast some doubt upon the correctness (adequacy) of part of the data. The fraction of distrusted data depends to a large extent on a rigorous definition of the area of application of expert data. In most popular resources [10, 18, 17], a small number of physical quantities (vacuum wavenumbers in the case at hand) is not valid, the origin of part of data is not known (as a rule, they are not published), some of distrusted data are of fairly old age, and the user-expert feedback mechanism is not available. The above-listed disadvantages of expert data point to the importance of assessing the expert data trust in quantitative spectroscopy.

4 Content Trust of Expert Resources

The task of assessment of trust in expert resources is as follows. Let a physical quantity PQ describe a state or a transition in a physical system and uniqueness of states or transitions be determined by a factor qn_i. Let there be a set of expert values of the physical quantity $A = \{PQ(p_i, qn_i)\}$, such as an energy level, vacuum wavenumbers or line intensity, where p_i are values of the physical quantity and all values of qn_i are unique. Let $M(p_j^i, qn_j)$ be a multiset of all published measured values of PQ which contains only *valid* values, whereas $T(p_j^i, qn_j)$ is a multiset of *all published* calculated values of PQ. Here j numbers all pairs (p_j^i, qn_j) of values of physical quantities and their associated quantum numbers. The index i is the number of publication from which the value of the pair (p_j^i, qn_j) was retrieved. The value of $p_j^i (i = 1, \ldots, n)$ for a fixed value of j may vary. Let D_k be a maximum permissible difference between the expert value of a physical quantity and the value of the physical quantity given in a primary data source. Let D_k vary in the range of change of PQ from A by virtue of the fact that measuring instruments operate on different principles. There may be other reasons for specifying part of the range of change of PQ to determine a permissible deviation of expert values of PQ from identical values of PQ from $M(p_j^i, qn_j)$ and $T(p_j^i, qn_j)$ according to the publishing criterion. The task is to find the number of values of PQ from A that satisfy or fail to satisfy the publishing criterion ($E(p_j^i, qn_j)$ and $F(p_j^i, qn_j)$, respectively) and determine the ranges of change of (E) and (F) in each of the ranges of change of PQ characterized by D_k with the proviso that the procedure used to obtain expert values is implicit and uncontrollable.

Examined below are two tasks: (1) formulation of quantitative restrictions found in the publishing criteria in different ranges of change of physical quantities and (2) decomposition of expert data.

4.1   Restrictions on Physical Quantities in a Publishing Criterion

A publishing criterion is based on the inequality $|p_{i,expert} - p_{i,primary}| < D_k$, where $p_{i,expert}$ and $p_{i,primary}$ are the expert and primary values of physical quantities, respectively, and D_k is the deviation satisfying the publishing criterion in the spectral range of interest. In view of the fact that the operation of measuring instruments used in quantitative spectroscopy is based on different physical principles, the permissible deviation will be different for different ranges of change of the physical quantities under consideration.

Decomposition is performed in three ways: decomposition into experimental primary data, into theoretical primary data and into experimental and theoretical primary data. This principle is independent of the physical quantity used in the decomposition. The comparison of expert data with primary data according to the publishing criterion performed here for vacuum wavenumbers makes use of division of the range of change of wavenumbers (from 0 to 100,000 cm^{-1}) into twelve subranges. The limiting accuracy that determines the areas of application of the publishing criterion in checking an expert dataset for a fit to the criterion is related to each of the subranges. In the microwave region, the limiting accuracy is 0.00001 cm^{-1}, in the far, long-wave, middle, near infrared and visible regions is 0.005 cm^{-1}, whereas in the short-wave infrared, it is 0.01 cm^{-1}.

4.2   A Decomposition Task

A representation of the results (E, F) obtained from decomposition that allows for the breakdown of expert data into computed and measured values provides a quantitative characterization of trust. In the overwhelming majority of cases, trust in measured characteristics of transitions in quantitative spectroscopy is much higher than trust in computed values.

Table 1 gives the number of distrusted transitions $F(p_j^i, qn_j)$ in the expert data from [10–12, 17, 19] for water and carbon dioxide isotopologues and hydrogen sulfide. Using the main water isotopologue as an example, we show the way the number of distrusted transitions changed, as new versions of information resources were created by two expert groups in 2005–2011. Trust in vacuum wavenumbers in the visible is seen to increase dramatically. Column "All Regions" comprises a complete number of distrusted transitions in the expert data examined.

The following abbreviated forms were used in the table for decomposition ranges: L.W.IR for long-wave infrared and S.W.IR for short-wave infrared. The blue rows of the table show the number of distrusted transitions in the region of interest. The numbers opposite chemical formulas of molecular isotopologues correspond to the number of transitions available in the publication containing associated expert data.

Assessment of trust in information resources for carbon dioxide is indicative of a high degree of trust in resources for the $^{12}C^{16}O_2$, $^{12}C^{16}O^{18}O$ and $^{13}C^{16}O_2$ isotopologues [17].

Accordingly, this is evidence that resources based on a considerable body of measured data evoke a higher degree of trust.

Assessment of trust in resources for the hydrogen sulfide molecule has shown that about 40% of transitions are distrusted for the values of D_i given in Section 4.1. The ranges of change of distrusted vacuum wavenumbers are specified along with distrusted transitions for hydrogen sulfide.

5   An Ontological Representation of Assessment of Trust

The OWL ontology of assessment of trust in expert data comprises taxonomies of classes and properties and a set of individuals. The taxonomy of classes and the structure of individuals are described below. Here no consideration is given to the properties. However, certain properties are shown in Fig. 3 to describe the structure of an individual. A description of the properties and classes is available in the code of the ontology (see http://wadis.saga.iao.ru).

5.1   The Structure of Individuals

The structure of an individual $\mathbf{A_1}$ describing a complete assessment of trust in an expert data source is shown in Fig. 2 where the trust is assessed for expert data from [17] as an example for the hydrogen sulphide molecule. Notably, the structure is the same for all molecules. The minimum cardinality of property *has-VacuumWavenumberDescriptionClassifiedByPrimaryInformationSource* is 1, whereas its maximum cardinality is 3. The value of this property is an individual $\mathbf{B}$ describing one of three expert data decomposition techniques. Figure 2 shows one value of this property (namely, $\mathbf{B_1}$) describing results obtained from decomposition into primary measured data. This example has no other individuals related to this property, because calculated published data for this molecule are

Decomposition Group	Vacuum Wavenumbers, cm⁻¹									
	RF	Microwave	Far IR	L.W. IR	Middle IR	S.W. IR	Near IR	Visible	Near UV	All Regions
H_2O	2011_JaCrArBo [1] (41147), 2008_JaScChCr [26] (41148)									
Distrusted Data	2009_RoGoBaBe [6] (37432)	16	616	426	1242	1909	1335	359	2	5905
Distrusted Data	2005_RoJaBaBe [25] (32365)	6	612	462	1131	1343	521	3	0	4079
Distrusted Data	2005_JaScChGa [24] (36701)	6	612	462	1131	1343	605	520	2	4682
Distrusted Data		16	619	420	1337	2691	2221	516	2	7822
$H_2^{17}O$	2009_RoGoBaBe (6992)		117	45	171	377	412	64		1186
$H_2^{18}O$	2009_RoGoBaBe (9753)	28	139	66	130	153	936	3		1456
HDO	2009_RoGoBaBe (13238)	24	523	84	204	520	59	76		1603
$^{12}C^{16}O_2$	2009_RoGoBaBe [6] (128170)		13	53	84	26	27			202
$^{13}C^{16}O^{18}O$	2009_RoGoBaBe (19264)		38	187	29	926	0			1180
$^{12}C^{16}O^{18}O$	2009_RoGoBaBe (79958)		79	944	214	433	0			1677
$^{13}C^{16}O_2$	2009_RoGoBaBe (49777)		0	0	81	41	1			123
$^{13}C^{18}O^{16}O$	2009_RoGoBaBe (2953)		0	0	590	0	127			
$H_2^{32}S$	2009_RoGoBaBe (12330)		127	364						
		2.985	15.683	994.127	1.250.024	3.303.930				2.985
		7.624	609.328	1.249.221	3.033.307	4.256.547				4.256.547
		8	969	62	1446	2504				4989

Table 1. Results of decomposition of expert data for four water and five carbon dioxide isotopologues and hydrogen sulfide

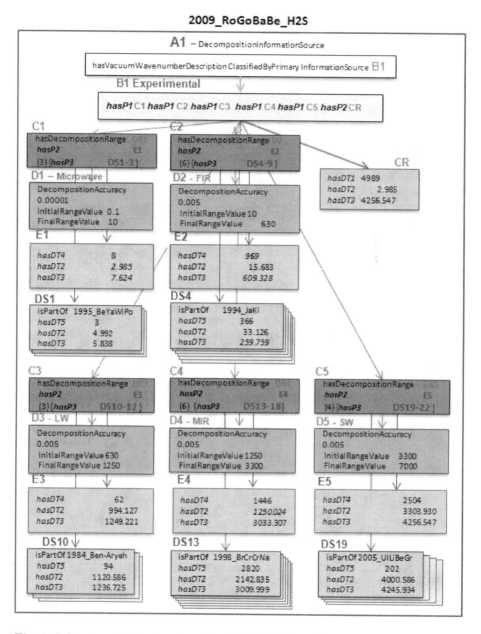

Fig. 2. Subject-predicate structure of an individual describing the assessment of trust in the expert data on vacuum wavenumbers for the H_2S molecule

lacking. The maximum cardinality of property *hasVacuumWavenumberDecompositionDescriptionClassifiedByRange* corresponding to *hasP1* in Fig. 2 is 12, whereas its minimum cardinality is 1. The values of this property are individuals ($\mathbf{C_n}$)

describing the assessment of trust in a certain range of change of vacuum wavenumbers. The values of property *hasDistrustedTransitionDescription* corresponding to *hasP2* in Fig. 2 are individuals **CR** and E_n specifying the entire range of change of vacuum wavenumbers or typical regions (microwave, visible, etc.) where the wavenumbers available in the expert data are found, respectively. Individuals **CR** and E_n represent the number of values of distrusted physical quantities and the ranges of their change. Finally, the value of property *hasTrustedTransitionDescription* (corresponding to *hasP3* in Fig. 2) is an individual **DS** specifying the number of trusted transitions and range of their change.

Figure 3 shows a fragment of Fig. 2 describing the structure of an individual C_5 of class DECOMPOSITIONINSHORTWAVEINFRAREDRANGEDESCRIPTION. This individual has three properties whose values are individuals DR_n, DS_n and E_n specifying the decomposition range and trusted and distrusted transitions in the expert data in this range, respectively. The trusted characteristics refer to each of the primary data sources that contain identical transitions with expert data. The wavenumbers of these transitions satisfy the restrictions imposed by the publishing criterion for this range.

Figure 3 demonstrates properties of one of the individuals (DS_n). The properties of an individual **2005_UlLiBeGr** are not shown. The latter individual **2005_UlLiBeGr** is an information source describing the solution to task $T6$ published in [27] and includes about 100 axioms.

Considering the other individuals characterizing trusted transitions of expert data and similar individuals corresponding to other decomposition ranges and decompositions into different combinations of primary datasets, we will arrive at a detailed description of the trusted part of transitions for decomposition into vacuum wavenumbers.

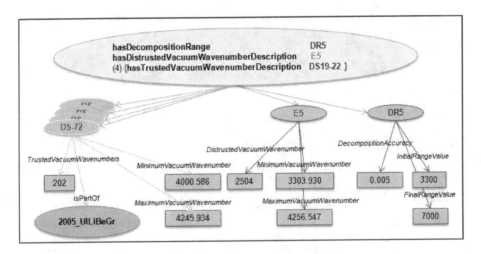

Fig. 3. Fragment of Fig. 2 with a detailed subject-predicate structure of an individual C_5 of a class DECOMPOSITIONSHORTWAVEINFRAREDRANGEDESCRIPTION

5.2 Taxonomy and an Instance of a Class Definition

Results obtained from an analysis of trust in information resources in the ontology of information resources are individuals of class DECOMPOSITIONINFORMATIONSOURCE (here the terminology of ontology version 6 is used). Four classes are associated with decomposition techniques (e.g., DESCRIPTIONUNDEREXPERIMENTALPRIMARYINFORMATIONSOURCEDECOMPOSITION), and thirteen classes are associated with decomposition ranges (e.g., DECOMPOSITIONVISIBLERANGEDESCRIPTION). Two classes (TRUSTEDTRANSITIONDESCRIPTION and DISTRUSTEDTRANSITIONDESCRIPTION) contain elements specifying the number of trusted and distrusted vacuum wavenumbers and ranges of change of the wavenumbers.

For the most part the classes are defined by a set of restrictions on the property values. Restrictions for class DECOMPOSITIONVISIBLERANGEDESCRIPTION using the Manchester syntax can be exemplified in the following way:

$$(\textit{hasTrustedDescription} \textbf{ some } \text{TRUSTEDVACUUMWAVENUMBERDESCRIPTION} \textbf{ or}$$
$$\textit{hasUntrustedDescription} \textbf{ some } \text{UNTRUSTEDVACUUMWAVENUMBERDESCRIPTION})$$
$$\textbf{and } (\textit{hasDecompositionRange} \textbf{ value } \text{VISIBLEDECOMPOSITIONRANGE})$$

This class includes individuals each of which specifies the number of trusted and distrusted transitions, associated ranges of change of trusted and distrusted transitions in the visible for one molecule and one expert data source.

The ontology of assessment trust in expert resources for quantitative spectroscopy comprises 19 classes, 14 properties and 9 types of structure of an individual describing the assessment of trust depending on the molecule under study, spectral range of expert data relating to this molecule and number of primary sources which may vary between 20 and 150.

6 Summary

The quality of expert resources in quantitative spectroscopy has been assessed. Use was made of primary data sources retrieved from more than 2000 publications. The primary data sources were uploaded to information system W@DIS and provided with semantic annotations [8]. The annotations contain information on the validity and degree of consistency of spectral data and are available for users in tabular form and OWL ontology.

To assess trust in expert resources, we applied a publishing criterion whose quantitative values vary in twelve ranges of vacuum wavenumbers. The structure of an individual characterizing the assessment of trust in expert resources is described. The former contains information for trusted and distrusted vacuum wavenumbers. Examples of assessment of trust in expert resources are expert values of vacuum wavenumbers.

Work is under way to apply the computed ontological knowledge base to development of an expert system for an assessment of and a semantic search for information resources in quantitative spectroscopy and to the Virtual Atomic and Molecular Data Centre [7]. A knowledge base of this type makes it possible to perform an analysis of data obtained by other experts for a number of molecules, on the one hand, and to form expert data aligned with published expert data, on the other. Thus experts will have quantitative assessments of validity of and trust in resources of this type at their disposal.

The work was supported by Russian Foundation for Basic Research (Grants 110700660 and 130700411).

References

1. Akhlyostin, A., Kozodoev, A., Lavrentiev, N., Privezentsev, A., Fazliev, A.: Computed knowledge base for description of information resourses of molecular spectroscopy 4. Software. Russian Digital Library Journal 15(3) (2012)
2. Artz, D., Gil, Y.: A survey of trust in computer science and the Semantic Web. Journal of Web Semantics 5(2), 58–71 (2007)
3. Bizer, C., Oldakowski, R.: Using context- and content-based trust policies on the semantic web. In: Proceedings of the 13th International World Wide Web Conference on Alternate Track Papers & Posters, WWW Alt. 2004, pp. 228–229. ACM, New York (2004)
4. Cami, J., van Malderen, R., Markwick, A.J.: SpectraFactory.net: A Database of Molecular Model Spectra. The Astrophysical Journal Supplement 187, 409–415 (2010)
5. Chance, K., Kurucz, R.L.: An improved high-resolution solar reference spectrum for earth's atmosphere measurements in the ultraviolet, visible, and near infrared. Journal of Quantitative Spectroscopy and Radiative Transfer 111, 1289–1295 (2010)
6. Ciolek, T.M.: The six quests for the electronic grail: Current approaches to information quality in www resources. Review Informatique et Statistique dans les Sciences Humaines (RISSH) 1(4), 45–71 (1996)
7. Dubernet, M., Boudon, V., Culhane, J., Dimitrijevic, M., Fazliev, A., Joblin, C., Kupka, F., Leto, G., Sidaner, P.L., Loboda, P., et al.: Virtual atomic and molecular data centre. Journal of Quantitative Spectroscopy and Radiative Transfer 111(15), 2151–2159 (2010)
8. Fazliev, A., Privezentsev, A., Tsarkov, D.: Computed knowledge base for quantitative spectroscopy. In: Proc. of Knowledge Engineering and Semantic Web Conference (KESW 2012), Saint-Petersburg, Russia (2012)
9. Gil, Y., Artz, D.: Towards content trust of web resources. Journal of Web Semantics 5(4), 227–239 (2007)
10. Jacquinet-Husson, N., Crepeau, L., Armante, R., Boutammine, C., Chédin, A., Scott, N., Crevoisier, C., Capelle, V., Boone, C., et al.: The 2009 edition of the GEISA spectroscopic database. Journal of Quantitative Spectroscopy and Radiative Transfer 112(15), 2395–2445 (2011)
11. Jacquinet-Husson, N., Scott, N., Chédin, A., Crépeau, L., Armante, R., Capelle, V., Orphal, J., Coustenis, A., Boonne, C., Poulet-Crovisier, N., et al.: The GEISA spectroscopic database: Current and future archive for Earth and planetary atmosphere studies. Journal of Quantitative Spectroscopy and Radiative Transfer 109(6), 1043–1059 (2008)
12. Jacquinet-Husson, N., Scott, N., Chédin, A., Garceran, K., Armante, R., Chursin, A., Barbe, A., Birk, M., Brown, L., Camy-Peyret, C., et al.: The 2003 edition of the GEISA/IASI spectroscopic database. Journal of Quantitative Spectroscopy and Radiative Transfer 95(4), 429–467 (2005)

13. Kozodoev, A., Fazliev, A.: Information system for molecular spectroscopy. 2. Array operations for transformation of data on spectral line parameters. Journal of Atmospheric and Oceanic Optics 18(9), 680–684 (2005)

14. Lavrentiev, N.A., Makogon, M.M., Fazliev, A.Z.: Comparison of the HITRAN and GEISA spectral databases taking into account the restriction on publication of spectral data. Journal of Atmospheric and Oceanic Optics 24(5), 436–451 (2011)

15. O'Hara, K., Alani, H., Kalfoglou, Y., Shadbolt, N.: Trust strategies for the semantic web. In: Golbeck, J., Bonatti, P.A., Nejdl, W., Olmedilla, D., Winslett, M. (eds.) ISWC Workshop on Trust, Security, and Reputation on the Semantic Web. CEUR Workshop Proceedings, vol. 127, CEUR-WS.org (2004)

16. Polovtseva, E.R., Lavrentiev, N.A., Voronina, S.S., Naumenko, O.V., Fazliev, A.Z.: Information system for molecular spectroscopy. 5. Ro-vibrational transitions and energy levels of the hydrogen sulfide molecule. Journal of Atmospheric and Oceanic Optics 25(2), 157–165 (2012)

17. Rothman, L., Gordon, I., Barbe, A., Benner, D., Bernath, P., Birk, M., Boudon, V., Brown, L., Campargue, A., Champion, J., et al.: The HITRAN 2008 molecular spectroscopic database. Journal of Quantitative Spectroscopy and Radiative Transfer 110(9-10), 533–572 (2009)

18. Rothman, L., Gordon, I., Barber, R., Dothe, H., Gamache, R., Goldman, A., Perevalov, V., Tashkun, S., Tennyson, J.: HITEMP, the high-temperature molecular spectroscopic database. Journal of Quantitative Spectroscopy and Radiative Transfer 111(15), 2139–2150 (2010)

19. Rothman, L.S., Jacquemart, D., Barbe, A., Benner, D.C., Birk, M., Brown, L., Carleer, M.R., Chackerian Jr., C., Chance, K., Coudert, L.H., et al.: The HITRAN 2004 molecular spectroscopic database. Journal of Quantitative Spectroscopy and Radiative Transfer 96(2), 139–204 (2005)

20. de Roure, D., Jennings, N.R., Shadbolt, N.: The Semantic Grid: A future e-Science infrastructure. In: Berman, F., Fox, G., Hey, A. (eds.) Grid Computing – Making the Global Infrastructure a Reality, pp. 437–470. John Wiley and Sons Ltd. (2003)

21. Sabater, J., Sierra, C.: Review on computational trust and reputation models. Journal of Artificial Intelligence Reviews 24(1), 33–60 (2005)

22. Tashkun, S., Velichko, T., Mikhailenko, S.: Critical evaluation of measured pure-rotation and rotation-vibration line positions and an experimental dataset of energy levels of $^{12}C^{16}O$ in $X^1\Sigma^+$ state. Journal of Quantitative Spectroscopy and Radiative Transfer 111(9), 1106–1116 (2010)

23. Tennyson, J., Bernath, P., Brown, L., Campargue, A., Carleer, M., Császár, A., Gamache, R., Hodges, J., Jenouvrier, A., Naumenko, O., et al.: IUPAC critical evaluation of the rotational-vibrational spectra of water vapor. Part I. Energy levels and transition wavenumbers for $H_2{}^{17}O$ and $H_2{}^{18}O$. Journal of Quantitative Spectroscopy and Radiative Transfer 110(9-10), 573–596 (2009)

24. Tennyson, J., Bernath, P., Brown, L., Campargue, A., Császár, A., Daumont, L., Gamache, R., Hodges, J., Naumenko, O., Polyansky, O., et al.: IUPAC critical evaluation of the rotational-vibrational spectra of water vapor. Part II: Energy levels and transition wavenumbers for $HD^{16}O$, $HD^{17}O$, and $HD^{18}O$. Journal of Quantitative Spectroscopy and Radiative Transfer 111(15), 2160–2184 (2010)

25. Tennyson, J., Bernath, P., Brown, L., Campargue, A., Császár, A., Daumont, L., Gamache, R., Hodges, J., Naumenko, O., Polyansky, O., et al.: IUPAC critical evaluation of the rotational-vibrational spectra of water vapor. Part III: Energy levels and transition wavenumbers for $H_2{}^{16}O$. Journal of Quantitative Spectroscopy and Radiative Transfer 117, 29–58 (2013)

26. Toth, R., Brown, L., Miller, C., Malathy, D.V., Benner, D.C.: Spectroscopic database of CO_2 line parameters: 4300–7000 cm^{-1}. Journal of Quantitative Spectroscopy and Radiative Transfer 109(6), 906–921 (2008)
27. Ulenikov, O., Liu, A.W., Bekhtereva, E., Gromova, O., Hao, L.Y., Hu, S.M.: High-resolution Fourier transform spectrum of H_2S in the region of the second hexade. Journal of Molecular Spectroscopy 234(2), 270–278 (2005)

Measuring Psychological Impact on Group Ontology Design and Development: An Empirical Approach

Tatiana Gavrilova[1], Ekaterina Bolotnikova[2], Irina Leshcheva[1],
Evgeny Blagov[1], and Anna Yanson[1]

[1] Saint Petersburg State University
199004, Volkhovsky per., 1-3
Saint Petersburg, Russian Federation
{gavrilova,leshcheva,blagove}@gsom.pu.ru,
annayanson@list.ru
[2] Saint Petersburg State Polytechnic University
195251, Polytechnicheskaya ul., 29
Saint Petersburg, Russian Federation
bolotnikovakate@gmail.com

Abstract. This paper describes the interdisciplinary problems of group ontology design. It highlights the importance of studying individual features of cognitive style and their influence on the specifics of collaborative group ontology design and development. The paper describes the preliminary results of the research project focused on working out a new paradigm for structuring data and knowledge with respect to individual cognitive styles, using recent advances in knowledge engineering and conceptual structuring, aimed at creating new consistent and structurally holistic knowledge bases for various domains. The results of this research effort can be applied to organizing the group ontology design (especially for learning purposes), data structuring and other collaborative analytical work.

Keywords: ontology, cognitive science, knowledge engineering.

1 Introduction

One of the main objectives of the pedagogical process is achieving the maximal effectiveness of knowledge transfer. This effectiveness can be measured by quality and speed of memorization of principal concepts of a particular domain and of the linkages between these concepts. Wide evidence exists that using visual thinking to address the subject of learning is positively linked to the memorization quality and speed, and thus to the effectiveness of learning as such, especially when the students are engaged in group knowledge sharing and creation processes considering continuous feedback.

During the last decade, visual knowledge representation has become one of the key considerations in e-learning methodology and it is heavily associated with ontology design and development. These ontologies, which are built on conceptual skeleton of the teaching domain, might serve various purposes such as better understanding, knowledge sharing, and collaborative learning, problem solving, seeking advice, or

P. Klinov and D. Mouromtsev (Eds.): KESW 2013, CCIS 394, pp. 29–43, 2013.
© Springer-Verlag Berlin Heidelberg 2013

developing competences by learning from peers. Recently, ontological engineering perspective has gained interest in the domain of computer-aided learning and cognitive psychology involving the study of the structure and patterns of knowledge. These studies rely heavily on theory and tools from knowledge engineering analysis that has already a longstanding tradition in the knowledge-based systems domain [1]. The tools and techniques developed in this domain can be applied fruitfully in the field of learning structuring and design [2-6], Semantic Web applications [7]. The ideas of using ontologies and visual structuring in educational e-learning were discussed in many works [8], [9] and now are implemented in several software tools.

One of the most prospective methods enabling such conditions appears to be the group ontology design. The KOMET (Knowledge and Content Structuring via Methods of group ontology design) project is developing methods of using group ontology design in learning with regards to the students' individual cognitive styles that are important factors influencing the memorization quality and speed as such.

The aim of the KOMET project is to develop a paradigm of data and knowledge structuring with regard to individual cognitive styles, using recent advances in knowledge engineering and conceptual structuring, aimed at creating new consistent and structurally holistic knowledge bases for the various areas of science and technology. This aim is decomposed to such objectives as a research of correlations between the expert's individual cognitive style and the peculiarities of expert's subject domain ontology development, a research of correlations between the expert's individual cognitive style and the group ontology design (including the design performed in groups consisting of experts either of similar or of different cognitive styles), and a research of formal ontology evaluation methods from the cognitive ergonomics point of view.

The influence of the expert's individual cognitive style on the ontology development was being researched in four consecutive steps: Firstly, the significant individual cognitive style characteristics have been identified on the basis of the on-line testing results; secondly, the test persons have created the "Informatics" domain ontologies using the PROTÉGÉ (Protégé) tool; thirdly, the metrics of the resulting ontologies have been counted using the COAT software environment [10]. Fourthly, statistical analysis has been performed to find out significant relationships between the experts' individual cognitive style characteristics and the ontology metrics.

KOMET-DILIGENT collective ontology development methodology developed within the KOMET project uses the algorithm [11]:

1. Preliminary individual ontology development by the participants and consequent mutual ontology matching;
2. Ontologies analysis, merging and alignment;
3. Ontology revision and redesign.

In the KOMET project specificity of the collective ontology development both in pairs and in groups of 3-5 people has been researched. The test sample consisted of the students of the Saint Petersburg State Polytechnic University, Institute of Information Technology and Control Systems (IITCS), attending the intelligent systems development course. It was their 4-th year of study at the bachelor program.

The experiments were aimed to figure out how the collective categorization style is being developed.

2   Background and Methods

The idea of using visual structuring of information to improve the quality of student's learning and understanding is not new. For more than twenty years concept mapping [12-14] has been used for providing structures and mental models that support the process of teaching and learning. As such, the visual representation of general domain concepts facilitates and supports student understanding of both substantive and syntactic knowledge. Many teachers, especially those who teach sciences and engineering courses, operate as a knowledge analysts or knowledge engineers by making visible the skeleton of the studied discipline and showing the domain's conceptual structure [15]. Often this structure is called "ontology".

From a philosophical viewpoint, "ontology" is the branch of philosophy which deals with the nature and the organization of reality. Now ontologies aim at capturing domain knowledge in a generic way and providing a commonly agreed understanding of a domain, which may be reused and shared across applications and groups [16]. Neches and colleagues [17] gave the classical definition as follows: "An ontology defines the basic terms and relations comprising the vocabulary of a topic area as well as the rules for combining terms and relations to define extensions to the vocabulary".

An ontology is a set of distinctions we make in understanding and viewing the world. Visual approach to present ontology is not only compact but also very comprehensive. It makes ontology a powerful mind tool [13], [18].

By formal definition, ontology is a declarative representation of a certain domain precise specification, including the glossary of the domain terms and the logical expressions describing the meanings and the relationships of these terms, thus allowing structured sharing of knowledge related to the domain. The relationships between the concepts in ontologies can be of different types, e.g., "is", "has a property of", etc. The concepts and relationships are universal for a certain class of objects of a subject area. Conceptual model visualization methods such as ontologies in learning have been developed for a number of disciplines [9], [19], [20].

However, ontology-based approach to knowledge representation in pedagogy is a relatively new development. There are numerous definitions of this milestone term [17], [21-23]. Together, these definitions clarify the ontological approach to knowledge structuring while giving enough freedom to open-ended, creative thinking. Many researchers and practitioners argue about distinctions between ontology and a conceptual model. We suppose that ontology corresponds to the analyst's view of the conceptual model, but is not de facto the model itself. There are more than one hundred of the techniques and notations that help to define and to visualize the conceptual models. Ontologies now supposed to be the most universal and sharable forms of such modeling.

Ontologies are useful structuring tools, in that they provide an organizing axis along which every student can mentally mark his vision in the information hyperspace of domain knowledge. Frequently, it is impossible to express the information as a single ontology. Accordingly, subject knowledge storage provides for a set of related ontologies. Some problems may occur when moving from one ontological space to another, but constructing meta-ontologies may help to resolve these problems.

Meta-ontology provides more general description dealing with higher level abstractions. Figure 1 illustrates different ontology classifications in the form of the mind map. Mind-mapping [24] and concept mapping [25] are now widely used for visualizing of the ontologies at the design stage.

A mind map is a diagram used to represent words, ideas, tasks, or other items linked to and arranged around a central key word or idea. The central topic sits in the middle with related topics branching out from it. Ideas are further broken down and extended until you've fully explored each branch of your map. Mind maps are used to generate, visualize, structure, and classify ideas, and as an aid in study, organization, and writing. The elements of a given mind map are arranged intuitively according to the importance of the concepts, and are classified into groupings, branches, or areas, with the goal of representing semantic or other connections between portions of information.

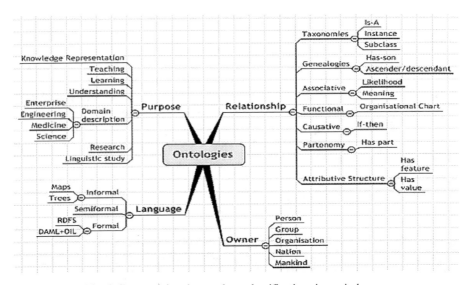

Fig. 1. Summarizing the ontology classifications in a mind-map

A concept map is a diagram showing the relationships among concepts. Such maps are graphical tools for organizing and representing knowledge. They include concepts, usually enclosed in circles or boxes of some type, and relationships between concepts indicated by a connecting line linking two concepts. One way to use concept maps for instruction is to have students create maps before and after each instructional activity in a unit. This allows teachers to determine the level of knowledge prior to teaching and to determine whether the desired objectives were met after instruction while allowing students to review their knowledge.

For both formative and summative assessment purposes, students, through creating ontologies and explaining the processes involved, can clearly indicate the extent and nature of their knowledge and understanding. Knowledge entities that represent static knowledge of the domain are stored in the hierarchical order in the knowledge repository and can be reused by others. At the same time those knowledge entities can be also reused in description of the properties or methodological approach as applied in the context of another related knowledge entity.

Of course, the ontologies are inevitably subjective to a certain extent, as knowledge does by definition include a component of personal subjective perception; however, using the ontologies developed by others is a convenient and compact means of acquiring new knowledge. From the other side, collective ontology development experience allows the participants of the process to get the most possibly full understanding of the subject area.

3   Expert's Individual Cognitive Style and Ontology Development

The aim of the KOMET project is to develop a paradigm of structuring data and knowledge with regard to individual cognitive styles, using recent advances in knowledge engineering and conceptual structuring, aimed at creating new consistent and structurally holistic knowledge bases for the various areas of science and technology.

The research of expert's individual cognitive style and ontology development objective has been divided into three consecutive parts:

- Identifying the significant individual cognitive style characteristics on the basis of the on-line testing results [26];
- Creating the "Informatics" domain ontologies using the PROTÉGÉ (Protégé) tool and estimating the ontology metrics using the COAT software environment [10].
- Performing statistical analysis to find out significant relationships between the experts' individual cognitive style characteristics and the ontology metrics.

From the plethora of cognitive style characteristics described in literature [27] three characteristics have been chosen: field dependence/ field independence (FD/FID), impulsivity/ reflectivity, and narrowness/ breadth of the category.

By definition of Witkin [28], FD/FID is "a structuring ability of perception". The FD/FID characteristic can be interpreted as a proxy of the structuring capability of an individual mind. The characteristic of this style does influence the structuring process as a whole (e.g., ontology development "from scratch" in the research setting described in this paper), and even more it influences the restructuration process (respectively, the individual ontologies merging). FD/FID exerts considerable influence on the collective problem solving process. In dyads where members have cognitive styles different by the FD/FID characteristic, the final solution is usually closer to the variant suggested by the FID participant. The FID dyads are experiencing hardships in developing common decisions on arguable points, while the FD dyads are more successful in coming to agreements in collective problem solving.

The impulsivity / reflectivity characteristic considers the amount of information collected prior to making a decision: the impulsive individuals are able to make decisions on considerably bounded information basis, while the reflective individuals are more inclined to make decisions considering the maximally full information on the respective situation. For assessing the test persons' impulsivity/ reflectivity, the "Similar pictures comparison" [29] method has been used.

As for the narrowness/breadth of the category, the main difference between the extreme points of this characteristic is that the narrowly categorizing individuals are inclined to restrict the area of application of a certain category, while the broad categorizers are, conversely, inclined to include a plethora of more-or-less related examples into a single category.

The second part of the research has been performed using the same test sample and included ontology development in/with the use of the Protégé (Protégé) tool. All the tested students were given a task to develop an ontology of the "Informatics" domain.

The quality of the developed ontologies can be assessed by two methods:

- An expert method, where the ontology analyst and domain experts assess the quality by such criteria as completeness, imbalance, "relevance", etc.
- A formalized method, where any ontology is assessed by the same set of quantitative metrics.

The formalized method is more preferable due to being free from experts' and analysts' subjective interpretations and to the possibility of being automated.

3.1   The Main Metrics

In our research the developed ontologies have been assessed by an augmented set of metrics (such as minimal depth, absolute breadth, etc.) suggested in [30].

The legend used to describe the metrics is the following:

"g" — a graph representing an ontology; the concepts (classes and exemplars/ of the ontology are the graph vertices, the relationships between the concepts are the graph links;

"G" — a set of all the vertices g;

"E" — a set of all the ribs g.

- A minimal depth:

$$m = N_{j \in P}, \forall i (N_{j \in P} \leq N_{i \in P}) \qquad (1)$$

where $N_{j \in P}$ and $N_{i \in P}$ are the path lengths j and i from the set of paths P of the graph g.

- An absolute breadth:

$$m = \sum_{j}^{L} N_{j \in L} \qquad (2)$$

where $N_{j \in L}$ is a number of vertices of the degree j from the set of vertices L of the graph g.

- An average breadth:

$$m = \frac{1}{n_{L \subseteq g}} \sum_{j}^{L} N_{j \in L} \qquad (3)$$

where $N_{j \in L}$ is a number of vertices of the degree j from the set of degrees L of the graph g, $n_{L \subseteq g}$— a number of all the degrees of the graph (a maximal graph depth augmented by 1, if considering only a chosen dominant relationship).

- 90% line depth:

$$m = P_{90}(N_{j \in P}) \qquad (4)$$

where $P_{90}(N_{j \in P})$ is a 90% percentile of the graph depth (possible value of the graph path length, not exceeding the length of 90% of the graph paths).

- Root-mean-square deviation of neighbouring levels/degrees breadth ratio:

$$m = \frac{\sum_{i=2}^{n_{L \subseteq g}} \left(\frac{N_{l_i \in L}}{N_{l_{i-1} \in L}} - \frac{1}{n_{L \subseteq g}-1} \sum_{i=2}^{n_{L \subseteq g}} \frac{N_{l_i \in L}}{N_{l_{i-1} \in L}} \right)^2}{n_{L \subseteq g}-1} \qquad (5)$$

- Complexity metric:

A number of vertices with multiple inheritance to the set of all the graph vertices:

$$m = \frac{N_{v \in MI}}{n_G} \qquad (6)$$

where $MI = \{v \in G | \exists a_1, a_2 (isa(v, a_1) \wedge isa(v, a_2))\}$ is a set of all the graph vertices with more than one "is-a" relationship arc, $N_{v \in MI}$ is a number of all the elements of this set, n_G is a number of the graph vertices.

- Average number of the parent vertices of a graph vertice:

$$m = \frac{1}{n_G} \sum_{v}^{G} N_{S_{v \in G}} \qquad (7)$$

where $S_{v \in G} = \{a \in G | isa(v, a)\}$ is a set of all the parents of the vertice v, $N_{S_{v \in G}}$ is a number of all the parent vertices of the vertice v, n_G is a number of the graph vertices.

3.2   Analysis of the Individual Ontology Construction

As we wrote in the introduction section the sample of the research consisted of 79 students of the 4-th year of bachelor program of the Saint Petersburg State Polytechnic University, Institute of Information Technology and Control Systems (IITCS), attending the intelligent systems development course. Due to the professional specificity of the sample, a bias toward narrow, reflective and field-independent test persons is present in the sample. However, a statistically significant Spearman's ρ negative correlation between the FID score and the time of the first answer in the Kagan test has been figured out, showing, among all, that the sample is dominated by the fast FID and slow FD respondents. All the tested students were given a task to develop an ontology of the "Informatics" domain.

The quality of the developed ontologies can be assessed by two methods:

- An expert method, where the ontology analyst and domain experts assess the quality by such criteria as completeness, imbalance, "relevance", etc.
- A formalized method, where any ontology is assessed by the same set of quantitative metrics.

The formalized method is more preferable due to being free from experts' and analysts' subjective interpretations and to the possibility of being automated.

4   Cognitive Style Influence on Ontology Construction

4.1   The Main Hypotheses Regarding Individual Ontology Construction

On the basis of the literature review and the practical ontology development experience the following hypotheses have been suggested:

Hypothesis 1. Individuals belonging to the FID extreme point of the FD/FID cognitive style characteristic tend to have highly developed cognitive structuring capabilities; thus, the quality of ontologies developed by the FID individuals would be higher.

Hypothesis 2. Impulsive individuals tend to develop superficial ontologies lacking sufficient categorization on the upper level, while the reflective individuals tend to develop ontologies of greater depth.

Hypothesis 3. Ontologies developed by the individuals being "imprecise" in the Kagan impulsivity/reflectivity test results tend to be more complex.

Hypothesis 4. The "narrowness/ breadth of the category" cognitive style characteristic exerts significant influence on the ontology breadth: the "broad categorizers" tend to develop ontologies of greater breadth.

The correlation between the cognitive style and ontology metrics values has been assessed by the Spearman's ρ (rank correlation) coefficient. For example, the Spearman's ρ for the "Average number of parents of a graph vertice" metric and the number of mistakes in the Kagan impulsivity/reflectivity test is 0.75, with the confidence interval r (0.63; 0.87), that shows the significant direct relationship between the values of these metrics in the sample.

4.2   Analysis of the Individual Ontology Construction

The Hypothesis 1 has not been supported, as no significant correlation between the FD/FID metric and the ontologies quality has been found; this result arouses optimistic feelings about the whole project, as it shows that it is possible to teach any individual to develop ontologies of high quality.

The Hypothesis 2 has been partially supported: the "90% line depth" metric has demonstrated significant positive correlations with the time of the first answer in the Kagan test, thus showing that reflective test persons tend to develop ontologies of greater depth; however, no significant negative correlation between the time of the first answer and the ontology breadth has been found.

The Hypothesis 3 has been supported, as the number of mistakes in the Kagan test has demonstrated a significant positive correlation with the values of the "Average number of parents of a graph node" metric that characterizes the ontology complexity.

Besides that, the number of mistakes in the Kagan test has demonstrated significant positive correlations with the metrics of the "Minimal depth of the ontology" and the "Families branching coefficient" and significant negative correlation with the weighted leaves branching coefficient.

The Hypothesis 4 has been fully supported: the broad categorizers have developed the ontologies of greater size in terms of the number of concepts, that has been achieved mainly by greater number of "children" of each parent concept.

Respectively, the results of the "Average judgments" test have demonstrated significant correlations with such metrics as the "Average ontology breadth", "Number of leaves", "Absolute power of families", etc. Besides that, these results have demonstrated significant correlation with the root-mean-square deviation of the average ontology breadth. This correlation shows that the number of concepts belonging to the neighboring levels and to different branches is significantly different, thus telling about imbalance of ontologies developed by the broad categorizers. Despite the objectivity of the quantitative metrics-based method of ontology assessment, this method has a significant drawback of being too formalized and lacking semantic analysis elements. Having augmented the quantitative metrics-based analysis by a semantic analysis performed manually, we have found that the ontologies developed by the field-independent test persons tend to have simpler and clearer structure. However, these simplicity and clarity tend to be achieved by truncating the concepts that don't fit into the developed ontology, thus sacrificing the ontology's completeness and integrity for formal logical consistency.

As for the collective ontology development, including wide categorizers into a group together with a FID individual can be useful, with the wide categorizers generating a plethora of subclasses and the FID participant restructuring these. This hypothesis has been tested on the stage of research dedicated to the collective ontology development.

So, the following relationships between the experts' individual cognitive styles and the peculiarities of experts' subject domain ontology development have been figured out as a result of the research:

— Considering the "impulsivity/reflectivity" scale, the reflective individuals tend to develop ontologies of greater depth;
— The ontologies developed by the individuals "imprecise" in the Kagan test persons tend to be more complex;
— The "narrowness/ breadth of the category" cognitive style exerts influence on the ontology branching coefficient, i.e., the ontology breadth.

Table 1. A correlation matrix of the ontology metrics and the chosen cognitive style characteristics

Ontology metrics	Cognitive style characteristics test results		
	I/R		N/BC
	Time of response	Number of mistakes	Category breadth
Number of classes			0,44
Number of leaves			0,46
Absolute depth			0,39
Minimal depth		0,54	
90% line depth	0,34		
Average breadth			0,48
Average breadth root-mean-square deviation			0,48
Average number of parents of a graph node		0,47	
Absolute power of families			0,44
Families branching coefficient		0,50	
Absolute power of leaves			0,46
Weighted leaves branching coefficient		-0,39	

4.3   Collective Ontology Design

As to specificity of the collective ontology development has also been researched, both in dyads as well as the groups of 3-5 persons. An objective of this study was to figure out how the collective categorization style is being developed.

KOMET-DILIGENT collective ontology development methodology developed within the KOMET project uses the algorithm [11]:

1. Preliminary individual ontology development by the participants and consequent mutual ontology matching;
2. Ontologies analysis, merging and alignment;
3. Ontology revision and redesign.

Students first develop individual ontologies and then were asked to develop the collective common ontology of the same topic "Informatics'. The given time was 1 hour.

The experiments were aimed to figure out how the collective categorization style is being developed. Two strategies have been figured out at that:

S1 – a strategy of collective ontology development "from the scratch", and

S2 – a strategy of common ontology development on the basis of two or more individual drafts.

These strategies influence the peculiarities of analyzing and merging individual ontologies in the collective ontology development methodology, suggested and explained by the authors hereinbefore.

The second strategy S2 is of greater practical interest. In its case the analysts nearly consequently apply all the three basic ontology engineering operations (matching, merging and alignment).

The experiments have shown that merging usually follows either of the two scenarios:

— Absorption scenario (60-70 % of all the tested groups);
— Compromise (synthesis) scenario (30-40 % of the tested groups).

The absorption scenario has been researched by us in more details, as this scenario was used more often than the others. Researching this scenario, we have been able to figure out two models of its implication:

— A conjunctive model, with the higher power ontology absorbing the lower power one and further merging of the same-degree vertices in the resulting ontology.
— A disjunctive model, with the vertices reduction leading to the resulting ontology including only the disjunction or interception of the same-degree vertices.

Comparison of these scenarios with the cognitive styles of the test persons has revealed the following relationships:

— Field-independent (FID) test persons tend to prefer the disjunctive scenaria;
— The field-dependent (FD) test persons tend to prefer the conjunctive scenaria.

5   Conclusion

The use of visual paradigm to represent and support the teaching process not only helps a professional tutor to concentrate on the problem rather than on details, but also enables learners and students to process and understand great volumes of information. The development of beautiful knowledge structures in the form of ontologies provide learning supports and scaffolds that may improve student understanding of substantive and syntactic knowledge. As such, they can play a part in the overall pattern of learning by facilitating for example analysis, comparison, generalization, and transferability of understanding to analogous problems. Therefore, the visual knowledge structure editors provide is a two dimensional, iconic model that represents the teacher's understanding of key elements in the subject.

As an assessment tool, ontologies can be used to visualize and analyze the student's knowledge and understanding. Through visual inspection of the ontology it is possible to detect gaps and misunderstandings in the student's cognitive model of the learnt knowledge. However, there is not much consensus yet about the designing and orchestrating of the courseware structure that should be used. Furthermore, in many cases it is not known what the structure of socially legitimate knowledge pattern looks like and how a particular instance of a knowledge model is deviating from that "ideal" state (e.g. teacher's view). But teachers are individuals, and they may disagree among themselves.

The stages of the KOMET research project dedicated to the inquiry into the influence of the expert's individual cognitive style parameters on the group ontology design strategies has shown the following results.

Group ontology design, both in dyads or groups of more than two participants, is performed either "from scratch" or on the basis of the drafts prepared by the members of the group individually.

Merging of the individual drafts into single group ontology follows either the absorption or the compromise, or synthesis scenario. The absorption scenario of the ontologies merging can be implied according to either a conjunctive or a disjunctive model.

From the group participants of different cognitive styles, the field-dependent participants tend to prefer the conjunctive model of the ontologies merging, with the higher power ontology absorbing the lower power one and further merging of the same-level nodes in the resulting ontology.

Respectively, the field-independent participants tend to prefer the disjunctive model, with the nodes reduction leading to the resulting ontology including only the disjunction or interception of the same-level nodes. The research of individual cognitive styles, primarily, field independence/ field dependence (FID/FD), influence on the peculiarities of team ontology development, has shown the following results.

When developing a common ontology on the basis of two or more individual drafts, the field-dependent test persons tend to prefer the conjunctive model of the ontologies merging, with the higher power ontology absorbing the lower power one and further merging of the same-level nodes in the resulting ontology.

Respectively, the field-independent test persons tend to prefer the disjunctive model, with the nodes reduction leading to the resulting ontology including only the disjunction or interception of the same-level nodes.

In team problem solving in dyads with participants of different cognitive styles, the final solution is usually closer to the variant suggested by the field-independent participant. However, the dyads consisting of two field-independent persons are experiencing hardships in developing common decisions on arguable points, while the field-dependent dyads are more successful in coming to agreements in cooperative problem solving.

Despite the preliminary character of the research results, all the findings can be used in organizing the team ontology development, data structuring and other team analytical work. Taking into consideration the students' cognitive styles when organizing students into groups for collective ontology development, the instructor enhances her or his ability of guiding the ontology development process to reach deeper levels of students' understanding of the subject domain.

6   Possible Applications

The first most obvious possible application of the results can be in learning on different levels of education. Indeed, team ontology development by the students can lead these students to deeper and more holistic understanding of the respective subject domains, especially when the instructor takes into consideration the students' cognitive styles when organizing students into groups for team ontology development.

Besides that, the influence of individual cognitive styles on team ontology development can be taken into consideration in all the possible areas where team intellectual work with ontology development as a possible method can be used, e.g., fundamental science, R&D or management consulting.

Comparison of the conjunctive and disjunctive models of the absorption scenario with the cognitive styles of the test persons has revealed the following relationships:

1. Field-independent (FID) test persons tend to prefer the disjunctive model;
2. The field-dependent (FD) test persons tend to prefer the conjunctive model.

Following the ideas of A. Witkin, we can interpret FID/FD as a proxy of the structuring capability of an individual mind.

This cognitive style does exert significant influence on the process of collective problem solving. For example, in cases of problem solving in dyads with participants of different cognitive styles, the final solution is usually closer to the variant suggested by the FID participant. However, the dyads consisting of two FID persons are experiencing hardships in developing common decisions on arguable points, while the FD dyads are more successful in coming to agreements in cooperative problem solving.

Acknowledgements. The KOMET project is funded by Russian Foundation for Basic Research (RFBR), grant 11-07-00140.

References

1. Mizoguchi, R., Bourdeau, J.: Using Ontological Engineering to Overcome Common AI-ED Problems. International Journal of Artificial Intelligence in Education 11(2), 107–121 (2000)
2. Schreiber, G.: Knowledge Engineering and Management: The CommonKADS Methodology. MIT Press, Cambridge (2000)
3. Dicheva, D., Aroyo, L.: Concepts and Ontologies in Web-based Educational Systems. Int. J. Cont. Engineering Education and Life-long Learning 14(3), 187–190 (2004)
4. Dicheva, D., Dichev, C.: Authoring Educational Topic Maps: Can We Make It Easier? In: Proceedings of ICALT, pp. 216–219 (2005)
5. Dicheva, D., Dichev, C.: Helping Courseware Authors to Build Ontologies: The Case of TM4L. In: 13th Int. Conference on Artificial Intelligence in Education, California, July 9-13, pp. 77–84 (2007)

6. Knight, C., Gašević, D., Richards, G.: An Ontology-Based Framework for Bridging Learning Design and Learning Content. Educational Technology & Society 9(1), 23–37 (2006)
7. Davies, J., van Harmelen, F., Fensel, D. (eds.): Towards the Semantic Web: Ontology-Driven Knowledge Management. John Wiley & Sons, Inc., New York (2002)
8. Gavrilova, T.: Teaching via Using Ontological Engineering. In: Proceedings of XI Int. Conf. Powerful ICT for Teaching and Learning PEG 2003, St.Petersburg, pp. 23–26 (2003)
9. Gavrilova, T., Leshcheva, I., Strakhovich, E.: The use of visual conceptual models in teaching. In: Vestnik of Saint Petersburg University. Management Series, vol. (4), pp. 125–151 (2011)
10. Gavrilova, T., Gorovoy, V., Bolotnikova, E.: Evaluation of collective ergonomics of ontology based on the analysis of the graph. Russian Academy of Sciences Journal "Artificial Intelligence and Decision Making" 3, 33–41 (2009)
11. Gavrilova, T., Bolotnikova, E., Leshcheva, I., Strakhovich, E.: Collective corporate ontologies development. In: The XVth Scientific and Practical Conference Reengineering of Business Processes Based on Contemporary Information Technologies. Systems of knowledge management, Moscow, pp. 39–42 (2012)
12. Sowa, J.F.: Conceptual Structures: Information Processing in Mind and Machine. Addison-Wesley, Reading (1994)
13. Jonassen, D.H.: Designing constructivist learning environments. In: Reigeluth, C.M. (ed.) Instructional Design Models and Strategies, 2nd edn. Lawrence Erlbaum, Mahwah (1998)
14. Conlon, T.: Towards Diversity: Advancing Knowledge-based Modelling with Knowledge Acquisition. In: Proceedings of 8th International PEG Conference, Sozopol, Bulgaria, pp. 379–386 (1997)
15. Kinchin, I.M., De-Leij, F.A.A.M., Hay, D.B.: The evolution of a collaborative concept mapping activity for undergraduate microbiology. Journal of Further and Higher Education 29(1), 1–14 (2005)
16. Chandrasekaran, B., Johnson, T.R., Benjamins, V.R.: Ontologies: what are they? why do we need them? IEEE Intelligent Systems and Their Applications. Special Issue on Ontologies 14(1), 20–26 (1999)
17. Neches, et al.: Enabling Technology for Knowledge Sharing. AI Magazine, 36–56 (Winter 1991)
18. Gavrilova, T.A., Voinov, A.: Visualized Conceptual Structuring for Heterogeneous Knowledge Acquisition. In: Proceedings of International Conference on Educational Multimedia and Hypermedia, EDMEDIA 1996, pp. 258–264. MIT, Boston (1996)
19. Gavrilova, T., Leshcheva, I., Bolotnikova, E.: Using visual conceptual models in teaching. In: Proceedings of the 8th International Conference on Education, ICE-2012, pp. 191–197. Research and Training Institute of East Aegean, Greece (2012)
20. Strakhovich, E., Gavrilova, T.: Cognitive aspects of educational ontologies design. New Trends in Software Methodologies, Tools, and Techniques. In: Proceedings of the Tenth SoMet 2011, pp. 227–233. IOS Press (2011)
21. Gruber, T.: A translation approach to portable ontology specifications. Knowledge Acquisition 5, 199–220 (1993)
22. Guarino, N., Giaretta, P.: Ontologies and Knowledge Bases: Towards a Terminological Clarification. In: Towards Very Large Knowledge Bases: Knowledge Building & Knowledge Sharing, pp. 25–32 (1998)
23. Gómez-Pérez, A., Fernández-López, M., Corcho, O.: Ontological Engineering with examples from the areas of Knowledge Management, e-Commerce and the Semantic Web. Springer, London (2004)

24. Buzan, T.: Mind Map handbook. Thorsons (2005)
25. Novak, J.D., Cañas, A.J.: The Theory Underlying Concept Maps and How to Construct Them. Technical Report IHMC CmapTools 2006-01, Florida Institute for Human and Machine Cognition (2006), http://cmap.ihmc.us/Publications/ResearchPapers/TheoryUnderlyingConceptMaps.pdf
26. Leshcheva, I., Kotova, E.: Investigation of the relationship between expert's cognitive style and ontologies built by expert. In: Proceedings of the 1st International Symposium Hybrid and Synergistic Intelligent Systems: Theory and Practice, GISIS 2012. The Publishing House of the Immanuel Kant Baltic Federal University (2012)
27. Kholodnaya, M.: Cognitive styles. On the nature of the individual mind, 2nd edn., Piter, Saint Petersburg (2004)
28. Witkin, H.A., Moore, C.A., Goodenough, D.R., Cox, P.W.: Field-dependent and field-independent cognitive styles and their educational implications. Review of Educational Research 47, 1–64 (1977)
29. Kagan, J.: Reflection-impulsivity: The generality and dynamics of conceptual tempo. Journal of Abnormal Psychology 71(1), 17–24 (1966)
30. Bolotnikova, E., Gavrilova, T., Gorovoy, V.: A method for evaluation of ontologies. Izvestiya RAN, The Theory and Systems of Management 3, 98–110 (2011)

Applied Semantics for Integration and Analytics

Sergey Gorshkov

Business Semantics, Bazhova 89,
620075 Ekaterinburg, Russia
serge@business-semantic.ru

Abstract. There are two major trends of industrial application for semantic technologies: integration and analytics. The integration potential of semantics was the first one which came to industrial implementation, particularly due to adoption of semantic platform by ISO 15926 standard. But there are certain problems in practical use of this standard, so integration is often built without using it. We will show an example of implementation of semantic Enterprise Service Bus in RosEnergoTrans company, and discuss whether it was better to rely on ISO 15926 ontologies for this project.

Adding analytic features to semantic solution gives it much more business value that integration itself can offer. We will discuss semantic solutions from this point of view, and compare analytical potential of ISO 15926 data models with "simple" semantics.

Keywords: ISO 15926, integration, analytics, business value.

1 Introduction

Semantic Web technologies are one of the most current trends of industrial data processing software development. Particularly, they are known in oil & gas and other industries due to promotion of the ISO 15926 standard. Expert's attention is now mostly focused on constructing industry-wide thesauri, such as the JORD project. They are providing reference data for modeling objects and processes in the industry. But the main question – how to use these models? – is often shadowed behind discussions of conceptual opportunities of various modeling approaches. Meanwhile, the practical usability of the model is a crucial factor of its success.

We see two major ways of practical usage of semantic data models. One of them is data conversion to the "universal", system-neutral form, for transferring information between applications. Implementations of this idea for integration (or interoperability) purposes may face some performance-related issues.

Another way of use of semantically expressed data is creating analytical applications, using graph search and reasoning. This allows building decision support systems, and a new generation of data warehouses and data mining applications. Development of such technologies is an obvious trend in the modern IT (Facebook Graph Search is a well-known example), that the industry cannot ignore.

P. Klinov and D. Mouromtsev (Eds.): KESW 2013, CCIS 394, pp. 44–53, 2013.
© Springer-Verlag Berlin Heidelberg 2013

2   Use Case Description

Let us start with description of the real industrial use case, which will be used in this article to test practical usability of discussed implementation approaches. RosEnergo-Trans company, part of SverdlovElektro group, is a manufacturing plant, producing electrical transformers and other equipment. One of important parts of business process of this company is working with client requests (calls for tender participation, etc). Each such request contains a specification of equipment required, that has to be reviewed by engineers for price calculation. Sales managers are putting requests for calculation of electrical transformers into the CRM (MySQL-based application). These requests, together with attached files and other information, are transferring to engineering software (Oracle-based application). There, engineers are performing calculations. The result – a price estimate – has to be approved. Then it returns to CRM, where sales manager receives it and uses to negotiate with customer. The whole integration process has to be completely transparent: manager needs to see in CRM, how his request is processing in engineering software. A manager should interact with an engineer by exchanging comments and request amendments. Each of them is working only in his own application, not being aware what application is used by his counterpart. In fact, requests processing is done simultaneously in both applications. A simplified look of request processing flow is shown on the Fig. 1.

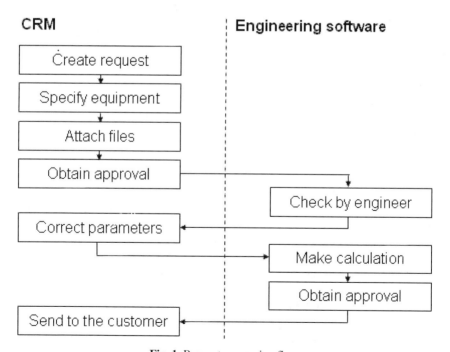

Fig. 1. Request processing flow

Data structures of these applications do not have a full symmetry. There is a quite different set of tables in both underlying databases. For example, CRM has one table to store requests and requested products, while engineering software has two. In total, almost 50% of entities (tables and properties) of both databases cannot be mapped directly with one-to-one relations. In addition, data structures in both applications tend to change from time to time, reflecting changes in the business process.

This leads to an idea of using semantic-based enterprise service bus as a mediator. Common semantic data model will provide an application-independent way of representing data transferred, and simplify entities mapping. Enterprise service bus offers transparent and real-time data exchange. We have used our Business Semantics software as an Enterprise Service Bus solution, as it has connectors for both Oracle and MySQL DB. The main question, however, lays in ontology and mapping design.

3   Standard-Based Ontologies vs. Generic Ontologies

There is the standard covering various aspects of ontology modeling, and even technical ways of semantic data exchange: ISO 15926. It offers a top-level ontology (201 types), a concept of Reference Data Library, intended to store commonly used entity types, and a concept of templates, used for expressing events and complex relations between information objects. Its obvious advantage is a status of ISO standard; however, its implementations are not wide spread, particularly due to high complexity of modeling and mapping. Obviously, use of this standard may make sense in case of data exchange (or interoperability) between enterprises. In our case, however, it is known that data exchange will never cross corporative DMZ boundary.

Another important factor of choice is a complexity and computability of the model, which affects simplicity of mappings, and ability to build some analytic features based on the model in the future. Analytics aren't included in the list of primary tasks of the project; however, it may become necessary, so the right choice of modeling approach is important from the beginning.

The question of choosing ISO 15926 as an ontology modeling basis worth discussion, because of a significant trend in industrial automation, promoting it as the best and proven practice [1]. It forces to select the modeling approach carefully and justify it for the industrial customer, taking into account technological and economical consequences. Despite oil & gas industry origin, ISO 15926 is widely used in electrical energy industry, particularly in Rosatom corporation [2], Areva etc.

To prove our choice, we have conducted some analysis of ISO 15926-based ontological models versus generic ones. Let's turn to another example, to clearly demonstrate ISO 15926 modeling features. We have built a sample model, containing description of one event, and all entities involved in it. This example is taken from ISO 15926 "native" area – oil & gas industry, because area is well covered by commonly accepted modeling practices and examples, and it provides a more diverse sample environment than our real use case.

So, let's describe the installation of a pump into a pipeline. This event may be represented as a simple semantic model like this:

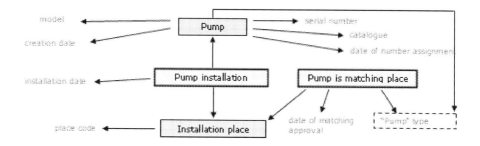

Fig. 2. Sample generic data model

On this image, boxes with thick borders are representing instances of events, boxes with thin borders – instances of physical objects, box with dashed border – a type definition from reference data. In fact, all these items are just a graph vertices; difference between them lies only at the logical level. Elements without borders are literals, arrows are representing graph edges.

Putting this model from OWL to triple store, we will have 5 entities and 11 relations (including literals), that give us 16 triples (+1 triple defining each entity's type). This model can be queried using rather simple SPARQL queries. For example, if we want to know in which place the pump with certain serial number was installed, we will have to examine three graph edges.

Using ISO 15926 approach, model will have the structure shown below.

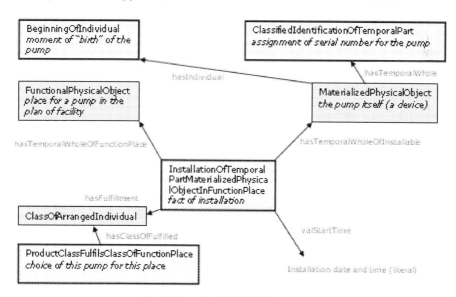

Fig. 3. Sample ISO 15926 data model

Here, boxes with thick borders are template instances, boxes with thin borders – object instances. Names in the boxes are representing class names – entity types.

This simple example gives us ability to describe and measure differences between ISO 15926-based model, and the "simple" (generic) one. ISO 15926 model, having the same amount of information than generic model shown above, has 7 entities and 29 relations, which give us 36 triples (2 times more). The same querying task will require looking at four graph edges instead of three.

A given example clearly shows the cause of complexity of ISO 15926 models: it is an inevitable consequence of introducing temporal parts as separate entities, use of templates to represent complex relations (mainly events), and introducing a complex entities classifications. However, there are other possible ways to express time-stamped data using semantic technologies [3]. In our particular case, we are not dealing with time-stamped data: although some entities are having attributes of datetime type, their values are not involved in any calculations or transfer logic.

This rise of complexity may be acceptable, if it would give meaningful opportunities in particular use case; however, in this case it does not. So, in the RosEnergo-Trans integration implementation, we have all reasons to use a generic ontology. As we know, similar approach is used in many other industrial applications (various implementations of SDShare protocol, for example by Bouvet company [4], projects of Det Norske Veritas company [5], and many others).

4   Integration or Interoperability?

Another important difference in approaches to semantic technologies usage in data exchange lies in data transfer mode. Generally, difference may be described as integration (which means duplicating some data from one system to another) versus interoperability (on-demand access to data sets stored in remote system). ISO 15926 standard, in general, promotes interoperability model, called federated data access. Part 9 of this standard, defining exchange implementation, states that interaction has to be performed between SPARQL endpoints (called "façades"), using two methods – pull (remote query for data), and push (active data transfer). So, ISO 15926 is defining the full stack of integration technologies, from modeling methodology to data transfer techniques. However, it does not mean that any dependency exist between modeling approach and data exchange methods. There are no technical reasons why ISO 15926 ontologies cannot be exchanged by another way, or why SPARQL "façades" cannot interact using generic ontologies.

An alternative may be a usage of semantic data encoding for data transfer using enterprise service bus, which implies at least partial data synchronization (master data management). In most cases, when we are talking about close interaction between operational applications, a true integration is required instead of interoperability, because data access speed become crucial. Due to this reason, in RosEnergoTrans case integration was required instead of interoperability: it is impossible to access another application each time when data on particular document needs to be involved in some query.

If semantic data model is built mostly for analytical purposes, data exchange schema has to be changed. In this case, it is most likely that we need to build a kind of semantic data warehouse. Designing architecture of data warehouse, we have to choose from similar alternatives: to replicate all required data into a single triple store, or to leave data where they are, building a logical semantic layer above existing storages. The last approach is on the edge of development now. Implementations (such as Optique project, www.optique-project.eu) tend to use semantic model as a core for a user interface, allowing building queries. Each element of semantic model has a mapping to relational database, where the real data is stored. The SPARQL query constructed by user is automatically converted to a joint SQL query, its result is mapped back to semantic model terms, and returned to the user. Obvious drawbacks of this approach are low execution speed (due to excessive complexity of queries, and its execution on remote servers), and the need to keep mappings up to date when changing database structure (that happens regularly in business process management applications databases). Examples of such challenges were demonstrated, for example, on Siemens applications of Optique project [6]. Depending on usage context, these drawbacks may overweight the main opportunity of discussed approach – absence of data duplication.

In the RosEnergoTrans project, we have undoubtedly selected integration (synchronization) schema, having necessity to provide real-time transparent data exchange in automating operational tasks, and being unable to isolate data of each type in single application.

5   Implementation Details

Now let us show some details regarding integration implementation in our use case. The diagram of entity types defined in ontology is shown below.

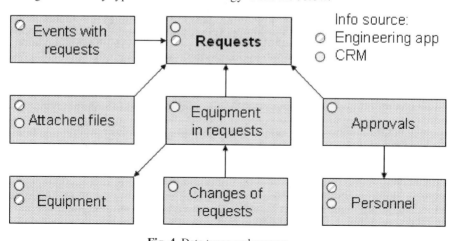

Fig. 4. Data types and sources

There are 8 entity types, having about 100 properties. Note that entities of a half of these types may be created/changed/deleted from both applications integrated.

Various tools may be used for ontology creation: we've started with Protégé, but then turned to Cognitum FluentEditor. It is a Controlled Natural Language tool [7], which allows creating ontologies using such interface:

```
1   Namespace: 'http://business-semantic.ru/'.
2
3   Every request is something.
4   Every approval is something.
5
6   Every request has-delivery-address one (some-value).
7   Every approval has-request one approval.
```

Fig. 5. Data types and sources

The result may be saved as an OWL file, and imported into Business Semantics server configuration interface. Server propagates ontology to client modules.

It is interesting to see how entities of those types are stored in both databases, to determine, how they can be mapped to ontology elements. If we would try to map databases directly, we will have the following image:

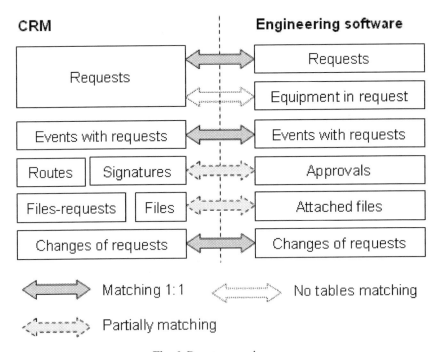

Fig. 6. Data types and sources

Equipment and personnel tables, not shown at this diagram, may be mapped direct-ly. One-to-one mapping between tables storing the same type of information, of course, does not mean that direct mapping is possible between properties: for exam-ple, a "Customer" property of the request in CRM is pointing to "Customers" table, which is storing customer's address and other information; in engineering software, customer and its address are just a textual fields in the properties of request.

But we are not establishing direct mapping between elements of two databases – instead, we are mapping elements of each database with ontology entities and their properties. We should do that using Business Semantics client configuration interface, for each integrating application separately.

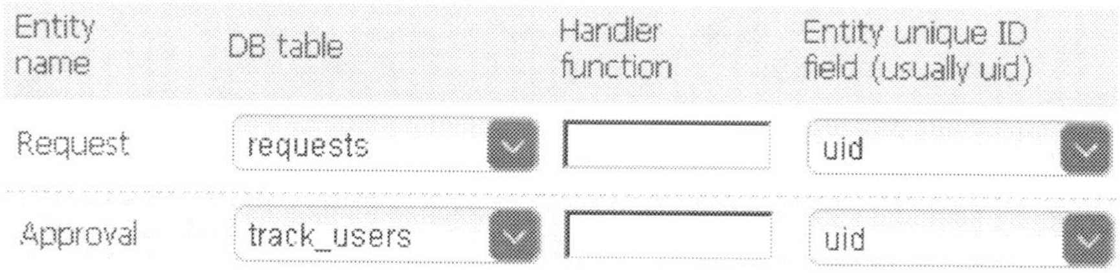

Entity name	DB table	Handler function	Entity unique ID field (usually uid)
Request	requests ⌄		uid ⌄
Approval	track_users ⌄		uid ⌄

Fig. 7. Mapping entities to tables in Business Semantics configuration interface

Next, we need to set up mappings between model properties, and database fields.

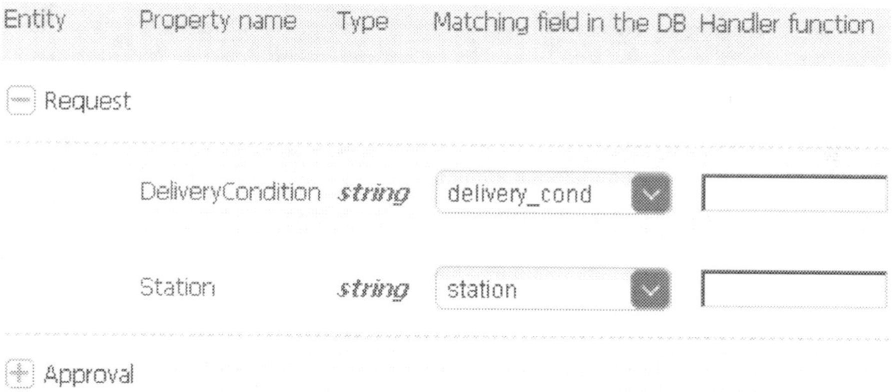

Entity	Property name	Type	Matching field in the DB	Handler function
⊖ Request				
	DeliveryCondition	*string*	delivery_cond ⌄	
	Station	*string*	station ⌄	
⊕ Approval				

Fig. 8. Mapping properties to fields in Business Semantics configuration interface

If we cannot map directly an entity to the table, or a property to the field, we should define a handler function. This function, written in the client system native language, has to be defined according to the rules described in Business Semantics documentation. It can perform custom actions, necessary to convert ontology ele-ments to the local storage structures, and back.

After these settings are done, we should set subscriptions and access rights for on-tology elements on the Business Semantics server.

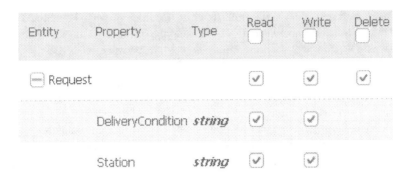

Fig. 9. Defining access rights

After that, the integration process can be run. Business Semantics client tracks changes in the source database using triggers, pushing changed data items into queue. Queue is processed each few seconds – client software encodes data into semantic form (triples expressed in Turtle syntax), and sending it to the server using SOAP interface. Server checks data integrity, and routes data to all subscribed applications. Client modules on that application's side, in its turn, are interpreting semantically encoded data back to relational storages.

The described integration schema is used in production environment. There are no performance issues, primarily due to not very intensive data flow (~10 000 triples daily). We have conducted performance stress-tests to prove system's ability to handle sufficiently higher load, and have achieved a maximum performance of 720 000 triples per hour (with one low-performance server).

The project is constantly developing. There is an interest to include company's ERP system in exchange process, to extend number of data types exchanged. As a prospective, we see development of semantic data warehouse for analytical purposes, as a way to extract additional business value from the use of semantic technologies in the corporate IT environment.

6   Conclusions

Semantic technologies allow achieving significant benefits in the project of integrating CRM system and engineering software in RosEnergoTrans company. We were able to avoid writing a large amount of program code, strictly bound to the database structure on both sides. Despite absence of simple mapping between databases, we were able to implement required transformations in the most general way, using semantic form of information representation as a mediator. In addition, such integration schema is much easier to support than thousands of lines of complex custom program code, which would inevitably appear in case of other integration solutions. For a user, integration is completely transparent. A user working in one application sees data processing as if it were performed only in this application. Any information, entered in one application, immediately appears in another.

Finding appropriate method of data modeling and implementing integration, a system engineer has to consider various aspects of model usability. Depending on usage scope, required level of analytical features, acceptable level of model complexity, standard-based or generic modeling approach may be chosen.

Another thing to choose is a data exchange approach. Integration offers more benefits in operational environments, but requires data duplication; interoperability keeps each data in a single source, but most probably will cause significant delays in applications execution. Building a semantic data model for analytical purposes, a system architect faces the same problem. It should be resolved regarding priorities of integration project.

A concept of semantic Enterprise Service Bus software is proven in the real industry use case.

References

1. Levenchuk, A.: Why ISO 15926 is resolving problems, that previous generations of the standards were unable to resolve. In: Capitalization of Oil & Gas Knowledge, `http://www.ngk-conf.ru/files/Anatoly_Levenchuk_Rus.pdf`
2. Berekzin, D.: Building an ontological industry-level glossary according to ISO 15926 standard. In: Hybrid and Synergies Intelligent Systems: Theory and Practice, Kaliningrad, pp. 245–254 (2012)
3. Artale, A., Kontchakov, R., Wolter, F., Zakharyaschev, M.: Temporal Description Logic for Ontology-Based Data Access. In: International Joint Conference on Artificial Intelligence, Beijing (to appear, 2013)
4. Borge, A.: Hafslund SESAM - Semantic Integration in Practice. In: Semantic Days 2013 (2013), `https://www.posccaesar.org/svn/pub/SemanticDays/2013/Present ations/DAY%202/1030%20Axel%20Borge%20Semantic%20Intergration %20for%20Hafslund%20by%20Axel%20Borge%20-Bouvet.pdf`
5. Klüwer, J.W., Valen-Sendstad, M.: The Source for engineering information: Building Aibel's EPC ontology. In: Semantic Days 2013 (2013), `https://www.posccaesar.org/svn/pub/SemanticDays/2013/Present ations/DAY%203/0930%20DNV%20TheSource-SemDays2013.pdf`
6. Hubauer, T.: On challenges with time-stamped data in Siemens Energy Services. In: Semantic Days 2013 (2013), `https://www.posccaesar.org/svn/pub/ SemanticDays/2013/Presentations/DAY%203/Parallell%202/ Thomas%20Hubauer%20Optique%20- %20On%20challenges%20with%20time- stamped%20data%20in%20Siemens%20Energy%20Services.pdf`
7. Kaplanski, P., Wroblewska, A., Zieba, A., Zarzycki, P.: Practical applications of controlled natural language with description logics and OWL. FluentEditor and OASE (2012), `http://www.cognitum.eu/research/publications/Cognitum_Semant ics%20_CNL2012.pdf`

Technology of Ontology Visualization Based on Cognitive Frames for Graphical User Interface

Pavel Lomov and Maxim Shishaev

Establishment of Russian Academy of Sciences
Institute for Informatics and Mathematical Modeling of
Technological Processes of the Kola Science Center RAS
{lomov,shishaev}@iimm.kolasc.net.ru

Abstract. This paper is dedicated to the issue of visualization of OWL ontologies to help their comprehension. In a previous work we showed a process of simplifying OWL ontologies by transforming them into a form called the *User Presentation Ontology* (UPO). In this paper we discuss some aspects of visual representation of ontologies for better understanding by human users. We present the approach of combining some UPO elements with special fragments called *cognitive frames*. It is expected that showing cognitive frames during visualization instead of just showing any terms linked with the chosen term will be more useful for ontology understanding. We determine some requirements for cognitive frames, define their types, and consider formal algorithms for constructing the frames.

Keywords: ontology, semantic web, ontology comprehension, upper level ontology.

1 Introduction

Nowadays the use of ontologies for knowledge representation and semantic processing of information becomes very useful. There are many fields where ontologies can be applied including multi-agent systems, automatic extraction of knowledge from texts in a natural language, information search and others. It is also very beneficial to use ontologies as the base of graphical user interface (GUI). Such a GUI allows an end user to operate with familiar terms, discover subject domain in a simple way and support him during query formation. On the other hand the developers of GUI dont waste time on achieving knowledge of subject domain because it is presented in some ontology in a formal way.

At the same time, Web Ontology Language (OWL, Ontology Web Language) [6] got the increasing popularity. It owed its success, wealth of expressive features and at the same time the formal resolvability. Proposed and developed by a consortium W3C, OWL is by far the de facto standard for presenting ontologies for their use in the Internet. However, OWL ontology is, in fact, a system of description logic statements (axioms). This complicates their visual representation within the intuitive graphical user interface (GUI). To solve this problem,

P. Klinov and D. Mouromtsev (Eds.): KESW 2013, CCIS 394, pp. 54–68, 2013.
© Springer-Verlag Berlin Heidelberg 2013

the developer needs good background and skills in logic, ontology engineering, conceptual modeling, cognitive science.

Because of this, we need some technology for visualization ontologies within the GUI, which would allow the developer to avoid their detailed analysis. Created with the help of such technology GUI should help user to understand the meaning of the concepts defined by the developer of the ontology.

To date, there exists a number of the software tools for ontologies visualization: GraphViz [10], TGVizTab [18], OWLViz [2], OntoSphere [7]. However, they focus on displaying those OWL axioms, which can be represented as nodes and edges, i.e. as a graph. Such a graph-like ontologie representation technique though is universal, but leads to loss of concept semantics at visual presentation. Another approach concentrates on the analysis of the semantics of ontology axioms and allows reflecting the logical consequences for its modification. Software tools implementing such approach in the papers [5,4] are considered. However, they are intended mostly for ontology developers, not for software developers or end-users. In addition, in the studies mentioned, the visualization takes into account only the formal semantics, which directly follows from the axioms describing the concept.

A similar approach has been presented in the work [1] devoted to the problem in extracting viewpoints from the knowledge base: determining which facts are relevant to requested viewpoints. However it is focused on the application to the frame-based knowledge representation model, not OWL ontology. During visualization it can lead to the omission of some OWL axioms which can't be presented as a set of frames in a trivial way.

The main idea of the approach proposed in this work is the visualization of ontology with regard to the meaning of the concepts and relations invariant to subject domains. As its sources upper-level ontologies are regarded. It is suggested allocating in visualized ontology fragments the cognitive frames corresponding to concept chosen by the user and shown to him. This allows us to convey the concepts meaning that the author of ontology meant. For ease of the understanding it by the user, cognitive frames are formed with the general laws of the human perception of the visual information.

The structure of the paper is as follows: Section 2 outlines the main results of the previous research in this field. Section 3 presents formal definition of the cognitive frame and basic requirements to it. Section 4 discusses the algorithms for cognitive frames composing, and Section 5 presents conclusions and the future directions of our research.

2   Background

In the previous work [19] the issue of the automatic generation of the OWL-ontologies representation adapted for visualization has been considered. This representation called User Presentation Ontology (UPO) is based on the SKOS (Simple Knowledge Organization System) model [25]. SKOS model is simpler than the OWL model, and could be visualized as a graph structure without any preliminary analysis performed by the GUI developer.

The SKOS data model views a knowledge organization system as a concept scheme comprising a set of concepts. SKOS concepts are similar to OWL classes and present some notion of a subject domain. They can be connected among themselves via hierarchical and associative relations, such as "skos:broader"/ "skos:narrower", "skos:related", "closeMatch" and others. SKOS language, unlike OWL is not a formal knowledge representation language.

UPO was formed by presenting the original axioms of OWL-ontology as a set of SKOS model elements: concepts, relationships, and collections. To do this the axioms were divided into two types - simple and composite, in accordance with the complexity of their visual presentation. Simple axioms have on the right side one named or unnamed class defined by the constraint on a single property, while a composite axiom has several named and/or unnamed classes on the right. Simple axioms can be directly represented as a set of elements of the SKOS model.

The classes of OWL-ontology and object relations are presented as SKOS-concepts and SKOS-relationships. It assumes that for named OWL classes SKOS concepts are created. And SKOS concepts are linked together via some relations if there is OWL object property, which contains corresponding OWL classes in its domain and range. (Fig. 1).

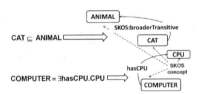

Fig. 1. Presentation of simple OWL-axioms in UPO

In the case of composite axioms a preliminary analysis has been produced. It consisted of bringing the axioms to disjunctive normal form, and representing any disjunct (we called it "subaxiom") as SKOS-concept (Fig. 2). The latter linked with SKOS-concept, corresponded to OWL-class defined by them, by SKOS-relation "related".

Thus, when rendering the UPO GUI developer is not required to analyze the components of the axioms and determine how to visualize them.

Later in the article, referring to the visualization of the ontology, we assume that the latter is transformed into an equivalent UPO, which can be represented as a graph structure. The nodes of such a structure would serve concepts, corresponding to the OWL-class of original ontology. Arcs will represent the relationship between OWL-classes.

3   The Definition of the Cognitive Frame

Typically, the process of submission of any data or knowledge within the interfaces of information systems consists in likening objects, processes and

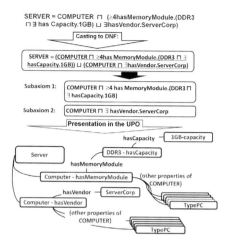

Fig. 2. Analysis and presentation of composite OWL-axioms in UPO

phenomena of the subject area, as well as relations between them to some visual images. These visual images serve as visualization metaphors. Thus, the metaphor can be defined as the mapping that assigns some system of the analogies to concepts of the modelled subject domain, and generating some set of the visual objects and methods of interaction with them[3].

In [26] the author emphasizes that visualization metaphor performs the basic cognitive function of GUI. This is reflected in the fact that through it, user can attach an image of an unknown fragment of reality to another image, known to him, and thereby provide a conceptualization of an unknown fragment in the existing system of concepts.

Widely used visualization metaphor for formal ontologies is a graph structure, i.e., the set of named nodes connected by edges. This is due to the fact that formal ontologies are approximately similar to semantic networks and for their visualization some graphical notations with the alphabet based on the elements of the graph are commonly used.

Note also that for the more accurate reproduction of the concept meaning (idea) which is embedded in it by the author of ontology corresponding visual image in addition to the concept itself should include the concept's context - neighbors-concepts, associated with it by some relation.

We will continue to refer such visual image as "cognitive frame", by analogy with the known notion of "frame" by Minsky [22]. Thus, Minsky defined the frame as a data structure for representing a stereotyped situation. That is, the frame is a kind of model of an object, phenomenon, event or process. In our case, cognitive frame refers to the graphical structure helping to understand the idea of representation of some entity existing in the ontology. Thus, cognitive frame provides a kind of meta-representation, promoting human perception of knowledge about objects, processes and phenomena from ontology.

The requirements to cognitive frame as a visual metaphor are determined by psychological limitations of the human's ability to process information. One of these limits is the Miller's "magical number" [21], , indicating the possibility of a short-term storage in the memory of man is not more than 7-9 objects. It defines a recommended limit in the number of cognitive frame components and conditions, cognitive frame compactness property. Following this limit allows a person to perceive simultaneously the idea transmitted by a cognitive frame without any additional mental operations, in particular - without partitioning a large number of components into groups.

Satisfying the requirement of compactness, cognitive frame, however, should provide complete information about the concept. The completeness and compactness of cognitive frames will allow a person to operate mainly a short-term memory, "downloading" individual frames as a whole, which requires much less mental effort than constructing a mental image by synthesizing several frames or decomposition.

It is clear that the requirements of completeness and compactness are contradictory. Their simultaneous satisfaction in cases where the full context of the concept has a lot of components is difficult. To solve this problem, it is possible to resort to alternative methods of forming the context [28], such as removing of unnecessary detail or releasing "orthogonal" (non-overlapping) perspectives and considering the creation of cognitive frames in a hierarchical structure.

An important requirement to cognitive frame is also its familiarity to a user. This is due to the fact that a cognitive frame serves as a visual metaphor that suggests an idea of some unknown object by means of a proxy object, which is known and understood by a user. The more you are familiar with a proxy object, the more the knowledge about it you will be able to shift to an unknown entity, and thus easier and better to know new entity and to operate with the knowledge of it.

Probably, this feature can be explained by the fact that people in the process of world perception, operate with so called cognitive structures.

Their nature is multifaceted and ambiguous. Cognitive structures reflect general principles of the categorization and information processing. The notion of cognitive structure is closely related to the idea of mental representation or mental model. It is defined as certain knowledge in the long-or short-term memory which structure corresponds to the structure of the represented situation[17].

Thus, as a result of the application of cognitive structures to information about the world man forms or supplements his mental models of objects, processes and events (Fig. 3).

Accordingly, the simpler the selection and application of a cognitive structure for processing data on the new facility, process or phenomenon, the less mental effort is spent on it. The metaphor in this case allows us to automatically re-apply to the perceived essence the same cognitive structure as that has already been explored in the role of metaphor. In this case a similar mental model is also produced. This new model is easier to reconcile with the existing models of

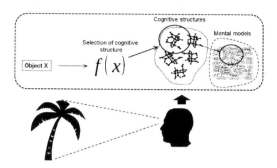

Fig. 3. Use of cognitive structures in the process of knowledge

other entities and to store in memory. Such effect appears in the fact that the conceptualized knowledge is remembered easier and for a longer period of time.

In accordance with the above considerations, it is possible to define at least two cases where the cognitive frame is familiar to the individual:

1. If the structural elements of the cognitive frame and the relationship between them and their visualization are a direct prototype of a mental model that already exists in the human mind (i.e. cognitive frame in this or a similar form is met in individual's previous mental practice);
2. If the perspective of the object under consideration within cognitive frame is familiar to the user, which provides an easy choice of an appropriate cognitive structure in the learning process.

The first condition is a condition of familiarity of any visual metaphors. But it is difficult to apply it to the cognitive frame, as a visual metaphor used for ontologies, and therefore for the cognitive frame, is a kind of abstract graph structure which is hardly to interpret. Thereupon, people will consider it at common position, without perceiving its subject area specificity.

The second condition forces on using certain generally accepted rules for visualization of ontology concepts. They have to define such manner of cognitive frame constructing, which would allow a person quickly and easily to select an adequate cognitive structure to make sense. In this case, it is possible to provide the meaning of unknown concepts in more detail and thus ensure its right interpreting.

Quite an important issue in this case is the formulation of generally accepted rules for ontology visualization that should define the various structures of cognitive frame. In this paper an upper-level ontology is considered to be the base for constructing such kind of rules.

The idea of the upper-level ontology is based on the fact that when generalization is performed in ontologies of multiple domains, we will come up with a small set of categories that is the same in all these domains[16]. This is due to the fact that in each subject area we deal with different species of some top-level entities: objects, processes, properties, relationships, space, time periods, roles, functions, etc. An upper-level ontology defines the top-level conceptual system of the most general concepts and relationships. It also sets a possible view of reality which determines certain ways of describing the knowledge of subject areas. Thus, upper-level ontology can be used as a source of rules to form a cognitive frame.

Let's note that the upper-level ontology is usually the result of the work of experts in different fields - linguistics, cognitive science, philosophy, semiotics and conceptual modeling. Therefore using an upper-level ontology as a basis for the development of domain ontologies makes it possible to represent specific concepts familiarly to experts in the various fields of knowledge. Accordingly, the cognitive frame formation rules based on the upper-level ontology guaranties a wide acceptance of such rules and as a result the familiarity of cognitive frame.

4   Constructing Cognitive Frames

This section describes construction of the cognitive frames of different types. We also present some examples of the frames formation for the concepts of our network device ontology which uses DOLCE ontology as the basis.

Let's consider cognitive frame as some subgraph - fragment of the UPO. Its vertices present concepts and its arches present the relations between them. Thereby, it should be noticed for clarity that for now we will consider ontology as a set of concepts, linked with some hierarchic, associative and domain specific relations.

A cognitive frame is determined by a target concept which meaning it has to convey and also by the selection criteria of the concepts related to it.

For formal definition of a cognitive frame we will define the term *"n-location of concept t by relation of kind R"* with which we will designate a set of the concepts connected with t by the relation of kind R through n-intermediate concepts.

Let's designate a set of all types of the relations in ontology:

$$H = \{R_1, ... R_n\}, \tag{1}$$

where V - set of all concepts of UPO, $R_m = \{r_z(k_i, o_j) : k_i, \ o_j \in V\}$, $r_z(k_i, o_j)$ - designates that exist some relation r_z between concepts k_i and o_j $R_n \cap R_m = \varnothing$, $r \neq n$.

Let's define a *n-location* of concept t by relations of the kind R_m inductively as follows:

1. $L_0^{R_m}(t) = t$;
2. $L_n^{R_m}(t) = \left\{ o_j : \exists r_l(k_i, o_j) \land k_i \in L_{n-1}^{R_m}(t) \land r_l \in R_m \right\}$, where $L_n^{R_m}(t)$ - n-location of the concept t by relations of the kind R_m, o_j and k_i - concepts of ontology.

Let's designate formal representation of the general cognitive frame as follows:

$$KF(t) = \langle O, Z \rangle, \tag{2}$$

where t - target concept of cognitive frame, Z - set of relations, that directly and indirectly connect concepts of ontology with the target concept,

$$O \subseteq \left\{ o_i : o_i \in \bigcup_{\substack{R_m \in H, \\ n \in \mathbb{N}}} L_n^{R_m}(t) \right\}, \ Z = \left\{ r_c\left(o_i, o_j\right) : o_i \in L_{f-1}^{R_m}(t), o_j \in L_f^{R_m}(t) \right\}.$$

Thus, a general definition of cognitive frame will include target concept and some concepts directly and indirectly related with target concept.

The general formation of cognitive frame for target concept t algorithm consisting of 3 steps will look like:

1. $KF(t) = \langle O, Z \rangle$, where $n = 1$, $O = E_1 := L_1^R(t)$,

$$Q_1 = Z = \left\{ \langle t, o_i \rangle : o_i \in \bigcup_{R_m \in U \subseteq H} L_1^{R_m}(t) \right\};$$

2. If $\left| E_n \cup L_{n+1}^{R_m}(t) \right| \le LM$, where LM - limit quantity of elements in cognitive frame, then $E_{n+1} = E_n \cup L_{n+1}^{R_m}(t)$,
   $Q_{n+1} = Q_n \cup \{\langle k_j, o_i \rangle : k_j \in E_n, o_i \in E_{n+1}\}$, else $E_{n+1} = E_n$;
3. If $E_{n+1} = E_n$, then $O = E_n$, $Z = Q_n$ and algorithm is finished, else $n = n+1$ and goes to second step.

According to this algorithm all the concepts connected with target directly will be included in a cognitive frame at the first stage(from the 1st location). At the second stage the attempt to include concepts from the 2nd and subsequent locations will be made. In that case if it becomes impossible because of the elements quantity restriction, additions do not happened, and the algorithm comes to an end.

Let's notice that at each stage all concepts of location, instead of their part are added. Such way of the cognitive frame expansion allows to display entirely all concepts of one level of hierarchy by some type of the relations. Such concepts have a similar importance for sense representation of the target concept, but each of them reflects its separate fragment. Thus, representing all of them makes possible to provide a semantic integrity of a cognitive frame. The method of visualization for a resultant cognitive frame is a node-link diagram.

Further in this work we will analyse common types of relations used in existing upper-level ontologies, such as DOLCE[20], BFO[13], GFO[15], CYC[9], SUMO[24], and consider a question of cognitive frame formation, based on them. In the presented ontologies main types of the relations are:

- *inheritance relation* - points that some concept (sub-concept) is a version of another one(super-concept). In this case the sub-concept inherits all relations of its super-concept;
- *meronymy relation* - relation between concepts designating a part of something and a concept designating the whole thing;
- *dependence relation* - designates that existence of one essence depends on existence another in some aspect;

The majority of the other types of the relations are, usually, their subtypes. Considering the main relations during the process of forming cognitive frames corresponding to some concept, will allow to present it from the various points of view. It will relieve the user of need to organize information mentally and, thereby, facilitate its understanding.

The first kind of the relations we consider will be inheritance. This type of relations is transitive and, as a rule, by means of the relations of this type the hierarchy of concepts of ontology is defined. This relation allows to receive information on a category of concept by his ancestor concept, and also about its versions by means of his concepts descendants. The cognitive frame corresponding to this type of relations can be created by means of the general algorithm presented earlier.

The next important type of the relations used in concepts definitions in various subject domains is meronymy. However, unlike the inheritance relations, the formation of the cognitive frame corresponding to a meronymy is not so obvious. It is connected with the existence of the subtypes of the meronymy relations[27,12], such as *component-integral object* (pedal-bike), *member-collection* (ship-fleet), *portion-mass* (slice-pie), *stuff-object* (steel-car), *feature-activity* (paying-shopping), *place-area* (Everglades-Florida).

In some cases it can lead to transitivity paradoxes. For example: From "Concert has-part Conductor", "Conductor has-part Hand", follow "Concert has-part Hand". Certainly, the existence of such paradoxes in the cognitive frame, will negatively influence its understanding.

To resolve this problem some rules of computing transitive closure are offered:

1. To consider transitivity of only one kind of meronymy relations[27];
2. To consider transitivity of meronymy only between one type objects [8];
3. To consider transitivity only between basic types of meronymy relations [23]: "component-integral object", "portion-mass", "feature-activity", "place-area".

Considering that, generally, meronymy types aren't presented in ontologies obviously the most expedient from the point of view of universality of application is the second rule.

It assumes additional condition while adding concepts-parts into cognitive frame at the second stage of general algorithm of its formation. It will include the requirement of a number of identical super-concepts of an added concept and a target one. The demanded quantity of identical super-concepts is defined depending on the top part of class hierarchy of concrete ontology or the upper-level ontology chosen as its basis. For example, in case of using upper-level ontology BFO this number will be not less than 4. It will allow to avoid the establishment of a wrong meronymy transitivity between the concepts "Continuant" and "Occurrent", and also their sub-concepts.

Thus, the algorithm of the formation of a cognitive frame on the meronymy relations will look like this:

1. $KF(t) = \langle O, Z \rangle$, where $O = E_1 := L_1^{R_m}(t)$, R_m - meronymy relations,
   $Q_1 = Z = \left\{ \langle t, o_i \rangle : o_i \in L_1^{R_m}(t) \right\}$, $n = 1$;

2. If $\left| E_n \cup \left(L_{n+1}^{R_m}(t) \setminus P \right) \right| \leq LM$,

   $P = \left\{ o_i : o_i \in L_{n+1}^{R_m}(t) \wedge |SC(t) \cap SC(o_i)| \leq LC \right\}$, where $SC(t)$, $SC(o_i)$ -
   set of super-concepts for concept t and o_i, LC - demanded quantity of the
   equal super-concepts, then $E_{n+1} = E_n \cup \left(L_{n+1}^{R_m}(t) \setminus P \right)$,
   $Q_{n+1} = Q_n \cup \{ \langle k_j, o_i \rangle : k_j \in E_n, o_i \in E_{n+1} \}$, else $E_{n+1} = E_n$;

3. If $E_{n+1} = E_n$, then $O = E_n$, $Z = Q_n$ and algorithm is finished, else $n = n+1$
   and goes to second step.

Let us consider the example of the cognitive frame formation based on the
meronymy relations (Fig. 4). At the first stage the concepts having relation *part*

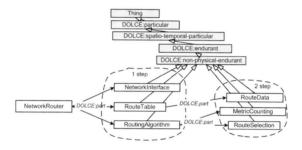

Fig. 4. Formation of the cognitive frame based on the meronymy relations

with the target concept are added to the frame. At the second stage there are
three concepts which are mediated parts of the target concept. These concepts
also have 5 similar super-concepts as well as ones added at the previous stage.
Such quality of equal super-concept is enough for DOLCE ontology to avoid the
transitivity paradoxes therefore the concept is added to the frame. Then the
second stage is repeated one more time. But there are no any concepts linked by
the meronymy relation with ones added at the previous stage, so the formation
of the frame is over.

Further we will consider a cognitive frame formation on the basis of the relations of dependence. Relations of this type are shown when existence or important qualities of one concepts depend on the existence of other concepts. In this
case it is expedient to add in cognitive frame concepts, which the target concept
depends on. The relations of dependence are defined in all existing upper-level
ontologies. However, their representation is carried out differently. It is mostly
caused by the existence of different types of things dependence, and also by various view points of the authors of ontologies on the importance of different types
of dependence.

Generally, in upper-level ontologies the following types of dependence are
presented:

- Generic and specific/rigid dependence. Generic dependence indicates dependence of one thing on existence of any other belonging to some class (dependence between a car and its engine, in this case the engine can be replaced). Specific/rigid dependence indicates dependence on existence of concrete individual belonging to some class (dependence between person and his brain);
- Conceptual dependence[20,11] - dependence of a certain quality on essence bearing it. For example, quality "to have color" depends on existence of the car which it characterizes.
- Constant/temporal dependence. Constant dependence is shown constantly between thing. Temporal dependence indicates the need of existence of one thing before emergence another one;
- External dependence[14] opposed to internal dependence. It defines dependence from external things, which are not parts or qualities.

Let's notice that number of the kinds of the dependence relations in top-level ontologies is less, than the types of dependence. It is due to that one relation can reflect some types of dependence, unrepugnant each other.

Establishing the transitive closure on the dependence relations during cognitive frame formation, it makes sense to consider relation of one type. This matches the modified first rule of establishment of the transitive closure for meronymy relations. It makes sense to apply the first rule, instead of the second, as in case of a meronymy because dependence more often than the meronymy connects the essence of absolutely different types.

Let's designate a set of all types of the dependence relations in ontology as $D = \{R_1, ...R_n\} \subseteq H$. In the algorithm of forming of cognitive frame corresponding to this relation at the 1st stage the concepts connected by any kinds of the dependence relation with target concept will be added. At the 2nd stage and farther their neighbors concepts, connected with them by the same type of the dependence relations will be added. Formally, the algorithm looks as follows:

1. $KF(t) = \langle O, Z \rangle$, where
$$O = E_1 = \bigcup_{R_m \in D} L_1^{R_m}(t) \ , \ Q_1 = Z = \bigcup_{R_m \in D} \left\{ \langle t, o_i \rangle : o_i \in L_1^{R_m}(t) \right\}, n = 1;$$

2. If $|E_n \cup F| \le LM$, where LM - quantity limit of the elements in the cognitive frame,
$$F = \bigcup_{R_m \in D} \left\{ f_p : f_p \in L_{n+1}^{R_m}(t) \wedge \exists r_k \, (n_j, f_p) \in R_m \wedge n_j \in L_n^{R_m}(t) \right\}, \text{ then}$$
$E_{n+1} = E_n \cup F, Q_{n+1} = Q_n \cup \{\langle k_j, o_i \rangle : k_j \in E_n, o_i \in E_{n+1}\}$, else $E_{n+1} = E_n$;

3. If $E_{n+1} = E_n$, then $O = E_n$, $Z = Q_n$ and algorithm is finished, else $n = n+1$ and goes to the second step.

Let us consider the following example of the formation cognitive frame based on dependence relations for the concept *Network router* (Fig. 5).

At the first step the concepts directly connected to target one by relation *generic-dependent* are added to the frame. At the second stage an attempt to

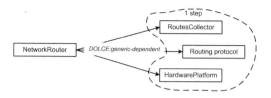

Fig. 5. Formation of the cognitive frame based on the dependence relations

find the concepts has dependence relation with ones added at the first stage. But there are no any concepts like these, so algorithm is over.

The considered algorithms cognitive frame formation based on relations invariant to subject domains, define some kind of general visual forms of concepts representation. However, in applied OWL ontologies of the subject domain concepts can possess special semantics. Generally, it is concluded in the specific relations and also OWL-axioms of equivalence and the inheritance, containing in the parts some logical expression defining an anonymous class. It is important to represent such semantics by means of the cognitive frame.

Taking into account representation features of OWL-axioms in the UPO reviewed in the background section we will consider an OWL-axiom as a set of subaxioms-concepts connected with the target concept by SKOS relation called "related". (Fig. 2). Their visualization will be carried out by specialized cognitive frames.

Besides subaxioms-concepts, specialized cognitive frame will include the concepts connected with target one by the domain specific relations, not categorized as meronymy, dependency or inheritance. Thus, in order to avoid cognitive frame "overload" at the first stage only concepts connected with target concept by such kind of relations not inherited from super-concepts will be included. The concepts related by the inherited relations will be added further. That is at each stage the addition of the concepts connected with the target relation inherited from super - concept of higher level of hierarchy will be considered.

Formally, the algorithm of special cognitive frame formation is defined as follows:

1. $KF(t) = \langle O, Z \rangle$, where $O = E_1 = L_1^{SR}(t) \cup A \cup J$, SR - type of the relations with subaxiom-concept, $SR \in H$,

$$A = \bigcup_{n \in N} \left\{ a_i : \exists r(g_j, a_i) \wedge g_j \in L_n^{SR}(t) \wedge a_i \in L_{n+1}^{SR}(t) \right\}$$ - set of the subaxiom-concepts connected with target concept indirectly,

$$J = P(t) \setminus \bigcup_{u_k \in SC(t)} P(u_k), \quad Q_1 = Z = \left\{ \langle t, o_i \rangle : o_i \in \bigcup_{R_m \in H} L_1^{R_m}(t) \right\}, \quad P(t) -$$
set of the concepts connected with target t by the domain specific relations, $SC(t)$ - set of super-concepts for concept t,

$Q_1 = Z = \left\{ \langle t, o_i \rangle : o_i \in J \vee o_i \in L_1^{SR}(t) \right\} \cup \left\{ \langle h_j, b_k \rangle : h_i, b_k \in A \wedge h_i \neq b_k \right\}$
$n = 1$;

2. If $|E_n \cup J_{n+1}| \leq LM$ where
$$J_{n+1} = P(t) \setminus \bigcup_{u_k \in SC(b_n)} P(u_k),$$
LM - quantity limit of the elements in the cognitive frame, b_n - the super-concept for target concept t from the n-th closest level of hierarchy, then $E_{n+1} = E_n \cup J_{n+1}, Q_{n+1} = Q_n \cup \{\langle k_j, o_i \rangle : k_j \in E_n, o_i \in E_{n+1}\}$, else $E_{n+1} = E_n$;

3. If $E_{n+1} = E_n$, then $O = E_n$, $Z = Q_n$ and algorithm is finished, else $n = n+1$ and go to second step.

For example the formation of special cognitive frame for the concept *Network router* is present on Figure 6. At the 1 stage two subaxioms-concepts are added

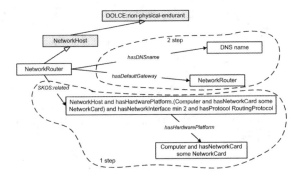

Fig. 6. Formation of the special cognitive frame

to the frame. So, because there is no concept connected with a target one by a domain specific relation the algorithm goes to the second stage. Then two concepts - *DNS name* and *Network router* with the corresponding domain-specific relation are added. It happens because these relations are inherited from the first nearest super-concept -*Network host*. Then the 2nd stage is performed again and the analysis of the domain specific relations of the second nearest super-concept *non-physical-endurant* is proceeded. But because it has not any domain specific relations algorithm comes to an end.

5   Conclusions and Future Work

In this work we considered the problem of visualization of conceptual system of the ontology used as a basis of a graphic user interface. It is offered to make visual representation of concepts by means of special structures - cognitive frames. Algorithms of their formation taking into account features of human perception of visual information and the main relations of upper level ontology are presented in the article. Their application during visualization allows to consider concept of ontology from various viewpoints and simplifies understanding of its meaning.

The main difference of the presented visualization technology from the existing one, is our orientation more on applied semantics of elements describing some concept, but not just formal semantics.

During the analysis of upper level ontologies only the formation of cognitive frames on the basis of their main relations was considered. However, it is also sensible to consider their main classes to which concepts of the applied ontologies developed on their basis can be referred.

Along with it there was not resolved a problem of an assessment of cognitive support features of the visualization, made on the basis of cognitive frames. In further work it is supposed to develop the formalized criteria of an assessment of cognitive support features on the basis of comparison of user knowledge about considered concepts and author's definition in ontology.

Acknowledgments. The work has been supported by the grant №13-07-01016 provided by the Russian Foundation for Basic Research (RFFI).

References

1. Acker, L., Porter, B.: Extracting viewpoints from knowledge bases. In: The 12th National Conference on Artificial Intelligence, pp. 547–552 (1994)
2. Alani, H.: TGVizTab: An Ontology Visualisation Extension for Protege, Knowledge Capture 03. In: Workshop on Visualizing Information in Knowledge Engineering, pp. 2–7 (2003)
3. Averbukh, V.L.: Toward formal definition of conception adequacy in visualization. In: IEEE Symposium on Visual Languages, The Isle of Capri, Italy, pp. 46–47 (1997)
4. Bauer, J.: Model exploration to support understanding of ontologies. Master thesis, Technische Universität Dresden (2009)
5. Bergh, J.R.: Ontology comprehension, University of Stellenbosch. Master Thesis (2010)
6. Bernardo, C.G., Horrocks, I., Motik, B., Parsia, B., Patel-Schneider, P.F., Sattler, U.: OWL 2: The next step for OWL. J. Web Sem. 6(4), 309–322 (2008)
7. Bosca, A., Bonino, D., Pellegrino, P.: OntoSphere: More than a 3D ontology visualization tool. In: SWAP, The 2nd Italian Semantic Web Workshop (2005)
8. Cruse, D.: Lexical Semantics. University Press, Cambridge (1986)
9. Cyc Ontology Guide: Introduction, http://www.cyc.com/ (retrieved)
10. Ellson, J., Gansner, E., Koutsofios, L., North, S.C., Woodhull, G.: Graphviz - open source graph drawing tools. In: Mutzel, P., Jünger, M., Leipert, S. (eds.) GD 2001. LNCS, vol. 2265, pp. 483–484. Springer, Heidelberg (2002)
11. Gangemi, A., Navigli, R., Velardi, P.: The OntoWordNet project: extension and axiomatisation of conceptual relations in wordnet. In: International Conference on Ontologies, Databases and Applications of Semantics, Catania, Italy (2003)
12. Gerstl, P., Pribennow, S.: A conceptual theory of part-whole relations and its applications. Data and Knowledge Engineering 20, 305–322 (1996)
13. Grenon, P.: Spatio-temporality in Basic Formal Ontology: SNAP and SPAN, Upper-Level Ontology, and Framework for Formalization: PART I. IFOMIS Report 05/2003, Institute for Formal Ontology and Medical Information Science (IFOMIS), University of Leipzig, Leipzig, Germany (2003)

14. Guarino, N., Welty, C.: A Formal Ontology of Properties. In: Dieng, R., Corby, O. (eds.) EKAW 2000. LNCS (LNAI), vol. 1937, pp. 97–112. Springer, Heidelberg (2000)

15. Herre, H.: General Formal Ontology (GFO): A Foundational Ontology for Conceptual Modelling. In: Theory and Applications of Ontology: Computer Applications, pp. 297–345 (2010)

16. Hoehndorf R. What is an upper level ontology?, http://ontogenesis.knowledgeblog.org/740 (retrieved)

17. Johnson-Laird, P.N.: Mental Models: Towards a cognitive science of language, inference and consciousness. Harvard University Press, Cambridge (1983)

18. Katifori, A., Halatsis, C., Lepouras, G., Vassilakis, C., Giannopoulou, E.: Ontology visualization methods: A survey. ACM Computing Surveys 39(4), 10 (2007)

19. Lomov, P.A.: OWL-ontology transformation for visualization and use as a basis of the user interface. In: Lomov, P.A., Shishaev, M.G., Dikovitskiy, V.V. (eds.) Scientific Magazine "Design Ontology", pp. 49–61. Novaya Tehnika, Samara (2012) (in Russian) ISSN 2223-9537

20. Masolo, C., Borgo, S., Gangemi, A., Guarino, N., Oltramari, A., Shneider, L.: WonderWeb. Final Report. Deliverable D18 (2003)

21. Miller, G.A.: The magical number seven, plus or minus two: Some limits on our capacity for processing information. Psychological Review 63(2), 81–97 (1956)

22. Minsky, M.: A Framework for Representing Knowledge. In: Winston, P.H. (ed.) The Psychology of Computer Vision. McGraw-Hill, New York (1975)

23. Motschnig-Pitrik, R., Kaasboll, J.: Part-Whole Relationship Categories and their Application in Object-Oriented Analysis. IEEE TSE 11(5), 779–797 (1999)

24. Niles, I., Pease, A.: Towards a Standard Upper Ontology. In: The 2nd International Conference on Formal Ontology in Information Systems, Ogunquit, Maine, pp. 17–19 (2001)

25. SKOS Simple Knowledge Organization System Reference, W3C Recommendation (2009), http://www.w3.org/TR/skos-reference (retrieved)

26. Valkman, J.R.: Cognitive graphic metaphors. In: International Conference Znaniya-Dialog-Resheniye, Yalta, pp. 261–272 (1995) (in Russian)

27. Winston, M., Chaffin, R., Herrmann, D.: A Taxonomy of Part-Whole Relations. Cognitive Science 11, 417–444 (1987)

28. Zybin, V.E.: Graphic and text forms of the specification of difficult managing directors of algorithms: irreconcilable opposition or cooperation? In: The 7th International Conference on Electronic Publications, Novosibirsk, pp. 32–45 (2003) (in Russian)

SRelation: Fast RDF Graph Traversal

Ján Mojžiš and Michal Laclavík

Institute of Informatics, Slovak Academy of Sciences, Bratislava, Slovakia
{jan.mojzis,laclavik.ui}@savba.sk

Abstract. Linked Data in the RDF format can be viewed as a set of interlinked data on the web. Particular tasks, which are computed upon this data includes text based searching for entities, relations or performing various queries using querying languages like SPARQL. Such interlinked data can be interpreted as a graph with edges and vertexes. For the current SPARQL 1.1 standard, there is support for graph traversal, proposed and announced by SPARQL working group. Regarding performance, the property path task is the problem in current solutions. This paper describes an innovative and time efficient method of the graph traversal task - SRelation. First we discuss current approaches for SPARQL 1.1 graph traversal. For data access we mention local and distributed solutions, disk-based, mixed and whole-in-memory data storage aspects. We debate pros and cons of various approaches and suggest our new method SRelation to fit in the field of in-memory concept. To support this, we present our experiments on selected Linked Data datasets.

Keywords: RDF graph, graph traversal, property path, SPARQL 1.1, Jena, Sesame, OWLIM-Lite, in-memory.

1 Introduction

Linked Data is a set of best practices for publishing and connecting structured data on the Web [1] based on Berners-Lee recommendations. Graph data can be represented by RDF triple statements in one of formats (RDF/XML, N3, Turtle, etc.).

For the simplicity; under the statement, we consider simple text line with 3 elements on it; a subject, a predicate and an object. Subject denotes the entity; predicate describes the property and object is for a value of the property. There are even ontological RDF formats. Semantic Web standards as well as RDF are works of W3C working groups [2]. One of groups is SPARQL Working group, and its work focus on the development of new SPARQL standards. Like SQL is a query language for relational databases, SPARQL operates on triple stores and over corresponding RDF graphs.

SPARQL standard describes many properties and operations, which differ in performance among various implementations (like FILTER, [3]). The last completed SPARQL standard of the working group is SPARQL 1.1 standard. Among other properties, the standard defines property paths [22]. Using property path we can write queries to find out the relations in the RDF graphs, perform breadth first traversal [5]

P. Klinov and D. Mouromtsev (Eds.): KESW 2013, CCIS 394, pp. 69–82, 2013.
© Springer-Verlag Berlin Heidelberg 2013

and evaluate the performance of the particular SPARQL 1.1 supporting engines. SPARQL property path [22] is related to graph traversal problem, which we trying to address in this paper.

1.1 Parallel vs. Single Machine Approaches

A current design leads toward parallelism and distributed computing in big Linked Data (like Wikipedia [12]). It profits from combined computational power, memory resources and shared disks in distributed stores.

Some developers of triple stores state that their systems are intended to not load more than 10^8 statements into the main memory, like Ontotext states for OWLIM-Lite [13], but this depends highly on the architecture of the store itself, the available memory resources and on the purpose. Main limitations are (1) memory; (2) maximum entries that can be stored (for 32 bit systems 2^32, or 64 bit 2^64 possible different values); (3) limited computational power based only on one single system.

As for the advantage, in single machine systems, we do not solve problems such as synchronization, communication, distribution of tasks or combination of results.

On the other side, distributed systems are commonly used to compute large-scale data. They can benefit, in comparison to single machine systems, from their combined memory capacity and computational power. They can (and often) have together much more memory and computational power. Furthermore, one distributed system can link various architectures (32 with 64 bit), operational systems and, etc. Moreover, if properly designed, the architecture allows quick addition/removal working machines (workers).

However, as parallel computation runs among many machines, we need to take care of synchronization, communication, distributing and merging. Especially, graph computations (edges, vertexes) are not easily handled. The properties in graph problems computed in parallel are well covered in [8].

1.2 The Single Machine Store Concept

Despite to disadvantages, mentioned in the previous section, we think, that even a single machine store can be useful, even for big data. Dataset on single machine store cannot link to other comparable stores to get more information. So the more information the single store has, the more it is useful. Single machine stores can, like distributed stores, index, sort or align RDF data in order to find data quickly. A most used storage schemes are debated in [9].

To get the data as quickly as possible, we propose to have data stored in memory. This approach does not interact with disk I/O operations, such as seek or read, and is generally faster. However, if the data loaded into main memory are changed in any way and not then saved to disk, the changes made to the data are lost. Fortunately, this is not our case, and our memory-loaded data can be saved in each moment to the hard disk.

In this paper, we propose SRelation; our stand-alone solution for fast RDF graph traversal compatible with selected SPARQL 1.1 features. We aim to outperform current in-memory triplestore solutions in both the capacity of loaded statements and the graph traversal query time performance (as we show, SRelation's time of query execution is sublinear and fastest). It is possible, for at least our benchmark (as we show in the proposed paper), to improve current implementations of SPARQL 1.1 property paths from the both memory and query time performance. We do not use any clustering or partitioning, our solution is single machine store, which is sufficient enough to get results faster with less memory requirements in comparison to current single machine stores. We aim to implement and support the following operations of SPARQL 1.1: (1) property path traversal [22]; (2) FILTER and DISTINCT [23].

To test and prove SRelation's effectiveness we evaluate its performance on the Wikipedia page links dataset in comparison to current single machine SPARQL triplestores, supporting property paths: Jena, Sesame and OWLIM-Lite. The result of our work is, as we show, that current single machine in-memory triplestores are not appropriate for storing and searching in large RDF datasets (containing more than 100M of RDF statements), when graph traversal operation are needed. This is the case in applications like search and navigation in big RDF/LinkedData.

2   State of the Art

The single machine stores, supporting SPARQL, for example, are commercial AllegroGraph or the free of charge solutions OpenLink Virtuoso, Jena[1], Sesame[2] or, already mentored, OWLIM-Lite[3].

Not all stores supporting SPARQL actually have support for property paths (Virtuoso 6). Those stores are not included in our benchmark, due to the scope of this paper oriented on SPARQL 1.1 property paths.

Jena and Sesame are stand-alone triple stores and frameworks (APIs) with the support for SPARQL 1.1 property paths. They can be used to store RDF data as well as the back-end frameworks for other solutions (to access AllegroGraph server or OWLIM-Lite).

OWLIM-Lite on the other side is rather a pure Java library without any user interface. Thus prior to use it, we need Sesame 2 or Jena.

Jena, Sesame and OWLIM-Lite support both disk based or all-in-memory approach, mapping elements to hashes, indexing data either in some forms of trees, linked lists or some other high effective data structures (e.g. TDB format of Jena).

Jena and Sesame uses trees or linked lists to index data. Both B+ and B-trees are known to have (similar) logarithmic $O(log_b \, n)$ access time, enabling us to quickly find or insert new record [16]. The definition of B-trees can be found in [17].

Unlike Jena's mixed memory and disk TDB format (higher capacity for a price of slower query performance), we use only the main memory.

We have not decided to actually extend any existing open-source store, primary because of: (1) time. It would require far more time to learn about necessary changes and there would be possibly too much to change; (2) testing purposes only. Our goal was to verify our concept in practice as soon as possible, making extension of current stores only a future step in the future work, if the results are as expecting.

---

[1]   http://jena.apache.org/
[2]   http://www.openrdf.org/
[3]   http://www.ontotext.com/OWLIM

2.1   The Selection of Stores

For the selection of stores to evaluate with, we place the following conditions: (1) freely available; (2) property path support; (3) support to load all data into the main memory; (3) the ability to load and handle more than 100 million triples; (4) is run under the Java runtime environment (SRelation is also run under Java). Based on the filter above and on the results published in [4, 13, we chose Jena and Sesame.

There is a major difference between various OWLIM versions, which is that a Lite version is a fast in-memory repository whereas SE and Enterprise are high scalable or clustered infrastructures [14].

For the software platform, we chose Java programming language, due to its rich palette of libraries and functions. Java implements binary (2-order) trees found in TreeMap and TreeSet classes, which guaranteed $O(log\ n)$ time for item search, insertion and removal [18]. We found that, for the graph traversal tasks, we need fast lookups, but not insertions/removals, because that we use traversal only to find items and not to modify them. We thus created a sorted list class, descending from ArrayList, which keeps its items sorted all the time. Time for lookup is guaranteed and tested to be $O(log\ n)$. We found, that the list saves more memory compared to TreeMaps. The drawbacks, however, are: (1) the slower insertion/removal items from the list; (2) ArrayList needs more time to fill (reallocation of the whole array for the 1 new item or if new item is inserted into the middle of the list, all items up to the list size-1 needs to be shifted).

To get the best time performance, it is important that the lookup operation in all lists (Fig.2, a), b) and c)) is at least $O(log\ n)$.

Regarding Java's internal strings handling and our implementation in Java, we further discovered, that storing text representations of nodes as a byte arrays instead of strings saves more memory (there is actually no reason to encode ASCII characters as 2 byte UTF-16 strings, and even if it is, we can easily translate UTF-16 strings into UTF-8 bytes).

2.2   RDF Graph Data Structure and Path Traversal

The graph navigation and traversal is very important in our projects. For our work, the graph traversal is the same operation as the SPARQL 1.1 definition for the property path [22]. We need to select distinct entries (DISTINCT) and to filter entries based on conditions (FILTER). More formal definition of SPARQL 1.1 graph pattern and property path, along with description and notes, can be found in [11].

2.3   Algorithm for RDF Graph Traversal

Algorithm is a breadth-first property path traversal with the use of stack and indexations from Fig. 2. Breadth first traversal is a graph traversal, which searches first for neighboring nodes of the given node, then it advances 1 level to 1 neighbor and the procedure repeats [5]. Our algorithm supports 2 functions of SPARQL 1.1 (aside property path traversal): FILTER[4] and DISTINCT[5], which filters results and prevents duplicate results per 1 query. Our algorithm takes 3 parameters:

Breadth-first level, textual representation of subject (node) S1 and the *array of permitted predicate edges* (textual representation).

Algorithm uses and returns a *stack of triples* (*PI, OI, L*) connected to *S1* through corresponding *breadth-first level*. Note that "triple" is not actually an RDF triple, rather a set of 3 elements (integral predicate identifier *PI*, integral object identifier *OI* and level *L*).

Algorithm further uses a *list of visited objects* and mapped *array of permitted predicate edges* (list of PI) and *highest level*, which is initially set to 1. Array of permitted predicate edges tells the algorithm, whether it can navigate through particular predicates, when traversing. For List of visited objects we need also fast insertion (beside of fast lookup), so we chose Java's TreeSet (instead of our sorted list). Both operations, search and insert, are O (log n) complex.

Algorithm is divided into 2 separate stages. In the first stage:

1. Map textual S1 to its integral identifier SI1 and all textual predicates, in the array, to their corresponding PI integral identifiers (with the use of list on Fig. 2a). Mapped predicates are stored in *permitted predicate edges* (list of PI). Go to 2.
2. For given subject SI get its sub-list of connected predicates and objects from the adjacency list (Fig. 2c). Go to 3.
3. Iterate over the pairs in sub-list. If the pair contains predicate, which is in the (integral mapped PI) list of permitted predicates, insert new triple (PI, OI, L) to the end of the stack, where L is the level and is set to 1.

The second stage is the loop over the triples (PI, OI, L) contained in the stack, removing the triples from the beginning of the stack while the stack is not empty. Stack can be continuously refilled, while the condition *level = breadth-first level* is not true.

1. If the stack is not empty, remove the triple (PI, OI, L) from the beginning of the stack and go to 2, else terminate.
2. If *L = breadth-first level*, return previously removed triple back to the stack and terminate, else continue to 3.
3. If *L is > highest level*, increment L by 1. Go to 4.
4. Map OI to its corresponding SI, if the mapping does not exist, return to 1, else continue to 5.
5. For given subject SI get its sub-list of connected predicates and objects from the adjacency list (Fig. 2c), if the sub-list does not exist or is empty, return to 1.
6. Iterate over the sub-list's pairs (PI, OI). If PI is in the (integral mapped PI) list of permitted predicates, continue to 7, else repeat 6 with the next pair.
7. If the *highest level +1 = breadth-first level*, continue 8, else continue 10.
8. Map OI to its corresponding SI (Fig. 2c). If the mapping exists and SI = SI1 return to 6, else continue to 9 (FILTER).

---

4 http://www.w3.org/TR/rdf-sparql-query/#tests
5 http://www.w3.org/TR/rdf-sparql-query/#modDuplicates

9. If OI is in the *list of visited objects*, return to 6, else add OI to the *list of visited objects* and continue to 10 (DISTINCT).

10. Insert new triple (PI, OI, L) to the end of the stack, where L is the level and is set to *highest level +1*.

When the algorithm terminates, it returns (filled or empty) *stack* (list) of triples (PI, OI, L) which are connected to S1 through corresponding *breadth-first level*. The actual connected objects and their connecting predicates can be easily retrieved, as the stack contains ascending sorted triples by their level L. The minimum level is *breadth-first level*, where the algorithm stopped (step 2 of second stage).

Presented Algorithm is Perhaps a Bit Intuitive, But Still we get the Best Performance in time, with the Minimal Memory Footprint

3   Architecture

Our design of the RDF store presents all in-memory approach. All triple statements have to be loaded into the main memory before any operation on the data can be started. We chose the memory concept due to fast random memory access and the lack of the input/output performance drawbacks (hard disk). Random access memory allows us to create connections between RDF graph's vertexes without the worry for the disk access time. When traversing RDF graph, navigating from subject to subject, searching for connections using predicates, access time to 1 subject can be critical.

The limit factor for SRelation is the capacity of the main memory. Although designed to be 32-bit and, as we will see, the number of statements is more than 100 million, the actual number of distinct subjects and objects hardly reaches 20 million. To code relations, we chose the adjacency list. The adjacency list is also proposed in [15]. Base architecture of SRelation is shown in Figure 1.

Main component is the **Sorted List Store module**, which maintains adjacency lists of subjects. The subjects in the list are sorted based on subject's key (subject is identified by its integral identifier SI). Key feature of this module is to provide fast lookups for subjects during path traversal. Each subject, which is connected, has its adjacency written in its sub-list. The overview of subjects list and their sub-lists of connected vertices and edges is on Figure 2.

Another main module is the **Mappings module**, which is responsible for mapping textual representation of elements to their integral representation (identifiers). It is highly needed during query preparation, because all textual representations (subjects, objects or predicates) in the query need to be mapped to integers, in order to find them in the Sorted List Store module. The architecture of the Mappings module is depicted in Figure 3.

RDF Graph Traversal API	
RDF Graph Traversal Alg.	
RDF Graph Abstraction	
Sorted List Store	Mappings

Fig. 1. Architecture of SRelation

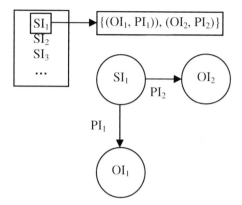

Fig. 2. Sorted List Store of subject integral keys (SI) and their corresponding adjacency lists with predicates (integral identifiers PI) and objects (integral identifiers OI). A sequence of SI, PI and OI represents a complete RDF triple.

RDF Graph Abstraction API enables users to directly manipulate with the underlying graph structure: iterate over mapping sets (Fig.3) and adjacency in Sorted List (Fig.2). This module can be used also for editing: either adding or removing subjects from adjacency list.

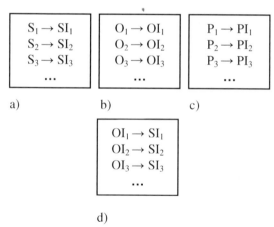

Fig. 3. a) Mappings module maps textual representation of subjects, objects and predicates (a, b, c) to their corresponding integral representation. d) is a mapping, which contains a list with information, whether a given object is not literal/blank node and can be traversed (and is pointing to its equivalent subject via its SI).

RDF Graph Traversal API is the layer, with which the user interacts, when he wants to perform the graph traversal operations. He can design queries, specify conditions (select traversable predicates and even their levels in path). The user can test SRelation on whole sets of starting subjects. The results can be then iterated over much like in Jena and Sesame.

Under the Graph Traversal API is the core traversal algorithm, the **RDF Graph Traversal Algorithm**. The algorithm uses the adjacency (Fig.2) and mappings (Fig.3). Based on conditions from RDF Graph Traversal API, performs graph traversal tasks and returns the results, which can be then iterated over.

3.1   Notes to Mappings Module

To save the memory, we could merge list b) into a). Because none of the lists support duplicate keys, we would gain the profit of removing duplicate entries. Duplicate entries are entries, which are contained in both list a) and b). The only duplicate entries are non-blank and non-literal entries in b). After merging, there would be only lists a) and b). The mapping d) would no longer be needed, because there is not objects list, so we can save even more memory by removing it.

The merging brings, however, one drawback; whenever it is needed to search for objects, we cannot. The objects and subjects are no longer distinguishable.

As we will see, the merging actually is less effective, than expected (for smaller datasets, Fig.4d). We include this changed module in the graphs for comparison.

4   Experiments and Evaluation

For the RDF dataset we selected Wikipedia page links[6] in n3 format (22 GBytes on disk, 158 million triples). We split the dataset based on triple count to create smaller dumps.

The whole benchmark was launched on the machine with the following configuration: OS Linux 3.2.0-29-generic 64 bit, RAM 32 GB, CPU 24 × 2 GHz. Due to the memory capacity of 32 GB (not counting the disk swap cache), we chose, for all stores, to use as much as 29 GB (the Java –Xmx2900M) constraint (we decided to keep the small amount of RAM for critical background processes).

The benchmark query is:

```
select distinct ?property where {
  ?s ?p ?property.
  FILTER (?s != ?property)

}
```

The distinct and filter are compatible functions with SRelation's path traversal algorithm. ?p is the predicate path and for level 2 property path traversal, it is:

```
dbpedia:wikiPageWikiLink / dbpediawikiPageWikiLink
```

and level 3:

```
dbpedia:wikiPageWikiLink / dbpedia:wikiPageWikiLink /
dbpedia:wikiPageWikiLink
```

---

[6] http://downloads.dbpedia.org/3.8/en/page_links_en.nt.bz2, actual version during the experiments was the version from July 25 2012.

To test property path level 2 extensively and evaluate the performance, we ran the above query on the selected pattern of 150,000 subjects from the given dataset. We assured, that all stores give the correct results (based on the result count and the fact that all results matched). Because Jena's memory requirements were much higher than Sesame and SRelation's, Jena required far more memory than we could supply (more than 29 GB of ram on 100% wikipedia page links load), the information on memory load at 100% is missing for Jena.

4.1   The Results

We evaluated and compared following parameters of all tested triplestores: load-time, query-time and memory usage after dataset loading. The evaluation is split to level 2 and level 3 queries. Jena, Sesame and OWLIM needed some time and memory to compile queries and prepare them before the execution itself. This time does not count to the final query time. The final results were surprising, because no tested triplestore could outperform SRelation in both query time performance and memory requirements, regardless of dataset size.

Despite to 29 GBytes of RAM, we were unable to load 100% size of Wikipedia dataset into Jena.

Evaluation was performed on Wikipedia page links datsets (various sizes) and 150,000 subjects for level 2. Here, the exceptions on 158 million dataset are: (1) although we were able to load 158 million statements into OWLIM, we found, that the query time would easily overlap 2 hours timeframe, which we decided not to cross; and (2) Jena would require more than 29 GB of RAM to load all 158 million triples (Table 1 and Fig.4a, c and d).

For level 3 we tested 1000 subjects on 4 datasets (Table 2 and Fig.4b).

The time performance is almost linear, with the exception of OWLIM-Lite. This could be due to its hash table index, where there is allocated memory for indices, which are not yet used.

SRelation performs better and requires less memory than other stores. For details see Fig.4.

Jena returned the results with better overall performance compared to Sesame. Even the results in [4] points that Jena starts to outperform Sesame in larger datasets (above 10 million triples). The worst performance of OWLIM-Lite, in our evaluation, is a bit surprising, because it is using Sesame's SAIL (The Storage And Inference Layer) and implements its own TRREE engine's edition called SwiftTRREE. However it has somewhat cheaper memory consumption than Jena and Sesame (we noted that on datasets with more than 32 million triples). We have tested individual query executions with OWLIM-Lite, using either "GettingStarted" unit or packed "sesame_owlim" and measured times to ensure, that the settings for OWLIM were correct. We decided to stop evaluation on 50% (79 millions), because for all 150k subjects, it would take more than 2 hours to complete.

Jena started to consume high amounts of memory (noticeable after more than 32 million triples are loaded) and there 29 GB constraint was not enough to load all 158 million triples.

In the memory, for 158 million triples dataset, SRelation consumes by 5 about GB less of memory than Sesame. This could be due to Sesame additional indexing (SPO, POS, OSP)[7] and the String instead of byte representation of texts.

In the time comparison, for level 2 query and 1.5M triples, SRelation is faster than Jena by 29.65 seconds. On 15M triples it is faster by 485.23 seconds and on 79M by 439.76 seconds (Table 1), making SRelation faster by about 1.43 ×. The 29 GB of RAM was not enough to load all 158 million triples into Jena.

We evaluated level 3 queries also, this time only for 1000 subjects. We decided to perform tests on fewer subjects because of the observation, where the equivalent query on level 2 would take by about 1.96 × more time to complete for Sesame (1.69 × times slower than SRelation).

Table 1. Average query time performance (in seconds) for 150,000 subjects and level 2 queries

Triples count	SRelation	Jena	Sesame	OWLIM-Lite
1,583,739	17,217	46,864	85,228	134,564
15,837,397	563,710	1,048,939	1,923,008	3,184,396
31,674,794	765,821	1,235,233	2,126,656	3,578,324
79,186,986	1,028,047	1,467,810	2,424,432	4,285,073
158,373,972	1,450,678		2,520,753	

Table 2. Average query time performance (in seconds) for 1000 subjects and level 3 queries

Triples count	SRelation	Jena	Sesame	OWLIM-Lite
1,583,739	0.92	2.96	2.97	7.34
15,837,397	553.15	1,209.96	1,573.33	2,968.94
31,674,794	717.38	1,417.35	1,833.37	3,529.15
79,186,986	1,120.88	1,828.82	2,287.92	4,720.28

For level 3 query and 1.5M triples, the difference between times of Jena and SRelation is 2.04 seconds, but for 79M triples the difference is 707.94 seconds (Table 2), making SRelation faster than Jena by about 1.63 ×. The result is that Jena performs better on level 2, but worse on level 3 (compared to SRelation).

---

[7]   Triple Clustering For Jena, TDB Architecture
    http://users.ecs.soton.ac.uk/ao/www2009.ppt, retrieved May 30 2013.

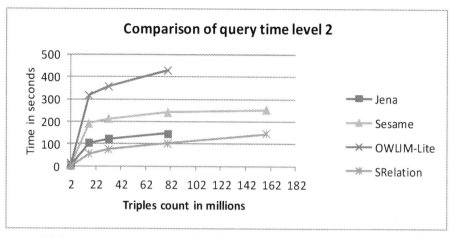

(a) Average query execution time (in seconds) for path traversal, level 2

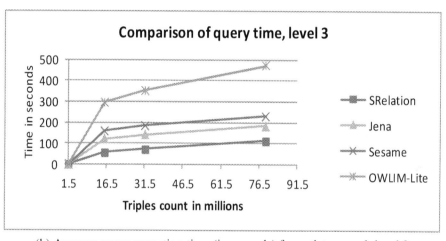

(b) Average query execution time (in seconds) for path traversal, level 3

Fig. 4. Charts comparing the average query execution times (a) for 150,000 subjects and (b) for 1000 subjects; (b) shows the final memory consumption after each dataset load. Datasets are colored on the legend, starting from 15.8 million triples. We see Jena and SRelation's characteristic sublinear query time (level 3). We excluded Jena and OWLIM from the 158 million dataset test, because of either time or memory constraint.

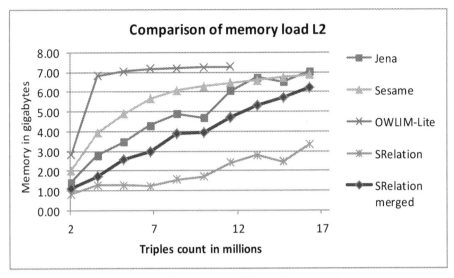

(c) Memory requirements (in GBytes) for small datasets

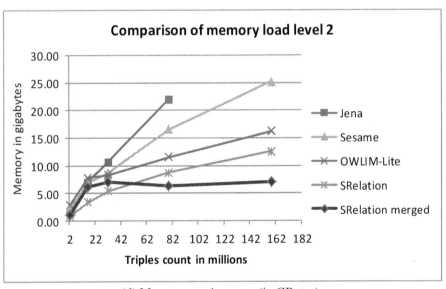

(d) Memory requirements (in GBytes)

Fig. 4. (*continued*)

With the SRelation's objects merging (from Section 4.1) the memory requirements are further lowered, but only after the larger dataset is loaded (more than 42 million triples, Fig.2b).

5   Conclusion and Future Work

We have tested our new algorithm for RDF property path graph traversal on Wikipedia page links dataset. We tested level 2 and 3 queries (for level 2, 150,000 and for level 3, 1000 subjects) and the result is that SRelation performed queries faster and with smallest memory requirements (Fig.4c and d).

We have successfully designed and implemented SRelation, a store used for fast RDF graph traversal (compatible with SPARQL property path [22]). We support both additional SPARQL operations: DISTINCT and FILTER (Section 4, Algorithm, second stage), from which FILTER was the subject of testing in [3] with the result of performance slowdown. SRelation outperformed all tested solutions with either its cheaper memory consumption (Fig.2c and d) or query performance (Fig.2a and b). We thus propose SRelation for performing fast RDF graph traversal tasks.

The capacity of SRelation seems to be well suited for high-scale RDF datasets. We will load more RDF data into SRelation to further test its limits. The capacity can be increased further by merging objects to subjects (Section 4.1) or by combination with Lucene [7], where the texts from Fig.3 would move into Lucene index, freeing further memory.

Our algorithm can be easily extended to support shortest path searching, useful for social networks [6]. In our design and implementation we do not use any partitioning schemas [10], which, when used, could further increase the query time performance.

In the future, we plan to evaluate the SRelation on bigger and richer datasets with multiple predicates and extended queries, in which the predicate path will be bound to the selected level (level 1 = predicate 1, level 2 = predicate 2, and so on). We even can set some predicates to be alternative paths only.

Much of the work, however, we would like to invest in, is the new (and promising) parallel computational model, known as Pregel [19] and its Java implementation, Sedge [20]. Although Sedge is already useable and can perform tasks as PageRank or shortest path search, we need to make a several changes to suit our needs. First, we need to implement RDF graph traversal; second, we need the data to be permanently loaded in the main memory. We already have the RDF graph traversal implemented and currently work on the second stage. The main motivation for us is to search and navigate in large diverse datasets such as the Semantic Web Challenge [21] or [24].

Acknowledgements. This work is supported by projects VEGA 2/0185/13, TRA-DICE APVV-0208-10 and ITMS: 26240220072.

References

1. Berners-Lee, T.: Linked Data - Design Issues, http://www.w3.org/DesignIssues/LinkedData.html (retrieved May 28, 2013)
2. W3C consortium, http://www.w3.org/Consortium/ (retrieved May 28, 2013)
3. Schmidt, M., Hornung, T., Lausen, G., Pinkel, C.: SP^2Bench: a SPARQL Performance Benchmark. In: The 25th IEEE International Conference on Data Engineering, pp. 222–233. IEEE (2009)

4. Bizer, C., Schultz, A.: The Berlin Sparql Benchmark. International Journal on Semantic Web and Information Systems 5(2), 1–24 (2009)
5. Even, S.: Graph algorithms. Cambridge University Press (2011)
6. Bahmani, B., Goel, A.: Partitioned Multi-Indexing: Bringing Order to Social Search. In: The 21st International Conference on World Wide Web, pp. 399–408. ACM (2012)
7. Hatcher, E., Gospodnetic, O., Mccandless, M.: Lucene in Action. Manning Publications Co., Greenwich (2004)
8. Lumsdaine, A., Gregor, D., Hendrickson, B., Berry, J.: Challenges in Parallel Graph Processing. Parallel Processing Letters 17(1), 5–20 (2007)
9. Schmidt, M., Hornung, T., Küchlin, N., Lausen, G., Pinkel, C.: An Experimental Comparison of RDF Data Management Approaches in a SPARQL Benchmark Scenario. In: Sheth, A.P., Staab, S., Dean, M., Paolucci, M., Maynard, D., Finin, T., Thirunarayan, K. (eds.) ISWC 2008. LNCS, vol. 5318, pp. 82–97. Springer, Heidelberg (2008)
10. Abadi, D.J., Marcus, A., Madden, S.R., Hollenbach, K.: Scalable Semantic Web Data Management Using Vertical Partitioning. In: The 33rd International Conference on Very Large Data Bases, pp. 411–422 (2007)
11. Arenas, M., Conca, S., Pérez, J.: Counting Beyond a Yottabyte, or How SPARQL 1.1 Property Paths Will Prevent Adoption of the Standard. In: Proceedings of the 21st International Conference on World Wide Web, pp. 629–638 (2012)
12. Mituzas, D.: Wikipedia: Site Internals, Configuration and Code Examples and Management Issues (2007)
13. DB-Engines Ranking, http://db-engines.com/en/ranking/rdf+store (retrieved July 9, 2013)
14. http://www.ontotext.com/owlim/editions (retrieved July 8, 2013)
15. Heese, R., Leser, U., Quilitz, B., Rothe, C.: Index Support for SPARQL. In: European Semantic Web Conference, Innsbruck, Austria (2007)
16. Lehman, P.L.: Efficient Locking for Concurrent Operations on B-Trees. ACM Transactions on Database Systems (TODS) 6(4), 650–670 (1981)
17. Bayer, R.: Symmetric Binary B-Trees: Data Structure and Maintenance Algorithms. Acta Informatica 1(4), 290–306 (1972)
18. Oracle Documents, http://docs.oracle.com/javase/6/docs/api/java/util/TreeMap.html (retrieved July 1, 2013)
19. Malewicz, G., Austern, M.H., Bik, A.J., Dehnert, J.C., Horn, I., Leiser, N., Czajkowski, G.: Pregel: A System for Large-Scale Graph Processing. In: The ACM SIGMOD International Conference on Management of Data, pp. 135–146 (2010)
20. Yang, S., Yan, X., Zong, B., Khan, A.: Towards effective partition management for large graphs. In: The ACM SIGMOD International Conference on Management of Data, pp. 517–528 (2012)
21. Semantic Web Challenge, http://challenge.semanticweb.org/2013/ (retrieved June 18, 2013)
22. W3C consortium, SPARQL 1.1 Property Paths, http://www.w3.org/TR/sparql11-property-paths/ (retrieved July 18, 2013)
23. W3C consortium, SPARQL 1.1 Query Language, http://www.w3.org/TR/sparql11-query/ (retrieved July 18, 2013)
24. Web Data Commons, http://www.webdatacommons.org/ (retrieved July 25, 2013)

An Approach to Improving the Classification of the New York Times Annotated Corpus

Elena Mozzherina

Saint Petersburg State University
7-9, Universitetskaya nab., St.Petersburg, 199034, Russia

Abstract. The New York Times Annotated Corpus contains over 1.5 million of manually tagged articles. It could become a useful source for evaluation of algorithms for documents clustering. Since documents have been labeled over twenty years, it is argued that the classification may contains errors due to a possible dissent between experts and the necessity to add tags over time. This paper presents an approach to improving the classification quality by using assigned tags as a starting point.

It is assumed that tags can be described by a set of features. These features are selected based on the value of mutual information between the tag and stems from documents with it. An algorithm for reassigning tags in case the document does not contain features of its labels is presented. Experiments were performed on about ninety thousand articles published by the New York Times in 2005. Results of applying the algorithm to the collection are discussed.

Keywords: document classification, classification improvement, classification evaluation, mutual information.

1 Introduction

The New York Times Annotated Corpus [1] contains documents from the historical archive of The New York Times and includes articles published between January 1, 1987 and June 19, 2007. As part of the indexing procedures, over 1.5 million articles were manually summarized and tagged by a staff of library scientists.

The process of manual tagging is time and labor consuming. It is supposed by default that manual tags assignment delivers high-quality results, and classification or clustering accuracies are compared on manually tagged collections. In many papers (e.g. in [2]) experiments were performed using the classic Reuters-21578 collection of newswire articles, originally labeled by Carnegie Group, Inc., and Reuters, Ltd. [3]. Quality of labels in TREC collections [4] are also out of question.

Therefore, not much work has been done in the field of manually tagged collections analysis. However, there are some reasons to review manually assigned tags. Firstly, the corpus covers a period of more than twenty years, and some new tags were added occasionally. A set of tags had changed over time, but recently added tag also can be applicable to the reviewed documents.

P. Klinov and D. Mouromtsev (Eds.): KESW 2013, CCIS 394, pp. 83–91, 2013.
© Springer-Verlag Berlin Heidelberg 2013

Secondly, the process of assigning tags can be easily controlled and managed when the number of tags is small, and they are clearly distinguishable – an ideal situation, that cannot be always gained in real life. In this paper, we perform experiments on a subset of the New York Times annotated corpus – a collection of articles published by The New York Times in 2005. In this collection, more than five thousand documents (about 18% of the total number) contains duplicate tags. Usually such situation happens, when tags are close to each other by meaning, or due to the number of assigned tags, e.g. some documents were labeled with 26 tags.

Table 1 presents two documents from the collection with their tags. Both documents are about the same situation, but the latter received one additional tag. Although articles report about unexpected death of twins, tag "Multiple Births" was assigned.

Table 1. Example of tags assignment

	First document	Second document
Title	Twins Die Mysteriously After a Nap at Home	Autopsy Results Awaited in Death of Twins
Author	Michael Wilson and Ann Farmer	Nina Bernstein
Tags	Twins, Multiple Births	Babies, Twins, Multiple Births
Text extract	Twin boys just 3 months old died in Brooklyn yesterday after their mother found them unconscious in separate cribs in their bedroom, the police said. ⟨..⟩	The crib deaths of 3-month-old twin boys in Brooklyn remained a mystery yesterday, as grief-stricken family members awaited autopsy results. ⟨..⟩

Finally, it is known that experts sometimes disagree about tags, and human relevance judgments are quite idiosyncratic [5]. Since these tags are going to be considered as a gold standard for clustering or classification algorithms evaluation, this paper presents an approach to improve classification quality by using manually assigned tags as a starting point.

It should be noted, that from experts' point of view, they solve a classification task when assign tags to the article. Most of the tags are known in advance, and the goal is to describe all topics mentioned in the document. As a result, on the one hand, all documents with the same tag have something in common. On the other hand, librarians are also trying to distinguish this document from the others – as we mentioned above, sometimes by assigning up to 26 tags to the document, or even introducing a new tag.

The main idea of clustering text documents is to group them into subsets in such a way that documents within a cluster are as similar as possible, and at the same time, they can be clearly distinguished from documents in other clusters.

According to Manning et al. [5] the difference between clustering and classification is great, since the former is an example of unsupervised learning, while the latter is a form of supervised. In fact, if it is granted that human supervisor was not always right, the difference between clustering and classification may not seem so great.

Thus, we claim that each tag generates a cluster of documents labeled with this tag, and information about these clusters can be used to detect problems with the classification.

Clustering algorithms are divided into flat and hierarchical, hard and soft [5]. Unlike hierarchical, flat clustering model does not create any explicit structure between clusters. If only one tag is assigned to the document, hard clustering model is presented. If several tags are allowed for the same document, it is possible to consider each tag as a generative feature of its own cluster and refer to this model as a soft clustering. Hereinafter, we consider flat soft clustering model.

Hence, the problem of classification improvement of the assigned tags can be reformulated. Given the clusters of documents formed by tags as an initial assignment, we want to recalculate the proposed clusters of documents.

Section 2 provides a brief state-of-the-art in document clustering, methods of clustering results evaluation, and techniques of selecting features of clusters. Description of the suggested approach can be found in section 3. Section 4 characterizes the collection used in the experiments, presents achieved results, and discusses some limitations of the approach. Section 5 concludes the paper.

2   Related Work

2.1   Clustering Techniques

Flat clustering of documents can be defined as follows. Given a set of documents $D = \{d_1, ..., d_N\}$, a number of clusters K, an objective function γ, find an assignment $\gamma : D \to \{1, ..., K\}$ that minimizes (or maximizes) the objective function. In most cases γ is defined in terms of similarity between documents, and supposed to be surjective. As soon as we consider soft clustering, one document can be assigned to several clusters with different probability.

One of the difficult issues in clustering is determining cardinality K. Since an initial assignment to clusters is given by experts, we suppose that K is determined correctly.

Popular approaches to soft document clustering are soft K-means and model-based approaches. The latter group assumes documents were generated by a model and tries to recover that original model from the data. One of the algorithms, which uses an idea of model-based clustering is expectation-maximization (EM) algorithm. EM can be applied to different types of probabilistic modeling, including the Bernoulli model (for details refer to [5]).

2.2   Feature Selection

Running experiments on text documents collection raises a problem of extracting features of clusters. Apparently, the characteristic features of documents are tokens or words they contain. Therefore, without deep analysis of the linguistic content of the documents, the most frequent tokens can be chosen to describe each document [6].

Since clusters are formed by documents, they can also be described by tokens, and some methods using variations of well-known term frequency – inverse document frequency $(tf-idf)$ formulation have been suggested to compute weightings of frequent tokens for cluster labels (e.g. in [7]).

In addition to the frequency-based approaches, feature selection can be done with information-based approach for phrase extraction (proposed in [8]).

Another common feature selection method is based on computing mutual information (MI) between terms from documents and clusters. Terms with highest value of MI are selected as features of clusters [5]. It should be noted, that calculating MI between each term and cluster is a time-consuming task, and preliminary dictionary reduction is needed. This approach was applied in our experiments.

2.3   Clustering Evaluation

There are two different criterions of cluster quality. Internal criterion (or internal measure) [9] allows to compare different sets of clusters without using any external knowledge source. According to this criterion, the goal is to achieve high similarity between documents within one cluster, and low similarity between documents from different clusters.

External criterion, by contrast, evaluate clustering results by comparing them to known in advance classes. Normalized Mutual Information and Entropy (in [5] and [9] , respectively) based on information-theoretic approach, or F-Measure [10] adopted from Information Retrieval are widely accepted criterions from this class. Since it is proposed, that clustering benchmark may contain errors, external measures are not applicable and internal criterion is the only way to assess the results of tags assignment.

Detailed study of widely used internal clustering validation measures is presented in [11,12]. Taking into account cluster hypothesis, most of the internal validation measures are based on two criteria – compactness and separation. The former measures how close are the objects in a cluster to each other. The latter measures how distinct is the cluster from others.

Since we are applying soft clustering model, measures that trying to separate clusters from each other would not provide good results. The Root-mean-square standard deviation (RMSSTD) is the square root of the pooled sample variance of all the features, and this measure is aimed only at compactness.

3   The Suggested Approach

Given the clusters of documents formed by tags as an initial assignment, we want to recalculate the proposed clusters of documents in a way to improve initial classification. We are going to use MI to select features of clusters, and RMSSTD measure to assess the results.

First of all some necessary text processing (including tokenization and lemmatization with the Porter stemmer [13]) is applied to the document collection $D = \{d_1, ..., d_N\}$. Let V be an extracted vocabulary, consisting of stems from all documents $V = \{t_1, ..., t_m\}$, and C a set of clusters $C = \{c_1, ..., c_K\}$.

In literature Porter stemmer is called aggressive [6]. It also makes some mistakes because of words ambiguity. However, the use of it is reasonable. Firstly, such aggressive stemming reduces the number of types in the collection significantly, making distributional statistics of stems over clusters more reliable. Secondly, if term's distribution is the same in the cluster and in the collection as a whole, then MI would be equal to zero. MI reaches its high values if the term is present in a document if and only if the document belong to the cluster; and some errors in stemming will not have a profound effect.

On the first step of iteration process mutual information between each stem and cluster is calculated as follows (adapted from [5]).

$$MI(t; c) = \frac{N_{tc}}{N} log_2 \frac{NN_{tc}}{N_t N_c} + \frac{N_{\bar{t}c}}{N} log_2 \frac{NN_{\bar{t}c}}{N_{\bar{t}} N_c} + \frac{N_{t\bar{c}}}{N} log_2 \frac{NN_{t\bar{c}}}{N_t N_{\bar{c}}} + \frac{N_{\bar{t}\bar{c}}}{N} log_2 \frac{NN_{\bar{t}\bar{c}}}{N_{\bar{t}} N_{\bar{c}}} \quad (1)$$

In the equation N_{tc} is a number of documents with stem t that belong to cluster c, $N_{t\bar{c}}$ is a number of documents with t and not in c, N_t is a number of documents with stem t independent of cluster membership, and so on.

On the second step, for each cluster c we select its features. A commonly used model of terms distribution in a collection is Zipf's law. It states that the collection frequency of the ith most common term is proportional to $1/i$ [5]. We assumed that this model would be valid also for the stems' values of MI as follows.

$$MI_i^j \propto \frac{1}{i}, i = \overline{1, V}, j = \overline{1, K} \quad (2)$$

Thus, MI for ith stem in jth cluster, when stems are ordered by decreasing the value of MI, is proportional to $1/i$ with some coefficient. As features for the cluster, we select stems with value of MI above some threshold. This threshold is different for each cluster; in other words, we select stems while the function of MI values continue to decrease rapidly (for details see Fig. 1).

On the next step, quality measure is calculated. Assume we agree with the Bernoulli model. When classifying a document, the Bernoulli model uses binary occurrence information, ignoring the number of occurrences. It generates an indicator for each feature of the cluster – either 1 indicating presence of feature in the document, or 0 indicating absence. Then distance between the document and the center of the cluster can be calculated as a number of cluster's features absent in the document divided to the total number of cluster's features. In this case, distance equals to 0 when all features were found in the document, and 1 if none.

RMSSTD can be calculated as follows.

$$RMSSTD = \sqrt{\sum_{i=1}^{K} \frac{\sum_{x \in C_i} d(x; c_i)}{n_i - 1}} \tag{3}$$

Here n_i is the number of documents in cluster C_i, c_i is the center of the cluster – a vector with 1 on a position of cluster's features and 0 on other positions, distance d between the document and the center of the cluster is calculated as discussed above.

On the final step of the iteration each document can be "relocated" to another cluster. We calculate distance from each document to centers of clusters. If the distance is above some threshold, then the document is added to the cluster.

We use number of iterations as a stop condition for this procedure, although a more complex condition can be applied.

Hence, the following algorithm is suggested.

```
ReClassification(D)
1   V <- ExtractVocabulary(D)
2   C <- ExtractClusters(D)
3   repeat
4       MI <- CalculateMI(C, V, D)
5       for each c in C
6       do F(c) <- ExtractFeatures(c, MI)
8       RMSSTD <- CalculateMeasure(F, V, D)
7       for each d in D
8       do Relocate(d, C, F)
9   until StopConditionIsReached
10  return C
```

4   Experimental Results

We run our experiments using a subset of articles from The New York Times Annotated Corpus, that were written and published in 2005. Table 2 provides some statistics about the collection.

Table 2. Description of the collection

Parameter	Value
No. of documents	89'975
Ave. length of documents (in words)	724.395
No. of stems in the collection	260'737
No. of tagged documents	56'681
No. of tags	1'529
Ave. no. of tags per document	3.402

It should be noted, that 5'126 documents in the collection contains duplicate "document-tag" relation (in meta-information of the document the same tag is mentioned several times). It can be considered as an implicit sign of errors in the assigned tags.

Despite the fact that total number of tags is over 1'500, the number of tags belonging to more than 100 documents is only 331. These tags can cover 55'624 documents – almost all documents that have tags. The other 1'057 documents belong to small clusters. For example, cluster "Music" contains 2'834 documents. Close cluster "Reggae Music" contains only 12 documents, "Gospel Music" contains even less – 8 documents. There are clusters with only one document in it. The suggested approach is statistical, it is argued that clusters with less than 100 documents are small and should be left as they are, without any recalculation. Thus, the number of documents $N = 55624$ and the number of clusters $K = 331$.

As it was mentioned above, the process of calculating MI between all stems and clusters is time-consuming to be an iterative procedure. On a machine with 8 cores and 14 GB of memory it takes about 13 hours.

In section 3 we made an assumption, that function of stems' MI (when stems are ordered by decreasing values of MI) would be of the form of Zipf's law. Fig. 1 illustrates that for three selected clusters. Function's behavior is the same for all of them – rapid decrease followed by a slow reduction. Thus, each cluster can be described by 20-25 terms with several highest values of MI.

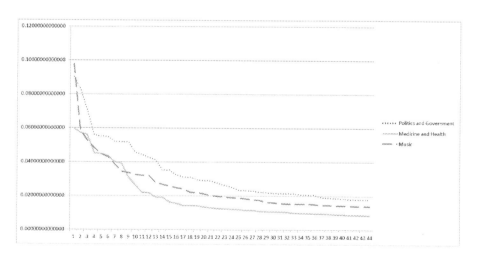

Fig. 1. Values of mutual information for the top 45 features

MI between all stems and clusters was calculated only once in order to down-size the vocabulary – we selected stems only with MI >0.001. The threshold was selected in such a way as to reduce the vocabulary as much as possible, but also to keep 30-35 stems for each cluster. Thus, with this threshold V consists of 12'244 stems.

Five top stems extracted as features by function "ExtractFeatures" for three popular tags are presented in Table 3.

Table 3. Features of tags

Name of tag	Extracted feature	MI
Politics and Government	elect	0.090255997
	democrat	0.082704254
	polit	0.070441557
	iraq	0.055800083
	republican	0.055189898
Medicine and Health	patient	0.059828043
	medic	0.057260097
	health	0.056043122
	diseas	0.045078527
	doctor	0.044837314
Music	music	0.097682959
	song	0.058235618
	album	0.052836975
	concert	0.048163433
	musician	0.044743533

Initial value of RMSSTD was 13.91. As a threshold value for relocating procedure we use 0.75. With this threshold most of the documents stayed in the original clusters, as long as experts' errors are rare enough. After three iterations RMSSTD decreased to 11.47, and the number of "document-cluster" relations decreased from 167'652 to 148'200. Thus, clusters became more compact.

5   Conclusions

We apply the suggested approach to a subset of articles from The New York Times Annotated Corpus, and according to the calculated quality measure, achieved some improvement.

However, the suggested approach has some limitations. First, it cannot deal with small clusters. In our experiments, we did not consider clusters with less than 100 documents. This border is conditional enough and could be changed so long as documents would provide enough information about their clusters and extracted cluster features would seem relevant.

Second, since the Bernoulli model ignore the number of stem's occurrences, it typically makes many mistakes when classifying long documents. Thus, the approach can be review by using another model, or terms (not stems) as cluster features. The latter approach would also require some linguistic analysis.

Finally, the main disadvantage is that calculating mutual information takes some time even with reduced dictionary. It can be avoided by recalculating it only every 5 or 10 iterations of documents relocation.

References

1. Sandhaus, E.: The New York Times annotated corpus. Linguistic Data Consortium, Philadelphia (2008)
2. Torkkola, K.: Discriminative features for text document classification. Pattern Analysis and Applications 6(4), 301–308 (2003)
3. Reuters-21578 Test Collection,
   http://www.daviddlewis.com/resources/testcollections/reuters21578/
4. Text Retrieval Conference, http://trec.nist.gov/
5. Manning, C., Raghavan, P., Schtze, H.: Introduction to Information Retrieval. Cambridge University Press, NY (2008)
6. Weiss, M.S., Indurkhya, N., Zhang, T., Damerau, F.J.: Text Mining: Predictive Methods for Analyzing Unstructured Information. Springer Science+Business Media, Inc., NY (2005)
7. Neto, J.L., Santos, A.D., Kaestner, C.A.A., Freitas, A.A.: Document clustering and text summarization. In: International Conference Practical Applications of Knowledge Discovery and Data Mining, pp. 41–55 (2000)
8. Bakus, J., Kamel, M.S., Carey, T.: Extraction of text phrases using hierarchical grammar. In: Cohen, R., Spencer, B. (eds.) Canadian AI 2002. LNCS (LNAI), vol. 2338, pp. 319–324. Springer, Heidelberg (2002)
9. Steinbach, M., Karypis, G., Kumar, V.: A comparison of document clustering techniques. In: KDD Workshop on Text Mining (2000)
10. Larsen, B., Aone, C.: Fast and effective text mining using linear-time document clustering. In: ACM SIGKDD International Conference on Knowledge Discovery and Data Mining, pp. 16–22 (1999)
11. Steinbach, M., Karypis, G., Kumar, V.: A comparison of document clustering techniques. In: KDD Workshop on Text Mining (2000)
12. Liu, Y., Li, Z., Xiong, H., Gao, X., Wue, J.: Understanding of internal clustering validation measures. In: IEEE International Conference on Data Mining, pp. 911–916 (2010)
13. Porter stemmer, http://tartarus.org/martin/PorterStemmer/

Applying the Latent Semantic Analysis to the Issue of Automatic Extraction of Collocations from the Domain Texts

Aliya Nugumanova[1] and Igor Bessmertny[2]

[1] Eastern Kazakhstan State Technical University, Oskemen, Kazakhstan
[2] National Research University of ITMO, Saint-Petersburg, Russia
`yalisha@ya.ru`, `Igor_bessmertny@hotmail.com`

Abstract. The aim of this paper is to study possibilities of latent semantic analysis for automatic extraction of word pair collocations from domain texts. The basic idea of this work consists in a search of collocations among pairs of words with strong (stable) relations since collocations are nothing else than steady combinations of words. Results of experiments on a corpus of texts from a Russian online newspaper demonstrate that applying latent semantic analysis to collocation extraction significantly decreases information noise and strengthens the words associations. The proposed method will be used for an automatic building thesaurus for a domain.

Keywords: Latent Semantic Analysis, Natural Language Processing, Collocations, Domain Knowledge.

1 Introduction

Latent semantic analysis (LSA) is a powerful algebraic statistical method that allows extracting latent semantic relations from natural language texts automatically without applying of any artificially built ontology. The method is based on a mathematical procedure of singular value decomposition (SVD) of matrices, used in many areas of applied mathematics. The method's essence consists in approximation of a matrix describing occurrence of words in considered texts by a matrix of a smaller rank by means of singular decomposition [1]. Consequently, the level of information noise in the frequency matrix is decreased. This means that the significance of irrelevant words in analyzed texts decreases, while the significance of occurrence of relevant words increases. As a result, latent links between words and texts can be revealed.

Primarily, LSA was used only as a method that raises accuracy of classification (ranking) of documents via decrease of information noise in the classification space features [1, 2, and 3]. In particular, in the paper, now acknowledged as classical [2], it was proved that using of this method raises quality of information retrieval by 30% as compared with standard search techniques.

The idea of LSA was developed in the more powerful and effective methods of analysis, such as probabilistic LSA (PLSA) and Latent Dirichlet allocation (LDA). In [4], it was argued that PLSA approach "is more principled than standard LSA, since it

P. Klinov and D. Mouromtsev (Eds.): KESW 2013, CCIS 394, pp. 92–101, 2013.
© Springer-Verlag Berlin Heidelberg 2013

possesses a sound statistical foundation". In [5], it was shown that LDA outperforms PLSA in text classification tasks with medium-size document collections. In [6], the new generalized learning algorithm for probabilistic topic models (PTM) was introduced. All of these benefits occur when a collection of documents are extensive and multi-thematic. In this study we have a limited size collection of documents from one domain. In this case, LSA is not inferior to its probabilistic extensions such as PLSA and LDA. Moreover, using a simple method, we only work with a matrix of relations and get rid of additional probabilistic variables.

The aim of this paper is to study possibilities of LSA for automated extraction of two words collocations from domain texts. Collocation means a combination of words that are often used together and compose syntactically and semantically complete unit of speech. For example, expressions like "hard nut", "strong tea", "Near East" are collocations (hereinafter translated from Russian), while expressions "strong nut", "hard tea", "Near South" are not.

Statistical methods have well proved themselves in automatic extraction of collocations. They are based on an idea of calculating frequencies of co-occurrence of words and differ only in ways of computing. For example, in [7], the method based on a measure of mutual information was used to identify collocations (to compute the co-occurrence of words). In [8], chi-square statistical criterion of co-occurrence was used for the same purpose. In [9], the likelihood ratio criterion was used for extraction of collocations. In [10], relations between words are defined according to an original semantic similarity measure learnt from a huge corpus.

The main difference of the approach proposed here is that it allows sifting out a large amount of words that are insignificant for the domain and then to reveal only essential (the most stable) pairs among words of the selected set. Thus, the basic idea of this work consists in that it is reasonable to search collocations among pairs of words revealed by LSA method with strong (stable) links since collocations are nothing else than steady combinations of words.

According to the aim mentioned above the paper is structured as follows. In section 2 we describe the method of latent semantic analysis and its basic results. In section 3 we describe our specific approach, which allows using LSA for automated extraction of collocations. The experimental part of the work is described in section 4. Section 5 concludes and outlines ways of further research.

2   Latent Semantic Analysis and Its Main Points

Let us have a corpus of documents referring to the given subject domain. We consider a corpus as any collection of text documents unified according to a common factor (language, genre, author, or time of creation). In our case, such factor is the thematic (subject) content of documents.

For the execution of the LSA on the set of documents of the corpus we construct a matrix "terms-by-documents", which rows correspond to words (terms) of the corpus, and columns – to documents. On the crossing of a row (term) and a column (document) of the matrix we put the frequency of occurrence of given term in given document. As a result, we obtain the sparse matrix of large scale because it is obvious that most of words occur not in all documents of the corpus, but only in their minority.

Each row of this matrix is a vector corresponding to a word and reflecting frequencies of this word in documents of the corpus, while each column is a vector corresponding to a document and reflecting frequencies of words in this document.

			Texts (documents)						
		d_1	d_2			d_j			d_m
	t_1								
	t_2								
Words (terms)	t_i					a_{ij}			
	t_m								

Fig. 1. The matrix "terms-by-documents"

According to the theorem of singular decomposition [11], the obtained matrix can be presented in the form of product of three matrices.

$$A = U \times S \times V^T \tag{1},$$

where A is an initial matrix, U and V are orthogonal matrices, S is a orthogonal matrix whose diagonal elements are decreasingly ordered and non-diagonal elements are equal to 0. Diagonal elements of matrix S are called singular numbers of the matrix A and are equal to arithmetic values of square roots of corresponding eigenvalues of the matrix AA^T.

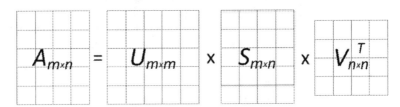

Fig. 2. Singular decomposition of the matrix "terms-by-documents"

Such decomposition possesses a property that if in matrix S only k largest singular values are left, and in matrixes U and V – only columns corresponding to these values and rows are left then product of obtained matrices (matrix A') will be the best approximation of rank k of the initial matrix A [3]. Thus, due to neglect of small singular values the part of information contained in the original matrix A, is discarded, so the new matrix A' contains less "information noise" than original matrix A.

Such decomposition possesses a property that if in matrix S only k largest singular values are left, and in matrixes U and V – only columns corresponding to these values and rows are left then product of obtained matrices (matrix A') will be the best approximation of rank k of the initial matrix A [3]. Thus, due to neglect of small singular values the part of information contained in the original matrix A, is discarded, so the new matrix A' contains less "information noise" than original matrix A.

The main issue of the LSA is that singular decomposition via decrease of rank of a matrix allows obtaining a new matrix, where basic associative links between words and documents are more evidently expressed and less important links are ignored [3].

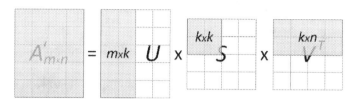

Fig. 3. Approximation of the matrix "terms-by-documents"

Thus, arising from the new matrix, we can estimate more precisely proximity between a word and a document, a word and a word, a document and a document as a distance between corresponding vectors. For calculation of a distance it is possible to use a cosine measure.

Therefore, LSA acts as a high-aperture lens in photography that blurs the background and enhances the information of the picture foreground. Similarly, against the fuzzy background, the overbearing issues in the text intensify.

3   Using LSA for Extraction of Collocations

Let words t_i and t_j $(i, j = 1 \ldots m)$ to be represented in the matrix A' by vectors $\bar{t}_i = [a'_{i,1} \ldots a'_{i,n}]$ and $\bar{t}_j = [a'_{j,1} \ldots a'_{j,n}]$. Then proximity between vectors can be defined by the cosine measure:

$$c_{i,j} = cos\left(\widehat{\bar{t}_i, \bar{t}_j}\right) =$$

$$\frac{a'_{i,1} \cdot a'_{j,1} + \ldots + a'_{i,n} \cdot a'_{j,n}}{\sqrt{a'^2_{i,1} + \ldots + a'^2_{i,n}} * \sqrt{a'^2_{j,1} + \ldots + a'^2_{j,n}}} \qquad (2).$$

After calculating the cosine measure for each pair of vectors representing words we can proceed from the matrix A' "terms-by-documents" to the matrix C "terms-by-terms" whose elements describe the strength of pairwise proximity of words. The matrix C is symmetric, and its diagonal elements are equal to 1. The more semantic proximity of the words, the closer to 1 is the value of a corresponding element of the matrix C.

If we choose from elements of the matrix "terms-by-terms" only pairs of words having proximity strength larger than 0.5, then we receive pairs-candidates that probably are collocations. It can be interpreted geometrically as a choice of those pairs of close words the angle between corresponding vectors is less than 60 degrees.

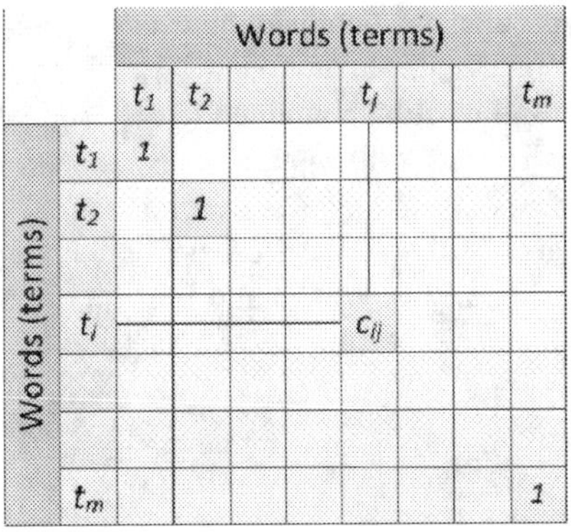

Fig. 4. The matrix "terms-by-terms"

In order to check out whether the pair-candidate is a collocation, we choose all documents in which this pair occurs. In each document, we measure a distance between the specified words as a number of other words between them. If the pair of words is a collocation, then, as a rule, these words are used either together or at a distance of 1-2 words (for instance, "result of negligence", "result of criminal negligence"), unlike such pairs, as «eastern - east», «automobile – car», which, despite the high strength of proximity, never can be used in conjunction.

For each pair of words, we calculate an average distance across all documents where these words occur. We set up the threshold value that should not exceed the average distance and obtain required pairs.

Accuracy of the proposed method is estimated by means of errors of the first and second type. Let the experimental sample to contain $P=PP+NP$ pairs, where PP is a quantity of pairs that are collocations, and PN is a quantity of pairs that are not collocations. We register an error of the first type FN or the false omission when the pair of words which is a collocation, is erroneously not detected. An error of the second type or the false detection FP is registered when the pair of words which is not a collocation is erroneously considered as a collocation. Using these values, it is possible to calculate a percentage of errors of the first type $Err1$ and the second type $Err2$.

$$Err1 = \frac{FN}{PP} * 100\% \qquad (3)$$

$$Err2 = \frac{FP}{PN} * 100\% \qquad (4)$$

4   Experiments

For carrying out of experiments we have chosen a subject domain "Traffic". We have prepared a training collection consisting of 1000 documents representing articles, published on the Russian website http://www.gazeta.ru/. Half of the documents concerned to the domain "Traffic", another half concerned to other domains (culture, science, finance etc.).

As a result of preliminary processing of texts from the training collection a dictionary of the volume of 53745 normalized words has been generated. The chi-square criterion was applied to words of the generated dictionary that allows us to allocate 567 key words of the domain "Traffic" from the dictionary. The way of application of the criterion is described in detail in [12]. Table 1 demonstrates the first 35 words translated to English with the highest value of the chi-square criterion.

Table 1. Top of keywords of domain "Traffic"

Word	Criteria
Automobile	1303,05
Car	859,96
Driver	665,37
Police	485,39
Road	458,34
Accident	396,17
Transport	352,87
Crash	300,38
Kilometer	298,01
Lanes	247,24
Wheel	241,44
Speed	232,22
Newspaper	231,69
Auto	222,89
To occur	219,35
Traffic	207,16
Automobilist	203,11
Owner	186,99
Criminal	185,90
Passenger	180,26
To suffer	178,37
To drive	178,12
To die	175,61
Region	175,46
Outlander	166,85
Jam	164,52
Automaker	162,16
Violation	156,41
Foreign	155,54
Article	151,77
Officer	151,13
To sue	148,91
Patrol	147,07
Trauma	146,25
Highway	141,86

Further, a matrix "terms-by-documents" with the dimension of 567x1000 (according to the number of key words and the number of documents of the training collection referred to the topic "Traffic") has been generated. Matrix cells contain frequencies of occurrence of words in documents.

By applying singular decomposition this matrix is approximated by a matrix of a rank 200. Fragments of the matrix "terms-by-documents" before and after the singular decomposition are shown on figures 5-6.

$$
\begin{pmatrix}
8 & 7 & 0 & 0 & 0 & 5 & 0 & \dots \\
1 & 0 & 0 & 0 & 0 & 0 & 0 & \dots \\
7 & 0 & 0 & 0 & 0 & 0 & 0 & \dots \\
1 & 1 & 3 & 4 & 2 & 0 & 16 & \dots \\
4 & 1 & 0 & 1 & 2 & 0 & 0 & \dots \\
3 & 1 & 0 & 1 & 3 & 0 & 0 & \dots \\
2 & 0 & 0 & 0 & 0 & 0 & 0 & \dots \\
\dots & \dots & \dots & \dots & \dots & \dots & \dots & \dots
\end{pmatrix}
$$

Fig. 5. The matrix "terms-by-documents" before SVD

As can be seen from Figures 5-6, by approximating the original sparse matrix "terms-by-documents", we are able to get rid of the noise information and enhance the essential links between words and documents.

$$
\begin{pmatrix}
8,052 & 7,098 & -0,001 & -0,133 & -0,081 & 4,929 & 0,024 & \dots \\
1,368 & -0,097 & 0,097 & 0,434 & -0,102 & 0,025 & 0,001 & \dots \\
6,348 & -0,035 & 0,083 & 0,140 & -0,171 & -0,103 & -0,117 & \dots \\
1,012 & 1,025 & 3,021 & 4,074 & 1,989 & 0,029 & 15,933 & \dots \\
4,190 & 1,151 & -0,076 & 1,100 & 2,067 & -0,109 & -0,044 & \dots \\
2,834 & 0,932 & 0,071 & 0,957 & 3,003 & 0,018 & 0,016 & \dots \\
1,522 & 0,338 & 0,064 & 0,026 & 0,133 & -0,092 & 0,026 & \dots \\
\dots & \dots & \dots & \dots & \dots & \dots & \dots & \dots
\end{pmatrix}
$$

Fig. 6. The matrix "terms-by-documents" after SVD

Then, using the cosine measure, we calculate the pairwise proximity of words in given row vectors in the new matrix. A fragment of the matrix "terms-by-terms" is shown on figure 7.

$$
\begin{pmatrix}
1 & 0,22 & 0,30 & 0,20 & 0,39 & 0,40 & 0,28 & \ldots \\
0,22 & 1 & 0,199 & 0,16 & 0,34 & 0,29 & 0,19 & \ldots \\
0,30 & 0,20 & 1 & 0,10 & 0,20 & 0,19 & 0,27 & \ldots \\
0,20 & 0,16 & 0,096 & 1 & 0,15 & 0,21 & 0,13 & \ldots \\
0,39 & 0,34 & 0,198 & 0,15 & 1 & 0,77 & 0,56 & \ldots \\
0,40 & 0,29 & 0,19 & 0,21 & 0,77 & 1 & 0,586 & \ldots \\
0,28 & 0,19 & 0,27 & 0,13 & 0,56 & 0,586 & 1 & \ldots \\
\ldots & \ldots & \ldots & \ldots & \ldots & \ldots & \ldots & \ldots
\end{pmatrix}
$$

Fig. 7. The matrix "terms-by-terms" of pairwise proximity of words

After that we have chosen from the elements of the matrix "terms-by-terms" only pairs of words having the value of proximity strength more than 0.5. Table 2 demonstrates the first 20 pairs of words with the highest value of proximity. Only 948 pairs were found.

Table 2. Top of semantic pairs of domain "Traffic"

First word	Second word	Proximity
Result	Negligence	0,959
Alcohol	Blood	0,952
To suffer	Victim	0,950
Metr	Metric	0,944
Blue	Bucket	0,938
Driver	License	0,892
Drunk	Drink	0,878
To die	Casualty	0,876
Law-enforcement	Agency	0,875
Article	PC (the Penal Code)	0,874
Audio	Signal	0,867
Liter	Petrolic	0,860
Statistic	Accident rate	0,857
Eyewitness	Testimony	0,849
Fuel	Benzene	0,829
Production	Auto	0,807
Engine	Petrol	0,802
Accident	Crash	0,801
Light	Flasher	0,794
Landscaping	Sidewalk	0,792

Each of the 948 found semantic relations was analyzed. To this end, all the documents of the corpus were reviewed for such occurrences, and amount of pairs with the distance of 1 or 2 intermediate words was calculated. We have found 322 collocations. Table 3 demonstrates top 30 collocations with the highest value of frequency.

Table 3. Top collocations of domain "Traffic"

First word	Second word	Collocation
Driver	License	Driver license
Law-enforcement	Agency	Law-enforcement Agency
Blue	Bucket	Blue Buckets (*A protest movement that has emerged in Russia as a response to arbitrary, unauthorized use of rotating beacon by bureaucrats*)
Accident	Statistics	Accident statistics
Eyewitness	Testimony	Eyewitness testimony
Medical	Aid	Medical aid
Head-on	Collision	Head-on collision
Kill	People	People killed
Take	Hospital	Taken to hospital
Deprived	Rights	Deprived of rights
Permissible	Limit	Permissible limit
Pedestrian	Zebra	Pedestrian zebra
Hit	Crosswalk	Hit in crosswalk
Hit	Pedestrian	Pedestrian hit
Mile-long	Jam	Mile-long jam
Front	Seat	Front seat
Back	Seat	Back seat
Registration	Number	Registration number
Inspector	Police	Traffic officer
Brain	Injury	Brain injury
Occur	Accident	Accident occurred
Lose	Control	Lost control
Passenger	Car	Passenger car
Alcohol	Test	Blood alcohol test

To assess the accuracy of the proposed method we have analyzed all 948 candidates to collocation pairs. As we said above, 322 of 343 collocations were found automatically, so the percentage of the first type errors is 6%. It is indicative that there are no second type errors.

5   Conclusion

The main difference between the approach which described in this paper and existing approaches is the use of factorization technique. First, we form a matrix of relations of document collection (between terms and terms, between terms and documents, between documents and documents), then use the factorization technique, and get the matrix that is free from the random relations. Among the obtained stable relations we are looking for two-word collocations.

As a factorization method we use latent semantic analysis based on singular value decomposition technique. The results of presented research demonstrate that latent semantic analysis is very useful tool for elimination of noise before applying statistical measures for assessment semantic links between words. The resulting matrix could have several purposes. Being transformed to "term-by-term" or to "document-by-document" this matrix al-lows assess links between words or similarity of documents respectively. And all this comes without an information noise.

However, we assume that the study of other methods of factorization such as PLSA or non-negative matrix factorization is very promising. Authors develop this method to solve a task of automatic building of thesaurus for a domain that is a part of the project of extremist content detection in social networks.

References

1. Deerwester, S.C., Dumais, S.T., Landauer, T.K., Furnas, G.W., Harshman, R.A.: Indexing By Latent Semantic Analysis. Journal of the American Society of Information Science 41(6), 391–407 (1990)
2. Dumais, S.: Enhancing Performance in Latent Semantic Indexing, Behaviour Research Methods. Instruments, & Computers 23(2), 229–236 (1990)
3. Dumais, S.T.: Latent Semantic Indexing (LSI): TREC-3 Report. In: The 3rd Text Retrieval Conference, vol. 500(226), pp. 219–230. Nist Special Publication (1995)
4. Hofmann, T.: Probabilistic Latent Semantic Indexing. In: The 22nd Annual International SIGIR Conference on Research and Development in Information Retrieval, pp. 50–57 (1999)
5. Blei, D.M., Ng, A.Y., Jordan, M.I.: Latent Dirichlet allocation. Journal of Machine Learning Research 3(5), 993–1022 (2003)
6. Potapenko, A., Vorontsov, K.: Robust PLSA performs better than LDA. In: Serdyukov, P., Braslavski, P., Kuznetsov, S.O., Kamps, J., Rüger, S., Agichtein, E., Segalovich, I., Yilmaz, E. (eds.) ECIR 2013. LNCS, vol. 7814, pp. 784–787. Springer, Heidelberg (2013)
7. Church, W.K., Hanks, P.: Word association norms, mutual information and lexicography. In: The 27th Meeting of the Association of Computational Linguistics, pp. 76–83 (1989)
8. Church, W.K., Gale, A.W.: Concordance for parallel text. In: The 7th Annual Conference of the UW Centre for New OED and Text Research, Oxford, pp. 40–62 (1991)
9. Lin, D.: Extracting collocations from text corpora. In: Workshop on Computational Terminology, Montreal, Canada, pp. 57–63 (1998)
10. Panchenko, A., Romanov, P., Morozova, O., Naets, H., Philippovich, A., Romanov, A., Fairon, C.: Serelex: Search and Visualization of Semantically Related Words. In: Serdyukov, P., Braslavski, P., Kuznetsov, S.O., Kamps, J., Rüger, S., Agichtein, E., Segalovich, I., Yilmaz, E. (eds.) ECIR 2013. LNCS, vol. 7814, pp. 837–840. Springer, Heidelberg (2013)
11. De Lathauwer, L., De Moor, B., Vandewalle, J.: A multilinear singular value decomposition. SIAM J. Matrix Anal. Appl. 21(4), 1253–1278 (2000)
12. Manning, C.D., Raghavan, P., Schütze, H.: Introduction to Information Retrieval. Cambridge University Press (2008)

Exploring Automated Reasoning in First-Order Logic: Tools, Techniques and Application Areas

Vladimir Pavlov, Alexander Schukin, and Tanzilia Cherkasova

St. Petersburg State Polytechnical University
Department of Management and Information Technology
195251 St. Petersburg, Russia
Vladimir.Alexandrovich@yahoo.com

Abstract. This paper describes state-of-the-art automated reasoning techniques and applications. We explore mainly first-order logic theorem proving, though our discussion also covers other domains: higher-order logic, propositional logic. We review applications of theorem proving systems in mathematics, formal verification, and other areas.

It is known that resolution is the most popular reasoning technique in first-order logic. Nevertheless, studying other algorithms could facilitate the development of automated reasoning. This article presents a survey of some promising methods. In particular, we give a detailed description of Maslov's inverse method that is applicable to a broad range of theories and also can be used as a decision procedure. However, this method is not well studied and its real potential is yet to be realized. We describe the architecture of our reasoning system that we use to compare the inverse method with the resolution method in practice. We also present some actual results of experiments.

Keywords: automated reasoning, automated theorem proving, resolution, inverse method, first-order logic.

1 Introduction

Automated reasoning is concerned with the development of computer programs that automate reasoning (i.e. the process of making inferences). The most advanced subfields of automated reasoning are automated theorem proving and automated proof checking. The former field deals with the automation of mathematical proofs, whereas the latter aims at mechanizing the process of checking proofs for correctness. In automated theorem proving, term "reasoning" is largely identified with deductive inference. This means that inferences are made within a certain formal system (e.g. propositional logic, first-order logic, intuitionist logic) in the form of deriving conclusions from a set of premises. Formal systems are rigorous and precise, so they are perfectly suit for mechanizing inferences. Computer programs that can automatically prove theorems within some formal system called theorem proving systems (inference engines, reasoning engines, or simply provers).

P. Klinov and D. Mouromtsev (Eds.): KESW 2013, CCIS 394, pp. 102–116, 2013.
© Springer-Verlag Berlin Heidelberg 2013

2   Theorem Provers and Their Applications

There are two main types of automated theorem proving systems (ATP systems):

1. Fully automatic theorem provers. These are reasoning engines which complete all parts of the proof without a user's assistance. A user of an automated prover provides a set of premises and a conjecture to be proven, and the system independently performs all further steps trying to derive the conjecture from premises and axioms. Depending on the particular system, a user can preset some additional options: time limit for a proof search, maximal proof tree depth, tactics to be used and other parameters. In common, fully automatic theorem provers work in first-order logic or first-order logic with equality. More sophisticated logical calculi are too complex for full automation of proofs [6]. Today the most powerful theorem prover for first-order logic is Vampire[1] that is dominant in the FOF division (First-Order-Form non-propositional theorems) at the CADE ATP system competition[2] since 2002.

2. Interactive theorem provers, or proof assistants. Proof assistants interact with their users during the process of making inferences. A user guides the proof by splitting the task of proving the complex theorem into smaller parts, providing hints or proof sketches to the program. This type of prover can serve as an intelligent assistant for mathematicians by automating some routine parts of the proof and automatically checking proposed hypotheses. Interactive theorem provers usually work in higher-order logic (type theory) or in first-order set theory [18].

Both types of theorem proving systems have certain advantages and disadvantages. Fully automatic theorem provers are more convenient and easy-to-use, but they have essential limits on the underlying logical calculi and don't allow user to guide the process of proof search. Interactive theorem provers are more flexible and powerful, but one needs to have sufficient experience and knowledge to use them properly and efficiently. Moreover, different interactive systems could have different user interfaces, proof languages, structures and features of background theories, tactics and options of the proof search. It means that a user of a proof assistant should be an expert not only in the mathematics and proof theory, but also in the techniques and languages that are specific for the used system (see [43] for an illustration). All these difficulties make using of such systems burdensome and restrict their application areas. Therefore, the urgent problems of modern proof assistants include development of convenient user interfaces and increasing the level of proof automation. There is also an extensive work on integrating advanced automatic theorem provers into proof assistants [8, 34]. On the other hand, modern resolution-based provers need to deal with the fact that unrestricted resolution can quickly generate so many clauses that the proof search space will become intractable. In fact, early attempts to prove even simple theorems using pure resolution techniques had been unsuccessful until the appropriate heuristics were developed [5]. Later it was discovered that different heuristics suit to the different classes of problems [6]. Modern automated reasoning systems are

---

[1] http://www.vprover.org/
[2] http://www.cs.miami.edu/~tptp/CASC/

able to manipulate with over a hundred of heuristics [41], but dealing with the substantial real-world problems is still a challenging task [25, 43, and 47].

2.1 Mathematics

After the first ATP systems appeared, there were great expectations on using ATP systems for solving open problems in mathematics. However, this goal turned to be too ambitious, and still there are no existing approaches that are capable of solving automatically a wide range of mathematical problems. Even for some relatively simple theorems the proof search space grows so quickly that their proof could not be found on the most powerful computers.

On the other hand, it seems to be a more easily attained goal to employ ATP systems as auxiliary tools for mathematicians. Modern proof assistants are well suited for this task, as they can partially automate proofs of complicated theorems and automatically verify the correctness of proofs found by a human. Proof system allows a user to construct the proof from sketch, without going into the details and routine verifications. This fruitful way of using ATP systems can be illustrated by several examples.

In 1996, an American computer scientist and mathematician William McCune used the computer program EQP for deriving the proof of the Robbins conjecture [33]. This hypothesis was posed in 1933 by Herbert Robbins, who suggested the new system of axioms for Boolean algebra. Robbins, Edward Huntington, Alfred Tarski and other mathematicians worked on this problem. Nevertheless, it hadn't been proved or refuted till the automated proof was published. The traditional proof was later constructed on the basis of computer-aided proof.

Another prominent example is the proof of the four color theorem that was proposed in 1852 by Francis Guthrie. In short, it states that every planar map, separated into contiguous regions, could be colored using at most four colors so that any two adjacent regions have different colors. The first mechanical proof of this theorem was obtained in 1976 by Kenneth Appel and Wolfgang Haken. However, their proof was not largely accepted by mathematicians because it was too complicated to check by hand (the proof contained more than 2000 diagrams, several hundreds of supplementary hand analysis and extensive amount of computer-aided analysis). The latest proof obtained in 2005 by Georges Gonthier by the means of the general-purpose proof assistant Coq[3], is far much simpler but still cannot be checked by traditional methods (the proof length is approximately 60000 lines) [14]. At the same time, this proof clarified most doubts on the validity of the four color theorem. An additional positive argument is the fact that the formal proof script was fully checked by the same Coq prover.

Otter[4], a fully automatic theorem prover for first order logic, has been used by the mathematician Kenneth Kunen to establish some facts in the theory of quasi-groups. Otter has also been used to obtain some interesting axiomatizations in other mathematical domains, e.g. lattice theory, ternary Boolean algebra, algebraic geometry.

---

[3] http://coq.inria.fr/
[4] http://www.cs.unm.edu/~mccune/otter/

The computer program Geometry Expert[5] for proving and discovering geometric theorems, has been applied to establish new results in Euclidean geometry. This system incorporates the most advanced techniques for automated theorem proving in geometry: the deductive base method, Wu's method, the area method, the Groebner basis method, the vector method, and the full-angle method.

Other successful results of applying ATP systems in mathematics include formalizations of the Jordan Curve Theorem within Mizar[6], the Prime Number Theorem within Isabelle[7] proof assistant, and 17-point version of the Happy End Problem [27, 1, 46]. This list has recently been expanded with computer-assisted formal proof of the Feit-Thompson Theorem (also known as the Odd Order Theorem), a central theorem in group theory [15]. The proof was completed with Coq by Georges Gonthier.

It is worth mentioning that one of the actual problems is making machine-generated proofs more compact and easier to understand. Especially for complex theorems automatically obtained proofs are too long and cumbersome to be understood by a human. Indeed, it is true for the examples above (the proof of the Robbins conjecture by EQP is an encouraging exception).

2.2   Formal Verification

Formal verification of computer systems (i.e. software, hardware circuits and security protocols) is an attractive application field for ATP systems. Reliability of software and hardware components is a crucial issue, since they are used in dangerous or safety critical areas: health care, nuclear plants, space- and aircraft control systems. Flaws in computer components can lead to distressing consequences and large expenses. For example, FDIV bug in early Intel Pentium processors [38] has the financial impact of $475 million. Similar losses resulted from the destruction of Ariane 5 rocket in 1996 due to the programming fault.

At the same time, even careful and sophisticated testing cannot guarantee that a program (or a hardware device) always performs its intended function. The ideas of proving software correctness rigorously first came in the 1970's. After discovery of FDIV bug, the largest microelectronics manufacturers, including Intel, AMD and IBM, started to use formal methods for circuit design verification. For instance, papers [19, 20] describe formal verification of floating-point operations in IA-64 architecture using HOL-Light[8] interactive prover.

The two basic approaches to formal verification are deductive reasoning and model checking [39]. Using a deductive reasoning, a verification task is stated as the problem of proving the theorems, which correspond to the specification requirements for a system behavior. With a model checking approach, a simplified abstract model of a finite state system is constructed to represent possible system's states and transitions between them. Then this model is used to check the compliance with the system specification, usually by exhaustive search of the whole state space of the system.

---

[5] http://www.mmrc.iss.ac.cn/gex/
[6] http://mizar.uwb.edu.pl/
[7] http://www.cl.cam.ac.uk/research/hvg/Isabelle/
[8] http://www.cl.cam.ac.uk/~jrh13/hol-light/

A deductive reasoning is more general method, as it can be used for infinite state systems. However, in general case this approach is only partially automatable. A model checking is limited to finite state concurrent systems, but at the same time it is fully automatable [39].

The task of hardware verification is more amenable to automation in comparison with software verification [18]. In common, a deductive approach for hardware verification is used. A verification task is formulated as a SAT problem (Boolean satisfiability problem), and a number of efficient algorithms have been developed to solve it. Specialized SAT solvers are developing extremely fast, but the used algorithms are merely enhanced versions of the DPLL algorithm [9] (Davis–Putnam–Logemann–Loveland). Indeed, the most powerful modern SAT solvers are based on either MiniSAT[9] or PicoSAT[10] (PrecoSAT[11]), which are in turn improve advanced DPLL implementations from Chaff[12] and GRASP[13] solvers. Some new algorithms are also developed, e.g. local search stochastic algorithms like WalkSAT [22]. More efficient solving of a SAT problem is achieved by the several means: using portfolio-based approach to join the strengths of multiple algorithms (SATZilla[14]), applying machine learning techniques (Glucose[15] and other solvers), running multiple solvers concurrently and performing distributed calculations. Quite apart stands the approach of conflict-driven answer set solving, which allows combining advanced techniques form constraint solving and satisfiability checking [13].

Model checking is a general approach to formal verification, and it can be used for verifying finite state systems such as hardware, software and communication protocols.

Combining the strong qualities of model checking with the generality of deductive reasoning is an attractive goal. Several attempts towards this goal have been made already: the verification system PVS[16] integrates symbolic model checking into reasoning procedure; the STeP[17] system combines both approaches on the basis of temporal logic.

2.3   Other Application Areas

There are also several interesting applications of automated theorem proving, which lie aside of the mainstream direction. One of them is reasoning over semantic web and OWL [23], which can help to find errors in ontologies, discover dependencies and

---

[9] http://minisat.se/MiniSat.html
[10] http://fmv.jku.at/picosat/
[11] http://fmv.jku.at/precosat/
[12] http://www.princeton.edu/~chaff/zchaff.html
[13] http://vlsicad.eecs.umich.edu/BK/Slots/cache/
     sat.inesc.pt/~jpms/grasp/
[14] http://www.cs.ubc.ca/labs/beta/Projects/SATzilla/
[15] https://www.lri.fr/~simon/?page=glucose
[16] http://pvs.csl.sri.com/
[17] http://www-step.stanford.edu/

unknown facts from the already presented in the ontology. OWL reasoning engines, such as HermiT[18] and Pellet[19], work mostly in the description logic.

Several attempts were made to apply automated theorem proving in artificial intelligence systems, such as computer vision and sentient computing systems. The ability to check the model of consistency could be used in the task of matching 3D-objects with their abstract representation, in the sensor systems to check the consistency of the world models according to a real life situation. For example, see paper [24] for description of model checking approach to the context-aware systems.

3   Theorem Proving Algorithms

3.1   Resolution

The resolution method was developed by J. A. Robinson in 1965 [40]. Resolution is a refutation theorem proving technique for propositional logic and first-order logic, i.e. resolution tries to prove a theorem by showing the unsatisfiability of its negation. Before applying the resolution rule, the formula must be converted to conjunctive normal form (which is equivalent to a set of clauses). The resolution technique includes only single inference rule that produces a new clause from a pair of clauses containing contrary literals. The resolution rule is applied sequentially until the empty clause is found. In this case the original clause set is unsatisfiable.

Resolution is the most widespread reasoning algorithm for first-order logic, now used by the vast majority of the modern automated theorem provers. Resolution has a lot of invariants; various strategies were developed to improve its efficiency: unit deletion, linear resolution, set of support, hyper resolution, UR-resolution, term ordering etc. In first order logic with equality resolution is augmented with special techniques to handle equality: paramodulation, term rewriting and superposition. Paramodulation can be seen as generalization of term rewriting that is based on replacing equal terms in formulas to simplify the subsequent calculations [21]. Superposition is a restricted instance of paramodulation rule and it has also become popular in equational theorem proving [2]. There are several refinements of resolution for various fragments of first-order logic and propositional logic. For example, SLD resolution is a popular technique used in logic programming for reasoning over Horn clauses [28]. In this paper, we will not describe resolution and related techniques in detail, as there are a lot of comprehensive literature on this topic (see, for example, [3], [7] and [21]).

Resolution is sound and complete as a refutation procedure [3]. The latter means that, if an initial set of clauses is unsatisfiable, resolution procedure will eventually discover this fact. However, resolution is non-terminating in the general case, as first-order logic is only semi-decidable.

---

[18] http://www.hermit-reasoner.com/
[19] http://clarkparsia.com/pellet/

3.2   Maslov's Inverse Method

The inverse method [7, 32, 30, 10, and 35] was invented by Soviet mathematician Sergey Maslov in 1964, not long before discovery of the resolution method by J. A. Robinson. However, the former method hasn't become so widespread for a number of reasons. Some of them are complexity of the original inverse method formulations by Maslov, mostly theoretical orientation of related papers by Maslov and his associates, and very little attention paid to the development of the practical issues.

The inverse method is a forward-chaining algorithm, in the opposite to backward-chaining methods like the method of analytic tableaux. While backward-chaining algorithms work from the goal to the axioms or premises, i.e. in the "upwards" direction within the proof tree, forward-chaining methods start from the axioms and premises, i.e. they work in the "downwards" direction.

The inverse method for first-order logic works as follows. It takes formulas of the form

$$F = \exists x_1 \ldots \exists x_n (D_1 \wedge \ldots \wedge D_\delta) \qquad (1)$$

In the Formula 1: $D_1, \ldots, D_\delta$ are disjunctions of literals (or simply clauses).

For the given formula, the corresponding calculus of favorable F-sets is built. Let ξ be the number of literals in the formula; and let all literals in the formula be indexed by the numbers from 1 to ξ. We will denote literals from the formula by $L_1, \ldots, L_\xi$. Then, an F-set is defined as an expression of the form

$$[(i_1, \theta_1); \ldots; (i_q, \theta_q)] \qquad (2)$$

In the Formula 2: q is a subscript for the element in the F-set ($q \geq 0$), $i_1, \ldots, i_q$ are indexes of disjunctions from the Formula 1 ($1 \leq i_1, \ldots, i_q \leq \xi$), and $\theta_1, \ldots, \theta_q$ are substitutions for the variables $x_1, \ldots, x_n$.

Finally, the calculus of favorable F-sets is built using the following inference rules:

1. Rule "A". Let L_i and L_j be arbitrary literals in the Formula 1; let θ_i and θ_j be arbitrary substitutions for the variables $x_1, \ldots, x_n$. Then, if the expression $L_i\theta_i \vee L_j\theta_j$ is a tautology, the corresponding F-set $[(i, \theta_i); (j, \theta_j)]$ is favorable.

2. Rule "B". Let $[H_1; C_1], \ldots, [H_f; C_f]$ be arbitrary F-sets, where each set $[H_k; C_k], 1 \leq k \leq f$ consists of the "head" H_k, and the "tail" C_k of the form $[(i_{k1}, \theta_{k1}); \ldots; (i_{kl_k}, \theta_{kl_k})]$ (hence l_k will be the length of the "tail" C_k). Next, let the following condition (we will refer to it further as "tail condition") to hold: for each disjunction $D_i, 1 \leq i \leq \delta$ exists such a set $[H_j; C_j], 1 \leq j \leq f$ that all the indexes $i_{j1}, \ldots, i_{jl_j}$ from its "tail" C_j correspond to literals in the disjunction D_i. Then, the F-set $[H_1\eta_1; \ldots; H_f\eta_f]$ is favorable, where $\eta_1, \ldots, \eta_f$ are such substitutions for the variables $x_1, \ldots, x_n$ that $\theta_k = \theta_{k1}\eta_k = \cdots = \theta_{kl_k}\eta_k, 1 \leq k \leq f$ and at the same time $\theta_1\eta_1 = \cdots = \theta_f\eta_f$.

The basic algorithm of the inverse method is simple: the calculus of favorable F-sets is built by applying the rules "A" and "B" sequentially, until the empty set is found. Derivability of the empty set is equivalent to derivability of the original formula F.

The rule "A" is used to build initial favorable sets for the given formula. In other words, the rule "A" forms a collection of the useful axioms to deduce the particular formula F. The rule "B" is the main inference rule; it constructs new favorable sets from already existing ones. In the rule "B", the "head" H_k can be an empty set.

For the clearer understanding of the inverse method, it is important to note that the F-set is interpreted as a disjunction of literals, which are the products of the substitutions $\theta_1, \dots, \theta_q$ into the literals with indexes $i_1, \dots, i_q$. In the rule "B", the substitutions $\eta_1, \dots, \eta_f$ play the same role as unifiers in resolution step. Therefore, the rule "B" could be rephrased shortly using the terms of resolvent and unifier: we make a resolvent of the sets $[H_1; C_1], \dots, [H_f; C_f]$ by unifying their "tails" $C_1, \dots, C_f$. The key aspects here are: a number f of input sets could vary (resolution step takes exactly two clauses); rejected "tails" of sets could have different lengths (in resolution, only one literal from each input clause is rejected); additional restrictions on rejected "tails" exist.

The "tail condition" from the rule "B" could be reformulated in the following way: for each disjunction $D_i, 1 \le i \le \delta$ from the Formula 1 there exist sets $[H_{j_1}; C_{j_1}], \dots, [H_{j_t}; C_{j_t}]$ $(1 \le j_1 < \dots < j_t \le f)$ such that the disjunction D_i is a logical consequence of the rejected "tails" $C_{j_1}, \dots, C_{j_t}$. This interpretation is more suitable for theoretical purposes, since it allows describing an algorithm that will automate logical inferences in first-order logic while being capable to serve for discovering wide classes of deducible formulas.

Maslov's inverse method has some advantages over the resolution method [32].

- The inverse method can be modified to accept arbitrary first-order formulas, not only Skolemized ones. This ability is crucial to the algorithm efficiency, since Skolemization could severely enlarge original formulas.
- The inverse method can be generalized on other logical calculi with reversible rules (e.g. first order logic with equality, constructive logic). The only restriction is that a suitable calculus must satisfy subformula property.
- Maslov's method allows implementing the effective proof search algorithm which at the same time can be used as the decision procedure for broad classes of first-order formulas. A decision procedure for a certain class of formulas is considered as an algorithm which takes an arbitrary formula from this class and necessarily terminates with an answer "yes" or "no", depending on the formula derivability. In other words, the inverse method is both a practical algorithm and a theoretical instrument, as it can be used to discover classes of deducible formulas. This is an important distinction from resolution and many other methods for first-order logic.
- In the inverse method, the proof search is directed towards the formula to be proven. A calculus of favorable sets is built exclusively for each given formula, so the inferences are constructed using the information from the formula itself.
- The inverse method can be used to simulate other methods of logical inference. Furthermore, it can be used in conjunction with the resolution method.

3.3   Other Algorithms

Except resolution, popular techniques of automated theorem proving in first-order logic include the method of analytic tableaux and the model elimination method. Both tableaux and model elimination belong to the class of global methods as they treat formula variables globally, and variable instantiations affect all parts of the proof. On the other hand, resolution and Maslov's inverse method are local methods: they treat all variables as universally quantified so that every instantiation is local to the certain branch of the proof [21].

Tableaux. Tableaux methods ([42], also [29, 21, 17]) are especially good for non-classical calculi like description and modal logics [17, 12]. There are different tableaux procedures for propositional logic, first order logic and modal logics. Tableau is usually represented as a tree-like structure. Initially, tableau consists only from the one branch, containing the set of premises and the negated conjecture. During the proof search tableau is branching; the way of branching depends on the properties of logical connectives in the tableau. For example, in simple refutational tableaux for propositional logic, the conjunction of two formulas is expanded into the two siblings of the same tableau branch; the disjunction splits the branch into the two separate branches. Similarly, other connectives are treated using their semantics. The branch is called closed, if it contains contrary literals. Therefore, if all the branches in tableau are closed, the original formula set is unsatisfiable.

Despite the fact that tableau calculi have been developed since fifties, they became popular only in recent two or three decades [12]. Now tableaux methods successfully embedded into several theorem provers[20], Isabelle proof assistant is among them [34].

Tableaux as a global methods have an essential difficulties with handling the equality. A special form of tableaux, called hyper tableaux, does not have this drawback [4]. Hyper tableaux incorporate the strong features of analytic tableaux with the ideas from hyper resolution.

Model Elimination. The model elimination method was developed by Donald Loveland in 1968 [31]. This method combines the features of both resolution and tableau calculi [21]. In logic programming, model elimination was the predecessor of the SLD resolution [28], which is used by logic programming language Prolog. By now, the model elimination method is largely replaced by SLD resolution. Nevertheless, some refinements of the model elimination have been developed during the past decade [16, 29, 37]. There are a number of theorem provers based on the model elimination, among which are PTTP[21] (Prolog Technology Theorem Prover), SETHEO[22], and METEOR[23].

---

[20] An extensive list of provers for description logic, modal logic, and related logics can be found here: http://www.cs.man.ac.uk/~schmidt/tools/

[21] http://www.ai.sri.com/~stickel/pttp.html

[22] http://www2.tcs.ifi.lmu.de/~letz/TU/setheo/

[23] http://www.cs.duke.edu/~ola/meteor.html

Evolutionary Algorithms. In addition to the mentioned algorithms, there are also several little known but interesting reasoning methods, which could be fruitful for improving the flexibility of the modern theorem proving systems. One of them is genetic reasoning [36], which seems to be a good alternative to ad-hoc proving techniques, which use heuristics to guide the reasoning process. Genetic reasoning applies the ideas of genetic programming to the problem of theorem proving. Genetic algorithms are well suited for solving complex optimization and search problems. These algorithms turned to be extremely effective on the number of problems, where conventional algorithms work very slowly or even could not find the solution at all. Since the general problem of automated reasoning can be considered as a complex proof-search problem, the genetic reasoning could make a big difference there. The main idea of genetic reasoning is to treat the proof as a program, composed of functions which correspond to the inference rules of the theory. The input of this program is the conjecture to be proven, and the output is the "simplified" expression which is evaluated by applying the chain of inference rules. In the case of completed proof, the output is either an axiom or a contradiction. Genetic reasoning algorithm starts from an arbitrary population, which elements are sets of functions (inference rules). This population is evolved using regular genetic operators: crossover and random mutation. The fitness function for each individual is the length of the produced expression after applying the corresponding inference rules. Thus, the genetic algorithm tries to simplify the expression until it matches one of the shortest statements, which are the constants "true" or "false".

Paper [11] presents another variant of evolutionary algorithm for reasoning in propositional logic. In this algorithm, inference rules of the theory play the role of evolutionary operators: Modus Ponens rule is recombination operator, substitution rule is mutation operator. The algorithm starts from a random set of substitutions that forms the initial population of substitutions. The initial population of theorems is obtained by randomly making these substitutions in the axioms of theory. Subsequent generations of theorems are obtained iteratively by applying Modus Ponens rule and making random mutations of individual theorems using substitution rule. During this process the population of substitutions may remain stable or may be modified by a genetic procedure. The algorithm works until the population of theorems contains the target formula, or a certain termination condition holds. In the first case the target formula is a theorem, and the formal proof may be obtained from the chain of applied evolutionary operators. This algorithm can be enhanced by using more flexible fitness function, effective selection procedures and survival mechanisms.

Machine Learning. Another tendency, which is already common among SAT provers, is using the machine learning techniques. An interesting attempt to extend the theorem prover E (for first-order logic with equality) with machine learning algorithms can be found in [6]. The author explored the ability of machine learning algorithms to automate a heuristics choice during the proof search. It turned out that effective classification is possible even on a few features of theorems. Heuristics selection based on learning techniques showed to be better than any single heuristics. However, the main limitation of the work is rather small set of heuristics used in learning. Only five heuristics were used in this work, while modern reasoning systems operate with tens and even hundreds heuristics. For example, classification of problems for over a hundred of strategies was manually made by Stephan Schulz in E[24] theorem prover. In spite of this limitation, the discussed work can be seen as the initial step in the real automation of heuristics selection problem. More applications of machine learning in automated theorem proving in first-order logic and even more sophisticated theories can be found in [48, 26].

4   Designing the Reasoning System

In the experimental part of our work we intended to explore practical features of the inverse method and to estimate its potential for applying in theorem proving systems. First of all, this task cannot be performed without a working reasoning system based on Maslov's method. Such system may be used to discover important practical characteristics of the inverse method, e.g. classes of problems that are most effectively solved with this method. On the other hand, the most interesting issue is correspondence between behavior of the inverse method and the resolution method. Taking into account the objective distinctions between the two methods, it is natural to suppose that each of the methods will show its best results at some specific kind of problems.

To the authors' knowledge, there are no existing open-source implementations of the inverse method for first-order logic. At least, known literature on Maslov's inverse method and its modifications (e.g. [3, 10]) lacks any appropriate references. Therefore, we had to implement our theorem proving system based on Maslov's method to be able to carry out the planned experiments. Further, it would be incorrect way to compare our small system with modern resolution theorem provers, which use hundreds of heuristics, sophisticated optimization algorithms and data structures. Finally, we decided to include both methods in our tool to compare them fairly.

Architecture Description. In the design of our reasoning tool, we provided the ability of using different axiom sets and adding some other reasoning methods. The system contains a uniform platform that allows sharing common data structures and logical framework among all methods under investigation. In our system design, some approaches were used from the popular resolution-based reasoning systems for first-order logic, such as E and Otter. At the same time, the special software architecture was developed for combining several distinct methods in the single system. The first version of the tool worked in propositional logic, later it was extended to first-order logic.

The theorem proving system is written in C++ using an object-oriented approach. The ATP system consists of the three main parts: the logical framework (a library of classes to handle logical operations), linked logical inference modules and the reasoning core.

---

[24] http://www4.informatik.tu-muenchen.de/~schulz/E/E.html

The logical framework is a class library to handle operations on formulas; it contains the classes for an internal formula representation in the form of syntactic trees, the classes for formula processing and converting to the standard forms, the classes for checking formulas on syntactical correctness, the classes for formula parsing and printing etc. The system allows to link different modules of logical inference, which could be implemented at the high level using the logical framework. The reasoning core interacts with the inference modules, providing them already prepared formulas and obtaining the results of the proof.

The logical framework was developed with the basic facilities for propositional logic and first-order logic. In propositional logic, both modules for the resolution method and for the inverse method were implemented. In first-order logic, the resolution method was finished, and the inverse method is yet being developed.

Experiments. A series of experiments was made using the developed system. Fig.1 illustrates the results of the comparative tests between Maslov's inverse method and the resolution method for propositional logic. During the test, randomly generated propositional formulas (tautologies) of the different length (from 20 to 100 symbols) were fed to the input of both methods, and the resulting proof length from each method was analyzed. Along the X axis, the formula length in symbols is plotted. Along the Y axis the proof length (a number of generated clauses) is plotted.

It can be seen on the Fig. 1 that on the test formulas the inverse method is even overcame resolution by the shortness of the proof. Since both methods work within the single ATP system, and use the common logical framework, the correlation of the proof times is the same. During the tests, Maslov's inverse method has shown a slow increasing of the time taken to prove the conjecture with increasing of the formula length. Certainly, this result rather roughly estimates the properties of both methods, because we tested them on the custom-generated problems and we do not use special tactics for resolution method that can significantly improve its performance. Yet our experiments can serve as the basis for further explorations. For first-order logic, we plan to carry out the full-fledged experiments on the problems from TPTP library [45], which is the established benchmarking library for ATP systems.

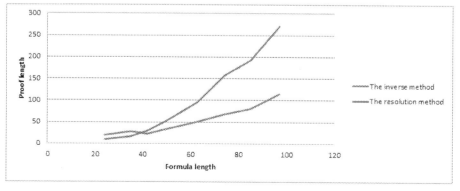

Fig. 1. Dependence of the proof length on the input formula length

5   Conclusions and Related Work

In this paper, we reviewed applications of automated reasoning, discussed open problems and challenging tasks in this area, analyzed reasoning algorithms that can be fruitful for first-order logic reasoning. We also presented the architecture of our reasoning engine and reusable logical framework. Presented results of our experiments with resolution and Maslov's method can serve as the basis for further explorations. We plan to extend our research on first-order logic and test different tactics for both methods. It also looks fruitful to extend the logical framework with non-classical logical calculi, as well as to try other reasoning methods.

References

1. Avigad, J., et al.: A formally verified proof of the prime number theorem. ACM Transactions on Computational Logic (TOCL) 9(1) (2007)
2. Bachmair, L.: Paramodulation, superposition, and simplification. In: Gottlob, G., Leitsch, A., Mundici, D. (eds.) KGC 1997. LNCS, vol. 1289, pp. 1–3. Springer, Heidelberg (1997)
3. Bachmair, L., Ganzinger, H.: Resolution theorem proving. In: Robinson, A., Voronkov, A. (eds.) Handbook of Automated Reasoning, vol. 1, pp. 19–99 (2001)
4. Baumgartner, P., Furbach, U., Niemelä, I.: Hyper tableaux. In: Orłowska, E., Alferes, J.J., Moniz Pereira, L. (eds.) JELIA 1996. LNCS, vol. 1126, pp. 1–17. Springer, Heidelberg (1996)
5. Bledsoe, W.W.: Non-resolution theorem proving. Artificial Intelligence 9(1), 1–35 (1977)
6. Bridge, J.P.: Machine learning and automated theorem proving. Technical Report, Cambridge (2010), http://www.cl.cam.ac.uk/techreports/UCAM-CL-TR-792.pdf
7. Chen, C., Li, R.: Matematicheskaya logika I avtomaticheskoe dokazatel'stvo teorem (Russian) (Mathematical Logic and Automatic Theorem Proving). In: Translated from English by Davydov, G. V., Mints, G. E., Sochilina, A. V. Edited by Maslov, S.Y. With appendixes by Maslov, S.Y., Mints, G.E., Orevkov, V. P. Nauka, Moscow (1983)
8. Chlipala, A., Necula, G.C.: Cooperative Integration of an Interactive Proof Assistant and an Automated Prover. In: Proceedings of the 6th International Workshop on Strategies in Automated Deduction, STRATEGIES 2006 (2006)
9. Davis, M., Logemann, G., Loveland, D.: A Machine Program for Theorem Proving. Communications of the ACM 5(7), 394–397 (1962)
10. Degtyarev, A., Voronkov, A.: The inverse method. In: Robinson, A., Voronkov, A. (eds.) Handbook of Automated Reasoning, vol. 1, pp. 179–272 (2001)
11. Dumitrescu, D., Oltean, M.: An Evolutionary Algorithm for Theorem Proving in Propositional Logic. Studia Universitatis Babes-Bolyai, Informatica 44(2), 87–98 (1999)
12. Furbach, U., Obermaier, C.: Applications of Automated Reasoning. In: Freksa, C., Kohlhase, M., Schill, K. (eds.) KI 2006. LNCS (LNAI), vol. 4314, pp. 174–187. Springer, Heidelberg (2007)
13. Gebser, M., et al.: Conflict-driven answer set solving. In: Proceedings of the 20th International Joint Conference on Artificial Intelligence (IJCAI 2007), pp. 386–392 (2007)
14. Gonthier, G.: A computer-checked proof of the Four Colour Theorem. Microsoft Research Cambridge (2005), http://research.microsoft.com/en-us/um/people/gonthier/4colproof.pdf

15. Gonthier, G.: Engineering mathematics: the odd order theorem proof. In: POPL 2013, pp. 1–2 (2013)
16. Hagen, R.A., Goodwin, S., Sattar, A.: Code improvements for model elimination based reasoning systems. In: Proceedings of the 27th Australasian Conference on Computer Science, ACSC 2004, vol. 26, pp. 233–240 (2004)
17. Hähnle, R.: Tableaux and Related Methods. In: Robinson, A., Voronkov, A. (eds.) Handbook of Automated Reasoning, vol. 1, pp. 101–177 (2001)
18. Harrison, J.: A short survey of automated reasoning. In: Anai, H., Horimoto, K., Kutsia, T. (eds.) AB 2007. LNCS, vol. 4545, pp. 334–349. Springer, Heidelberg (2007)
19. Harrison, J.: Floating-Point Verification using Theorem Proving. In: Bernardo, M., Cimatti, A. (eds.) SFM 2006. LNCS, vol. 3965, pp. 211–242. Springer, Heidelberg (2006)
20. Harrison, J.: Formal verification of IA-64 division algorithms. In: Aagaard, M.D., Harrison, J. (eds.) TPHOLs 2000. LNCS, vol. 1869, pp. 234–251. Springer, Heidelberg (2000)
21. Harrison, J.: Handbook of Practical Logic and Automated Reasoning. Cambridge University Press, New York (2009)
22. Hoops, H.H., Stützle, T.: Local Search Algorithms for SAT: An Empirical Evaluation. Journal of Automated Reasoning 24(4), 421–481 (2000)
23. Horrocks, I., Patel-Schneider, P.F.: Knowledge Representation and Reasoning on the Semantic Web: OWL. In: Domingue, J., Fensel, D., Hendler, J.A. (eds.) Handbook of Semantic Web Technologies, pp. 365–398. Springer (2011)
24. Katsiri, E., Mycroft, A.: Model checking for sentient computing: An axiomatic approach. In: Proceedings of the 1st Workshop on Semantics for Mobile Environments, SME 2005 (2005), http://www.cl.cam.ac.uk/research/dtg/www/files/publications/public/ek236/satisfiability6.pdf
25. Kaufmann, M., Moore, J.S.: Some Key Research Problems in Automated Theorem Proving for Hardware and Software Verification. In: Revista de la Real Academia de Ciencias Exactas, Físicas y Naturales. Serie A: Matemáticas (RACSAM) 98(1/2), 181–195 (2004) ISSN 1578-7303
26. Khalifa, M., Raafat, H., Almulla, M.: Machine Learning Approach to Enhance the Design of Automated Theorem Provers. In: Huang, T., Zeng, Z., Li, C., Leung, C.S. (eds.) ICONIP 2012, Part II. LNCS, vol. 7664, pp. 673–682. Springer, Heidelberg (2012)
27. Kornilowicz, A.: Formalization of the Jordan Curve Theorem in Mizar. In: International Congress of Mathematicians, Volume of Abstracts, p. 611 (2006)
28. Kowalski, R.: Predicate Logic as a Programming Language. In: Proceedings of the IFIP Congress, pp. 569–574 (1974)
29. Letz, R., Stenz, G.: Model elimination and connection tableau procedures. In: Robinson, A., Voronkov, A. (eds.) Handbook of Automated Reasoning, pp. 2015–2112 (2001)
30. Lifschitz, V.: What is the inverse method? Journal of Automated Reasoning 5(1), 1–23 (1989)
31. Loveland, D.W.: Mechanical Theorem-Proving by Model Elimination. Journal of the ACM 15(2), 236–251 (1968)
32. Maslov, S.Y.: The inverse method for establishing deducibility for logical calculi. Logical and logical-mathematical calculus (Russian). Trudy Mat. Inst. Steklov. 98(pt.I), 26–87 (1968)
33. McCune, W.: Solution of the Robbins problem. Journal of Automated Reasoning 19(3), 263–276 (1997)
34. Meng, J.: Integration of interactive and automatic provers. In: Second CologNet Workshop on Implementation Technology Computational Logic Systems (2003)

35. Mints, G.: Decidability of the Class E by Maslov''s Inverse Method. In: Blass, A., Dershowitz, N., Reisig, W. (eds.) Gurevich Festschrift. LNCS, vol. 6300, pp. 529–537. Springer, Heidelberg (2010)

36. Nordin, P., Eriksson, A., Nordahl, M.G.: Genetic Reasoning: Evolutionary Induction of Mathematical Proofs. In: Langdon, W.B., Fogarty, T.C., Nordin, P., Poli, R. (eds.) EuroGP 1999. LNCS, vol. 1598, pp. 221–231. Springer, Heidelberg (1999)

37. Paskevich, A.: Connection Tableaux with Lazy Paramodulation. Journal of Automated Reasoning 40(2-3), 179–194 (2008)

38. Pratt, V.R.: Anatomy of the Pentium bug. In: Mosses, P.D., Nielsen, M. (eds.) CAAP 1995, FASE 1995, and TAPSOFT 1995. LNCS, vol. 915, pp. 97–107. Springer, Heidelberg (1995)

39. Reed, J.N., Sinclair, J.E., Guigand, F.: Deductive Reasoning versus Model Checking: Two Formal Approaches for System Development. In: Proceedings of the 1st International Conference on Integrated Formal Methods (IFM), pp. 375–394 (1999)

40. Robinson, J.A.: A Machine-Oriented Logic Based on the Resolution Principle. Communications of the ACM 5, 23–41 (1965)

41. Schulz, S.: E – A Brainiac Theorem Prover. Journal of AI Communications 15(2/3), 111–126 (2002)

42. Smullyan, R.M.: First-Order Logic. Courier Dover Publications (1995)

43. Stump, A.: Programming with Proofs: Language-Based Approaches to Totally Correct Software. In: Meyer, B., Woodcock, J. (eds.) VSTTE 2005. LNCS, vol. 4171, pp. 502–509. Springer, Heidelberg (2008)

44. Sutcliffe, J.: Automated theorem proving: theory and practice. AI Magazine 23(1), 121–122 (2002)

45. Sutcliffe, J., Suttner, C.: The TPTP Problem Library. Journal of Automated Reasoning 21(2), 177–203 (1988)

46. Szekeres, G., Peters, L.: Computer solution to the 17-point Erdős-Szekeres problem. ANZIAM Journal 48(2), 151–164 (2006)

47. Tiwari, A., Gulwani, S.: Logical interpretation: Static program analysis using theorem proving. In: Pfenning, F. (ed.) CADE 2007. LNCS (LNAI), vol. 4603, pp. 147–166. Springer, Heidelberg (2007)

48. Urban, J., Sutcliffe, G., Pudlák, P., Vyskočil, J.: MaLARea SG1 - Machine Learner for Automated Reasoning with Semantic Guidance. In: Armando, A., Baumgartner, P., Dowek, G. (eds.) IJCAR 2008. LNCS (LNAI), vol. 5195, pp. 441–456. Springer, Heidelberg (2008)

OntoQuad: Native High-Speed RDF DBMS for Semantic Web

Alexander Potocki[1], Anton Polukhin[1], Grigory Drobyazko[2], Daniel Hladky[2], Victor Klintsov[2], and Jörg Unbehauen[3]

[1] Eventos, Moscow, Russia
{alexander.potocki,anton.polukhin}@my-eventos.com
[2] National Research University - Higher School of Economics (NRU HSE), Moscow, Russia
{gdrobyazko,vklintsov,daniel.hladky}@hse.ru
[3] Universität Leipzig, Institut für Informatik, Leipzig, Germany
unbehauen@informatik.uni-leipzig.de

Abstract. In the last years native RDF stores made enormous progress in closing the performance gap compared to RDBMS. This albeit smaller gap, however, still prevents adoption of RDF stores in scenarios with high requirements on responsiveness. We try to bridge the gap and present a native RDF store "OntoQuad" and its fundamental design principles. Basing on previous researches, we develop a vector database schema for quadruples, its realization on index data structures, and ways to efficiently implement the joining of two and more data sets simultaneously. We also offer approaches to optimizing the SPARQL query execution plan which is based on its heuristic transformations. The query performance efficiency is checked and proved on BSBM tests. The study results can be taken into consideration during the development of RDF DBMS's suitable for storing large volumes of Semantic Web data, as well as for the creation of large-scale repositories of semantic data.

Keywords: RDF, SPARQL, index, multiple joins, query optimization.

1 Introduction

The *research goals* addressed in this article are: creation of a native RDF DBMS that is efficient in terms of its performance, does not require the use of a relational DB and translation of SPARQL into SQL, and supports such recommendations of the World Wide Web Consortium (W3C) as RDF, SPARQL 1.1 [1], SPARQL protocol[1]; elaboration on existing approaches to the creation of a native RDF DBMS information architecture; development of new heuristic algorithms for optimizing query execution plans. An RDF data representation model is one of the foundations of the Semantic Web concept developed and being promoted by the W3C. Accordingly, an RDF DBMS is one of its fundamental underlying tools. The efficiency of any given RDF DBMS depends on its capabilities tailored

---

[1] http://www.w3.org/standards/semanticweb/

P. Klinov and D. Mouromtsev (Eds.): KESW 2013, CCIS 394, pp. 117–131, 2013.
© Springer-Verlag Berlin Heidelberg 2013

to a specific range of tasks. These are, first of all, volumes of processed data, and performance, i.e., the ability to efficiently execute advanced queries on such data. Although there are already RDF DBMS's designed to process voluminous data (hundreds and thousands of billions triples), a task of searching and developing optimal storage structures and RDF data processing algorithms continues to be relevant. *The main contributions* of this paper are: (a) evolvement of a vector model representing triples into a vector model representing quadruples and its efficient implementation by means of index structures for the quadruple data storage and retrieval; (b) presentation of the *multiple join* query execution plan operator implemented by the *zig-zag join* method for joining several data sets simultaneously; (c) a set of heuristics for the static optimization of SPARQL queries. The work has resulted in the practical embodiment of (a), (b) and (c) as an efficient native RDF DBMS "OntoQuad"[2] that can be used for creating large-scale Semantic Web data repositories.

2   Related Works

In a series of works by Harth et al. [2,3,4] focused on the YARS2 system development there is a discussion of issues related to the building of a complete index on SPOC[3] quadruples, or quads. This approach enables direct lookups by multiple dimensions with no need for joins. The total number of quad indices is determined, such indices being necessary for performing the full search by all possible complete quadruple patterns (16 patterns, 16 complete quad indices). They are then reduced to six indices with an alternative ordering on the assumption that the indices can be used to support prefix search that enables lookups with a partial key in case of incomplete quads. A problem of choosing index structure variants for the implementation of selected indices is investigated, and a sparse index variant is proposed. A similar method is presented by Baolin et al. in [5] where, proceeding from all possible SPO[3] triple patterns, a three-index system is proposed ensuring the prefix lookups. Weiss et al. in [6] presented an approach and evaluation of a prototype of one of the column-oriented vertical-partitioning (COVP) method variants. In this approach the fundamentals of vertical partitioning (see Abadi et al. [7]) and multi-indexing (see Wood et al. [8] and Harth et al. [2]) systems are taken. An RDF triple of the SPO type is indexed within a multiple-index construct that associates two value vectors with every RDF element, one vector per each of the two remaining RDF triple elements. A six-index structure is proposed for indexing RDF data, such indices being used to materialize any orders of precedence consisting of three SPO-type RDF elements. Pursuing the elaboration of the multiple-index approach proposed in [2,8] and improved in the Hexastore solution [6], we have created a database structure supporting certain permutations of a set of elements not only for SPO triples, but also for quads belonging within SPOG[3] relations. We develop a

---

[2] Developed on C++, trial RPM is
  http://www.ontoquad.ru/repository/RHEL/trial/ontoquad.repo
[3] Here, "S" stands for Subject, "P" for Predicate, "O" for Object, and "G" for Graph

vector model of the Hexastore to represent triples, and extend it onto the quadruple representation.

The next important problem we solved in the course of creating the Onto-Quad RDF DBMS was a problem of generating a query execution plan (QEP) that would ensure a better query execution time in comparison to an initial performance plan produced by the SPARQL parser. QEP optimization issues were formerly addressed by several researchers. Neumann et al. [9,10] proposed the query optimizer which mostly focuses on join order when generating execution plans. It uses dynamic programming for the plan enumeration, with a cost model based on RDF-specific statistical synopses. Stocker et al. [11] offered SPARQL query optimization methods based on static optimization using the Basic Graph Pattern (BGP) method to optimize triple pattern join sequences. The QEP optimization is performed before its efficiency is evaluated, and is achieved by means of the triple-pattern join selectivity estimation heuristics along with generalized statistics on RDF data to support those heuristics. In Hartig et al. [12] the SPARQL Query Graph Model (SQGM) was proposed supporting all phases of the query execution process. The optimization consists in transforming the initial SQGM into a semantically equivalent one to implement a better execution strategy. Such transformation is performed by means of a set of the Rewrite Rules included in the heuristics on transforming the initial SQGM into a resulting model, which ensures the achievement of a specific query transformation goal. Pérez et al. [13] presented an approach to formalize the semantics of the SPARQL core. The work defines a set of equivalence expressions allowing to transform any SPARQL query into a simple normal form consisting of the union of graph patterns. Gomathi et al. [14] described a multi-query optimization process that splits an input query into clusters using the K-means method based on the common sub-expression in the queries constituting an input set of queries. During our research we examined equivalent query plan transformations based on heuristic rules worked out using computational complexities of algorithms for implementing operations, experimentally as well as through the observation of the system response times for various QEP configurations. Proceeding in this direction, we developed a set of heuristics never referred to in the works examined by us, and used it for the static optimization of the initial QEP.

3   Database Organization

Definition 1. *Under a given set R of URI hyperlinks, set B of blank nodes and set L of literals, a triple $(s, p, o) \in (R \cup B) \times R \times (R \cup B \cup L)$ is named an "RDF triple". A pair (t, c) with a triple t and $c \in (R \cup B)$ is named a "triple in context c". A triple ((s, p, o), c) in context c is treated as a quadruple (s, p, o, c) [2].*

In the (s, p, o) triple, s is named a "subject", p is named a "predicate" or "attribute", o is named an "object". A concept of context is introduced to trace the origin of a triple in an aggregating graph G.

In our work we elaborate on the vector representation of triples proposed for the Hexastore [6], by expanding it onto quadruple representation. This model consists of four levels corresponding to the positions of elements in a quad; on each of these levels a vector of the element values is generated. The root level (level 1) contains a vector of all values of four elements S, P, O, G. Level 2 of the model contains groups of vectors, where each group has one of the level 1 element values as its parent. For every element (S, P, O, G) admissible at the first level there exist three vectors consisting of values corresponding to three admissible remaining elements of a quadruple (e.g., if an instance of element P is chosen at level 1, then vectors of values of the S, O and G elements will conform to it at level 2). Two vectors of values corresponding to the two admissible remaining elements of a quadruple will conform to an element value at the second level (e.g., if an instance of element P is chosen at level 1, and an instance of element S is chosen at level 2, then vectors of values of the O and G elements will conform to it at level 3).

The DBMS creates several files for storing data, that correspond to the logical structure described above. Each file is meant for storing quadruple elements values belonging to only one of the levels. The file combines both a structure for storing data and an Key-Value index implemented as *B-trees*. We use *B-tree* because it ensures the support of prefix range lookups, and one index can be used for executing queries by several triple patterns (e.g. ?s ?p ?o, :s ?p ?o, :s :p ?o).

The *B-tree* index being created is a clustering index ([15]), and its search key defines the ordering of the entries, thus ensuring the efficient performance of join operations. Four separate files corresponding to the S, P, O and G quadruple elements are created for the first level. For the second and subsequent levels, vectors of values corresponding to the S, P and G elements are placed into one file, while vectors corresponding to the O element are placed into another separate file. The DBMS keeps all unique values in a separate *Vocabulary* file, and Key-Value indexes contain referenses (fixed-length identifiers) to the *Vocabulary* items.

Vocabulary is a comprehensive lexicon of URI's and literals that are "known" to the base which associates the values of S, P, O and G with their vocabulary ID's that are unique within a DB instance. By introducing the *Vocabulary* we achieve: (a) acceleration of the work with types instances placed in the *Vocabulary* during data write-read operations; (b) reduction of space occupied by DB index files on HDD and in memory due to the fact that a long value is stored in the *Vocabulary* as a unique copy, while indices use a short numeral reference to it.

Fig. 1 shows a fragment of a quadruple index structure. Let us inspect it closer. The key of the first level is a reference to a S, P, O or G value stored in the system *Vocabulary*. For each value of the first-level key there exist three unique auto-incremental numbers serving as indicators of three possible quadruple elements that correspond at the second level to the element of the first level. For example, for each instance of P there are three unique numbers designating S, G and O elements. Thus, such numbers for the instance P_j in Fig. 1 are designated as k_1^p, k_2^p and k_3^p.

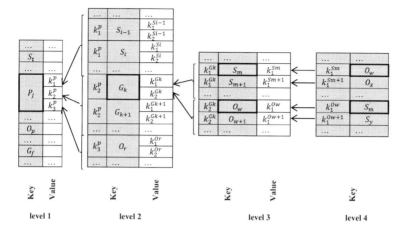

Fig. 1. Quadruples index structure fragment

At the second level a key is an object consisting of two fields: reference to the value of a "parental" instance residing at the first level, and reference to a value stored in the system *Vocabulary*. For each value of the second-level key there exist two unique auto-incremental numbers serving as indicators of two possible quadruple elements that correspond at the third level to the element of the second level. For example, for each instance of G that refers to the first-level instance of P there are two unique numbers designating O and S elements. Thus, such numbers for the instance G_k in Fig. 1 are designated as $k_1^G k$ and $k_2^G k$. And so on, through to the fourth level.

Our data storage structure is a variant of a method of the vertical partitioning of SPOG quadruple instances into subsets. Vertical partitioning the RDF data was offered by Abadi et al. [7] in order to increase the efficiency of search query responses. As distinct from [7] where it is proposed to create separate tables for every predicate P with two columns S and O, each of the four SPOG elements in our schema is an peer entity, and a quadruple is partitioned vertically as described above. Such a structure resembles the data organization used in a column-oriented DBMS [16]. The difference between our storage schema and the column-oriented DBMS lies in a method of binding data from the same tuple. While a traditional columnar storage schema implies, for every data element instance, the presence of a pointer to a tuple to which this element belongs, such a pointer in our schema points at an element preceding the selected element in the quadruple tuple. Since the columns of our database contain not the values themselves but references to the *Vocabulary* items, one can take advantage of the column-oriented approach and efficiently compress files on disk and in RAM. [17].

Thus, we implemented a vector model for storing data that was initially proposed for triples in the Hexastore and afterwards expanded by us onto the quadruple column-oriented storage schema.

4   Architecture and Implementation

4.1   DBMS Components

The main system components and their interaction when executing queries described below. The *SPARQL parser* is responsible for the syntactic analysis of queries and generation of the initial QEP tree [19]. The tree nodes contain operators implementing operations of relational algebra [15], the majority of which correspond to SPARQL algebra operators [1]. The main arguments of leaf operators are quad patterns and index files of the base. Higher-level operators in the execution plan tree may have one (e.g., *Order by* or *Distinct*), two (e.g., such operators as *join, Cartesian product*) or more (as in the *multiple join*) lower-level arguments/operators.

In our system the operators are implemented by *iterators* [19]. The *Iterator* is an object the interface of which includes such methods as *empty()* – check if the dataset is empty, *next()* – go to the next dataset record, *lowerBound()* – do logarithmic complexity search by ordered data, *setRange()* – do logarithmic complexity search of value ranges.

The QEP tree is processed in the following way. To obtain the SPARQL operator execution result, the *next()* method of the root iterator is called. This root iterator, in its turn, will call the *next()* method of the next iterator occupying a lower place in the execution plan tree. The process will go on until the leaf *iterators* working with database index files are reached.

The *Optimizer* is responsible for transforming the initial QEP into a new equivalent plan, more optimal in terms of performance time and resources. The *Optimizer* can choose one or another algorithm for instantiating relational algebra operators. When constructing a plan, the *Optimizer* uses knowledge about computational complexity and resource intensity of the *iterators*, as well as the *Vocabulary* and *indices*.

The *iterators* and the *Optimizer* interact with the *indices* (*Index Storage*) and *Vocabulary*. The *Functions* are either functions of the SPARQL language (e.g., *coalesce, if, sameTerm* and others [1]) or other custom functions. The *functions* are used by the *iterators* and retrieve variable values from the *Vocabulary*.

The *indices* and *Vocabulary* store their objects in the *Database File Storage*, in the *B-tree*. An intermediate layer between the *File Storage* and *Index Storage* and *Vocabulary* is a cache of database file pages (*Database Cache*).

4.2   Datasets Joining Iterators

We distinguish two types of iterators[4] responsible for joining datasets. These are the *Join* iterator family *(join)⋈ (L, R)* [15] performing the join of two (left and right) sets, and the *Multiple Join* iterator family *(multiple join)* ⋈$_M$ $(R_1, R_2, ..., R_n)$ performing the simultaneous join of several sets.

---

[4] Iterators below are written in prefix notation

We also distinguish between iterators with sorted and unsorted arguments, depending on whether the datasets we join are sorted or not. Thus, the iterator family *join* includes the following iterators: $\bowtie$ (*sorted, sorted*), $\bowtie$ (*unsorted, sorted*), $\bowtie$ (*unsorted, unsorted*). To use the *multiple join* iterators, the sorted dataset condition must be fulfilled for all arguments except, perhaps, for the first one: $\bowtie_M$ (*sorted, sorted, ..., sorted*) and $\bowtie_M$ (*unsorted, sorted, ..., sorted*).

Each iterator has two pointers to a current position in a dataset, the *begin* and the *end*. The *begin* pointer indicates the beginning of an ordered relation subrange, the *end* is a pointer to the end of the subrange. These pointers can be set using one of those techniques:

- by calling *lowerBound(key)* method of iterator. This will set a position of the *begin* to the beginning of an ordered relation subset, every tuple of which has a key fragment greater than or equal to a specified *key* value.
- by calling *setRange(key_begin, key_end)* method of iterator. This will set *begin* and *end* pointing to range *[key_begin, key_end)*.
- by calling *next()* iterator method. It shifts a position of the *begin* pointer by an entry next to the current one.

As practice shows, the *lowerBound* method is faster than the *setRange* method because it requires a less number of disk reads (only the upper boundary of the key needs to be found in a dataset, while the *setRange* method implies the search of both upper and lower boundaries).

4.3   Join of Two Datasets

Let us consider the $\bowtie$ (*sorted, sorted*) operator by the example of two joined patterns, $?s : p_1 ?o_1 ?g_1$ and $?s : p_2 ?o_2 : g_2$, and demonstrate the principles of such join. Here $: p_1, : p_2, : g_2$ – are pattern constants, and $?s$ is a variable by which the join of datasets is performed.

In case of such join, the transformation of patterns is performed at first, when constants in every pattern are "shifted" to the left and variables by which the join is executed are placed immediately following the constants: $: p_1 ?s ?o_1 ?g_1$ and $: p_2 : g_2 ?s ?o_2$.

For each pattern from the set of available indexes such a index is being chosen the key components of which in the left-to-right order correspond as fully as possible to the pattern constants. Thus, the PSOG and PGSO index files are to be chosen. Next, one of the leaf iterators (*indexScan*) is selected as a left (L) argument of join $\bowtie$, while the other iterator becomes a right (R) argument: $\bowtie_{s=s}$ (*indexScan$_L$(PGSO, key$_L$), indexScan$_R$(PSOG, key$_R$)*). It makes sense to choose such iterator in the capacity of L for which the condition $|L|<|R|$ is fulfilled, where $|L|$ and $|R|$ are dataset dimensions.

During the index scanning the keys key_L and key_R are generated. The beginning part of such key is formed by inserting constants from query patterns for L and R. These keys are then used by the leaf iterators for obtaining L and R dataset entries determined by specified patterns.

The join is performed in the following way. A process $\bowtie$ generates key_L from the pattern constants and join variables, then initiates a call to the $lowerBound(key_L)$ method of the leaf iterator $indexScan_L(key_L)$. The latter sets the scanning range $[begin,\ end)$ in L and uses the next() method to obtain the next tuple that is transferred to $\bowtie$. In $\bowtie$ a current value of the join variable $?s$ is extracted from the "left" tuple. This value participates in generating the key_R key to perform lookups in R.

Then the iterator $\bowtie$ calls the $lowerBound(key_R)$ method of the leaf iterator $indexScan_R(key_R)$, which, similar to the left index scan, sets the scanning range $[begin,\ end)$ in R and performs the index search of tuples with the key_R key. The ordering of R by join variables guarantees that, if such a range exists, a join variable value ($s2$) from the first tuple of this range will be $\geq$ the last specified join variable value ($s1$) from L. If the scanning range $[begin,\ end]$ for R is found, then, using the $next()$ method, all tuples will be extracted from it one-by-one and returned to $\bowtie$.

Current value of the join variable will be extracted from every such tuple, and if the join variable values of tuples "on the left" and "on the right" are identical, the iterator $\bowtie$ performs a join of a tuple having come from L with tuples having come from R. As soon as the tuples from the "left" or "right" range $[begin,\ end)$ become exhausted, the first out-of-this-range tuple is chosen from a dataset currently being scanned (it can be either L or R), on which in $\bowtie$ a current value of the join variable $?s$ is extracted from that tuple and becomes involved in the process of generating a key for lookups in an opposite set.

The process is repeated from the moment of setting a scanning range by means of the $lowerBound_i(key_i)$ method in an opposite dataset. In such a manner, the algorithm alternatively moves between entries of the left relation L and entries of the right relation R, resulting in the formation of a join of the left and right tuples provided that their values coincide in the positions specified by the join variables. The join algorithm terminates when, at the next $lowerBound(key_i)$ lookup attempt, a returned subset of tuples is empty. In case of the $\bowtie$ (*unsorted, sorted*) join, the whole left set can be scanned consistently, entry by entry, instead of setting a lower boundary by the left set $lowerBound(key_L)$.

Fig. 2 schematically shows the process of joining two ordered sets by variable $?s$. Judging by the look of the left/right dataset alternating scanning trajectory, the algorithm we use belongs to the *zig-zag join* type [15,18]. It allows us to avoid lookups (and disk readouts) of "unnecessary" tuples from the left and right sets, which is a common thing for the join and index based join algorithms [15], as well as does not require any re-sorting of the left and right sets in case of the leaf iterators because a properly chosen *B-tree* index guarantees that these datasets are properly sorted.

4.4   Multiple Join of Several Datasets

We extended the above-presented *zig-zag join* algorithm for two L and R sets onto the *multiple join* $\bowtie_M$ ($L_1, R_1, R_2, ..., R_n$) operation of joining several dataset simultaneously. Such a join is performed in a cascaded manner from left to right

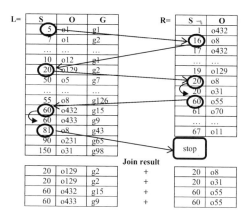

Fig. 2. Quadruples index structure fragment

when a join variable value retrieved from the L_1 is used to set a range scan key $[begin, end)$ by the *setRange* operator for R_1, join variable value retrieved from the R_1 tuple is used to set a range scan key for the R_2, and so on through to the last dataset participating in the join. The use of the *multiple join* $\bowtie_M$ operator is more efficient than the use of several sequentially executed operators $\bowtie (L, R)$. At that, the more datasets are participating in a *multiple join*, the higher its efficiency.

At first glance, the multijoin algorithm may look like the *Sideways Information Passing* technique [20] from RDF-3X. However, those two methods are quite different. In case of *multiple join* we use only a single thread of execution. Our technique does not store intermediate results, does not synchronize memory access, and has no thread managment overheads. Each iterator from *multiple join* knows next $max\{next(x)\}$ vaue to search to and entirely excludes any unnecessary join operations. We have no need in SIP as the value-gaps information is available for an iterator at any moment of time without any overhead.

4.5 Memory Requirements

Memory consumption mostly depends on two factors, one of which is the size of the database cache, and the second is the presence in QEP of iterators, which are memory consuming. One element of the quad takes on the average 40 bytes of RAM to store. Most iterators does not store data, so they do not use memory at all. It's true with the exception of some of the iterators (e.g. DISTINCT and SORTING) which do store data. Most of optimization heuristics know about memory consuming iterators and try to make the plan execution procedure more memory-efficient. Until the DBMS starts executing queries, most of the memory is allocated for caching pages of the database file. he database cache size is set as a parameter at the moment the DBMS starts.

Observations show that the more RAM is allocated for the cache, the better the DBMS performance is. Maximum performance is achieved when all the database files are put in the cache.

5 Execution Plan Optimization Based on Heuristics

Our system uses a static query optimizer based on heuristics and a transformation of an initial QEP D_0 into an equivalent plan D_1. These heuristics do not use preliminary calculated database statistics.

"Leaf iterator constants shift" heuristic. A similar heuristic was discussed in [11]. The optimizer looks for constants in triple pattern and "shifts" them within this pattern to the left, thus ensuring the use of sorted index structures. It is applicable only for the leaf iterators.

"Transform Cartesian product to join" heuristic. The optimizer tries to turn the *Cross-product (Cartesian product, ×)* [15] iterator into an iterator from the *Join* family ($\bowtie$) enabling the use of *indexScan(key)* (e.g., *zig-zag join*). Such transformation can be achieved if the sorting of tuples returned by at least either of the two arguments of the × operator is possible. The transformation pattern is: $\sigma_F(\times(L, R)) \Rightarrow \bowtie (L_{order_1}, R_{order_2})$, where the σ_F operator stands for the selection (*filter*) [15]. L and R are arguments of the × and $\bowtie$ operators designating the joined multisets. The $order_i \in \{sorted, unsorted\}$ signifies the $\bowtie$ sorting flag, *sorted* means a sorted dataset, and *unsorted* means an unsorted dataset. In order to apply $\bowtie$ with sorted arguments, the preliminary sorting of datasets must be ensured by any of the following methods: either by choosing an appropriate index, or by the multiset sorting operator τ_L [15].

"Reorder joins" heuristic. Suppose that there are two sequential joins with sorted and unsorted arguments. This transformation is applied in order to join the sorted multisets before joining the unsorted multisets by means of their relocation to lower node of QEP tree. The transformation patterns in this case are: $\bowtie (\bowtie (L_{1unsort}, R_{1sort})_{sort}, R_{2sort}) \Rightarrow \bowtie (\bowtie (L_{1sort}, R_{2sort})_{unsort}, R_{1sort})$ and $\bowtie (L_{2sort}, \bowtie (L_{1unsort}, R_{1sort})_{sort}) \Rightarrow \bowtie (\bowtie (L_{1sort}, L_{2sort})_{unsort}, R_{1sort})$. Here and further indexes *unsort* and *sort* stand for unsorted and sorted multisets.

"Sort Minus arguments" heuristic. The transformation is aimed at the replacement of the complete scan of the right R and left L arguments of the *minus* [1] operator by the index search operations. The transformation patterns in this case are: $minus(L_{unsort}, R_{unsort}) \Rightarrow minus(L_{unsort}, R_{sort})$, and $minus(L_{unsort}, R_{unsort}) \Rightarrow minus(L_{sort}, R_{sort})$. This transformation is achieved by the preliminary reordering of variables, selecting proper indices, or sorting the right R and, ideally, left L multiset entries.

"Sort outer join arguments" heuristic. The transformation is aimed at the replacement of the complete lookup of the right R and left L arguments of the *left outer join* ($\overset{\circ}{\bowtie}_L$) [15] operator by the index search operations. The transformation patterns in this case is: $\overset{\circ}{\bowtie}_L (L_{unsort}, R_{unsort}) \Rightarrow \overset{\circ}{\bowtie}_L (L_{unsort}, R_{sort})$. This transformation is achieved by the preliminary reordering of variables, selection of proper indices, or sorting of the right R and, ideally, left L relation-argument entries of the $\overset{\circ}{\bowtie}_L$ operator.

"Remove unrequired reordering" heuristic. The transformation is aimed at the removal from the QEP tree of a redundant iterator that performs the reordering of the columns of a resulting relation in case these resulting relation columns are already properly arranged.

"Execute the simplest union first" heuristic. If a SPARQL expression consists of several *Union* sections, a QEP tree needs to be reordered to ensure that the sections containing simpler statements are executed first. For example, sections are considered "simpler" if they contain the *Limit* operator and do not contain the *Filter* operator.

"Move Projection closer to leafs" heuristic. The heuristic tries to place a multiset projection operator π [15] before sorting operator τ_L and operator δ [15] performing the removal of duplicate tuples from that multiset. This allows to decrease the consumption of RAM used by the π and τ_L. The transformation patterns in this case are: $\pi_{j1,\dots,jn}(\delta(\Omega)) \Rightarrow \delta(\pi_{j1,\dots,jn}(\Omega))$, and $\pi_{j1,\dots,jn}(\tau_L(\Omega)) \Rightarrow \tau_L(\pi_{j1,\dots,jn}(\Omega))$.

"Move filters closer to leafs" heuristic. If a QEP tree contains the *join, outer join, Cartesian product, sort* operators, then the heuristic tries to move filter in the QEP tree closer to the leaf nodes, placing it before these operators. The transformation pattern in this case is: $\sigma_F(\dots op(L_1, R_1)\dots) \Rightarrow op(\dots(\dots\sigma_{F1}(\Omega_1)\dots\sigma_{F2}(\Omega_2)\dots)\dots)$, where the σ_F operator stands for the selection (*filter*), while the *op* operator stands for one of the $\bowtie$ (*join*), $\overset{\circ}{\bowtie}_L$ (*left outer join*), $\times$ (*Cartesian product*), τ_L (*Order by*) operators.

"Merge Distinct with Sorting" heuristic. If a *Select* clause contains the *Distinct* and *Order by* solution modifiers [1], we replace them by a new iterator performing simultaneously the duplicate tuple removal and sorting functions. This method allows to decrease the *Select* execution time, as well as to halve the demand for operative memory. The transformation pattern in this case is: $\tau_L(\delta(\Omega)) \Rightarrow \delta\tau_L(\Omega)$. Here, $\delta\tau_L$ stands for the operator simultaneously performing the duplicate tuple removal and sorting functions.

"Set sorted set limit" heuristic. If a *Select* clause contains the *Order by* and *Limit* solution modifiers, then we create a sorted set with a size specified in the *Limit* for storing resulting tuples. In accordance with the sorting conditions a new tuple read out by an iterator gets into an appropriate position of the set. When the sorting set becomes overflowed, extra tuple is removed from the end of the set.

"Chose optimal distinct algorithm" heuristic. To implement the *Distinct* solution modifier, we use two mechanisms, namely, the *hash map* table or *rb-tree* structure. If a QEP tree contains the *Distinct* solution modifiers, an attempt to use the *hash map* instead of *rb-tree* is made. The *hash map* works faster than *rb-tree*. However, in our implementation it requires the *Vocabulary* identifiers for

every variable from *Distinct* solution modifier, which is not mandatory in case of *rb-tree*. In other words, the use of *hash map* is possible when solution modifire does not contain variables generated by means of the *Bind* operator [1].

"Merge join with filter" heuristic. The heuristic tries to replace two iterators of the QEP tree, the *join* iterator with the embedded *filter* iterator, by the unified *join* iterator with the simultaneous filtering. The transformation pattern, subject to the specified conditions, is: $\bowtie_M (\sigma_F(R_1), R_2, ..., R_n) \Rightarrow \bowtie_{M\sigma_F} (R_1, R_2, ..., R_n)$, where the σ_F operator stands for the selection (*filter*), while the $\bowtie_{M\sigma_F}$ operator stands for the *multiple join* operator combined with the R_1 set filtering.

"Replace join with multiple join" heuristic. The *multiple join* operator can be used instead of the *join* operator even in case of just two input arguments. Even with two arguments *multiple join(unsorted, sorted)* is faster than *join(unsorted, sorted)*, because *multiple join* uses the *lowerBound(key)* method to specify a dataset scan range instead of the *setRange(key)* method. (It was mentioned earlier that the *lowerBound* method works faster than *setRange*). The transformation pattern is $\bowtie_{replaced} (L_{unsort}, R_{sort}) \Rightarrow \bowtie_M (L_{unsort}, R_{sort})$.

"Convert nested multiple joins to one multiple join" heuristic. Suppose there exist several nested *multiple join* operators with identically sorted join variables. Then, this transformation converts them into a single *multiple join* operator. The transformation pattern in this case is: $\bowtie (M_{1sort}, ..., M_{nsort}) \Rightarrow$ $\bowtie_M (M_{11sort}, ..., M_{1ksort}, ..., M_{n1sort}, ..., M_{nmsort})$. Here M_{isort} appears as $\bowtie (M_{i1sort}, ..., M_{ipsort})$, where M_{ij} is either a multiset or, in its turn, a nested join operator.

6   Evaluation

In this section we present the evaluation of the OntoQuad RDF store. We benchmarked our system using the Berlin SPARQL Benchmark (BSBM) using the Explore use case of specification V3.1. The Explore use case of BSBM simulates an e-business use case, where a user explores a dataset about products and their features linked with other types, like reviews and offers. Such a browsing session is referred to as a query mix and consists of 25 SPARQL queries.

For comparison, we also tested Virtuoso 6.1.6, Jena TDB (Fuseki 0.2.7) and BigData (Release 1.2.2). The benchmark machine is powered by one quad-core Intel i7-3770 CPU with 32GB of RAM. The storage layer is comprised of 2x 2 TB 7200rpm SATA hard drives, configured as software RAID 1. All systems were configured to use 22GB of main memory.

In our benchmark efforts we varied the database size (10 million triples, 100 million triples and 1 billion triples), used different levels of concurrencies with 1, 4, 8, 16 parallel clients. Each store was warmed up with 2000 query mixes before the actual testing was performed. Also, we varied the set of queries used,

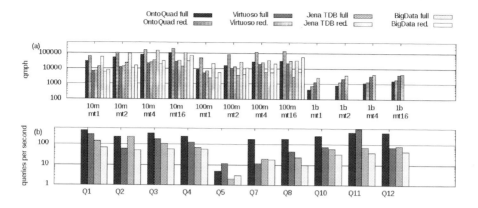

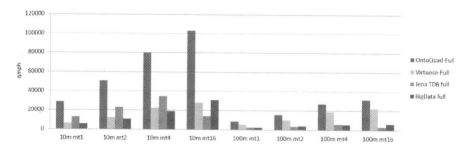

Fig. 3. (a) is total benchmark runtime in query mixes per hour (qmph) for the tested triple stores, dataset sizes and levels of parallelism on a logarithmic scale. (b) shows individual query runtime in queries per second for the 100m data set on a logarithmic scale.

Fig. 4. A near linear gain in performance with increasing thread count

as for large query sets BSBM query 5 dominates query run time due to its non-linear performance[5]. Therefore, one run with the full BSBM V3.1 query set and a reduced query set omitting query 5 was performed.

The overall benchmark results of these runs can be seen in Fig. 3 (a) where the total performance is given in query mixes per hour. In general, OntoQuad performs well in the comparison with the other state-of-the-art triple stores. In both the 10m and the 100m datasets OntoQuad is the best performing triple store, with performance gains up to an order of a magnitude. For the 1b dataset Virtuoso delivers the best performance, although the gap closes with increasing thread count.

In Fig. 3 (b) we display for the 100m dataset the individual query performance. Our efficient join execution strategy is reflected in the performance levels

---

[5] c.f.: http://lod2.eu/BlogPost/1584-big-data-rdf-store-benchmarking-experiences.html

we achieve in most queries, but is especially well observed in query 7. As a counter-example, query 11 does not contain a join, and is one of the two queries where OntoQuad is outperformed. Query 5 is an example where there is still room for improvement. Virtuoso executes a more efficient strategy here.

At all sizes we observe a near linear gain in performance for OntoQuad with increasing thread count, up to the point where the CPU is saturated (see in Fig. 4).

7   Conclusions and Further Work

In this paper we presented the native RDF DBMS OntoQuad solution and its internal architectural principles based on the vector model for representing quadruples. We described its efficient implementation by means of index structures as well as on a set of heuristics for the static optimization of SPARQL queries. The introduced approach ensures query processing speeds that are comparable to the results of other well-known industrial RDF database management systems. In our further elaboration on OntoQuad and continuation of the work, we intend to complete the following tasks: (a) database structure optimization at the data storage layer by means of removing some redundant links between the quadruple data representations; (b) further development of heuristics for QEP optimization in order to ensure the optimal performance of the BSBM BI test; (c) addition of a statistical estimator unit to the optimizer for evaluating performance efficiency of links and operators; (d) creation of the data store/DBMS cluster structure oriented towards the multi-platform processing of very-large-scale RDF data with a view to the development of Big Data-type semantic stores.

References

1. Harris, S., Seaborne, A.: SPARQL 1.1 Query Language. Technical report, W3C Recommendation (2013),
   http://www.w3.org/TR/2013/REC-sparql11-query-20130321/
2. Harth, A., Decker, S.: Optimized Index Structures for Querying RDF from the Web. In: LA-WEB (Latin American Web Congress) (2005)
3. Harth, A., Umbrich, J., Hogan, A., Decker, S.: YARS2: A Federated Repository for Querying Graph Structured Data from the Web. In: ISWG/ASWG, pp. 211–224 (2007)
4. Harth, A., Decker, S.: Yet Another RDF Store: Perfect Index Structures for Storing Semantic Web Data With Context, DERI Technical Report (2004)
5. Baolin, L., Bo, H.: HPRD: A High Performance RDF Database. In: NPG, pp. 364–374 (2007)
6. Weiss, C., Karras, P., Bernstein, A.: Sextuple Indexing for Semantic Web Data Management. PVLDB 1(1), 1008–1019 (2008)
7. Abadi, D.J., Marcus, A., Madden, S., Hollenbach, K.J.: Scalable Semantic Web Data Management Using Vertical Partitioning. In: VLDB, pp. 411–422 (2007)
8. Wood, D., Gearon, P., Adams, T.: Kowari: A Platform for Semantic Web Storage and Analysis. In: XTeGh (2005)

9. Neumann, T., Weikum, G.: The RDF-3X Engine for Scalable Management of RDF Data. Journal: The Vldb Journal - VLDB 19(1), 91–113 (2010)
10. Neumann, T., Weikum, G.: RDF-3X: a RISC-style Engine for RDF. PVLDB 1(1), 647–659 (2008)
11. Stocker, M., Seaborne, A., Bernstein, A., Kiefer, C., Reynolds, D.: SPARQL Basic Graph Pattern Optimization Using Selectivity Estimation. In: WWW 2008, pp. 595–604. ACM, New York (2008)
12. Hartig, O., Heese, R.: The SPARQL Query Graph Model for Query Optimization. In: Franconi, E., Kifer, M., May, W. (eds.) ESWC 2007. LNCS, vol. 4519, pp. 564–578. Springer, Heidelberg (2007)
13. Pérez, J., Arenas, M., Gutierrez, C.: Semantics and Complexity of SPARQL. In: Cruz, I., Decker, S., Allemang, D., Preist, C., Schwabe, D., Mika, P., Uschold, M., Aroyo, L.M. (eds.) ISWC 2006. LNCS, vol. 4273, pp. 30–43. Springer, Heidelberg (2006)
14. Gomathi, R., Sathya, C.: Efficient Optimization of Multiple SPARQL Queries. IOSR Journal of Computer Engineering (IOSR-JCE) 8(6), 97–101 (2013), www.iosrjournals.org e-ISSN: 2278-0661, p- ISSN: 2278-8727
15. Garcia-Molina, H., Ullman, J.D., Widom, J.: Database Systems: The Complete Book. Prentice Hall, Upper Saddle River (2002) ISBN 0130319953
16. Stonebraker, M., Çetintemel, U.: One Size Fits All: An Idea Whose Time Has Come and Gone. In: Proceedings of the International Conference on Data Engineering, IGDE (2005)
17. Stonebraker, M., Bear, C., Çetintemel, U., Cherniack, M., Ge, T., Hachem, N., Harizopoulos, S., Lifter, J., Rogers, J., Zdonik, S.: One Size Fits All? - Part 2: Benchmarking Results. In: Proc. Conference on Innovative Data Systems Research, CIDR (2007)
18. Antoshenkov, G., Ziauddin, M.: Query Processing and Optimization in Oracle Rdb. VLDB J. 5(4), 229–237 (1996)
19. Graefe, G.: Query Evaluation Techniques for Large Databases. ACM Comput. Surv. 25(2), 73–170 (1993)
20. Neumann, T., Weikum, G.: Scalable Join Processing on Very Large RDF Graphs. In: SIGMOD 2009, Providence, USA (2009)

A Comparison of Federation
over SPARQL Endpoints Frameworks

Nur Aini Rakhmawati, Jürgen Umbrich, Marcel Karnstedt,
Ali Hasnain, and Michael Hausenblas

Digital Enterprise Research Institute
National University of Ireland, Galway
{firstname.lastname}@deri.org

Abstract. The increasing amount of Linked Data and its inherent distributed nature have attracted significant attention throughout the research community and amongst practitioners to search data, in the past years. Inspired by research results from traditional distributed databases, different approaches for managing federation over SPARQL Endpoints have been introduced. SPARQL is the standardised query language for RDF, the default data model used in Linked Data deployments and SPARQL Endpoints are a popular access mechanism provided by many Linked Open Data (LOD) repositories. In this paper, we initially give an overview of the federation framework infrastructure and then proceed with a comparison of existing SPARQL federation frameworks. Finally, we highlight shortcomings in existing frameworks, which we hope helps spawning new research directions.

1 Introduction

The Resource Description Framework (RDF) was introduced since 1998 and now has become a standard for exchanging data in the Web. At present, huge amount of data has been converted to RDF. The SPARQL Protocol and RDF Query Language (SPARQL)[1] was officially introduced in 2008 to retrieve RDF data as easily as SQL does for relational databases. As Web of data grows and more applications rely on it, the number of SPARQL Endpoints constructing SPARQL queries over Web of Data using HTTP also grows fast. SPARQL Endpoint becomes main preferences to access data because it is a flexible way to interact with Web of Data by formulating query like SQL in traditional database. Additionally, it returns query answer in several formats, such as XML and JSON which are widely used as a data exchange standards in various applications. This situation has attracted people to aggregate data from multiple SPARQL Endpoints akin to conventional distributed databases. For instance, NeuroWiki[2] collects data from multiple life science RDF stores by utilizing LDIF framework [32] and RKBexplorer(http://www.rkbexplorer.com/explorer/) gathers research

---

[1] http://www.w3.org/TR/rdf-sparql-query/
[2] http://neurowiki.alleninstitute.org/

P. Klinov and D. Mouromtsev (Eds.): KESW 2013, CCIS 394, pp. 132–146, 2013.
© Springer-Verlag Berlin Heidelberg 2013

publication information from more than 20 datasets under rkbexplorer.com domain [20].

Contributions. In this study, we will focus primarily on the federation over
SPARQL Endpoint infrastructure, as the LOD cloud statistics[3] reports that
68.14% of the RDF repositories are equipped with SPARQL Endpoints. Aside
from giving an overview of querying over SPARQL Endpoints, we will compare
the existing federation frameworks based on their platform, infrastructure properties, query processing strategies, etc.—to chose any framework for small and
large-scale systems. Further, we highlight shortcomings in the current federation
frameworks that could open an avenue in the research of federated queries.

Related Works. More general investigations w.r.t. querying Linked Data have
been performed elsewhere [6, 9, 18]. [6] mentioned nine myths and five challenges arising in the Federation over Linked Data. Based on their observation,
they suggested to consider Linked Data as a service not as distributed data. [9]
explained the Federated SPARQL query infrastructure, whereas [18] focused on
the basics of federated query processing strategy.

A number of studies [23, 34] compares federation frameworks by evaluating
their performance. [23] tests federation frameworks by using FedBench [29] in
various networking environment and data distribution. Similar to [23], [34] con-
ducts an experiment in the FedBench to evaluate federation frameworks on large
scale Life Science datasets. In this survey, we investigate and compare more existing Federation over SPARQL Endpoint frameworks based on their strategy
such as source selection and execution plan.

Structure of the Paper. An overview of federation architectures of querying
over SPARQL Endpoints are presented in Section 2. Section 3 introduces the
existing federation frameworks, supporting either SPARQL 1.0 or 1.1[4]. We also
categorize them based on their architecture and querying process and investigate
features that should be added in the existing frameworks. Finally, we discover
challenges that should be considered in the future development of federation
query in Section 5. We conclude our findings in Section 6. For full version of this
paper we refer to [27].

2   Architecture of Federation over SPARQL Endpoints

SPARQL 1.1 is designed to tackle limitations of the SPARQL 1.0, including
updates operations, aggregates, or federation query support. As of this writing,
not all query engines support SPARQL 1.1. Therefore, we discuss the federation
frameworks that support either SPARQL 1.0 or SPARQL 1.1. There are three
kinds of architecture of federation over SPARQL Endpoints (Figure 1) namely
a) the framework has capability to execute SPARQL 1.1 query, b) the framework
accepts SPARQL query without specifying SPARQL Endpoint address, then it
rewrites query to SPARQL 1.1 syntax before passing it to the SPARQL 1.1 engine

---

[3] http://lod-cloud.net/state/
[4] http://www.w3.org/TR/sparql11-query/

Query 1.1. Example of Federated SPARQL Query in the SPARQL 1.0

```
SELECT ?drugname ?indication {
FROM <http://localhost/dbpedia.rdf> {     ?drug a dbpedia-owl:
    Drug .
          ?drug rdfs:label ?drugname .
          ?drug owl:sameAs ?drugbank . }
FROM <http://localhost/drugbank.rdf> {     ?drugbank drugbank:
    indication ?indication . }
}
```

Query 1.2. Example of Federated SPARQL Query in the SPARQL 1.1

```
SELECT ?drugname ?indication {
SERVICE <http://dbpedia.org/sparql> {     ?drug a dbpedia-owl:
    Drug .
          ?drug rdfs:label ?drugname .
          ?drug owl:sameAs ?drugbank . }
SERVICE <http://www4.wiwiss.fu-berlin.de/drugbank/sparql> { ?
    drugbank drugbank:indication ?indication . } }
```

and c) the framework handles SPARQL query without SERVICE keyword and processes the query in several phases by interacting with the SPARQL 1.0/1.1 engine of each SPARQL Endpoints. Those systems that have already supported SPARQL 1.1 allow user to execute query federation over SPARQL Endpoints by using *SERVICE* keyword (Figure 1.a). The query processor distributes each sub query to defined SPARQL Endpoints and join the result from SPARQL Endpoint. Basically, SPARQL 1.0 allows us to query data from remote data sources, however it does not retrieve specified remote SPARQL Endpoints. As described in the Query 1.1., it only fetches remote graphs or graphs with the name in a local store.

At present, the SPARQL 1.1 is the simplest solution to yield data from multiple sources. The W3C recommendation of the SPARQL 1.1 formalizes rules to query in multiple SPARQL Endpoints by using *SERVICE* operator. However, users must have prior knowledge regarding the data location before writing a query because the data location must be mentioned explicitly. As seen in the Query 1.2, the Drugbank and DBPedia SPARQL Endpoints are mentioned after SERVICE operator to obtain the list of drugs and their associated diseases. In order to assist users in term of data source address, it allows us to define a list of SPARQL Endpoints as data beforehand and attach the list of SPARQL Endpoint address as variable in the SPARQL query. Besides *SERVICE*, SPARQL 1.1 also introduces *VALUES* as one of the SPARQL Federation extension which can reduce the intermediate results during query execution by giving constrains from the previous query to the next query.

Query 1.3. Example of Federation SPARQL Query in the SPARQL 1.0 without SPARQL Endpoint specified

```
SELECT ?drugname ?indication {
?drug a dbpedia−owl:Drug . ?drug rdfs:label ?drugname .
?drug owl:sameAs ?drugbank . ?drugbank drugbank:indication ?
    indication . }
```

The lack of knowledge of data information is a main problem to execute federated query throughout multiple single RDF stores. Thus, several efforts have been introduced to address that issue (Figure 1.b). The user can write a query blindly without knowing the data location. These federation models can execute Query 1.2 or Query 1.1 without a SPARQL Endpoint declared. By removing SERVICE or FROM keywords, those two queries can be replaced by Query 1.3. These framework architectures provide an interface to translate query from SPARQL 1.0 to SPARQL 1.1 format. The core part of this interface is query rewriting component. After parsing and decomposing the query, this component adds destination address of this query by inserting *SERVICE* operators in each sub query. Further on, the result of query rewriter will be executed by internal SPARQL 1.1 processor system.

Since not all of the existing SPARQL Endpoints can handle SPARQL 1.1 query, several systems (Figure 1.c) developed query execution processor to execute the federated SPARQL query without SPARQL Endpoint address declared. The processor has responsibility to manage query processing such as maintain data catalogue, determine relevant sources, plan the query execution and join all results after retrieving data from SPARQL Endpoints. The details of phase

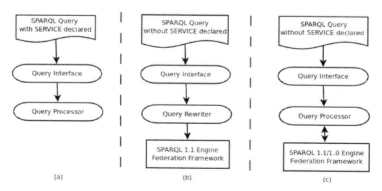

Fig. 1. Architecture of Federation over SPARQL Endpoint

of querying process in the Federated Over SPARQL Endpoint for architecture **b** and **c** can be found at [27].

3   The Existing Federation over SPARQL Endpoints Frameworks

This section presents the insight on existing federation over SPARQL Endpoint based on their architectures. To give better explanation, they will be classified based on their features. Ultimately, we propose several features that should be considered for next development.

3.1   The Existing Federation over SPARQL Endpoints Frameworks Based on Their Architecture

As described in the section 2, three federation architectures categories have been developed recently. We explain the existing federation based on those categories in this section.

Frameworks Support SPARQL 1.1 Federation Extension

As of this writing, several RDF store systems have been able to process federation query, but not all of them support *VALUES* keyword. Instead of handling *VALUES*, a number of frameworks has supported *BINDING* which is also addressed to reduce the size of intermediate results. The existing frameworks supporting SPARQL 1.1 are as follows:

ARQ[5], a query engine processor for Jena, has supported federated query by providing *SERVICE* and *VALUES* operator. ARQ implements nested loop join to gather retrieved result from multiple SPARQL Endpoints. In term of security, the credential value to connect ARQ service must be initialized in the pre-configuration[6].

Sesame. Previously, Sesame already supported federation SPARQL query by using SAIL AliBaba extension [7] at 2009, but Sesame can not execute SPARQL 1.1. Instead, SAIL Alibaba integrates multiple datasets into a virtual single repository to execute federated query in SPARQL 1.0. It can execute federation SPARQL query either RDF dump or SPARQL Endpoint by using its API. The data source must be registered in advance during setup phase. The simple configuration file only containing the list of SPARQL Endpoint address can cause poor performance since it sends query to all data sources without source selection. In order to optimize the query execution, Sesame offers additional features in the configuration file namely predicate and subject prefixes owned by one dataset. According to its configuration, Sesame can do prefix matching to predict the relevant source for a sub query. The join ordering is based on calculation of the size of basic graph pattern. The new version of Sesame (2.7)[8] is able to handle

---

[5] http://jena.apache.org/documentation/query/index.html

[6] http://jena.hpl.hp.com/Service#

[7] http://www.openrdf.org/doc/alibaba/2.0-alpha2/alibaba-sail-federation/index.html

[8] http://www.openrdf.org/index.jsp

SPARQL 1.1 which provides Federation extension features including *SERVICE* and *VALUES* operator.

SPARQL-FED Virtuoso. 6.1.6 allows to execute SPARQL queries to remote SPARQL Endpoint through SPARQL-FED[9]. The remote SPARQL Endpoint must be declared after SERVICE operator.

SPARQL-DQP. SPARQL-DQP is built on top of the OGSA-DAI [3] and OGSA-DQP [19] infrastructures. SPARQL-DQP transforms the incoming query from SPARQL to SQL, as it implements SQL optimization techniques to generate and optimize query plans. The optimization strategy is based on OGSA-DQP algorithm which does not need any statistic information from data sources. No SPARQL Endpoint registration is required because the SPARQL Endpoint must be written in the query. The OGSA-DAI manages a parallel hash join algorithm to reorder query execution plan.

Frameworks Supporting Federation Without Re-writing Queries to SPARQL 1.1

In order to overcome the lack of knowledge of data location, several federation frameworks have been developed recently without specifying SPARQL Endpoint address in the query. The federation framework acts as mediator [16] transferring SPARQL query from user to multiple data sources either RDF repository or SPARQL Endpoints. Before delivering a query to related source, it breaks down a query into sub queries and selects the destination of each sub query. In the end, the mediator must join the retrieved results from the SPARQL Endpoints. Following are overview of the current of federation frameworks and summarized in the Table 1.

DARQ(Distributed ARQ) [25] is an extension of ARQ which provides transparent query to access multiple distributed endpoints by adopting query mediator approach. The service description which consists of data description and statistical information has to declare in advance before query processing since it assists to predict where a sub query should go. According to the list of predicates in the service description, DARQ re-writes the query, creates sub query and designs the query planning execution. The query planning is based on estimated cardinality cost. DARQ implements two join strategies : Nested Loop Join and Bind Join.

Splendid [10] extends Sesame which employs VoID as data catalogue. The VoID of the dataset is loaded when the system started then the ASK SPARQL query is submitted to each dataset for verification. Once the query is arrived, the system builds sub queries and join order for optimization. Based on the statistical information, the bushy tree execution plan is generated by using dynamic programming [35]. Similar to DARQ, Splendid computes join cost based on cardinality estimation. It provides two join types: hash join and bind join to merge the results locally.

FedX [33] is also developed on top of the Sesame framework. It is able to run queries over either Sesame repositories or SPARQL Endpoints. During

---

[9] http://www.openlinksw.com/dataspace/dav/wiki/Main/VirtSparqlCxml

initial phase, it loads the list of data sources without its statistical information. The source selection is done by sending SPARQL ASK queries. The result of a SPARQL ASK query is stored in a cache to reduce communication for the successive query. The intermediate result size can be minimized by a rule based join optimizer. FedX implements Exclusive Groups to cluster related patterns for one relevant data source. Besides grouping patterns, it also groups related mapping by using single SPARQL UNION query. Those strategies can decrease the number of query transmission and eventually, it reduces the size of intermediate results. As complementary, it came with Information Workbench for demonstrating the federated approach to query processing with FedX.

ADERIS (Adaptive Distributed Endpoint RDF Integration System) [17] fetches the list of predicates provided by data source during setup stage. The predicate list can be used to decide destination source for each sub query pattern. During query execution, ADERIS constructs predicate tables to be added in query plan. One predicate table belongs to one sub query pattern. The predicate table consists of two columns: subject and object which is filled from the intermediate results. Once two predicate tables have been completed, the local joining will be started by using nested loop join algorithm. The predicate table will be deleted after query is processed. ADERIS is suitable for data source who does not expose data catalogue, but it only handles limited query patterns such as UNION and OPTIONAL. ADERIS provides a simple GUI for configuration and query execution.

Avalanche [4] does not maintain the data source registrations as its data source participants depends on third-parties such as search engines and web directories. Apart from that, it also stores sets of prefixes and schemas to special endpoints. The statistics of a data source is always up to date since Avalanche always requests the related data sources statistic to the search engine after query parsing. To detect the data sources that contributes to answer a sub query, Avalanche calculates the cardinality of each unbound variables. The combinations of sub queries are constructed by utilizing the best first search approach. All sub queries are executed in parallel processes. To reduce the query response time, Avalanche only retrieves the first K results from SPARQL Endpoints.

Graph Distributed SPARQL (GDS) [37] overcomes the limitation of their previous work [38] which can not handle multiple graphs. GDS is developed on top of Jena platform by implementing Minimum Spanning Tree (MST) algorithm and enhancing BGP representation. Based on Service Description, MST graph is generated by exploiting Kruskal algorithm. The MST graph estimates the minimum set of triple patterns evaluation and the lowest cost of execution order. The query planning execution can be done by either semi join or bind join which is assisted by a cache system.

Distributed SPARQL. In contrast to aforementioned frameworks, users must declare the SPARQL Endpoint explicitly in the SPARQL query at Distributed SPARQL [39]. Since it is developed for SPARQL 1.0 user, the SPARQL Endpoint address is mentioned after *FROM NAMED* clause. Consequently, this framework does not require any data catalogue to execute a query. As part of

Table 1. The existing frameworks support federation over SPARQL Endpoint without reformulating queries to SPARQL 1.1.

Framework	Catalogue	Platform	Source Selection	Cache	Query Execution	Source Tracking	GUI
DARQ	Service Description	Jena	Statistic of Predicate	✓	Bind Join or Nested Loop Join	Static	✗
ADERIS	Predicate List during setup phase	✗	Predicate List	✗	Nested Loop Join	Static	✓
FedX	✗	Sesame	ASK	✓	Bind Join parallelization	Dynamic	✓
Splendid	VoID	Sesame	Statistic + ASK	✗	Bind Join or Hash Join	Static	✗
GDS	Service Description	Jena	Statistic of Predicate	✓	Bind Join or Semi Join	Dynamic	✗
Avalanche	Search Engine	Avalanche	Statistic of predicates and ontologies	✓	Bind join	Dynamic	✗
Distributed SPARQL	✗	Sesame	✗	✗	Bind join	✗	✗

Networked Graphs [28], it is also built on the top of Sesame. To minimize the number of transmission query during execution, Distributed SPARQL applies distributed semi join in the query planning.

Frameworks Re-writing Queries to SPARQL 1.1

A number of frameworks were developed to accepts SPARQL query federation in SPARQL 1.0 format, but they are built on top of SPARQL query engine that support SPARQL 1.1 (Table 2.)

ANAPSID. ANAPSID [1] is a framework to manage query execution with respect to data availability and runtime condition for SPARQL 1.1 federation. ANAPSID enhances XJoin [36] operator and combines it with Symmetric Hash Join [8]. Both of them are non blocking operator that save the retrieved results to the hash table. Similar to others frameworks, ANAPSID also has data catalogue containing the list of predicates. Additionally, the execution time-out information of SPARQL Endpoint is added in the data catalogue. Therefore, the data catalogue is updated on the fly. Apart from updating data catalogue, ANAPSID also updates the execution plan at runtime. The Defender [21, 22] in ANAPSID has purpose to split up the query from SPARQL 1.0 format to SPARQL 1.1 format. Not only splitting up the query, Defender also composes related sub query in the same group by exploiting the bushy tree strategy.

SemWIQ. SemWIQ is another system building on top of ARQ and part of the Grid-enabled Semantic Data Access Middleware (G-SDAM). It provides

Table 2. The Existing Frameworks Supports Federation over SPARQL Endpoints, Reformulate query to SPARQL 1.1.

Framework	Catalogue	Platform	Source Selection	Cache	Query Execution	Source Tracking	GUI
SemWIQ	RdfStats+VoID	Jena	Statistic + Service	✓	Bind Join	Dynamic	✓
Anapsid	Predicate List and Endpoint status	Anapsid	Predicate List	✗	Symmetric Hash Join and XJoin	Dynamic	✓
WoDQA	VoID Stores	Jena	List of predicates and ontologies	✗	✗	Dynamic	✓

Query 1.4. Example of Link Predicate Problem

```
SELECT ?drug ?compoundname {
?drug drugbank:keggCompoundID ?compound .
?compound rdfs:label ?compoundname . }
```

a specific wrapper to allows data source without equipped SPARQL Endpoint connected. The query federation relies on data summaries in RDFStats and SDV[10]. RDFStats is always up-to-date statistic information since the monitoring component periodically collects information at runtime and stores it into a cache. As the RDFstats also covers histogram String, Blank Node etc, it is more beneficial for SemWIQ to be able to execute any kind of query pattern. SDV is based on VoID which is useful for data source registration. The query is parsed by Jena SPARQL processor ARQ before optimization process. SemWIQ applies several query optimisation methods based on a number of statistic cost estimations such as push-down of filter expressions, push down of optional group patterns, push-down of joins and join and union reordering. During optimization, the federator component inserts SERVICE keyword and SPARQL Endpoint for each sub query.

WoDQA. WoDQA (Web of Data Query Analyzer) [2] also uses ARQ as a query processor. The source selection is done by analysing metadata in the VoID stores such as CKAN[11] and VoIDStore[12]. The source observation is based on Internationalized Resource Identifier (IRI), linking predicate and shared variables. WoDQA does not exploit any statistic information in the VoID of each dataset, but it only compares IRI or linking predicate to subject, predicate and object. The same variables in the same position are grouped in one sub query. After detecting relevant sources for each sub query, the SERVICE keyword is appended following with SPARQL Endpoint address.

---

[10] http://purl.org/semwiq/mediator/sdv#
[11] http://ckan.net/
[12] http://void.rkbexplorer.com/

4   Desired Features

We have seen existing federation SPARQL frameworks along with their behaviours and properties. Based on our summary and experience, we suggest several features that could be added into their framework.

Hybrid Data Catalogue. As described in the section 3, the data source registration could be done by the mediator as well as third party such as search engine. In term of querying in the Linked Open Data, the data source registered should be not limited. The framework could combine static and dynamic data sources registration where the data source in the static registration is given higher priority than data source in the dynamic registration before delivering a query.

Link Predicate Awareness. Link predicate has ability to connect one entity to another entity in the different sources. The details of Link predicate definition can be found at [27]. For instance, the `drugbank:keggCompoundID` links the entity `drugbank:drugs` in the Drugbank dataset with the class `kegg_resource:Compound` in the Kegg dataset and `owl:sameAS` connects the entity `dbpedia-owl:Drug` in the DBpedia dataset with the entity `drugbank:drugs` in Drugbank. Assuming the link predicate connects two datasets, we should avoid to deliver the same destination of query patten containing the link predicate. In the case of Query 1.4, pattern *?compound rdfs:label ?compoundname* should not be sent to the Drugbank dataset as `drugbank:keggCompoundID` is a link predicate, even predicate *rdfs:label* occurs in all datasets.

5   Challenges

According to our investigation in Section 3, we note several challenges to be addressed in the future of federation framework development. Federation over SPARQL Endpoint has become actively developed over the last four years, especially in the source selection part. This field area is still infancy which faces several challenges that need to be tackled:

Data Access and Security. The data source and mediator are usually located in different locations, therefore the secure communication process among mediator and data sources should be concerned. Several SPARQL Endpoints provide authentication feature to restrict query access for limited user. However, the unauthorized interception between mediator and data sources have not been undertaken by any federation frameworks yet. The public key cryptography could be implemented in the federation frameworks where mediator and data source share public and private key for data encryption in the interaction process.

Data Allocation. Since several RDF stores crawl data from other data source, the data redundancy could not be avoided in the Linked Open Data Cloud. Consequently, the federation over SPARQL Endpoints framework detects relevant sources from multiple locations. This such condition could increase communication cost during selection source and query execution stage particularly for federation system employing data statistic from third-party. Furthermore, the redundancy data could increase the intermediate results as more data duplication from multiple source. On the one hand, using popular vocabulary allows user to query easily, but on the other hand, the source prediction for a query will be a hard task. As pointed out by [26] when popular entities and vocabularies are distributed over multiple data sources, the performance of federated query is getting worse.

Data Freshness. The freshness is one of important measurement in the querying data because each data source might have different freshness value. Having up-to-date data catalogue is a must in the federation framework to achieve high freshness value. The inaccurate results could arise from inaccurate data catalogue. Nevertheless, updating data catalogue is a costly operation in term of query execution and traffic between data source and mediator. Apart from data catalogue being static, the freshness could not be obtained when the high network latency occurs during communication process.

Benchmark. To date, benchmarks are generally proposed for single RDF stores such as LUBM [13], BSBM [7], and SP2Bench [31]. Hence, they are not suitable for distributed infrastructure. FedBench [30] is the only benchmark proposed for federated query which evaluated the federated query infrastructure performance including loading time and querying time. Those performance metrics are lack to evaluate federation framework. The federation framework benchmark should take into account several performance measurements from traditional distributed database such as query throughput. In addition, several metrics particularly occurring in the federation framework should be considered. For instance, the size of intermediate result, number of request, amount of data sent, etc. Apart from performance metric, due to heterogeneous data in the federated query, the evaluation of data quality become important measurement namely freshness, consistency, completeness and accuracy. [21] added two more FedBench measurements, namely Endpoint Selection time and completeness. Furthermore, it evaluated performance federation framework in various environment. Since the FedBench has static dataset and query set, it is difficult task to evaluate framework for other dataset. To address this problem, SPARQL Linked Open Data Query Generator (SPLODGE) [11] generates random query set for specified dataset. The query set generation is based on predicates statistic. Beside predicate statistic, it also considers the query structure and complexity such as number of join, the query shape, etc to produce the query set.

Overlapping Terminologies. The data is generated, presented and published using numerous expressions, namespaces, vocabularies and terminologies, that significantly contain duplicate or complementary data [24, 5]. As an example, there are multiple datasets in the LSLOD describing the concept *Molecule-* in Bio2RDFs kegg dataset, it is represented using *kegg:Compound* whereas in chebi, these are identified as *chebi:Compound* and in BioPax they are denoted as *biopax-level3.owl#SmallMolecule*, i.e, using different vocabularies and terminologies to explain the similar or related concepts [15]. Moreover, different datasets contains different fractions of data or predicates about the same entities e.g: Chebi dataset contains data regarding the mass or the charge of a Molecule whereas Kegg dataset explains Molecules interaction with biological entities such as Proteins. Conceptual overlap and different datasets share data about the same entities in LD4LS can be seen in the Figure 2 . Therefore, the mapping rules among heterogeneous schemas is highly required in the federated query. This task could be done by having global schema catalogue that maps related concepts or properties and generating more links among related entities.

Provenance. Apart from the number of sources, data redundancy often occurs in the Federation SPARQL query, particularly in Federation over Linked Open Data. It is because several publisher expose the same dataset. For example, Sindice contains DBpedia data: while a user is requesting DBpedia data, the DBpedia and Sindice SPARQL Endpoints are able to answer that query. The redundant result can not be avoided by Federation Framework using third party catalogue. Hence, the data provenance is the important factor in the Federation over SPARQL Endpointa. [14] explains a notable provenance implementation in the Federation System called OPENPHACTS (http://www.openphacts.org/). In order to tackle provenance issue, OPENPHACTS utilizes a Nanopublication [12] which supports provenance, annotation, attribution and citation.

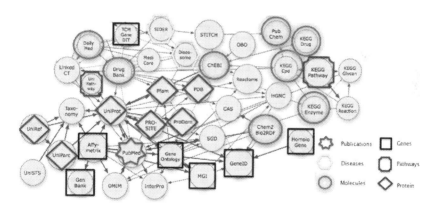

Fig. 2. Different Life Science Datasets talks about same concepts

6   Conclusion

Federation query over SPARQL Endpoints made a significant progress in the recent years. Although a number of federation frameworks have already been developed, the field is still relatively far from maturity. Based on our experience with the existing federation frameworks, the frameworks mostly focus on source selection and join optimization during query execution.

In this work, we have presented a list of federation frameworks over SPARQL Endpoints along with their features. According to this list, the user can have considerations to choose the suitable federation framework for their case. We have classified those frameworks into three categories: i) framework interprets SPARQL 1.1 query to execute federation SPARQL query covering *VALUES* and *SERVICE* operator; ii) framework handles SPARQL query without specifying SPARQL Endpoint address and has responsibility to find relevant source for a query and join the incoming results from SPARQL Endpoints; and iii) framework accepts SPARQL query without specifying SPARQL Endpoint address and translate the incoming query to SPARQL 1.1 format. Based on the current generation of federation frameworks surveyed in this paper, it still requires further improvements to make frameworks more effective in a broader range of applications. Finally, we point out challenges for future research directions.

Acknowledgement. This publication has emanated from research conducted with the financial support of Science Foundation Ireland (SFI) under Grant Number SFI/12/RC/2289.

References

[1] Acosta, M., Vidal, M.E.: Evaluating adaptive query processing techniques for federations of sparql endpoints. In: 10th International Semantic Web Conference (ISWC) Demo Session (November 2011)

[2] Akar, Z., Hala, T.G., Ekinci, E.E., Dikenelli, O.: Querying the web of interlinked datasets using void descriptions. In: Linked Data on the Web, LDOW 2012 (2012)

[3] Antonioletti, M., Hong, N.P.C., Hume, A.C., Jackson, M., Karasavvas, K., Krause, A., Schopf, J.M., Atkinson, M.P., Dobrzelecki, B., Illingworth, M., McDonnell, N., Parsons, M., Theocharopoulous, E.: Ogsa-dai 3.0 - the whats and whys. In: UK e-Science All Hands Meeting (2007)

[4] Basca, C., Bernstein, A.: Avalanche: Putting the spirit of the web back into semantic web querying. In: The 6th International Workshop on Scalable Semantic Web Knowledge Base Systems, SSWS 2010 (2010)

[5] Bechhofer, S., Buchan, I., De Roure, D., Missier, P., Ainsworth, J., Bhagat, J., Couch, P., Cruickshank, D., Delderfield, M., Dunlop, I., et al.: Why linked data is not enough for scientists. Future Generation Computer Systems (2011)

[6] Betz, H., Gropengieser, F., Hose, K., Sattler, K.U.: Learning from the history of distributed query processing - a heretic view on linked data management. In: Proceedings of the 3rd Consuming Linked Data Workshop, COLD 2012 (2012)

[7] Bizer, C., Schultz, A.: The berlin sparql benchmark. International Journal On Semantic Web and Information Systems (2009)

[8] Deshpande, A., Ives, Z., Raman, V.: Adaptive query processing. Found. Trends Databases 1(1), 1–140 (2007)

[9] Görlitz, O., Staab, S.: Federated Data Management and Query Optimization for Linked Open Data. In: Vakali, A., Jain, L.C. (eds.) New Directions in Web Data Management 1. SCI, vol. 331, pp. 109–137. Springer, Heidelberg (2011)

[10] Görlitz, O., Staab, S.: SPLENDID: SPARQL Endpoint Federation Exploiting VOID Descriptions. In: Proceedings of the 2nd International Workshop on Consuming Linked Data, Bonn, Germany (2011)

[11] Görlitz, O., Thimm, M., Staab, S.: SPLODGE: Systematic generation of SPARQL benchmark queries for linked open data. In: Cudré-Mauroux, P., Heflin, J., Sirin, E., Tudorache, T., Euzenat, J., Hauswirth, M., Parreira, J.X., Hendler, J., Schreiber, G., Bernstein, A., Blomqvist, E. (eds.) ISWC 2012, Part I. LNCS, vol. 7649, pp. 116–132. Springer, Heidelberg (2012)

[12] Groth, P., Gibson, A., Velterop, J.: The anatomy of a nanopublication. Inf. Serv. Use 30(1-2), 51–56 (2010)

[13] Guo, Y., Pan, Z., Heflin, J.: Lubm: A benchmark for owl knowledge base systems. Web Semantics: Science, Services and Agents on the World Wide Web 3(2-3), 158–182 (2005); selcted Papers from the International Semantic Web Conference, ISWC 2004

[14] Harland, L.: Open phacts: A semantic knowledge infrastructure for public and commercial drug discovery research. In: ten Teije, A., Völker, J., Handschuh, S., Stuckenschmidt, H., d'Acquin, M., Nikolov, A., Aussenac-Gilles, N., Hernandez, N. (eds.) EKAW 2012. LNCS, vol. 7603, pp. 1–7. Springer, Heidelberg (2012)

[15] Hasnain, A., Fox, R., Decker, S., Deus, H.F.: Cataloguing and Linking Life Sciences LOD Cloud. In: 18th International Conference on Knowledge Engineering and Knowledge Management (EKAW 2012), OEDW 2012 (2012)

[16] Hose, K., Schenkel, R., Theobald, M., Weikum, G.: Database foundations for scalable rdf processing. In: Polleres, A., d'Amato, C., Arenas, M., Handschuh, S., Kroner, P., Ossowski, S., Patel-Schneider, P. (eds.) Reasoning Web 2011. LNCS, vol. 6848, pp. 202–249. Springer, Heidelberg (2011)

[17] Lynden, S., Kojima, I., Matono, A., Tanimura, Y.: Adaptive integration of distributed semantic web data. In: Kikuchi, S., Sachdeva, S., Bhalla, S. (eds.) DNIS 2010. LNCS, vol. 5999, pp. 174–193. Springer, Heidelberg (2010)

[18] Ladwig, G., Tran, T.: Linked data query processing strategies. In: Patel-Schneider, P.F., Pan, Y., Hitzler, P., Mika, P., Zhang, L., Pan, J.Z., Horrocks, I., Glimm, B. (eds.) ISWC 2010, Part I. LNCS, vol. 6496, pp. 453–469. Springer, Heidelberg (2010)

[19] Lynden, S., Mukherjee, A., Hume, A.C., Fernandes, A.A.A., Paton, N.W., Sakellariou, R., Watson, P.: The design and implementation of ogsa-dqp: A service-based distributed query processor. Future Gener. Comput. Syst. 25(3), 224–236 (2009)

[20] Millard, I., Glaser, H., Salvadores, M., Shadbolt, N.: Consuming multiple linked data sources: Challenges and experiences. In: COLD (2010)

[21] Montoya, G., Vidal, M.E., Acosta, M.: Defender: a decomposer for queries against federations of endpoints. In: 9th Extended Semantic Web Conference (ESWC) Demo Session (Mai 2012)

[22] Montoya, G., Vidal, M.E., Acosta, M.: A heuristic-based approach for planning federated sparql queries. In: Proceedings of the 3rd Consuming Linked Data Workshop, COLD 2012 (2012)

[23] Montoya, G., Vidal, M.-E., Corcho, O., Ruckhaus, E., Buil-Aranda, C.: Benchmarking federated SPARQL query engines: Are existing testbeds enough? In: Cudré-Mauroux, P., Heflin, J., Sirin, E., Tudorache, T., Euzenat, J., Hauswirth, M., Parreira, J.X., Hendler, J., Schreiber, G., Bernstein, A., Blomqvist, E. (eds.) ISWC 2012, Part II. LNCS, vol. 7650, pp. 313–324. Springer, Heidelberg (2012)

[24] Quackenbush, J.: Standardizing the standards. Molecular Systems Biology 2(1) (2006)

[25] Quilitz, B., Leser, U.: Querying distributed rdf data sources with sparql. In: Bechhofer, S., Hauswirth, M., Hoffmann, J., Koubarakis, M. (eds.) ESWC 2008. LNCS, vol. 5021, pp. 524–538. Springer, Heidelberg (2008)

[26] Rakhmawati, N.A., Hausenblas, M.: On the impact of data distribution in federated sparql queries. In: 2012 IEEE Sixth International Conference on Semantic Computing (ICSC), pp. 255–260 (September 2012)

[27] Rakhmawati, N.A., Umbrich, J., Karnstedt, M., Hasnain, A., Hausenblas, M.: Querying over federated sparql endpoints - a state of the art survey. CoRR abs/1306.1723 (2013)

[28] Schenk, S., Staab, S.: Networked graphs: a declarative mechanism for sparql rules, sparql views and rdf data integration on the web. In: Proceedings of the 17th International Conference on World Wide Web, WWW 2008, pp. 585–594. ACM, New York (2008)

[29] Schmidt, M., Görlitz, O., Haase, P., Ladwig, G., Schwarte, A., Tran, T.: Fedbench: A benchmark suite for federated semantic data query processing. In: Aroyo, L., Welty, C., Alani, H., Taylor, J., Bernstein, A., Kagal, L., Noy, N., Blomqvist, E. (eds.) ISWC 2011, Part I. LNCS, vol. 7031, pp. 585–600. Springer, Heidelberg (2011)

[30] Schmidt, M., Görlitz, O., Haase, P., Ladwig, G., Schwarte, A., Tran, T.: FedBench: A benchmark suite for federated semantic data query processing. In: Aroyo, L., Welty, C., Alani, H., Taylor, J., Bernstein, A., Kagal, L., Noy, N., Blomqvist, E. (eds.) ISWC 2011, Part I. LNCS, vol. 7031, pp. 585–600. Springer, Heidelberg (2011)

[31] Schmidt, M., Hornung, T., Lausen, G., Pinkel, C.: Sp2bench: A sparql performance benchmark. CoRR abs/0806.4627 (2008)

[32] Schultz, A., Matteini, A., Isele, R., Mendes, P.N., Bizer, C., Becker, C.: LDIF - A Framework for Large-Scale Linked Data Integration. In: 21st International World Wide Web Conference (WWW2012), Developers Track (April 2012)

[33] Schwarte, A., Haase, P., Hose, K., Schenkel, R., Schmidt, M.: FedX: A federation layer for distributed query processing on linked open data. In: Antoniou, G., Grobelnik, M., Simperl, E., Parsia, B., Plexousakis, D., De Leenheer, P., Pan, J. (eds.) ESWC 2011, Part II. LNCS, vol. 6644, pp. 481–486. Springer, Heidelberg (2011)

[34] Schwarte, A., Haase, P., Schmidt, M., Hose, K., Schenkel, R.: An experience report of large scale federations. CoRR abs/1210.5403 (2012)

[35] Selinger, P.G., Astrahan, M.M., Chamberlin, D.D., Lorie, R.A., Price, T.G.: Access path selection in a relational database management system. In: Proceedings of the 1979 ACM SIGMOD International Conference on Management of Data, SIGMOD 1979, pp. 23–34. ACM, New York (1979)

[36] Urhan, T., Franklin, M.J.: XJoin: A reactively-scheduled pipelined join operator. IEEE Data Engineering Bulletin 23(2), 27–33 (2000)

[37] Wang, X., Tiropanis, T., Davis, H.: Querying the web of data with graph theory-based techniques. In: Web and Internet Science (2011)

[38] Wang, X., Tiropanis, T., Davis, H.C.: Evaluating graph traversal algorithms for distributed SPARQL query optimization. In: Pan, J.Z., Chen, H., Kim, H.-G., Li, J., Wu, Z., Horrocks, I., Mizoguchi, R., Wu, Z. (eds.) JIST 2011. LNCS, vol. 7185, pp. 210–225. Springer, Heidelberg (2012)

[39] Zemánek, J., Schenk, S.: Optimizing sparql queries over disparate rdf data sources through distributed semi-joins. In: International Semantic Web Conference (Posters & Demos) (2008)

Knowledge-Based Support for Complex Systems Exploration in Distributed Problem Solving Environments

Pavel A. Smirnov, Sergey V. Kovalchuk, and Alexander V. Boukhanovsky

Saint-Petersburg National University of Information Technologies,
Mechanics and Optics, Saint-Petersburg, Russia
`smirnp@niuitmo.ru`, `{kovalchuk,boukhanovsky}@mail.ifmo.ru`

Abstract. The work is aimed to the development of approaches to intelligent support of knowledge usage and generation process performed within simulation-based research. As contemporary e-Science tasks often require acquisition, integration and usage of complex knowledge belonging to different domains, the concept and technology for semantic integration and processing of knowledge used within complex systems simulation tasks were developed. Within proposed approach three main classes of knowledge considered are considered: domain-specific, IT, and general system-level knowledge. All these classes are needed to be integrated and coordinated to support the simulation process. Ontology-based technology is described as a core technique for unified multi-domain knowledge formalization and automatic or semi-automatic interconnection. Virtual Simulation Objects (VSO) concept and technology are described as a basic approach for development of domain-specific solutions to support of the whole simulation-based research process including model development, simulation running and results presentation.

Keywords: problem solving environment, e-science, complex system simulation, knowledge base, ontology.

1   Introduction

Modern level of information technologies enables solving complex and computational-intensive scientific tasks. Often such tasks are characterized by the complexity of its structure, which includes subtasks related to different problem domains. Moreover, frequently it is needed to combine different software and hardware technologies within single solution. Under such condition the emergence of e-Science concept [1] is forced by the idea of technological support of domain-specific research. This concept's goal is the development of a completely new kind of scientific approaches and tools for world exploration. Today one of the most popular solutions for building this kind of tools is presented by a concept of Problem Solving Environments (PSE) [2] which presents technological toolboxes for managing domain problems. On the other hand, solving complex scientific tasks often requires integration of different components into single solutions. Today popular technologies for composite solution build-

P. Klinov and D. Mouromtsev (Eds.): KESW 2013, CCIS 394, pp. 147–161, 2013.
© Springer-Verlag Berlin Heidelberg 2013

ing intensively exploit the idea of Service-Oriented Architecture (SOA) [3], which allows making the technological integration of different components over predefined interfaces. The modern scientific composite solutions are usually developed on the basis of workflow model [4] which enables interconnection of computing or information-providing services available within distributed environment. As a result workflow management systems (WFMS) [5] are often used as PSEs by providing a set of domain-specific services. Still most of modern solutions require a lot of knowledge from problem domain and IT area to be used. So the formalization of knowledge and its usage has become an important issue within e-Science area. One of the approaches to manage this issue was implemented within Intelligent PSE (iPSE) concept and technology [6]. Nevertheless the process of scientific exploration using e-Science tools can be considered much wider from the knowledge processing point of view. First of all, frequently e-Science solution explicitly use knowledge (both formal and informal), for support of simulation or data processing. Popular solutions use ontologies [7] for formal description of used services [8], modeling and simulation process [9] and high-level solution's architecture [10]. On the other hand, developed general solutions for complex e-Science tasks (e.g. WFMS) require a set of implicit knowledge (mostly IT-related) being used by the end-users, who usually are domain-area specialists without strong IT background. The complexity of such knowledge set predetermines an issue of end-users experience support to appear (see e.g. [11]). Within the presented work we try to identify the set of knowledge which can be formalized in order to bring more automation into PSEs and enriching the e-Science solutions to make them more usable for domain specialists.

2   Knowledge Processing

Considering the knowledge processing within e-Science solution several features can be identified (see fig. 1). First of all, living between problem domains and IT domain this area of knowledge is related to a) a set of technological solutions of IT areas – first of all, solutions for high performance and distributed computing and solution for data processing; b) declarative and imperative domain-specific knowledge, which are defined within particular problem domains. Today one of the important trends of science development is active collaboration of scientists which is forced mostly by the appearance of the Internet and corresponding communication technologies. This trend, which is often called Science 2.0 [12], exploits a significant role of interactive scientific society for knowledge generating as well as consuming. The e-Science area can be divided into methodological and technological subareas. Here the methodological subarea includes different technique for modeling and simulation as well as data analysis approaches. The technological subarea includes a set of technologies which allows to express methodological practices and to use native IT software and hardware solutions. Important technologies here are a) formal knowledge specification to translate knowledge from problem domain to machine-readable format; b) domain-specific languages, which allows the user to interact with machines in more convenient way; c) computational and data processing technologies used to call particular software (including WFMS).

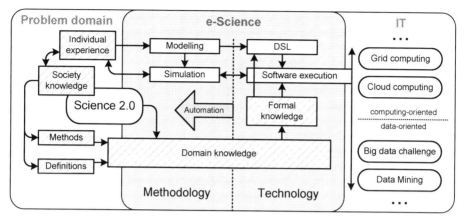

Fig. 1. Knowledge processing within e-Science simulation tasks

Generally speaking the main goal of the work is to discover the possible development of the e-Science technological subarea to move the borderline between subareas and allow the e-Science technologies to solve automatically the tasks which usually belong to methodological subarea. First of all, this goal includes knowledge-based support of modeling and simulation processes.

Different knowledge sources involved into scientific exploration process can be classified according to many characteristics:

— formal or informal;
— implicit or explicit;
— individual (personal) or collective (collaborative);
— personified (experts, colleagues) or anonymous (non-personified knowledge of the society);
— interactive (first of all, humans within society) or stored (formally or informally);
— active (having a significant influence on scientific exploration process) or passive (consulting or explanatory systems);
— etc.

Considering the knowledge sources within a framework of Science 2.0 concept the society knowledge has become aggregated knowledge source, which not only supports the scientific exploration process with its knowledge, but also is filled up with the knowledge, produced by the performed research. Within the Science 2.0 concept collaboration process is getting much more important as it enables knowledge exchange with society (globally – within the Internet; or locally – within the group of colleagues). Today the collaboration process often becomes a significant issue within general purpose e-Science solutions (see e.g. [10, 13, 14]). So, the society either local or global becomes an important source of knowledge which can become that power which allows to develop automatic solutions for methodological issues of e-Science.

Within the process of scientific task solving using iPSE approach [6] several stages can be defined: analysis of the problem, definition the particular task (meta-workflow (MWF) which formally define the requirements to the solutions); data preparation (including the analysis of existing data sources); solution development (it can be defined as an abstract workflow (AWF) – declarative structure without relation to certain services; computing (with mapping the abstract workflow to concrete services within concrete workflow (CWF)); and result acquisition and analysis. Each of these stages can be somehow supported by the knowledge from different sources (see Table 1). Comparing the experts as a traditional source of knowledge to the society as a new source, a ways to e-Science technological enrichment can be found in the knowledge acquisition from society. Firstly, this is supported by the available data sets and e-science experimental history (provenance – see, e.g. [14]). Secondary, the interactive society or collaborative environment becomes a source of non-formalized knowledge which becomes available through the society communication.

Table 1. Knowledge within scientific exploration process

№	Stage	Knowledge of experts		Knowledge of society	
		Stored	Interactive	Stored	Interactive
1	Analysis	Articles	AC	Provenance	Discussion (CVE), CS
2	Task definition	IS on MWF, ES	EC	IS/P on MWF	CVE
3	Data preparation	DM	EC	IS/P on DM	CVE
4	Solution development	IS on AWF, ES	EC	IS/P on AWF	CVE, CS
5	Computing	IS on CWF, explanation on monitoring	EC	IS/P on CWF, optimal explanation on monitoring	CVE
6	Results analysis	DM, cognitive visualization, articles references	EC, AC	Provenance enriching	Discussion (CVE), CS, results of analysis dissemination

IS – intelligent support; ES – explanation on solution; DM – data mining; AC – authors consult; EC –experts (knowledge base source) consult; IS/P – intelligent support using provenance analysis; CVE – collaboration within virtual environment; CS – comments of society.

Considering the e-Science area from this point of view the important issue for developing a knowledge-based problem-solving environment is to discover a way to define the technique which allows to formalize the collaborative knowledge in a form available for automatic intelligent support of the high-level processes within e-Science area. This kind of formal knowledge should allow interpretation (both by the user and by the machine); reusing (i.e. using within different domain tasks); expressing of declarative and imperative knowledge; structural analysis of knowledge and logical inference in order to identify the best solution.

2.1   E-Science Ontology Levels

Today ontologies become a powerful tool for knowledge formalization within different knowledge areas [7]. Considering the ontology as a formal specification of shared conceptualization within a context of e-Science task solving, we can define several levels of it (fig. 2).

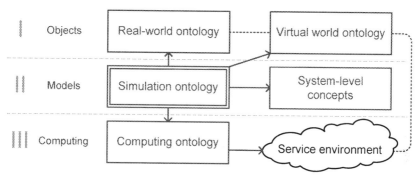

Fig. 2. E-Science ontological levels

First of all the ontological approach can be used to describe the objects which exist in real world. This descriptive goal is common for ontological approach. Within the framework of e-Science this part of ontological description can be used for informational support of the user providing the information of explored objects and their relationship. Nevertheless the concepts of this ontology can be related not only to the objects of real world, but with the objects of virtual simulation-based world. As the research is usually directed to the exploration of the real world, it is obvious that the real world and the virtual world are corresponded. But this correspondence isn't univocal. Firstly, virtual world is simplified since the models which are used to build it aren't full. Secondary, the virtual world is extended with cognitive concepts which allow the exploration of it. However, the approaches to work with the concepts of this level (I on fig. 2) are common to ontological approach and rather well-known.

On the other hand, the ontology can be used to describe services for computing or data accessing. There are a lot of projects (see e.g. [15, 16]) devoted to the description of distributed services and composite application. The description of this level (III on fig. 2) allows to bring automatic support to service searching, composition and running. Nevertheless, the key (from the point of view of semantic integration) concepts on this level are defined using separate problem domains or even IT domain. As a result in case of complex distributed service environment e-Science solution development still remains a complicated task.

The middle level of this multi-level concept (II on fig. 2) represents a semantic description of modeling and simulation process. This ontology should allow integrating the upper and the lower levels into continuous ontological solution. Moreover the concepts of this level can define system-level methodological approaches generally defined using basic concepts and then propagated onto the concepts of particular problem domain. The approach allows to develop solutions which will be focused more on system-level exploration of the domain-specific complex objects, then on particular IT-based procedures. The proposed idea gives ontology based answer on the issue of system-level science which can be considered as a modern trend of IT-side e-Science area [17].

2.2   Ontology Characteristics

Analyzing ontological approach a set of its properties [7-10, 18-20] can be identified which forms a good response to the requirements mentioned earlier.

1. *Interpretability.* Formal knowledge expressed as an ontological structure is readable to both the user and the machine. As the user is usually a domain specialist, he/she can understand the nature of concepts defined by the ontology. On the other hand, formality of the ontology allows to perform automatic operations using inference and classification technique. Within the considered task ontology existing on level II can form the basis to develop high-level solutions using domain-specific terminology with ease. This property of ontology allows to make it a powerful expressive tool for emitting knowledge modules interpretable for general purpose solutions.
2. *Reusability.* The knowledge within the ontological approach can be expressed in an unified way which allows the integration of different knowledge modules. This property makes the emitted knowledge modules a self-cost, while it can be used in completely different solutions even within multidisciplinary tasks. Moreover the modules can be extended or modified independently to the author. So the reusability property makes ontology a useful technology for collaborative knowledge exchange within scientific society.
3. *Declarative and imperative knowledge separation.* Ontological approach is mostly focused on declarative knowledge, while imperative knowledge can be defined implicitly (as constraints or rules) or linked with the ontology elements. E.g. this property helps to separate the process of declarative domain-specific knowledge description from imperative knowledge on service calling (which belongs to IT area). So this property of ontology simplifies the knowledge acquisition procedure by dividing it with relationship being kept and to give a way to describe unified procedures of knowledge classification and inference.
4. *Structural analysis.* The ontology initially claims the structure definition as one of the main goals. Within the trend to system-level science [17] this property gain more importance because the initial classification should be used for definition of the explored system's structure, which identify the task structure, which in turn extend the knowledge on the system and thus enrich its structure. So structural analysis is one of the most important properties of the ontological approach used within the work.
5. *Rating and relevance of knowledge.* The important issue of the knowledge-based scientific exploration is identification of the part of knowledge defining the relevant and best-fit solution. During the knowledge inference a set of possible solutions is analyzed according to the selected quality criteria (performance, precision, reliability etc.) to find the best variant for automatic implementation. Estimation according to these criteria should be performed according to current domain-specific task and a set of available services. Thus, the integration of all three ontology levels forms the basis for such inference.

3   Conceptual Structure

3.1   Virtual Simulation Objects

To form a basis of the proposed approach we developed Virtual Simulation Objects (VSO) concept and technology [21]. It allows to organize simulation and data analysis process around domain-specific semantic structure of the investigated system. Within VSO concept the system is described as a set of objects, which interact with each other. Each of the VSOs is related to some real-world object, which forms a real system. So the set of VSOs can be considered as an image of system to be investigated using simulation. This image includes the knowledge on domain-specific objects and their characteristics (level I), simulation procedures and objects interconnection within a model (level II), service calls and integration (level III). Internal structure of the VSO is formed using hierarchy of the following concepts:

1. *Simulated object*, which represents the main entity being explored. The object can be considered as a composite entity, or system of objects.
2. *Simulated model*, which describes a set of static and dynamic characteristics of the object and can be used to explore it.
3. *Method* can be defined as an imperative description of the model usage process. Methods are implemented in different simulation software as algorithms for solving some particular domain problem.
4. *Software packages* are used as implementations of the defined methods in form of an algorithm. Usually this software is developed by the domain specialists.
5. *Service* within a distributed computational environment (in case we are using SOA) can be considered as the software deployed on computational resource.

This hierarchy is developed to integrate the domain-specific concepts (1-3) and technological concepts (4-5). This continuous hierarchy allows to integrate knowledge which belongs to all three levels I-III mentioned earlier. Also it explains the computational and data analysis processes to the user with domain-specific terms.

Most modern distributed simulation environments work on level 5 (services) of this hierarchy. More advanced environments and PSEs get to the level 4 (software packages). General iPSE concept covers level 3 (methods) which allows to call domain-specific methods within AWFs. One of the extensions to iPSE concept [22] allows to compare and to select models and methods according to the quantitative domain-specific quality estimation based on the analysis of provided data and interactive dialog with the user. So this extension permits operating on levels 2 and 3. Concerning this hierarchy the VSO concept is developed as the conceptual extension which works on levels 1 to 3.

3.2   Knowledge-Based Virtual Environment

This section describes usage of VSO for the purpose of virtual environment building. The developed toolbox for VSO-based virtual environment building can be considered as an extension to the basic technology. The toolbox a) enables more convenient description of the complex systems with a set of interacting objects of different classes acting within the single environment; b) presents more natural way of human-computer interaction by the use of semantically supported interactive environment-based visualization of simulation results; c) form a set of typical collaboration practices for knowledge expression and usage. This approach can be applied to the wide range of tasks including multi-agent simulation, virtual test-bed building etc.

One of the most powerful abilities provided by the VSO concept and technology is building virtual environments to explore the system using its virtual representation. The proposed concept defines semantic structure of virtual environment which (according to the specific of VSO concept) can be characterized with the following claims (see fig. 3):

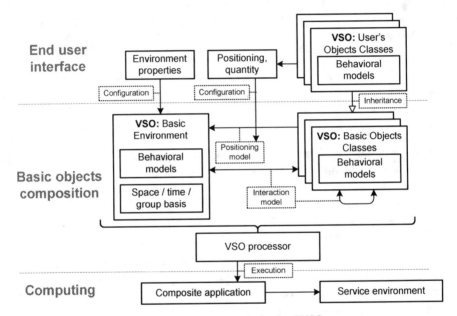

Fig. 3. Virtual environment on the basis of VSO concept

1. Explored system's structure is defined as a basic VSO representing the environment, and a set of basic VSOs representing typical objects which can be placed within the environment. The process of placement in that case defines the link (or transition models within VSO concept) between objects' characteristics and the environment, which defines mapping of the objects' bases (space, time or group) between two objects. The transition models also define process of objects interaction, which include exchange of properties between models of environment and models of basic objects according to bases mapping. Such a relationship allows to describe the basic scenario of environment-object interaction.

2. The user can manipulate the virtual environment in the following ways: a) the new objects inherited from basic can be defined by the user by adding specific properties, models or methods; b) the environment can be configured by the definition of existing properties; c) the objects of basic or inherited classes can be placed within

the environment (which can be done by the configuration of corresponding transition models). The most important thing here is the interpretability of the semantic structure: firstly, the end user interface can be developed using only domain-specific concepts (objects, their properties, models and methods); secondary, as the transition models are already preconfigured the completed structure of the explored system can be analyzed and mapped onto services automatically.

3. Constructed system's structure can be used on different stages of system's exploration process: analysis can be supported by presenting the knowledge set relevant to the particular task (according to objects' descriptions); the task is automatically defined by the model, constructed using basic and inherited objects; data preparation is supported by semantic search of relevant data sources; simulation solutions is developed automatically by the interpretation of the structure; computing is performed fully automatically; intelligent support of data analysis can be provided by the use of interpretable system's description.

Moreover, the semantic description of such system can be used to develop extended virtual environment solutions. E.g. virtual reality (interactive 3-D space) can be developed as a general solution for system's exploration. In that case the semantic description can be used as a background structure for 3-D scene definition:

1. By adding 3-D images to each VSO (including one that describes the environment) all the elements of the scene can be defined. Moreover, dynamic 3-D images can be used in order to show the evolution of objects properties.
2. The placement and interaction scenarios of the objects within the environment are already defined by transition models within the system's structure. So the complex dynamic scene can be built fully automatically.
3. The process of placement can be performed within virtual environment by the use a kind of "toolbox" with available objects which the user can place in any position within the 3-D scene.

4   Implementation Details

The proposed conceptual hierarchy (Section 3.1) was implemented as ontological structure using RDF/OWL. The technology allows the unification of knowledge description and enables integration with existing ontological descriptions which are a) high-level semantic description of real-world objects (e.g. SUMO [23]) to enrich automatic integration of virtual simulation objects; b) technological description of low level services (e.g. [15, 16]) to integrate the developed technology with different distributed computational environments. The main goal of the proposed ontological structure is semantic integration of separately described areas (problem domains and IT) to support automatic interpretation of the domain-specific user structures onto workflow, containing data processing procedures and calling of particular services within distributed environment.

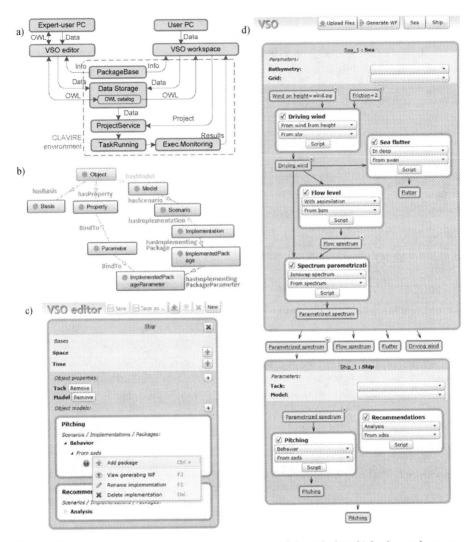

Fig. 4. VSO instrumental environment a) architecture of the solution; b) basic ontology concepts; c) VSO editor; d) VSO workspace

The implementation was integrated into cloud computing environment CLAVIRE [24], which allows performing automatic execution of composite applications described in form of AWF. Whole ontological structure contains the following elements:

— basic conceptual ontology, which define the core hierarchy of concepts;
— service integration ontology, which is automatically constructed using service descriptions available through the CLAVIRE environment;
— extendable domain-specific ontologies which define domain-specific virtual simulation objects, which can be developed by the domain experts.

The instrumental environment (fig. 4a) was developed, which uses the CLAVIRE as an underlying platform, which allows to get the information on available services and to perform the simulation by executing of automatically constructed workflows. The basic ontology concepts used by this environment are shown of the fig. 4b. Here the Object, Model, Scenario and ImplementedPackage concepts represents levels 1-4 of conceptual hierarchy presented in Section 3.1. Other concepts serve for the purpose of parameter processing (Basis, Property, Parameter, ImplementedPackageParameter) and hierarchy concepts linking (Implementation concept define detailed parameters of software calling within the particular method). The instrumental environment contains two main modules: a) VSO editor to allow the expert to develop the domain-specific VSO modules (fig. 4b); b) VSO workspace to allow the user to develop and modify the system's structure (fig. 4c) and run the simulation using CLAVIRE environment.

Each of these modules was implemented as a web application using Microsoft Silverlight technology which allows to access the system using web-browser. Developed instrumental environment to perform system's exploration by simulation the behavior of the system, described within the VSO workspace. E.g. system's structure presented on the fig. 4b allows performing simulation ship's behavior on the waved sea. This example includes two VSOs from different problem domain: Sea object allows to perform the waves simulation by the use of SWAN software [25]; Ship object allows ship behavior simulation using ShipXDS software [26]. Here the object's interconnection can be done automatically on the basis of objects description by connecting semantically identical properties of the object (i.e. wave characteristics) which are output parameters for models of one object and input parameters for another object.

4.1   Virtual Environment Test Case

Last works within the VSO project are devoted to the development of virtual environment framework according to the description presented in Section 3.2. The test case considered within this development includes the application which allows simulation of crowd behavior within the city environment. The corresponding composite application was developed within CLAVIRE environment (for more details on the application see [27]): initially data on the flash-mob action is collected during social network crawling; then the dataset describing formed crowd is generated; using generated data, a multi-agent simulation of crowd evacuation in case of panic is performed and visualized (see fig. 5a,b).

VSO can be used as a basic concept and technology for building virtual environment for this task in the following way (see fig. 5c).

1. The basic objects set include two main objects. The city environment, which mainly can be defined by the landscape (streets, buildings, rivers etc.). For the sake of simplicity within the task the object can be extended with the escape places which people are trying to reach in case of panic. The second object is a general citizen simulator, which is characterized by the simple behavior switching between regular and panic state. The citizens can be placed within the city environment according to some rules, which are represented by the transition model within the environment.

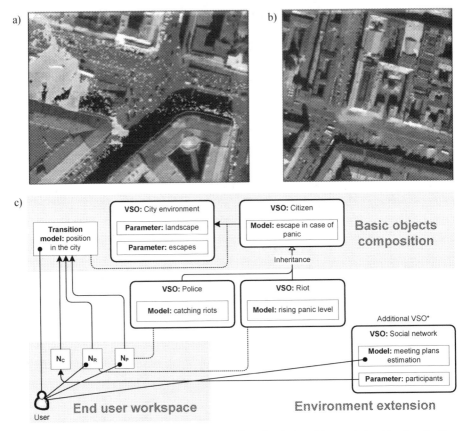

Fig. 5. Virtual environment test case a) evacuation simulation; b) crowd density visualization; c) high-level virtual environment construction

2. The basic variant of virtual environment can be extended by the advanced user with the following techniques:
   (a) Inheritance of the basic object allows to alter the objects models, method and properties keeping them able to behave like a parent object (i.e. be placed in the environment, interact with each other and the environment, etc.). In this test case the basic Citizen object might be extended as Riot object depicting the person who raised the level of panic in the crowd as well as Police object depicting the person with altered behavior who is trying to catch the Riot person.
   (b) Adding external VSOs which might be connected to the existing objects or transition models. E.g. the Social network object can be added to the environment in order to crowd specified social networks for their parameters analysis (i.e. estimation of planning crowd event).
3. On the last stage the virtual environment is configured by the user for the particular case exploration:
   (a) the quantity of individuals within the environment is defined for each class (if the quantity isn't defined by other VSOs);

(b) the placement of the objects is configured using available properties;
(c) all available objects are configured to satisfy the current task.

Being configured in such a way that virtual environment can run simulation (and related visualization automatically) using CLAVIRE environment by the same way as it was shown earlier.

5   Discussion

Today the e-Science is a rapidly developing area. One of the most powerful tendencies within this development is a knowledge-based automation of scientific exploration process. There are a lot of works trying to develop knowledge-based support for modeling and simulation process as well as distributed software composition (see e.g. [8-10, 14-16, 20]). Within our work we are trying to develop a comprehensive view of knowledge-base scientific exploration of complex system, which requires data analysis and simulation management. Considering this task the important thing is to focus on user-oriented toolbox development, where the user usually is a domain specialist without strong IT background [11]. As a result the main idea of the developed solution is to hide whole technological details of the simulation process behind the domain-specific task definition. This approach should allow the user to describe the system being investigated using domain-specific terms while the simulation, data analysis processes etc. should be hidden behind the scene and performed in an automatic way. This becomes possible in case the process of scientific exploration is supported by knowledge-based technologies on the whole way from analysis to final results processing. Considering the idea of complex multi-domain knowledge base development with automatic integration, interpretation and analysis capability the ontological approach [7-10, 18-20] can be used.

On the other hand, today a huge set of knowledge becomes accessible via the Internet environment. The most interesting part here is the availability of world-wide scientific society (the growing role of the society is outlined within such concepts like Science 2.0 [12]). Moreover modern technologies allow a huge part of society knowledge to be expressed and published in formal way. This discovers a completely new scale of knowledge acquisition: today the knowledge of society can be used within automatic systems. So the most interesting part of this work is devoted to the development of technology which enables the knowledge-based environments (PSEs, virtual environment) to be built using public knowledge.

6   Conclusion

Within the presented work we were trying to discover the possible ways to the automation of scientific exploration process. As it is usually related to the complicated simulation and data analysis process the main problem is to develop a knowledge base structure which allows integrating comprehensive knowledge on the e-Science solutions with information for automation of technological process. The developed solution is aimed to hide the whole technological complexity behind understandable domain-specific system's description, which can be built and interpreted using knowledge-based description. Important part of this work is devoted to the development of conceptual solution of knowledge processing within e-Science task. This conceptual solution allows developing knowledge-based frameworks for building scientific tools of different kind (problem-solving environments, virtual simulation environments etc.) are able to interact with the user using domain-specific concepts. The described technological solution for building virtual simulation environments with knowledge-based support of whole simulation lifecycle is currently developing using the mentioned conceptual and technological background.

Acknowledgements. This work is supported by the projects "Technology of system-level design and development of inter-disciplinary applications within cloud computing environment" (agreement 14.B37.21.1870), "Virtual testbed for complex system supercomputing simulation" (agreement 14.B37.21.0596) granted from the Ministry of Education and Science of the Russian Federation and project "Urgent Distributed Computing for Time-Critical Emergency Decision Support" performed under Decree 220 of Government of the Russian Federation.

References

1. Hey, T., Tansley, S., Tolle, K.: The Fourth Paradigm. Data-Intensive Scientific, Discovery, Microsoft, 252 (2009)
2. Rice, J.R., Boisvert, R.F.: From Scientific Software Libraries to Problem-Solving Environments. IEEE Computational Science & Engineering 3(3), 44–53 (1996)
3. Lublinsky, B.: Defining SOA as an architectural style (January 9, 2007), http://www.ibm.com/developerworks/architecture/library/ar-soastyle/
4. Gil, Y., et al.: Examining the Challenges of Scientific Workflows. IEEE Computer 40(12), 24–32 (2007)
5. Yu, J., Buyya, R.: A Taxonomy of Workflow Management Systems for Grid Computing. Journal of Grid Computing 3(3-4), 171–200 (2005)
6. Boukhanovsky, A.V., Kovalchuk, S.V., Maryin, S.V.: Intelligent Software Platform for Complex System Computer Simulation: Conception, Architecture and Implementation, Izvestiya VUZov. Priborostroenie 10, 5–24 (2009) (in Russian)
7. Chandrasekaran, B., Josephson, J.R., Benjamins, V.R.: What Are Ontologies, and Why Do We Need Them? IEEE Intelligent Systems 14(1), 20–26 (1999)
8. Chen, L., et al.: Semantics-assisted Problem Solving on the Semantic Grid. Journal of Computational Intelligence 21(2), 157–176 (2005)
9. Silver, G.A., Lacy, L.W., Miller, J.A.: Ontology Based Representations of Simulation Models Following the Process Interaction World View. In: Winter Simulation Conference, pp. 1168–1176 (2006)
10. Hu, J., Zhang, H.: Ontology Based Collaborative Simulation Framework Using HLA and Web Services. Computer Science and Information Engineering 5, 702–706 (2009)
11. McPhillips, T., Bowers, S., Zinn, D., Ludäscher, B.: Scientific workflow design for mere mortals. Future Generation Computer Systems 25(5), 541–551 (2009)
12. Shneiderman, B.: Science 2.0. Science 319, 1349–1350 (2008)

13. Belloum, A., et al.: Collaborative e-Science Experiments and Scientific Workflow. IEEE Internet Computing 15(4), 39–47 (2011)
14. Altintas, I., et al.: A Data Model for Analyzing User Collaborations in Workflow-Driven eScience. International Journal of Computers and Their Applications (IJCA), Special Issue on Scientific Workflows, Provenance and Their Applications 18(3), 160–180 (2011)
15. Konong, R., et al.: Using ontologies for resource description in the CineGrid Exchange. Future Generation Computer Systems 27(7), 960–965 (2011)
16. Vidal, A.C.T., et al.: Defining and exploring a grid system ontology. In: International Workshop on Middleware for Grid Computing, Melbourne, Australia, vol. 16 (2006)
17. Foster, I., Kesselman, C.: Scaling System-Level Science: Scientific Exploration and IT Implications. IEEE Computer 39(11), 31–39 (2006)
18. Mitrofanova, O.V., Konstantinova, N.S.: Ontologies as Knowledge Storing Systems, 54 (2008) (in Russian), http://window.edu.ru/resource/795/58795
19. Gavrilova, T.A., Malinovskaya, O.L.: Multilevel knowledge structuring and flexible conceptual atlases design, Uchenye zapiski Kazanskogo universiteta. Fiziko-matematicheskie Nauki 153(4), 189–202 (2011) (in Russian)
20. Agarwal, S., Petrie, C.: An Alternative to the Top-Down Semantic Web of Services. IEEE Internet Computing 16(5), 94–97 (2012)
21. Kovalchuk, S.V., et al.: Virtual Simulation Objects Concept as a Framework for System-Level Simulation. In: IEEE 8th International Conference on E-Science, pp. 1–8 (2012)
22. Kovalchuk, S., Larchenko, A., Boukhanovsky, A.: Knowledge-Based Resource Management for Distributed Problem Solving. In: Wang, Y., Li, T. (eds.) Knowledge Engineering and Management. AISC, vol. 123, pp. 121–128. Springer, Heidelberg (2011)
23. Suggested Upper Merged Ontology (SUMO), http://www.ontologyportal.org/
24. Knyazkov, K.V., et al.: CLAVIRE: e-Science infrastructure for data-driven computing. Journal of Computational Science 3(6), 504–510 (2012)
25. The official SWAN homepage, http://www.swan.tudelft.nl/
26. Bezgodov, A.A., Boukhanovsky, A.V.: Virtual testbed for exploration of extreme dynamics of marine objects in irregular sea, Izvestiya VUZov. Priborostroenie 5, 98–100 (2011) (in Russian)
27. Vasilev, V.N., et al.: CLAVIRE: cloud computing platform for data-driven computing. Informacionno-izmeritelnye i Upravlayushie Sistemy 10(11), 7–16 (2012) (in Russian)

Efficient Module Extraction for Large Ontologies

Venkata Krishna Chaitanya Turlapati and Sreenivasa Kumar Puligundla

Department of Computer Science & Engineering
Indian Institute of Technology Madras
Chennai, India
{chaitut,psk}@cse.iitm.ac.in

Abstract. Modularity of ontologies has gained importance due to its application in ontology reasoning, ontology reuse and other areas of ontology engineering. One technique for extracting modules is by using Atomic Decomposition (AD). This paper uses MGS-Labels (Minimal Globalising Signatures) to improve the state-of-the-art approach which uses MSS-Labels (Minimal Seed Signatures) in terms of pre-processing time and memory requirement. It also improves the module extraction-time by reducing the number of containment checks in the worst case. We further improve the algorithm by introducing the notion of MGS-Space. We propose uniqueness properties about MGS-Space that help us to build indices and extract modules using simple operations on integers.

1 Introduction

An ontology is a collection of axioms that describe a specific domain. As knowledge about the domain increases, the size of the ontology i.e. number of axioms in the ontology increases. For example, NCI ontology[1] consists of 422,953 axioms. Thus the tasks of maintenance, reuse and reasoning become difficult. More specifically, reasoning with the largest decidable ontology language OWL 2 DL is 2NEXPTIME-complete.

A *module* is a subset of ontology and contains information about (all of the entailments over) a specific set of terms, that the original ontology contains. This set of terms is called the *seed signature* of the module. Dividing an ontology into modules helps in better maintenance and reuse. Also, efficient reasoners like CHAINSAW are built based on modularity [9].

This flexibility of working with a subset of ontology does not come easily. Sometimes, module extraction may take more time than the time taken for reasoning with the whole ontology. As the module preserves all of the entailments over seed signature, ontology can be viewed as a *deductive conservative extension* (dCE) [3] of the module w.r.t. seed signature. But checking if an ontology is a dCE of a module is undecidable for ontologies in OWL 2 DL [5] and 2NEXPTIME-complete for light weight profiles such as OWL 2 EL [6]. Hence, the approach currently in use is *locality based modules* [1]. Especially, *syntactic*

---

[1] http://www.mindswap.org/2003/CancerOntology/nciOncology.owl

P. Klinov and D. Mouromtsev (Eds.): KESW 2013, CCIS 394, pp. 162–176, 2013.
© Springer-Verlag Berlin Heidelberg 2013

locality based modules are of interest because they can be generated in polynomial time [1, 2]. Axioms that are *local* for a given set of terms do not directly contain any *non-trivial information* about them. Hence, a module is a combination of the axioms that are non-local for given set of terms (and terms present in these non-local axioms). It requires loading the whole ontology and checking for locality of all axioms.

If an ontology has n terms, 2^n signatures are possible. This makes extracting and storing modules w.r.t. all possible signatures, a difficult task. Atomic Decomposition [11] is a polynomial representation of all the modules in the ontology. An *atom* is a set of axioms that is either present in full or is not present at all in any module. It is proved that any module is a union of atoms (but arbitrary union of atoms is not a module) [11]. Hence, module extraction algorithms can be proposed by checking the *inclusion* of an atom in the module w.r.t. a given signature Σ. These algorithms need not load the whole ontology into the memory. They can further achieve better performances using *dependency* properties of atoms. The first work on extracting modules using atoms is done by Del Vescovo et al. [10] by labeling each atom with its *minimal seed signatures*(MSS). It checks for *inclusion* of an atom in the module using its MSS-Label.

This paper improves the work done by Del Vescovo et al. by labeling atoms with their *Minimal globalising signatures* (MGS) [10]. MGS of an atom (or axiom) is a set of minimal signatures that the atom(axiom) is non-local for. This paper describes a sufficient condition for a combination of atoms to form a module based on their MGS-Labels. It improves the algorithm in [10] in terms of memory as MGS-Label of an atom is a subset of its MSS-Label. It improves the pre-processing time as computing MGS-Labels is an intermediate step in *labeling algorithm* for MSS [10]. It also improves the performance by reducing the number of *inclusion checks in the worst-case* for an atom.

This paper also introduces the notion of MGS-Space that is a union of MGS-Labels of all the atoms in the ontology. The observations we make in this paper about MGS-Space help in building indices that further improve the efficiency of the algorithm. Once the indices are built, we formulate a mechanism that converts module extraction task into simple operations on integers.

2   Preliminaries

This section introduces the notions of modules [1, 2] and atomic decomposition [11]. We assume that the reader is familiar with the notions of ontology, axioms, interpretation and signature. We use $\tilde{x}$ to denote the signature of x, where x is an axiom or a set of axioms. A term is a named element in the ontology's signature.

Definition 1 (Module). *Let $\mathcal{O}$ be an ontology and Σ be a signature. A set of axioms $\mathcal{M} \subseteq \mathcal{O}$ is said to be a module of $\mathcal{O}$ w.r.t. Σ if for all axioms α such that $\tilde{\alpha} \subseteq \Sigma$, $\mathcal{O} \models \alpha \Longleftrightarrow \mathcal{M} \models \alpha$.*

Checking if $\mathcal{M}$ is a module w.r.t. Σ is undecidable for ontologies in OWL 2 DL [5] and 2NEXPTIME-complete for light weight profiles such as OWL 2

EL [6]. Hence, approximations like syntactic locality based modules, that capture all entailments, have been proposed.

Syntactic locality is a technique that is used in identifying whether an axiom has non-trivial information about terms represented by a signature Σ. The grammar of syntactic $\bot$-locality guarantees that axioms that are syntactically $\bot$-local for Σ do not directly contain any non-trivial information about Σ. Hence, axioms that are non-local for the signature are to be considered. The signature will be extended with the terms in the newly added axioms and is again checked for locality. This process goes on until no new non-local axiom is found. Necessary discussion and proofs about syntactic $\bot$-locality are given in [1, 2].

Given a signature Σ, the following grammar defines two sets of concepts $\mathcal{C}_\Sigma^\top$ and $\mathcal{C}_\Sigma^\bot$ recursively [1, 7].

$$\mathcal{C}_\Sigma^\bot ::= \bot \mid A^\bot \mid \neg C^\top \mid C \sqcap C^\bot \mid C^\bot \sqcap C \mid \exists R^\bot.C \mid \exists R.C^\bot \mid \geq nR^\bot.C \mid \geq nR.C^\bot$$

$$\mathcal{C}_\Sigma^\top ::= \top \mid \neg C^\bot \mid C_1^\top \sqcup C_2^\top \mid \geq 0R.C$$

where $A^\bot$ is an atomic concept not in Σ, $R^\bot$ is a role not in Σ, R is any role, C is any concept, $C^\bot \in \mathcal{C}_\Sigma^\bot$, $C^\top \in \mathcal{C}_\Sigma^\top$, $C_1^\top \in \mathcal{C}_\Sigma^\top$ and $C_2^\top \in \mathcal{C}_\Sigma^\top$.

Definition 2 (Syntactic $\bot$-locality [1,2]). *Let Σ be a signature. An axiom α is syntactically $\bot$-local for Σ if it is in one of the following forms: $R^\bot \sqsubseteq R$ or $Trans(R^\bot)$ or $C^\bot \sqsubseteq C$ or $C \sqsubseteq C^\top$ or $C^\bot \equiv C^\bot$ or $C^\top \equiv C^\top$.*

In the rest of the paper, the word *locality* represents syntactic $\bot$-locality. An axiom that is not local for Σ is called a *non-local* axiom for Σ.

Informally, the set $\mathcal{C}_\Sigma^\bot$ consists of the concepts that become equivalent to $\bot$ and $\mathcal{C}_\Sigma^\top$ consists of concepts that become equivalent to $\top$ when all the terms $A^\bot \notin \Sigma$ and $R^\bot \notin \Sigma$ are replaced by $\bot$ and empty role respectively. The axioms which become syntactic tautologies after replacement are treated as local as tautologies have trivial information like $C \sqsubseteq \top$ or $\bot \sqsubseteq C$. All the entailments of an ontology remain the same with or without syntactic tautologies.

Consider the ontology $\mathcal{O}_{ex}$ in Figure 1 and the signature $\Sigma = \{Plant\}$. Axiom 5 is of the form $C^\bot \sqsubseteq C^\bot$ and is local for $\{Plant\}$. Axiom 3 is of the form $C \sqsubseteq C^\bot$ and is non-local for $\{Plant\}$. According to axiom 3, *Plant* is subsumed by *LivingThing*. Though axiom 4 contains the term *Plant*, it is of the form $C^\bot \equiv C^\bot$ and is local for it. Intuitively, it restricts the interpretations of $\{Plant, Animal\}$ together but it does not restrict any one of their interpretations individually. Hence, it is non-local for $\{Plant, Animal\}$.

Theorem 1. *Let $\mathcal{O}$ be an ontology and Σ be a signature. Let $\mathcal{M} \subseteq \mathcal{O}$ be a set of axioms such that $\mathcal{O} \backslash \mathcal{M}$ is $\bot$-local for $\Sigma \cup \widetilde{\mathcal{M}}$. Then $\mathcal{M}$ is said to be a $\bot$-locality based module for $\mathcal{O}$ w.r.t. Σ [2].*

Consider the signature $\{PizzaRestaurant\}$. The set of axioms $\mathcal{M} = \{1, 8\}$ is such that $\mathcal{O}_{ex} \backslash \mathcal{M}$ is local for $\{PizzaRestaurant, LivingThing, NonLivingThing, serves, Pizza\}$. Axiom 8 contains information about *PizzaRestaurant*. But Information about *NonLivingThing* is also needed in order to explain about *Piz-*

$$\text{LivingThing} \equiv \neg\text{NonLivingThing} \tag{1}$$

$$\text{Animal} \sqsubseteq \text{LivingThing} \sqcap \exists\text{eats}.\top \tag{2}$$

$$\text{Plant} \sqsubseteq \text{LivingThing} \tag{3}$$

$$\text{Plant} \sqcap \text{Animal} \equiv \bot \tag{4}$$

$$\text{Herbivore} \sqsubseteq \text{Animal} \tag{5}$$

$$\text{Herbivore} \sqsubseteq \forall\text{eats}.\ \text{Plant} \tag{6}$$

$$\text{Carnivore} \sqsubseteq \text{Animal} \sqcap \neg\text{Herbivore} \tag{7}$$

$$\text{PizzaRestaurant} \equiv \text{NonLivingThing} \sqcap \exists\text{serves}.\ \text{Pizza} \tag{8}$$

$$\text{ItalianPR} \sqsubseteq \text{PizzaRestaurant} \tag{9}$$

Fig. 1. Example ontology $\mathcal{O}_{ex}$

zaRestaurant. So, the required signature is expanded to $\{PizzaRestaurant, Non\text{-}LivingThing\}$ and axiom 1 is also included. Hence, $\mathcal{M}$ forms a module w.r.t. $\{PizzaRestaurant\}$. In the rest of the paper, we use the word *module* to denote syntactic locality based $\bot$-module and $\text{mod}(\Sigma, \mathcal{O})$ to represent the module of $\mathcal{O}$ w.r.t. signature Σ. The algorithms in this paper are also applicable to modules based on $\top$-locality.

Definition 3. *The following are the properties of $\bot$-locality based modules* [2,4].

- *Monotonicity: for any signature $\Sigma \subseteq \Sigma_1, \text{mod}(\Sigma, \mathcal{O}) \subseteq \text{mod}(\Sigma_1, \mathcal{O})$.*
- *Self-Containedness: for any signature Σ_1 such that $\Sigma \subseteq \Sigma_1 \subseteq \Sigma \cup \widetilde{\mathcal{M}}$, $\text{mod}(\Sigma, \mathcal{O}) = \text{mod}(\Sigma_1, \mathcal{O})$.*
- *Uniqueness: For a given signature Σ, the module obtained by the notion of $\bot$-locality is unique.*

There can be some axioms that are non-local for any signature. Such axioms are called *Global Axioms* [11].

Definition 4 (Global Axioms). *Global axioms is the set of axioms that are present in all the modules of $\mathcal{O}$ w.r.t. any $\Sigma \in PowerSet(\widetilde{\mathcal{O}})$. The set of global axioms of ontology $\mathcal{O}$ is denoted by $\mathcal{G}(\mathcal{O})$. The expression for $\mathcal{G}(\mathcal{O})$ is given by $\mathcal{G}(\mathcal{O}) = \text{mod}(\emptyset, \mathcal{O})$.*

In example $\mathcal{O}_{ex}$, axiom 1 is non-local for the empty signature $\emptyset$. Hence $\mathcal{G}(\mathcal{O}) = \{\text{LivingThing} \equiv \neg\text{NonLivingThing}\}$.

Definition 5 (Atoms [11]). *An atom $\mathfrak{a}$ is a set of axioms of the ontology $\mathcal{O}$ such that for every module $\mathcal{M}$ of $\mathcal{O}$, either $\mathfrak{a} \cap \mathcal{M} = \mathfrak{a}$ or $\mathfrak{a} \cap \mathcal{M} = \emptyset$.*

The notion of atoms is introduced in [11]. An atom $\mathfrak{a}$ can be formed by grouping axioms $\{\alpha_1, \alpha_2, \ldots, \alpha_n\}$ such that $\text{mod}(\widetilde{\alpha_1}, \mathcal{O}) = \text{mod}(\widetilde{\alpha_2}, \mathcal{O}) = \ldots =$

$mod(\widetilde{\mathfrak{a}_n}, \mathcal{O})$. Global axioms and syntactic tautologies are not included in any atom [11].

In example $\mathcal{O}_{ex}$, the atoms are $\{\mathfrak{a}_1 = \{2\}, \mathfrak{a}_2 = \{3\}, \mathfrak{a}_3 = \{4\}, \mathfrak{a}_4 = \{5, 6\}, \mathfrak{a}_5 = \{7\}, \mathfrak{a}_6 = \{8\}, \mathfrak{a}_7 = \{9\}\}$. We use $\mathcal{A}(\mathcal{O})$ to denote the atoms of an ontology $\mathcal{O}$ and $Atom(\alpha)$ to denote the atom containing α, where $\alpha \notin \mathcal{G}(\mathcal{O})$.

Definition 6 (Dependency of Atoms). *An atom $\mathfrak{a}$ is dependent on an atom $\mathfrak{b}$ $(\mathfrak{a} \succeq \mathfrak{b})$ if, for every module $\mathcal{M}$ if $\mathfrak{a} \subseteq \mathcal{M}$, then $\mathfrak{b} \subseteq \mathcal{M}$. $\mathfrak{a}$ and $\mathfrak{b}$ are independent if there exist two modules $\mathcal{M}_1$ and $\mathcal{M}_2$ such that $\mathfrak{a} \subseteq \mathcal{M}_1$ and $\mathfrak{b} \subseteq \mathcal{M}_2$ and $\mathcal{M}_1 \cap \mathcal{M}_2 = \emptyset$.*

In the above example, the atom $\{9\}$ needs *PizzaRestaurant* in atom $\{8\}$ to explain about *ItalianPR*. Hence the atom $\{9\}$ is dependent on $\{8\}$. The collection of atoms and relations between them is called *atomic decomposition* (AD).The relation $\succeq$ is a partial order over $\mathcal{A}(\mathcal{O})$ of an ontology $\mathcal{O}$ [11].

Definition 7 (Principal Ideal). *Principal ideal of an atom $\mathfrak{a}$ is denoted by $(\mathfrak{a}]$ and is given by $(\mathfrak{a}] = \{\alpha \in \mathfrak{b} \mid \mathfrak{a} \succeq \mathfrak{b}\}$.*

Proposition 1. *Let $\mathcal{O}$ be an ontology. For every atom $\mathfrak{a}$ in $\mathcal{A}(\mathcal{O})$, $(\mathfrak{a}]$ is a module [11].*

Definition 8 (Minimal Globalising Signatures [10]). *Minimal Globalising Signatures (MGS) of an axiom α, denoted by $\mathsf{MGS}(\alpha)$, is the set of all $\Sigma \subseteq \widetilde{\alpha}$ such that α is non-local for Σ and α is local for all $\Sigma_1 \subset \Sigma$. For an atom $\mathfrak{a}$, $\mathsf{MGS}(\mathfrak{a}) = \bigcup^*_{\alpha \in \mathfrak{a}} \mathsf{MGS}(\alpha)$, where $\bigcup^*$ retains Σ_1 if there are two signatures $\Sigma_1 \in \mathsf{MGS}(\alpha)$ and $\Sigma_2 \in \mathsf{MGS}(\beta)$ such that $\Sigma_1 \subseteq \Sigma_2$.*

For example, consider the atom $\mathfrak{a} = \{A \sqcap B \equiv C \sqcup D, C \equiv D \sqcap \exists R.E\}$. MGS of first axiom $=\{\{A, B\}, \{C\}, \{D\}\}$ and MGS of second axiom$=\{\{C\}, \{D, R, E\}\}$. MGS of atom $\mathfrak{a}$ is $\{\{A, B\}, \{C\}, \{D\}\}$. We use $\mathsf{MGS}(\mathfrak{a})$ to denote the MGS of atom $\mathfrak{a}$ and $\mathfrak{m}$ to denote a signature in $\mathsf{MGS}(\mathfrak{a})$.

Definition 9 (Minimal Seed Signatures [10]). *Let $\mathcal{O}$ be an ontology and $\mathfrak{a}$ be an atom in $\mathcal{A}(\mathcal{O})$. The set of minimal signatures $\{\mathfrak{m}_i\}$, such that $(\mathfrak{a}] = mod(\mathfrak{m}_i, \mathcal{O})$, is called minimal seed signatures (MSS) of a principal ideal $(\mathfrak{a}]$.*

In this paper, $\mathsf{MSS}(\mathfrak{a})$ of an atom $\mathfrak{a}$ denotes minimal seed signatures of $(\mathfrak{a}]$. We call it MSS-Label or simply MSS of the atom $\mathfrak{a}$. For the ontology $\mathcal{O}_{ex2} = \{A \equiv B \sqcup C, D \equiv E \sqcup F, G \equiv A \sqcap D\}$, the atoms formed are $\mathfrak{a} = \{G \equiv A \sqcap D\}$, $\mathfrak{b} = \{A \equiv B \sqcup C\}$ and $\mathfrak{c} = \{D \equiv E \sqcup F\}$. Here $\mathfrak{a} \succeq \mathfrak{b}$ and $\mathfrak{a} \succeq \mathfrak{c}$.

$\quad$ $\mathsf{MSS}(\mathfrak{b}) = \mathsf{MGS}(\mathfrak{b}) = \{\{A\}, \{B\}, \{C\}\}$

$\quad$ $\mathsf{MSS}(\mathfrak{c}) = \mathsf{MGS}(\mathfrak{c}) = \{\{D\}, \{E\}, \{F\}\}$

$\quad$ $\mathsf{MGS}(\mathfrak{a}) = \{\{G\}, \{A, D\}\}$

$\quad$ $\mathsf{MSS}(\mathfrak{a}) = \{\{G\}, \{A, D\}, \{A, E\}, \{A, F\}, \{B, D\}, \{B, E\}, \{B, F\}, \{C, D\}, \{C, E\}, \{C, F\}\}$.

The algorithm for finding MSS of an atom is given in [10] and its explanation is beyond the scope of this paper.

Algorithm 1. Original Module Extraction [1,2]

    Input: An ontology $\mathcal{O}$ and a signature Σ
    Output: A module $\mathcal{M}$ such that $\mathcal{M} = \mathrm{mod}(\Sigma, \mathcal{O})$
1   $\mathcal{M} := \emptyset$, $\Sigma := \Sigma_{input}$
2   **repeat**
3      $changed = false$
4   **for** $\alpha \in \mathcal{O} \backslash \mathcal{M}$ **do**
5   **if** α *is non-local for* Σ **then**
6            $\mathcal{M} := \mathcal{M} \cup \{\alpha\}$
7            $\Sigma := \Sigma \cup \widetilde{\alpha}$
8            $changed := true$
9   **until** $changed = false$
10   **return** $\mathcal{M}$

---

3 Existing Approaches for Module Extraction

This section describes the original module extraction algorithm in [1,2], an improvement of this algorithm by Tsarkov et al. [8] and an improved algorithm based on AD by Del Vescovo et al. [10].

3.1 Original Module Extraction Algorithm

The algorithm for original module extraction [1,2] is shown in Algorithm 1. It is a fix-point algorithm. Let Σ_{input} be the input signature. Σ is initialised with Σ_{input}. It starts with empty module. If an axiom α is non-local for Σ, then α is added to the module. As modules are self-contained, $\widetilde{\alpha}$ is added to the Σ. It terminates when no new axiom is found to be non-local w.r.t. Σ.

Algorithm 1 loads all the axioms in $\mathcal{O} \backslash \mathcal{M}$ into memory until a fix-point is reached. This would be difficult if ontologies are very large like GO, which consists of 386,643 axioms. It can not be used in modular reasoners [9] as module extraction takes more time than actual reasoning time.

An improved algorithm by Tsarkov et al. is given in [8]. According to this algorithm, given a signature Σ, an axiom α_i is checked for locality if $\Sigma \cap \widetilde{\alpha_i} \neq \emptyset$. But this algorithm did not exploit the fact that all the axioms in $(\mathfrak{a}_i]$ can be added to the module if an axiom $\alpha_j \in \mathfrak{a}_i$ is found to be non-local for Σ.

3.2 Fast Module Extraction

First work on Fast Module Extraction based on atomic decomposition (AD) was done by Del Vescovo et al. [10][2]. To the best of our knowledge, no other algorithm for Fast Module Extraction based on AD that is faster than this algorithm exists.

---

[2] Their implementation of this algorithm is available at
   http://tinyurl.com/bioportalFME [10]

According to this algorithm, each atom $\mathfrak{a}_i$ in $\mathcal{A}(\mathcal{O})$ is labeled with $\mathsf{MSS}(\mathfrak{a}_i)$. An atom $\mathfrak{a}_i$ is said to be relevant to a term e if there exists a signature $\mathfrak{m}_j$ in $\mathsf{MSS}(\mathfrak{a}_i)$ such that $e \in \mathfrak{m}_j$. Let Σ_{input} be the input signature. Signature Σ is initialised to Σ_{input}. The algorithm starts with an empty module $\mathcal{M}$. Relevant atoms are found by checking if a signature $\mathfrak{m}$, such that $\mathfrak{m} \subseteq \Sigma$, exists in their MSS-Labels. For each atom $\mathfrak{a}_i$ relevant to Σ, $(\mathfrak{a}_i]$ is added to $\mathcal{M}$. Now Σ is extended to $\Sigma \cup \widetilde{\mathcal{M}}$. This continues until no new terms are added to Σ. Finally, the set of global axioms is added to the module.

One case that is not covered by this algorithm is when there is an atom $\mathfrak{a}$ in $\mathcal{A}(\mathcal{O})$ such that there is a signature $\mathfrak{m} \in \mathsf{MSS}(\mathfrak{a})$ and $\mathfrak{m} \cap \widetilde{\mathcal{G}(\mathcal{O})} \neq \emptyset$. Consider the following ontology $\mathcal{O}_{ex3} = \{A \equiv \neg B, \ A \sqcap C \equiv D\}$. Here $\mathcal{G}(\mathcal{O}_{ex3}) = \{A \equiv \neg B\}$ and there is only one atom $\mathfrak{a} = \{A \sqcap C \equiv D\}$. $\mathsf{MSS}(\mathfrak{a}) = \{\{A, C\}, \{D\}\}$. Let the input signature Σ_{input} be $\{C\}$. There is no signature $\mathfrak{m} \in \mathsf{MSS}(\mathfrak{a})$ such that $\mathfrak{m} \subseteq \{C\}$. Hence, $\mathfrak{a}$ is not included and the module returned by the algorithm is $\{A \equiv \neg B\}$. But $\mathrm{mod}(\{C\}, \mathcal{O}_{ex3}) = \mathcal{O}_{ex3}$. This case occurs because signature of $\mathcal{G}(\mathcal{O}_{ex3})$ is not added to Σ during initialisation.

The performance of the algorithm decreases as the size of MSS of atoms increases. Consider the ontology $\mathcal{O}_{ex2}$ in Section 2. Let the input signature Σ be $\{C, F\}$. The atoms containing at least one term of $\{C, F\}$ in their MSS are $\mathfrak{a}, \mathfrak{b}$ and $\mathfrak{c}$. In the best case, it chooses $\mathfrak{c}$ first and performs one containment check to find that $\{C, F\}$ is present in $\mathsf{MSS}(\mathfrak{c})$ and returns $(\mathfrak{c}]$. The worst-case of this algorithm occurs when the signature $\mathfrak{m} \in \mathsf{MSS}(\mathfrak{a})$, such that $\mathfrak{m} \subseteq \Sigma$, is the last one to be checked for containment in $\mathsf{MSS}(\mathfrak{a})$ and $\mathfrak{a}$ is the last atom whose MSS-Label is checked. In the worst-case, the algorithm first searches $\mathsf{MSS}(\mathfrak{b})$ for containment in the order $\{B\}, \{A\}, \{C\}$ and $\mathsf{MSS}(\mathfrak{c})$ in the order $\{E\}, \{D\}, \{F\}$. If the signature $\{C, F\}$ is the last one to be checked in atom $\mathfrak{a}$, then the total number of checks is 16 (3 for $\mathfrak{b}$ and $\mathfrak{c}$ each and 10 for $\mathfrak{a}$).

If an atom $\mathfrak{a}$ has an axiom that is non-local for $\Sigma_1 \cup \Sigma_2 \cup \ldots \cup \Sigma_n$, where $\Sigma_i \in \mathsf{MSS}(\mathfrak{b}_i)$ and $\mathfrak{b}_i$ is a direct (non-transitive) dependency of $\mathfrak{a}$, then $|\mathsf{MSS}(\mathfrak{a})|$ is at least $|\mathsf{MGS}(\mathfrak{a})| + \prod_{i=1}^{n} |\mathsf{MSS}(\mathfrak{b}_i)| - 1$. If the input signature $\Sigma \supseteq \Sigma_1 \cup \Sigma_2 \cup \ldots \cup \Sigma_n$, the *number of containment checks in the worst-case* is at least $\prod_{i=1}^{n} |\mathsf{MSS}(\mathfrak{b}_i)|$ $+ \sum |\mathsf{MSS}(\mathfrak{b}_i)|$. If an atom $\mathfrak{a}$ has n overlapping direct-dependencies each with an MSS of size m, then the number of containment checks in the worst-case is $m^n + mn + 1$.

4   Proposed Algorithms

We propose algorithms based on MGS-Labels and improve the algorithm in [10] in terms of memory needed, preprocessing time and module extraction time.

Proposition 2. *If $\mathfrak{a} \in \mathcal{A}(\mathcal{O})$ and $\mathfrak{m} \in \mathsf{MGS}(\mathfrak{a})$, then $\mathrm{mod}(\mathfrak{m}, \mathcal{O}) = (\mathfrak{a}]$.*

Proof. Let $\mathfrak{a}$ be an atom and $\mathfrak{m} \in \mathsf{MGS}(\mathfrak{a})$. We prove that $(\mathfrak{a}] = \mathrm{mod}(\mathfrak{m}, \mathcal{O})$ by proving $\mathrm{mod}(\mathfrak{m}, \mathcal{O}) \subseteq (\mathfrak{a}]$ and $(\mathfrak{a}] \subseteq \mathrm{mod}(\mathfrak{m}, \mathcal{O})$.

According to Proposition 1, every principal ideal is a module. Hence $(\mathfrak{a}]$ is also a module. Self-containedness property implies that $(\mathfrak{a}] = \mathrm{mod}(\widetilde{(\mathfrak{a}]}, \mathcal{O})$. As

$m \in MGS(\mathfrak{a})$, $m \subseteq \widetilde{(\mathfrak{a}]}$. According to monotonicity property, if $m \subseteq \widetilde{(\mathfrak{a}]}$, then $mod(m, \mathcal{O}) \subseteq mod((\mathfrak{a}], \mathcal{O})$. Hence, $mod(m, \mathcal{O}) \subseteq (\mathfrak{a}]$.

As $m \in MGS(\mathfrak{a})$, there exists at least one axiom α in $\mathfrak{a}$ that is non-local for m. As a result, $mod(m, \mathcal{O})$ contains $\mathfrak{a}$. If $\mathfrak{a}$ is present in $mod(m, \mathcal{O})$, all its dependencies are also present in it. Hence $(\mathfrak{a}] \subseteq mod(m, \mathcal{O})$.

Hence, $m \in MGS(\mathfrak{a})$ implies that $(\mathfrak{a}] = mod(m, \mathcal{O})$. □

Proposition 3. *(i) If an axiom α is non-local for a signature Σ, then α is non-local for any signature $\Sigma_1 \supseteq \Sigma$. (ii) If an axiom α is local for a signature Σ, then α is local for any signature $\Sigma_1 \subseteq \Sigma$* [2].

Proposition 4. *If an axiom α is local for a signature Σ_A, then α is local for any signature $\Sigma_A \cup \Sigma_B$ such that $\Sigma_B \cap \widetilde{\alpha} = \emptyset$* [8].

Proposition 5. *An atom $\mathfrak{a}$ contains an axiom α that is non-local for a signature Σ if and only if $MGS(\mathfrak{a})$ contains some signature m such that $m \subseteq \Sigma$.*

Proof. Let $\mathfrak{a}$ be an atom that contains an axiom α that is non-local for Σ. We partition Σ into Σ_A and Σ_B such that $\Sigma_A \subseteq \widetilde{\alpha}$ and $\Sigma_B \cap \widetilde{\alpha} = \emptyset$.

1. a From Proposition 4, if α is local for Σ_A, then α is local for $\Sigma_A \cup \Sigma_B$ as $\Sigma_B \cap \widetilde{\alpha} = \emptyset$. So, for α to be non-local for $\Sigma_A \cup \Sigma_B$, α should be non-local for Σ_A. From the definition of $MGS(\alpha)$, if α is non-local for $\Sigma_A \subseteq \widetilde{\alpha}$, then $MGS(\alpha)$ contains some signature $m \subseteq \Sigma_A \subseteq \Sigma$.
   b If $\mathfrak{a}$ contains another axiom β that is non-local for Σ, then from the same argument, $MGS(\beta)$ contains a signature $p \subseteq \Sigma$. If $p \subseteq m$ or $m \subseteq p$, the smaller one is retained in $MGS(\mathfrak{a})$. If not, both are retained in $MGS(\mathfrak{a})$. In any case, $MGS(\mathfrak{a})$ contains some signature that is subset of Σ.
2. If a signature $m \subseteq \Sigma$ is in $MGS(\mathfrak{a})$, then $\mathfrak{a}$ contains an axiom α that is non-local for m. As $m \subseteq \Sigma$, from Proposition 3, α is non-local for Σ.

Hence, an atom $\mathfrak{a}$ contains an axiom non-local for a signature Σ if and only if $MGS(\mathfrak{a})$ contains some signature m such that $m \subseteq \Sigma$. □

Proposition 6. *If $\mathcal{M}_e$ is the module computed by Algorithm 1 and $\mathcal{M}_f$ is the set of axioms returned by Algorithm 2, then $\mathcal{M}_e = \mathcal{M}_f$.*

Proof. Let Σ_{input} be the input signature. Then $\mathcal{M}_e = mod(\Sigma_{input}, \mathcal{O})$. We prove $\mathcal{M}_e = \mathcal{M}_f$ by proving that $\mathcal{M}_f \subseteq \mathcal{M}_e$ and $\mathcal{M}_e \subseteq \mathcal{M}_f$.

To prove $\mathcal{M}_f \subseteq \mathcal{M}_e$: Suppose that Algorithm 2 starts with $\mathcal{M}_0 = \mathcal{G}(\mathcal{O})$ as the initial value of $\mathcal{M}$ and $\Sigma_0 = \Sigma_{input} \cup \widetilde{\mathcal{G}(\mathcal{O})} = \widetilde{\mathcal{M}_0}$ as the initial value of Σ. From the definition of $\mathcal{G}(\mathcal{O})$, $\mathcal{G}(\mathcal{O}) \subseteq \mathcal{M}_e$. As $\mathcal{G}(\mathcal{O}) \subseteq \mathcal{M}_e$, $\mathcal{M}_0 \subseteq \mathcal{M}_e$ and $\Sigma_0 \subseteq \Sigma_{input} \cup \widetilde{\mathcal{M}_e}$. Suppose that Algorithm 2 adds the principal ideals $(\mathfrak{a}_1], (\mathfrak{a}_2], (\mathfrak{a}_3], \cdots (\mathfrak{a}_f]$ to $\mathcal{M}_0$ in that order to form the sets of axioms $\mathcal{M}_1, \mathcal{M}_2, \mathcal{M}_3, \cdots, \mathcal{M}_f$. The signatures formed are $\Sigma_1, \Sigma_2, \Sigma_3, \cdots, \Sigma_f$. We can observe that whenever Σ is updated to Σ_i, $\Sigma_i = \Sigma_{input} \cup \widetilde{\mathcal{M}_i}$. As $\Sigma_i = \Sigma_{input} \cup \widetilde{\mathcal{M}_i}$, proving $\mathcal{M}_i \subseteq \mathcal{M}_e$ automatically proves that $\Sigma_i \subseteq \Sigma_{input} \cup \widetilde{\mathcal{M}_e}$.

We prove that $\mathcal{M}_f \subseteq \mathcal{M}_e$ and $\Sigma_f \subseteq \Sigma_{input} \cup \widetilde{\mathcal{M}_e}$ by proving the following statement by induction on i.

Let $\mathcal{M}_i$ be the value of $\mathcal{M}$ and Σ_i be the value of Σ at any point of time during the execution of Algorithm 2. Then, $\mathcal{M}_i \subseteq \mathcal{M}_e$ and $\Sigma_i \subseteq \Sigma_{input} \cup \widetilde{\mathcal{M}_e}$.

1. *Basis:* Initially, $\mathcal{M} = \mathcal{M}_0$ and $\Sigma_0 = \Sigma_{input} \cup \widetilde{\mathcal{G}(\mathcal{O})}$. Let $\mathfrak{a}_1$ be an atom whose MGS contains a signature $\mathfrak{m}_1 \subseteq \Sigma_0$. By Proposition 2, $\text{mod}(\mathfrak{m}_1, \mathcal{O}) = (\mathfrak{a}_1]$. By monotonicity property, as $\mathfrak{m}_1 \subseteq \Sigma_0$, $(\mathfrak{a}_1] \subseteq \text{mod}(\Sigma_0, \mathcal{O})$. From the statements $(\mathfrak{a}_1] \subseteq \text{mod}(\Sigma_0, \mathcal{O})$, $\text{mod}(\Sigma_0, \mathcal{O}) = \mathcal{M}_e$ and $\mathcal{M}_0 \subseteq \mathcal{M}_e$, we can say that $\mathcal{M}_1 = \mathcal{M}_0 \cup (\mathfrak{a}_1] \subseteq \mathcal{M}_e$ and $\Sigma_1 \subseteq \Sigma_{input} \cup \widetilde{\mathcal{M}_e}$.

2. *Inductive Step:* We assume that inductive hypothesis holds for $\mathcal{M} = \mathcal{M}_i$. So, $\mathcal{M}_i \subseteq \mathcal{M}_e$ and $\Sigma_i \subseteq \Sigma_{input} \cup \widetilde{\mathcal{M}_e}$. Now, we should prove that $\mathcal{M}_{i+1} \subseteq \mathcal{M}_e$ and $\Sigma_{i+1} \subseteq \Sigma_{input} \cup \widetilde{\mathcal{M}_e}$. By monotonicity property, as $\Sigma_i \subseteq \Sigma_{input} \cup \widetilde{\mathcal{M}_e}$ and $\mathcal{M}_e = \text{mod}(\Sigma_{input} \cup \widetilde{\mathcal{M}_e}, \mathcal{O})$, $\text{mod}(\Sigma_i, \mathcal{O}) \subseteq \mathcal{M}_e$. Now, Algorithm 2 chooses an atom $\mathfrak{a}_{i+1}$ such that there is a signature $\mathfrak{m}_{i+1} \in \text{MGS}(\mathfrak{a}_{i+1})$ and $\mathfrak{m}_{i+1} \subseteq \Sigma_i$, and adds $(\mathfrak{a}_{i+1}]$ to $\mathcal{M}_i$ to form $\mathcal{M}_{i+1}$. So, $\mathcal{M}_{i+1} = \mathcal{M}_i \cup (\mathfrak{a}_{i+1}]$. According to Proposition 2, $\text{mod}(\mathfrak{m}_{i+1}, \mathcal{O}) = (\mathfrak{a}_{i+1}]$. As $\mathfrak{m}_{i+1} \subseteq \Sigma_i$, by monotonicity property, $(\mathfrak{a}_{i+1}] \subseteq \text{mod}(\Sigma_i, \mathcal{O}) \subseteq \mathcal{M}_e$. As $(\mathfrak{a}_{i+1}] \subseteq \mathcal{M}_e$ and $\mathcal{M}_i \subseteq \mathcal{M}_e$, $(\mathfrak{a}_{i+1}] \cup \mathcal{M}_i \subseteq \mathcal{M}_e$. As $\mathcal{M}_{i+1} \subseteq \mathcal{M}_e$, $\Sigma_{i+1} \subseteq \Sigma_{input} \cup \widetilde{\mathcal{M}_e}$.

Hence, by mathematical induction, $\mathcal{M}_f \subseteq \mathcal{M}_e$ and $\Sigma_f \subseteq \Sigma_{input} \cup \widetilde{\mathcal{M}_e}$.

To prove $\mathcal{M}_e \subseteq \mathcal{M}_f$: Note that $\mathcal{M}_f$ is the set of axioms returned by Algorithm 2 upon termination and $\Sigma_f = \Sigma_{input} \cup \widetilde{\mathcal{M}_f}$. Algorithm 2 teminates if and only if there is no atom $\mathfrak{a}_{f+1}$, other than the ones included in $\mathcal{M}_f$, that has some signature $\mathfrak{m}_{f+1} \in \text{MGS}(\mathfrak{a}_{f+1})$ such that $\mathfrak{m}_{f+1} \subseteq \Sigma_{input} \cup \widetilde{\mathcal{M}_f}$. Hence, from Proposition 5, there is no axiom in $\mathcal{O} \setminus \mathcal{M}_f$ that is non-local for $\Sigma_{input} \cup \widetilde{\mathcal{M}_f}$. From Theorem 1, $\mathcal{M}_f$ is a module for $\Sigma_{input} \cup \widetilde{\mathcal{M}_f}$. As $\Sigma_{input} \subseteq \Sigma_{input} \cup \widetilde{\mathcal{M}_f}$, by monotonicity property, $\mathcal{M}_e = \text{mod}(\Sigma_{input}, \mathcal{O})$ is a subset of $\mathcal{M}_f$.
Form the statements $\mathcal{M}_e \subseteq \mathcal{M}_f$ and $\mathcal{M}_f \subseteq \mathcal{M}_e$, $\mathcal{M}_e = \mathcal{M}_f$. □

Algorithm 2 gives a naïve implementation of MGS based fast module extraction. It uses the dependency property of atoms and includes all the dependencies of $\mathfrak{a}$ if an atom $\mathfrak{a}$ is included. Hence, it terminates faster than Algorithm 1.

We compute MGS-Labels for each atom and store them. The set of atoms that contain the term e in a signature in their MGS-Labels is returned by *getContainingAtoms(e)*. Let Σ_{input} be the input signature. Σ is initialised to $\Sigma_{input} \cup \widetilde{\mathcal{G}(\mathcal{O})}$. Here, *included* represents the atoms that are included in the final module. For each term e in Σ, atoms returned by *getContainingAtoms(e)* and are not present in *included* are added to *candidateAtoms*. For each atom $\mathfrak{a}$ in *candidateAtoms*, the algorithm checks if any signature in its MGS is a subset of Σ. If yes, then atoms in $(\mathfrak{a}]$, given by *atomsIn($(\mathfrak{a}]$)*, are added to *included* and $(\mathfrak{a}]$ is added to Σ. It terminates when no new atoms are added to the module.

As $\widetilde{\mathcal{G}(\mathcal{O})}$ is added to Σ initially, for the ontology $\mathcal{O}_{ex3}$ and $\Sigma_{input} = \{C\}$, $\Sigma = \{A, B, C\}$. MGS($\mathfrak{a}$) contains $\{A, C\}$ which is a subset of Σ. Hence, $\mathfrak{a}$ is added to the module. The module returned will be $\mathcal{O}_{ex3}$ and is equal to $\text{mod}(\{C\}, \mathcal{O})$.

Algorithm 2. Naive implementation of MGS Based Module Extraction

Input: A set of terms Σ_{input}
Output: $\mathrm{mod}(\Sigma_{input}, \mathcal{O})$

1   $\Sigma := \Sigma_{input} \cup \widetilde{\mathcal{G}(\mathcal{O})}$, $included := \emptyset$, $\mathcal{M} := \mathcal{G}(\mathcal{O})$
2   **repeat**
3     $changed := false$
4     $candidateAtoms := \emptyset$
5   **for** $each\ e\ in\ \Sigma$ **do**
6       $candidateAtoms := candidateAtoms \cup getContainingAtoms(e)$
7     $candidateAtoms := candidateAtoms \setminus included$
8   **for** $each\ \mathfrak{a}\ in\ candidateAtoms$ **do**
9   **if** $there\ exists\ a\ signature\ \mathfrak{m} \in \mathsf{MGS}(\mathfrak{a})\ such\ that\ \mathfrak{m} \subseteq \Sigma$ **then**
10        $included := included \cup atomsIn((\mathfrak{a}])$
11        $\mathcal{M} := \mathcal{M} \cup (\mathfrak{a}]$
12        $\Sigma := \Sigma \cup \widetilde{(\mathfrak{a}]}$
13        $changed := true$
14 **until** $changed = false$
15 **return** $\mathcal{M}$

Consider the example ontology $\mathcal{O}_{ex2}$ from Section 2 and the input signature $\Sigma = \{C,\ F\}$. In the best case, the number of checks is 3 (when it checks in the order $\mathfrak{a}$, $\mathfrak{b}$, $\mathfrak{c}$). In the worst-case, the algorithm first checks the signatures of $candidateAtoms = \{\mathfrak{b},\ \mathfrak{c}\}$ for containment and it takes a total of 6 containment checks for $\mathfrak{b}$ and $\mathfrak{c}$. After adding $\widetilde{(\mathfrak{b}]}$ and $\widetilde{(\mathfrak{c}]}$ to Σ, $\Sigma = \{A,\ B,\ C,\ D,\ E,\ F\}$. Now $candidateAtoms = \{\mathfrak{a}\}$ and it takes 2 checks in the worst-case to check $\mathsf{MGS}(\mathfrak{a})$ for containment. $\mathsf{MGS}(\mathfrak{a})$ contains $\{A,\ D\}$ which is a subset of Σ. Hence, the module is $\mathfrak{a} \cup \mathfrak{b} \cup \mathfrak{c}$. Here, the total number of checks is reduced from 16 to 8. In general, number of checks in the worst-case is reduced from $\prod |\mathsf{MSS}(\mathfrak{b}_i)| + \sum |\mathsf{MSS}(\mathfrak{b}_i)|$ to $\sum |\mathsf{MGS}(\mathfrak{b}_i)| + |\mathsf{MGS}(\mathfrak{a})|$, where $\mathfrak{b}_i$ is a direct dependency of $\mathfrak{a}$.

The worst-case behavior of MGS based algorithm (MSS based algorithm) during module extraction arises due to the following fact. *Though an atom $\mathfrak{a}$ in candidateAtoms is found, checking if there is a signature $\mathfrak{m}_i \in \mathsf{MGS}(\mathfrak{a})$ such that $\mathfrak{m}_i \subseteq \Sigma$ takes $|\mathsf{MGS}(\mathfrak{a})|$ (or $|\mathsf{MSS}(\mathfrak{a})|$) containment checks in the worst-case.* This can be eliminated if we can individually identify each of the signatures in $\mathsf{MGS}^*(\mathcal{O})$ and work with them. The properties about MGS-Labels and MGS-Space that we define next provide a means of achieving that.

4.1   Properties of MGS-Labels and MGS-Space

We define the notion of *MGS-Space* that is a union of MGS-Labels of all the atoms in $\mathcal{A}(\mathcal{O})$.

Definition 10 (MGS-Space). *The MGS-Space, $\mathsf{MGS}^*(\mathcal{O})$, for an ontology $\mathcal{O}$, is given by $\mathsf{MGS}^*(\mathcal{O}) = \{\mathfrak{m}_j | \mathfrak{m}_j \in \mathsf{MGS}(\mathfrak{a}_i)\ and\ \mathfrak{a}_i \in \mathcal{A}(\mathcal{O})\}$.*

Signature	Terms	Atom	size	Term	Containing signature
m_1	{Animal}	a_1	1	Animal	m_1, m_3
m_2	{Plant}	a_2	1	Plant	m_2, m_3
m_3	{Plant, Animal}	a_3	2	Herbivore	m_4
m_4	{Herbivore}	a_4	1	Carnivore	m_5
m_5	{Carnivore}	a_5	1	PizzaRestaurant	m_6
m_6	{PizzaRestaurant}	a_6	1	NonLivingThing	m_7
m_7	{NonLivingThing, serves, Pizza}	a_6	3	serves	m_7
				Pizza	m_7
m_8	{ItalianPR}	a_7	1	ItalianPR	m_8

Fig. 2. Indices for ontology in example $\mathcal{O}_{ex}$

Proposition 7. *For any two distinct atoms* a *and* b, $\mathsf{MGS}(a) \cap \mathsf{MGS}(b) = \emptyset$.

Proof. Let $\mathcal{O}$ be an ontology, a and b be two distinct atoms in $\mathcal{A}(\mathcal{O})$ and m be a signature in $\mathsf{MGS}(a) \cap \mathsf{MGS}(b)$. Then $(a] = \mathrm{mod}(m, \mathcal{O})$ and $(b] = \mathrm{mod}(m, \mathcal{O})$. But as locality-based modules are unique for a particular signature (Definition 3), $(a] = (b]$. Hence, $a = b$, which is a contradiction as a and b are distinct. Thus, for any two distinct atoms a and b, $\mathsf{MGS}(a) \cap \mathsf{MGS}(b) = \emptyset$.   □

Corollary 1. *If* $\mathcal{O}$ *is an ontology, then* $|\mathsf{MGS}^*(\mathcal{O})| = \sum_{i=1}^{|\mathcal{A}(\mathcal{O})|} |\mathsf{MGS}(a_i)|$, *where* $a_i \in \mathcal{A}(\mathcal{O})$.

Proof. For any atom a_i, all the signatures in $\mathsf{MGS}(a_i)$ are distinct as $\bigcup^*$ disallows duplicates. Proposition 7 implies that for two distinct atoms a_i and a_j, $\mathsf{MGS}(a_i) \cap \mathsf{MGS}(a_j) = \emptyset$. Hence, there is no common signature m in MGS-Labels of two distinct atoms a_i and a_j which proves that $|\mathsf{MGS}^*(\mathcal{O})| = \sum_{i=1}^{|\mathcal{A}(\mathcal{O})|} |\mathsf{MGS}(a_i)|$.   □

As each $m \in \mathsf{MGS}^*(\mathcal{O})$ is distinct, Corollary 1 helps us to assign a unique id to each signature in $\mathsf{MGS}^*(\mathcal{O})$. Proposition 7 implies that given a signature $m \in \mathsf{MGS}^*(\mathcal{O})$, we can retrieve the atom whose MGS contains m. The memory needed is to load a set of ids (set of integers) instead of the whole ontology (set of axioms) or MSS-Labels (collections of terms) or atoms.

We create an inverted-index table *termToSigs*, such that *termToSigs*(e) returns the ids of signatures $m_i \in \mathsf{MGS}^*(\mathcal{O})$ such that the term $e \in m_i$. This prevents the worst-case of $\mathcal{O}_{ex2}$ as we can identify $m \in \mathsf{MGS}^*(\mathcal{O})$ that contains the term e instead of searching whole MGS-Labels of the atoms in *candidateAtoms*. For the ontology given in $\mathcal{O}_{ex}$, indices are shown in Figure 2. To compute principal ideals of atoms without loading AD into memory, we use labeled-atomic-decomposition graph in [9]. It consumes the space equal to $\sum_{i=1}^{|\mathcal{A}(\mathcal{O})|} |\tilde{a}_i|$ which is equal to space needed for AD in the worst-case in which all the atoms are independent.

Another implementation of Fast Module Extraction is given in Algorithm 3. It uses inverted indices explained in the above paragraph. In each iteration of lines 2-10, the algorithm assigns the value of *getAtomsInMod*(Σ) minus *included* to

---

Algorithm 3. MGS Based Fast Module Extraction (implementation 2)

Input: A set of terms Σ_{input}
Output: $mod(\underbrace{\Sigma_{input}}, \mathcal{O})$

1   $\Sigma := \Sigma_{input} \cup \widetilde{\mathcal{G}(\mathcal{O})}$, $\mathcal{M} := \mathcal{G}(\mathcal{O})$, $included := \emptyset$
2   **repeat**
3     $changed := false$
4     $atomsInMod := getAtomsInMod(\Sigma) \backslash included$
5   **if** $atomsInMod \neq \emptyset$ **then**
6       $changed := true$
7   **for** each atom $\mathfrak{a}$ in $atomsInMod$ **do**
8         $\Sigma := \Sigma \cup \widetilde{(\mathfrak{a}]}$
9         $included := included \cup atomsIn((\mathfrak{a}])$
10 **until** $changed = false$
11 **for** each $\mathfrak{b}$ in $included$ **do**
12     $\mathcal{M} := \mathcal{M} \cup \mathfrak{b}$
13 **return** $\mathcal{M}$

Algorithm 4. getAtomsInMod(Σ)

Input: A set of terms Σ
Output: A set of atoms($atomsInMod$) such that, for each atom
       $\mathfrak{a}_i \in atomsInMod$, $(\mathfrak{a}_i] \subseteq mod(\Sigma, \mathcal{O})$

1   $atomsInMod := \emptyset$
2   **for** each signature $\mathsf{m} \in \mathsf{MGS}^*(\mathcal{O})$ **do**
3     $\mathsf{m}.count := 0$
4   **for** each term $e \in \Sigma$ **do**
5   **for** each signature $\mathsf{m} \in termToSigs(e)$ **do**
6       $\mathsf{m}.count = \mathsf{m}.count + 1$
7   **if** $\mathsf{m}.size = \mathsf{m}.count$ **then**
8         $atomsInMod := atomsInMod \cup Atom(\mathsf{m})$
9   **return** $atomsInMod$

$atomsInMod$. Here, $getAtomsInMod(\Sigma)$ returns the set of atoms $\{\mathfrak{a}\}$ such that for each $\mathfrak{a}$, there exists some signature $\mathsf{m}_j \in \mathsf{MGS}(\mathfrak{a})$ and $\mathsf{m}_j \subseteq \Sigma$. For each atom $\mathfrak{a}$ in $atomsInMod$, $\widetilde{(\mathfrak{a}]}$ is added to Σ. The loop in lines 2-10 terminates when no new atom, not included in $included$, is returned by $getAtomsInMod(\Sigma)$.

The function $getAtomsInMod(\Sigma)$ works as follows. For each term e in Σ and for each signature m in $termToSigs(e)$, it increments the $count$ value of m. For each signature m in $\mathsf{MGS}^*(\mathcal{O})$ such that $\mathsf{m}.count = \mathsf{m}.size$, the atom $\mathfrak{a}$ such that $\mathsf{m} \in \mathsf{MGS}(\mathfrak{a})$ is added to the set $atomsInMod$. This is the the sufficient condition that $\mathsf{m} \subseteq \Sigma$. Finally, the set of atoms $atomsInMod$ is returned. Thus, the table $termToSigs$ and Proposition 7 convert module extraction task into simple operations on integers.

The following are the benefits of proposed algorithm over the fast module extraction algorithm proposed in [10].

1. *Preprocessing Time:* Preprocessing time is reduced as MGS computation is an intermediate step in MSS-Labeling algorithm [10].
2. *Memory Requirement:* From Proposition 2, if a signature $m \in MGS(a)$, then $mod(m, \mathcal{O}) = (a]$. From the definition of MSS, if $mod(m, \mathcal{O}) = (a]$, then $m \in MSS(a]$. Hence, MGS of an atom is a subset of its MSS.
3. *Module Extraction:* (i) Improved speedup (due to small number of containment checks in the worst-case and indices built). (ii) Accurate module size[3].

5   Empirical Evaluation

Algorithms 2 and 3 are implemented in Java. All the experiments are run on a machine with Intel Xeon processor (2.13GHz), with 32GB of RAM (out of which 16GB is used as Heap space for Java) running Windows Server 2008 (64-bit) operating system. 30,000 signatures, of sizes 2, 5 and 10 each, are generated in a random manner. Modules are extracted with MGS based algorithms and MSS based algorithm in [10] w.r.t. each of these signatures. The results obtained are averaged out and the speed-ups are given in Table 1.

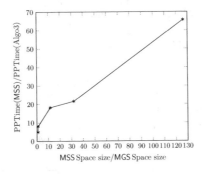

Fig. 3. Pre-processing time comparison

The column *% inclusions* shows percentage of modules extracted in which the atom with maximum-sized MSS-Label is included after containment checking. From the experimental evaluation, we can observe that the atoms that have maximum MSS size are checked for containment in almost all the modules generated. Also, the atom with the largest MSS of size 10258 in *myGrid* ontology is included in 99.8% of the modules. On average, for an atom with MSS of size 10258, 5129 containment checks are to be made. But MGS based algorithm makes an average

---

[3] Atoms whose MSS can not be computed before time-out (which is 5 seconds per atom according to Algorithm 1 in [10]) are called *dirty atoms*. A dirty atom ∂ is added to modules w.r.t. Σ without containment check if $\widetilde{\partial} \cap \Sigma \neq \emptyset$ [10].

Table 1. Module Extraction Time Comparison

Ontology	Sig. size	T_{MSS} (Sec)	Speedup $\frac{T_{MSS}}{T_{Algo2}}$	Speedup $\frac{T_{MSS}}{T_{Algo3}}$	$\frac{\|MSS^*\|}{\|MGS^*\|}$	Max MGS Size	Max MSS Size	% of modules
GO	2	0.1	2.6	5.9				
	5	0.2	3.4	12.2	1	1	1	-
	10	0.5	5.1	21.0				
NCI	2	0.02	3.29	3.87				
	5	0.04	7.23	7.9	1	1	1	-
	10	0.07	10.0	12.8				
ICNP	2	1.1	358.0	583.1				
	5	1.3	257.4	420.0	11.6	1	4940	99.2
	10	1.4	192.6	339.3				
TAMBIS full	2	0.11	447.2	858.6				
	5	0.15	931.3	1590.8	32.0	42	3794	96.5
	10	0.20	844.4	1480.7				
myGrid	2	1.0	9712.0	12803.0				
	5	1.3	6749.8	8966.5	126.2	9	10258	99.8
	10	1.8	5422.4	6549.2				
Small ontologies (Avg. over 91 ontologies)	2	0.016	6.1	7.29				
	5	0.025	5.2	8.23	-	-	-	-
	10	0.039	4.7	9.78				

% of modules = percentage of modules extracted in which the atom with maximum-sized MSS-Label is included after containment checking.

of 4.5 containment checks for *myGrid* ontology. Results demonstrate the same by showing huge speedups in case of ontologies with large MSS size.

For ontologies with MSS size of 1, for each atom $\mathfrak{a}$, $MSS(\mathfrak{a}) = MGS(\mathfrak{a})$. In such cases, MSS based algorithm is similar to Algorithm 2. But small speedups have been observed due to better implementation like using Java BitSets for costly operations like containment checking. Even for these ontologies, Algorithm 3 gives better speedups because of inverted indices proposed. Table 1 also shows the results for 91 small ontologies from ORE 2012[4] with varying MSS sizes.

Since both the MSS and MGS based algorithms load only labels into memory, we compared memory needed in terms of ratio of MSS Space size (union of all MSS-Labels) to MGS Space size. The column $\frac{\|MSS^*\|}{\|MGS^*\|}$ shows the ratio of MSS space size to MGS space size. Maximum improvement is observed in case of *myGrid* where the space needed for MSS-Labels is 126.2 times that of the space needed for MGS-Labels.

The graph in Figure 3 shows (for first 5 ontologies) that with increase in the ratio of MGS-space size to MSS-Space size, the ratio of preprocessing times

---

[4] http://www.cs.ox.ac.uk/isg/conferences/ORE2012/

(PPTime(MSS)/PPTime(Algo3)) increases. It shows that the pre-processing time for computing MSS is at least 5 times of that of Algorithm 3 (which includes MGS computation and building indices). The best speedup in pre-processing is observed for *myGrid* ontology when MSS Space size/MGS Space size is 126.2.

6   Conclusion

We proposed algorithms for module extraction for large ontologies using atomic decomposition. The proposed algorithms require less pre-processing time and memory. We proposed and proved properties of MGS and MGS-Space. Empirical evaluation confirmed that the proposed algorithms outperform the MSS based extractor. It also confirmed that the proposed algorithms perform better for ontologies that have atoms with huge MSS-Labels such as ICNP, myGrid and TAMBIS in terms of preprocessing time, memory needed and extraction time.

References

1. Grau, B.C., Horrocks, I., Kazakov, Y., Sattler, U.: Just the right amount: extracting modules from ontologies. In: WWW, pp. 717–726 (2007)
2. Grau, B.C., Horrocks, I., Kazakov, Y., Sattler, U.: Modular reuse of ontologies: Theory and practice. JAIR 31, 273–318 (2008)
3. Konev, B., Lutz, C., Walther, D., Wolter, F.: Formal Properties of Modularisation. In: Stuckenschmidt, H., Parent, C., Spaccapietra, S. (eds.) Modular Ontologies. LNCS, vol. 5445, pp. 25–66. Springer, Heidelberg (2009)
4. Kontchakov, R., Pulina, L., Sattler, U., Schneider, T., Selmer, P., Wolter, F., Zakharyaschev, M.: Minimal module extraction from dl-lite ontologies using qbf solvers. IJCAI, 836–841 (2009)
5. Lutz, C., Walther, D., Wolter, F.: Conservative extensions in expressive description logics. IJCAI, 453–458 (2007)
6. Lutz, C., Wolterinst, F.: Conservative extensions in the lightweight description logic EL. In: Pfenning, F. (ed.) CADE 2007. LNCS (LNAI), vol. 4603, pp. 84–99. Springer, Heidelberg (2007)
7. Sattler, U., Schneider, T., Zakharyaschev, M.: Which kind of module should i extract? In: Description Logics (2009)
8. Tsarkov, D.: Improved algorithms for module extraction and atomic decomposition. In: Description Logics (2012)
9. Tsarkov, D., Palmisano, I.: Divide et impera: Metareasoning for large ontologies. In: OWLED (2012)
10. Del Vescovo, C., Gessler, D.D.G., Klinov, P., Parsia, B., Sattler, U., Schneider, T., Winget, A.: Decomposition and modular structure of bioPortal ontologies. In: Aroyo, L., Welty, C., Alani, H., Taylor, J., Bernstein, A., Kagal, L., Noy, N., Blomqvist, E. (eds.) ISWC 2011, Part I. LNCS, vol. 7031, pp. 130–145. Springer, Heidelberg (2011)
11. Del Vescovo, C., Parsia, B., Sattler, U., Schneider, T.: The modular structure of an ontology: Atomic decomposition. IJCAI, 2232–2237 (2011)

Representation of Historical Sources on the Semantic Web by Means of Attempto Controlled English*

Aleksey Varfolomeyev[1] and Aleksandrs Ivanovs[2,3]

[1] Petrozavodsk State University, Petrozavodsk, Russia
avarf@petrsu.ru
[2] Daugavpils University, Daugavpils,
[3] Rezekne University, Rezekne, Latvia
aleksandrs.ivanovs@du.lv

Abstract. The paper discusses some promising approaches to the representation of the meta-information and the meaning of historical sources on the Semantic Web in order to provide researchers with appropriate tools for data capturing, semantic linkage of information, and automatic logical inference. It is desirable that the meaning of the sources is represented fully to aggregate their internal information within a definite semantic network and to link this information with the external data provided by ontologies. The authors propose to use controlled natural languages—namely, Attempto Controlled English (ACE)—to represent the meaning of historical sources on the Semantic Web. In the paper, both actual and potential possibilities of ACE in the representation of the contents of Old Russian charters are examined; therefore, a special attention is paid to ACE tools, especially to ACE Reasoner (RACE).

Keywords: digital humanities, historical sources, semantic publications, Semantic Web, controlled natural languages, Attempto Controlled English.

1 Introduction

Nowadays, the progress of Semantic Web technologies poses a number of challenges and, at the same time, offers new opportunities for digital humanities. This technological breakthrough might affect, first of all, the process of creation of the empirical basis for scholarly research by means of the representation (i.e. publication) of vast complexes of historical sources, collections of manuscripts, and corpora of literary texts on the Semantic Web. The representation should not be seen as an end in itself. It goes without saying that the representation of raster images and electronic texts – transcriptions – of the written historical records on the Web, as well as the creation of digital libraries and archives is a

---

* The work described in this paper has been partially supported by the Program of Strategic Development of Petrozavodsk State University for 2012–2016.

P. Klinov and D. Mouromtsev (Eds.): KESW 2013, CCIS 394, pp. 177–190, 2013.
© Springer-Verlag Berlin Heidelberg 2013

very important task in order to provide distant access to primary sources. However, modern computer technologies are very useful for conducting analytical and synthetic operations (source criticism), namely: information search, data capturing, aggregation and semantic linkage of information extracted from historical sources, automatic logical inference that can be performed by a computer, etc.

The above-mentioned operations can be performed applying Semantic Web technologies. It means that publications of historical sources on the Web should contain both the texts and additional information layers that display, on the one hand, the meta-information about historical sources (provenance, repository, paleographic features, etc.) and, on the other hand, the sense of the texts in a formalized way suitable for automatic processing [13]. Such publications of historical sources can be called semantic publications.

On the Web, the semantic publications are chiefly represented by research papers that are included in digital libraries and electronic journals. These publications have been already studied by specialists in information technologies [2], [8], [23], [24], [28]. Nowadays, the creation of semantic publications is based on different technological and methodological approaches; nevertheless, all the semantic publications are oriented to the formalized representation of the knowledge about the texts that is usually expressed in the form of domain ontologies [7], [17].

In the field of historical research, the problem of creation of specialized ontologies has recently been raised in scholarly papers [19]. Meanwhile, a number of specialized historical ontologies have been created within such projects as Pearl Harbor Project in the USA [9], CultureSampo Project in Finland [1], etc. Historical ontologies are usually based on the cultural heritage ontological framework CIDOC CRM [5]. Besides the elaboration of ontological models useful for the semantic description of research results, in humanities there has emerged a new task - production of the semantic publications of historical sources. This task is very important for the computer-based source studies [26]. Some principle approaches to the creation of the semantic publications of historical documents, as well as possible solutions have already been studied [13], [18]. It is noteworthy that comprehensive semantic publications of historical sources should be based on specialized ontologies, which are oriented to the exhaustive representation of the information about the documents, and a special attention should be paid to the links between these documents within a definite semantic network. Moreover, light-weighted tools for the creation of ontological models [15], [27] and formalized representation of the contents (or meaning) of historical sources should be developed.

To a certain extent, the formalized representation of the contents of historical sources can be performed by means of the text markup [21], [25]. For these purposes widely spread markup schemes TEI [31] and CEI [30] are usually used. On the basis of these schemes, not only structural parts and paleographic features of historical sources, but also diverse historical objects directly or indirectly mentioned in the texts - persons, place names, outdated terms, references to other documents, etc. - can be marked up. It means that due to this in-depth markup historical sources are integrated into a definite semantic network, which embraces different objects related to the texts. Unfortunately, the marked up objects do not exhaustively represent the sense of historical sources.

The authors of the paper argue that in the semantic publication the contents of historical sources can be directly represented by means of the so-called controlled natural languages, e.g., Attempto Controlled English [29]; thus, the sense of the texts recorded in such languages can be understood not only by a human-reader, but also by a computer. The authors propose to extend the existing markup schemes adding the texts of historical documents recorded in a controlled natural language to the original texts of the same documents. In this case, the texts in such languages might create additional information layers that represent the sense of the texts.

The empirical basis of the paper embraces the complex of the interconnected Old Russian charters, which reflect the course of relations between Riga and Smolensk in the 13th century [11]. This complex forms a constituent part of the vast collection of medieval and early modern records "Moscowitica-Ruthenica" kept in the Latvian State Historical Archives (Riga, Latvia) [10], [12].

2   Controlled Natural Languages

Nowadays, controlled natural languages for knowledge representation develop intensively [16]. These languages have simplified syntax and restricted semantics. The following controlled natural languages can be mentioned: Controlled English to Logic Translation (CELT) [20], Processable English (PENG) [22], Computer-Processable Language (CPL) [3], and Attempto Controlled English (ACE) [4]. Some of them are being developed; others can already provide some necessary tools for researchers, e.g., Processable English (PENG).

2.1   Attempto Controlled English

One of the most expressive and widely spread natural controlled languages is Attempto Controlled English (ACE). For these reasons, it has been chosen for the purposes of the representation of the sense of historical sources.

The following features that reflect the advantages of ACE can be mentioned:

First, ACE texts can be translated into the so-called Discourse Representation Structures (DRS) that can be directly correlated with first-order logic formulas [14]. It is clear that ordinary languages cannot be translated into logic formulas because of ambiguities of any discourse; therefore, the sense can be revealed only within a definite context. On the contrary, Discourse Representation Structures provide an unambiguous subset of a natural language due to the restricted vocabulary, comparatively simple syntax, and monosemy of phrases and sentences. As a result, DRS can be translated into formal languages that are based on first-order logic and are used for knowledge representation (e.g., OWL, Rule Markup Language, Semantic Web Rule Language, etc.). Thus, ACE may seem to be completely natural, but it is actually a formal language; more precisely, it is a first-order logic language with English syntax. This language is human and machine understandable.

Second, nowadays Attempto Controlled English is supported by a number of tools: the parser (Attempto Parsing Engine, APE) that translates ACE texts into Discourse Representation Structures; the reasoner (ACE Reasoner RACE) that makes logical inference from the statements represented in ACE; the editor that is used for the construction of ACE texts, etc. It is very important that when processing ACE texts it is possible to use different domain-specific lexicons. Furthermore, the texts of the documents in ACE can be processed using the reasoner, which can generate new hypotheses based on the facts revealed by a researcher. Therefore, this language is quite appropriate for the purposes of the production of the semantic publications of historical sources.

Third, ACE construction rules are rather simple. For instance, these rules require that each noun should be introduced by a determiner (a, every, no, some, etc.), with the exception of proper names, which are written with capital letters; anaphoric references can be used (He = Metropolitan), etc. Although this language puts some substantial restrictions on text rendering (e.g., the verbs can be used in the Present Indefinite Tense only), nevertheless, it seems that ACE construction rules can be applied to the texts of medieval charters. Unfortunately, the translation of the texts of the charters into ACE comprises, to a certain extent, researchers' interpretations of the meaning of the documents. It should be also noted that practical implementation of these rules sometimes poses rather difficult problems.

Nevertheless, the research conducted by the authors testifies that the sense of medieval records, even of those written in Old Russian, can be rather precisely rendered into ACE. In our pilot project, the translation into ACE has been made from the original Old Russian texts. The accuracy of this translation has been tested using APE (since the ACE texts can be successfully mapped into DRS, the translation is considered to be correct).

Some methodological comments on the above-mentioned operations, namely, the use of ACE for the representation of the contents of medieval documents, should be made. When performing such operations, one of the major methodological problems is a question about the applicability of the controlled natural languages to the purposes of the representation of original texts on the Web, since any translation to a certain extent alters the sense of the texts.

Actually, in this case ACE texts can be viewed as a mode of representation of the meta-information, i.e. researcher's interpretation of the meaning of the documents that is expressed in ACE. It can be also argued that rendering original texts into ACE does not substitute them for "surrogates": ACE texts are linked with the diplomatic transcriptions of manuscripts and supplement their original texts with computer processable information.

2.2   Binding together ACE Texts and XML-Markup

For research purposes, it is very important that the ACE texts can be bound up with the XML-markup of the same texts. The following example shows how this operation can be performed. This markup example is mainly based on CEI scheme, which is supplemented with a TEI element <s>...</s> – "sentence" (in TEI the <s> element contains a sentence-like division of a text; it may be used to mark orthographic sentences, or any other segmentation of a text). In addition, the attribute "ACEtext", which contains the translation of a definite fragment of the text into ACE, is also used.

```
<context>
<tei:s xml:id="ch6_s2" ACEtext="The metropolitan of Riga demands
that the prince of  Smolensk knows about a complaint that is
lodged against some inhabitants of Riga by some inhabitants of
Vitebsk. The metropolitan of Riga supposes that the inhabitants
of Vitebsk want to justify their actions to Helmich."> You
<lb n="4"/> should know about that complaint, which the
inhabitants of <placeName>Vitebsk</placeName><lb n="5"/> lodged
against Rigans in order <lb n="6"/> to set themselves right with
<persName>Helmich</persName>. </tei:s>

<tei:s xml:id="ch6_s3" ACEtext="The inhabitants of Vitebsk appeal
to the Prince of Briansk."> And their words were as follows:
<lb n="7"/> they wanted to justify themselves with those words.
</tei:s>

<tei:s xml:id="ch6_s4" ACEtext="The inhabitants of Vitebsk say
that 50 Rigans kill a man and grab 10 berkovets of wax."> And
<supplied>they</supplied> said <lb n="8"/> to <roleName>Prince
of <placeName>Briansk</placeName></roleName> that <lb n="9"/>
50 men had ridden out of <placeName>Riga</placeName>, and killed
a man, <lb n="10"/> and taken 10 <term>berkovets</term> of wax.
</tei:s><lb n="11"/>

<tei:s xml:id="ch6_s5" ACEtext="The metropolitan of Riga says
that the inhabitants of Vitebsk complain on the inhabitants of
Riga unjustly."> And now I, <roleName>Metropolitan</roleName>,
say that those <lb n="12"/> inhabitants of <placeName>Vitebsk
</placeName> unjustly complained on Rigans.</tei:s><lb n="13"/>
...
</context>
```

Listing 1. Fragment of CEI markup of the charter no. 6[1] that contains an additional attribute "ACEtext"

This markup example demonstrates that the ACE texts do not substitute the original texts of historical sources. These texts can be recorded in XML-files either using a simplified mode of transcription, or, if necessary, preserving some principal paleographic features of the originals. It is very important that the integrity of historical sources is preserved in XML-files. The initial markup that

---

[1] A conventional number of the document according to the latest publication [11].

reveals semantic and structural fragments of the texts, as well as paleographic features (e.g., line brakes in the manuscripts) is also preserved.

Thus, the additional attributes, which contain the ACE texts, supplement the traditional XML-markup with the meta-information. Actually, it means that such a markup integrates the texts of the documents into two different, however – at the same time – closely interconnected systems of semantic links. On the one side, there are the links that are predetermined by the set of CEI/TEI elements. On the other side, there are diverse, spontaneous, infinite links within the complex of medieval historical sources that are rendered into ACE.

2.3   Potentialities and Possibilities Offered by ACE Reasoner

The perspectives of using ACE as a tool for the representation of the contents of historical sources on the Semantic Web are closely connected with the possibilities to make a logic inference from ACE texts. For these purposes, a special attention should be devoted to ACE Reasoner – RACE [6].

ACE Reasoner RACE is a SOAP-based Web-service, which can run in 3 modes, namely:

– as a checker of consistency of a set of axioms,
– as a theorem prover,
– and as a question answering system.

The last mode – the question answering mode – is the most promising one for the purposes of semantic publishing.

The access to RACE can be gained by means of a query from a SOAP client (e.g., PHP script). However, the user interface on the ACE site can also provide possibility to use this tool.

The following simple example demonstrates, how does ACE Reasoner work: on the Fig. 1, there is the ACE Reasoner user interface. In the window "Axioms", there are 3 axioms recorded in ACE; in the field "Query", there is a researcher's question.

The second and the third axioms ("The metropolitan of Riga is an issuer of Charter_6" and "Charter_6 mentions Helmich") are actually the facts about charter no. 6, which are recorded in ACE. It is noteworthy that the first axiom should represent a part of a definite domain ontology, which establishes the rules that determine automatic logical inference. In this particularly case, on the basis of the first axiom – "if X is an issuer of Y then Y mentions X and X sends Y" – ACE Reasoner draws the following inference: "Charter_6 mentions the metropolitan of Riga and the metropolitan of Riga sends Charter_6". The combination of the first part of this inference ("Charter_6 mentions the metropolitan of Riga") with the third axiom ("Charter_6 mentions Helmich") makes it possible for ACE Reasoner to draw the conclusion that the metropolitan of Riga and Helmich are mentioned in charter no. 6.

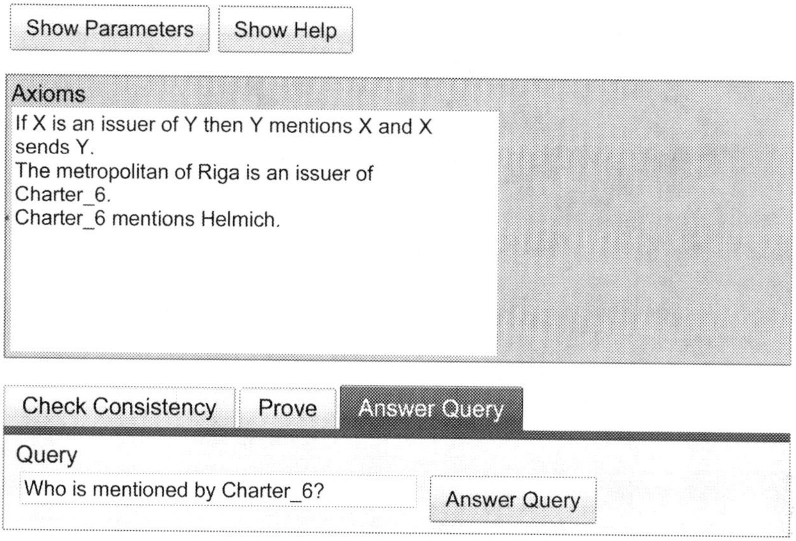

Show Parameters   Show Help

Axioms

If X is an issuer of Y then Y mentions X and X
sends Y.
The metropolitan of Riga is an issuer of
Charter_6.
Charter_6 mentions Helmich.

Check Consistency   Prove   Answer Query

Query

Who is mentioned by Charter_6?   Answer Query

Fig. 1. User interface of ACE Reasoner (http://attempto.ifi.uzh.ch/race/)

In this case, ACE Reasoner has made the inference in 0.05 seconds. All in all, it has provided three answers:

1. who = Helmich,
2. who = (at least 1) issuer,
3. who = (at least 1) metropolitan.

All of the above-mentioned answers are quite correct. The "issuer" is indirectly mentioned in the text of the charter: the issuer of the missive was the metropolitan (archbishop) of Riga. Unfortunately, the reasoner cannot automatically exclude answers, which are trivial and uninformative for researchers. Nevertheless, we hope that the post-processing of answers might make it possible to select the informative statements.

3   Representation of the Information of Historical Sources by Means of ACE

3.1   Representation of Semantic Links between the Charters within the Complex of Interconnected Historical Sources

The aforementioned querying and answering example shows that not only the texts of historical sources, but also the so-called "facts about the texts" (i.e. information related to the documents) can be recorded in ACE and processed using ACE Reasoner. The "facts about the texts" reflect, first and foremost, semantic interconnections between historical sources within a definite complex.[2] The facts about charter no. 6 recorded in ACE are as follows (these statements reflect the results of the research work performed by historians):

- Charter_6 mentions Charter_3a.
- Charter_6 mentions Charter_4 likely.
- The metropolitan of Riga is an issuer of Charter_6.
- The prince of Smolensk is an addressee of Charter_6.
- The governor of Smolensk is a recipient of Charter_6.
- Charter_6 mentions the prince of Bryansk.
- Charter_6 mentions Helmich.
- Charter_3a incorporates Charter_1.
- Charter_4 confirms Charter_3a.
- Charter_4 mentions Helmich.
- Charter_5 mentions Grigorii.
- Charter_4 mentions Artemii.
- Grigorii is the governor of Smolensk likely.
- Artemii is the governor of Smolensk likely.

When recording the "facts about the texts" in ACE a researcher should take into consideration that RACE Web Service uses a restricted set of nouns, verbs, adjectives, and adverbs. In order to change or supplement the vocabulary with additional words, ACE Reasoner should be modified; at the present stage of our research, it has not been done.

It is desirable that ACE Reasoner could make logic inference automatically on the basis of the above-mentioned set of the facts that describe the semantic links between charter no. 6 and other historical records of the complex. In this case, the automatic logic inference does not pose serious problems. It means that in perspective large amounts of facts related to historical sources, which should be entered and processed manually in the course of production of semantic publications on the basis of, e.g., Semantic MediaWiki [27], can be entered and processed automatically due to the opportunities offered by ACE.

Some additional examples can be provided to test this thesis. For instance, we can put a query in order to find out, what objects are mentioned in the charters. Within the set of the "facts about the texts" shown before, there can be selected the facts related either to persons, or to other charters. As a result, only four facts can be mentioned:

- Charter_6 mentions Charter_4 likely.
- Charter_6 mentions Charter_3a.

---

[2] Semantic publications should be based on "natural" (historical) complexes of interconnected historical sources. Such complexes represent integral parts of definite systems that documents form in the course of performing their initial functions. The main features of a natural complex of historical records are as follows: common origin (provenance) of the documents that belong to the complex, close historical interconnections between the components of the complex, and hierarchical disposition within the system. Any complex of sources comes into existence spontaneously.

– Charter_6 mentions Helmich.
– Charter_4 mentions Helmich.

Based on this set of the facts, the answer to the question "What does Charter_6 mention?" will be as follows: Charter_4, Charter_3a, Helmich.

In order to get to know, what objects are presumably (according to the researcher's interpretation; it is expressed by the adverb "likely") mentioned in charter no. 6; the question is to be changed and formulated as follows: "What does Charter_6 mention likely?" However, since ACE is based on the "open world assumption", the answer to the question "What does not Charter_6 mention likely?" cannot be given, because within ACE the set of the objects has no limits. That is why, for the purposes of the differentiation between the exact facts and the hypothetical ones, not only the adverb "likely", but also the adverb "exactly" should be used for the formulation of axioms.

To differentiate the persons from the documents (i.e. other charters of the complex) additional axioms are needed. These axioms do not represent the facts about charter no. 6; they represent domain ontology knowledge:

– Charter_4 is a document.
– Charter_3a is a document.
– Helmich is a person.

It is noteworthy that in this case we cannot receive an answer to the question "Which documents does Charter_6 mention?" It should be noted that this question is formulated according to ACE construction rules; however, this question refers to the set of documents on the whole, not to definite documents mentioned in the charter's text. The correct question can be formulated as follows: "What is a document that Charter_6 mentions?" The reasoner gives the following answer: Charter_4, Charter_3a.

Within the set of the "facts about the texts" only some references to persons and other charters are expressed by the verb "to mention", e.g., the fact "The prince of Smolensk is an addressee of Charter_6" supposedly means that "Charter_6 mentions the prince of Smolensk". This rule can be recorded as a domain ontology axiom: "If X is an addressee of Y then Y mentions X likely". Based on this axiom supplemented with the axiom that "The prince of Smolensk is a person", the answer to the question "What is a person that Charter_6 mentions?" will be as follows: "Helmich, the prince of Smolensk". Actually, there are two answers; both of them are correct.

The aforementioned examples testify that ACE is an appropriate tool useful for logic inference that is based on the sets of statements, which reveal interconnections between historical sources within a definite semantic network. Therefore, ACE can be employed for the purposes of creation of such networks. At the same time, the question, whether ACE tools can make a consistent logical inference from the texts as such, remains, since these texts are not as simple as the sentences mentioned before. Some potential possibilities of ACE in this sphere are discussed in the following section.

3.2   Representation of the Contents of the Charters

Processing the full texts of historical records, there have emerged some serious problems: the reasoner has failed to make logical inference from the statements that represent the full texts of the charters (despite the fact that the translation has been made correctly observing ACE construction rules). For instance, APE and RACE consistency checker have stated that the sentence "The metropolitan of Riga says that the inhabitants of Vitebsk complain on the inhabitants of Riga unjustly" is correctly constructed and provides a consistent statement. Meanwhile, ACE Reasoner has not provided a definite answer to the following question: "What does the metropolitan say?" We have received the following answer: "Query cannot be answered from axioms".

This problem definitely reflects the present-day level of the development of ACE Reasoner. RACE employs a great number of axioms that are recorded by means of Prolog language; these axioms establish different rules for sentence processing. Obviously, the existing set of the axioms is not sufficient to process the queries to complex sentences (such as, e.g., "Somebody says that...". We hope that in the future this problem will be solved; and the declaration that the new knowledge about historical sources (namely, new facts and hypotheses) can be acquired by means of automatic inference will be implemented to the full.

At present, only some fragments of the texts allow automatic logic inferring related to the contents of the documents. In this case, these fragments should be very simple. For instance, the shortest sentence in charter no. 6 is: "The inhabitants of Vitebsk appeal to the prince of Bryansk". The following questions can be asked about this sentence:

 - Who appeals to the prince?
 - Who appeals to somebody?
 - Who do the inhabitants appeal to?
 - Who does somebody appeal to?

Direct representation of the sense of historical sources within a semantic network using ACE calls for specially formulated inference rules that might make it possible to extract the "facts about the texts" from the texts (sentences) automatically. For instance, the inference rule "If X blesses somebody then X is an issuer" should be established to make automatic inference from the sentence that represents the so-called protocol (i.e. the beginning) of charter no. 6: "The metropolitan of Riga blesses the prince of Smolensk and the children of the prince of Smolensk...". In this case, as a result of the automatic logical inference, the reasoner provides a correct answer to the following question: "Who is an issuer?" The answer is: "The metropolitan of Riga", so it can be reformulated as a fact: "The metropolitan of Riga is an issuer of Charter_6". This new ("synthesized") fact about the text might be used in other queries.

One more example can be provided. The sense of the sentence "There is an agreement that is concluded by Riga and Smolensk" is quite understandable for a human: in this sentence, the author directly refers to another charter. However, two additional axioms are needed to make this fact understandable for a computer: "Every agreement is a document. If there is a document X then charter mentions X". Due to these axioms, the computer can give definite answers to the following questions: "Is there something that charter mentions?" and "What is a document that charter mentions?"

Unfortunately, the reasoner cannot process complex sentences. However, a "palliative" solution might be proposed for this problem. The texts of historical sources recorded in ACE can be simplified or fragmentized in order to process them using ACE Reasoner. Thus, the abovementioned sentence "The metropolitan of Riga says that the inhabitants of Vitebsk complain on the inhabitants of Riga unjustly" can be replaced by its simplified version: "The inhabitants of Vitebsk complain on the inhabitants of Riga unjustly". In this case, the following question can be posed: "What is a city whose inhabitants complain on somebody?"

It is clear that such simplified sentences alter the meaning of historical sources causing heavy losses of information. However, we can argue that even such mode of the simplified representation of the contents of historical sources can be conducive for historical research, and especially for analytical operations.

One more possible solution for the problem is the complication of the markup:

```
<tei:s xml:id="ch6_s5"><ACEText>The metropolitan of Riga says that
<idea xml:id="ch6_s5_i1" author= "metropolitan">the inhabitants of
Vitebsk complain on the inhabitants of Riga unjustly.</idea>
</ACEText>
<InitialText>And now I, <roleName> Metropolitan </roleName>, say
that those <lb n="12"/> inhabitants of <placeName> Vitebsk
</placeName> unjustly complained on Rigans.</InitialText></tei:s>
<lb n="13"/>
<tei:s xml:id="ch6_s6"><ACEText>The metropolitan of Riga knows
that <idea xml:id="ch6_s6_i1" author= "metropolitan">the
inhabitants of Riga are not guilty.</idea>
<InitialText> And now I know that Rigans <lb n="14"/> are not
guilty of that.</InitialText></tei:s>
```

Listing 2. Fragment of CEI markup of charter no. 6 with additional elements <ACEText> and <idea>

This markup is based on the CEI markup scheme. Sentences rendered in ACE are included into the elements <ACEText>. In order to markup the parts of the sentences that express opinions, thoughts, or words of the issuer – metropolitan of Riga, there can be used a special element <idea>, which has the attribute "author". In this case, the program that extracts the sentences in ACE from the XML-file and load them into ACE Reasoner can distinguish the attitudes of the person from the factual statements and process them separately.

4   Conclusion

In the paper, the possibilities of using controlled natural languages for the representation of the contents of historical sources in the semantic publications have been discussed. The authors have proposed an innovative approach to the creation of additional semantic layers in such publications by means of combining original texts of historical sources with their translations into Attempto Controlled English. The case study of applicability of ACE to the purposes of the representation of the contents of an Old Russian charter conducted by the authors has proved that ACE is an appropriate tool that can be used to record the so-called "facts about the texts". These facts form a basis for performing automatic logical inference and question answering. All in all, the potentialities of ACE revealed in the paper offer an opportunity to create software modules that might perform the functions of "intellectual assistants" to the researchers who use semantic publications of historical sources.

The paper also shows that at present the full texts of historical sources are too difficult for processing them using, e.g., ACE Reasoner. However, the fragmentation or simplification of such texts can, to a certain extent, solve the problem. It means that an in-depth research should be made in this field in order to choose an appropriate way of modification of the texts of historical sources so as to avoid drastic changes of the sense of the texts and, at the same time, to make the modified texts suitable for automatic processing.

It is beyond all doubt that the representation of the sense of historical sources by means of the controlled natural languages is a very promising trend in the development of the technologies of semantic publications that fully corresponds with the purposes of the Semantic Web paradigm adaptation for historical knowledge representation.

References

1. Ahonen, E., Hyvönen, E.: Publishing Historical Texts on the Semantic Web - A Case Study. In: IEEE International Conference on Semantic Computing, Berkeley CA, pp. 167–173 (2009)
2. Baruzzo, A., Casoto, P., Challapalli, P., Dattolo, A., Pudota, N., Tasso, C.: Toward Semantic Digital Libraries. Exploiting Web 2.0 and Semantic Services in Cultural Heritage. Journal of Digital Information 10(6) (2009)
3. Clark, P., Harrison, P., Jenkins, T., Thompson, J., Wojcik, R.: Acquiring and Using World Knowledge Using a Restricted Subset of English. In: The 18th International FLAIRS Conference (2005)
4. de Coi, J.L., Fuchs, N.E., Kaljurand, K., Kuhn, T.: Controlled English for Reasoning on the Semantic Web. In: Bry, F., Małuszyński, J. (eds.) Semantic Techniques for the Web. LNCS, vol. 5500, pp. 276–308. Springer, Heidelberg (2009)
5. Doerr, M., Kritsotaki, A.: Documenting Events in Metadata. In: International Symposium on Virtual Reality, Archaeology and Cultural Heritage (2006)
6. Fuchs, N.E.: First-Order Reasoning for Attempto Controlled English. In: Rosner, M., Fuchs, N.E. (eds.) CNL 2010. LNCS, vol. 7175, pp. 73–94. Springer, Heidelberg (2012)
7. García-Castro, L.J., Giraldo, O., García, A.: Using Annotations to Model Discourse. An Extension to the Annotation Ontology. In: Workshop on Semantic Publishing, Crete, pp. 13–22 (2012)

8. Groza, T., Handschuh, S., Möller, K., Decker, S.: SALT - Semantically Annotated LaTeX for Scientific Publications. In: Franconi, E., Kifer, M., May, W. (eds.) ESWC 2007. LNCS, vol. 4519, pp. 518–532. Springer, Heidelberg (2007)

9. Ide, N., Woolner, D.: Historical Ontologies. In: Words and Intelligence II. Essays in Honor of Yorick Wilks, pp. 137–152. Springer, Dordrecht (2007)

10. Ivanov, A.: Moscowitica - Ruthenica in the Latvian State Historical Archives. Ancient Russia 3, 47–54, 4, 94–106 (2004) (in Russian)

11. Ivanov, A., Kuznetsov, A.: Smolensk and Riga Charters. In: 13th - First Half of the 14th Century: Documents of the Complex Moscowitica-Ruthenica about the Relations between Smolensk and Riga. Latvian State Historical Archives, Riga (2009) (in Russian)

12. Ivanovs, A., Varfolomeyev, A.: Editing and Exploratory Analysis of Medieval Documents by Means of XML Technologies. The Case of the Documentary Source Complex Moscowitica-Ruthenica. In: International Conference of the Association for History and Computing, Amsterdam, pp. 155–160 (2005)

13. Ivanovs, A., Varfolomeyev, A.: Semantic Publications of Charter Corpora (The Case of a Diplomatic Edition of the Complex of Old Russian Charters Moscowitica - Ruthenica). In: International Conference Digital Diplomatics: Tools for the Digital Diplomatist, Naples, pp. 36–40 (2011)

14. Kamp, H., Reyle, U.: From Discourse to Logic. Introduction to Modeltheoretic Semantics of Natural Language, Formal Logic and Discourse Representation Theory. Kluwer Academic Publishers, Dordrecht (1993)

15. Krötzsch, M., Vrandecic, D., Völkel, M., Haller, H., Studer, R.: Semantic Wikipedia. Journal of Web Semantics 5(4), 251–261 (2007)

16. Kuhn, T.: A Survey and Classification of Controlled Natural Languages. In: Computational Linguistic, pp. 1–91 (to appear, 2013)

17. Marcondes, C.H.: A Semantic Model for Scholarly Electronic Publishing. In: Workshop on Semantic Publishing, Crete, pp. 47–58 (2011)

18. Meroño-Peñuela, A., Ashkpour, A., Rietveld, L., Hoekstra, R., Schlobach, S.: Linked Humanities Data: The Next Frontier? A Case-study in Historical Census Data. In: International Workshop on Linked Science 2012 - Tackling Big Data, Boston MA (2012)

19. Mirzaee, V., Iverson, L., Hamidzadeh, B.: Computational Representation of Semantics in Historical Documents. In: International Conference of the Association for History and Computing, Amsterdam, pp. 199–206 (2005)

20. Pease, A., Murray, W.: An English to Logic Translator for Ontology-Based Knowledge Representation Languages. In: IEEE International Conference on Natural Language Processing and Knowledge Engineering, Beijing, pp. 777–783 (2003)

21. Schmidt, D.: The Role of Markup in the Digital Humanities. Historical Social Research 37(3), 125–146 (2012)

22. Schwitter, R.: Processing Coordinated Structures in PENG Light. In: Wang, D., Reynolds, M. (eds.) AI 2011. LNCS, vol. 7106, pp. 658–667. Springer, Heidelberg (2011)

23. Shotton, D.: Semantic Publishing. The Coming Revolution in Scientific Journal Publishing. Learned Publishing 22(2), 85–94 (2009)

24. Shotton, D., Portwin, K., Klyne, G., Miles, A.: Adventures in Semantic Publishing. Exemplar Semantic Enhancements of a Research Article. PLoS Computational Biology 5(4) (2009)

25. Varfolomeyev, A., Ivanov, A.: Structural and Semantic Models of Historical Sources. Information Bulletin of the Association for History and Computing (A Special Issue) 37, 25–31 (2011) (in Russian)

26. Varfolomeyev, A., Ivanov, A.: Computer-based Source Studies. Semantic Linkage of Information in Representation and Criticism of Historical Records. Petrozavodsk State University, Petrozavodsk (2013) (in Russian)
27. Varfolomeyev, A., Ivanovs, A.: Wiki Technologies for Semantic Publication of Old Russian Charters. In: Meister, J.C. (ed.) Digital Humanities 2012, pp. 405–407. Hamburg University Press, Hamburg (2012)
28. de Waard, A.: From Proteins to Fairytales. Directions in Semantic Publishing. IEEE Intelligent Systems 25(2), 83–88 (2010)
29. The Attempto Project, http://attempto.ifi.uzh.ch
30. Charters Encoding Initiative, http://www.cei.lmu.de
31. Text Encoding Initiative, http://www.tei-c.org

Ontology Merging
in the Context of a Semantic Web Expert System

Olegs Verhodubs and Janis Grundspenkis

Riga Technical University, Riga, Latvia
Oleg.Verhodub@inbox.lv, Janis.Grundspenkis@rtu.lv

Abstract. The purpose of this paper is to describe the process of OWL ontology merging and member function assignment for ontology elements. Ontology merging and member function assignment are necessary for constructing a Semantic Web Expert System (SWES) knowledge base. We use the acronym SWES to refer to expert systems which are capable of processing OWL ontologies from the Web with the purpose to supplement or even to develop their knowledge base. To our knowledge, the tasks of ontology merging and member function assignment for SWES have not yet been investigated.

Keywords: Ontology Merging, Semantic Web, Expert Systems.

1   Introduction

The technological development of the World Wide Web has led to the appearance of new Semantic Web technologies that took up the challenge of the increasing volume of information in the Web. The Semantic Web and Semantic Web technologies offer a new approach to managing information and processes, the fundamental principle of which is the creation and use of semantic metadata [1]. Semantic metadata contrasts with today's Web, which is encoded in HTML (HyperText Markup Language) and which purely describes the format in which the information should be presented [1]. Semantic metadata give an opportunity to organize, find and use information based on meaning, not just text [1].

In this paper we will overview different types of ontology combination, we will choose the most appropriate one for SWES and we will describe it in details. These are the main purposes of this paper. It is important to inscribe the process of ontology combination in the whole process of knowledge base filling therefore we will develop the structure of SWES knowledge base, because combined ontology is the part of SWES knowledge base. The final goal of the research is to develop SWES. SWES is a new expert system, which will use semantic metadata (ontologies) from the Web to extract rules and to supplement its knowledge base in automatic mode. Combined ontology consists of several ontologies of one domain, and it is the basic part of SWES knowledge base. This combined ontology is used by Jena semantic reasoner to infer new knowledge according to a user request. So, the main purpose of SWES is to solve problems by means of reasoning on knowledge, obtained from the Web.

P. Klinov and D. Mouromtsev (Eds.): KESW 2013, CCIS 394, pp. 191–201, 2013.
© Springer-Verlag Berlin Heidelberg 2013

There are several types of ontology combination. They are ontology alignment, ontology integration, ontology merging and ontology mapping [1]. This paper explains that ontology merging is the most appropriate type of ontology combination for SWES and describes the process of ontology merging including member function assignment for ontology elements. The paper also presents the structure of SWES knowledge base, which is the place, where the combined ontology is stored.

The paper is organized as follows. The next section gives an overview of related work. Section III presents the main idea of SWES, describes the structure of its knowledge base and also shows the process of SWES knowledge base development. Section IV reflects ontology merging in the context of the Semantic Web Expert System. And finally conclusion is presented.

2   Related Work

The use of semantic metadata is crucial for information integration [1] that is why there are a lot of information sources on the topics of information integration (combination) and the use of semantic metadata. It is necessary to give an overview of these information sources for the purpose of choosing the most appropriate type of information combination for development of SWES. Let us scrutinize some information sources on this topic.

In [1] there are raised many relevant issues related to the Semantic Web Technologies. They are knowledge discovery for ontology construction, ontology evolution, reasoning with inconsistent ontologies, ontology engineering methodologies, the semantic web services and so on. That is this information source is rather complete and contains sufficient amount of information to familiarize with the main trends in the area of the Semantic Web. The book has special section, which is dedicated to ontology mapping, merging and aligning, too. This section contains comprehensive information, including definitions, explanations and references to the other information sources about ontology mapping, merging and aligning. This book is the main information source, which provides an opportunity to understand the different kinds of ontology combining and then to choose the most appropriate for SWES. However [1] does not define the concept of ontology integration.

In paper [2] there is also a brief survey of the approaches to semantic combination: ontology mapping, ontology alignment and ontology merging. In addition, this paper presents ontology integration as a separate ontology combining approach.

The purpose of ontology combining is to get a single ontology, which can be used to generate rules and to put this combined ontology with generated rules into the Jena semantic reasoner. This will provide new knowledge, based on user's request. In general there are several types of ontology combining, and it is necessary to overview all of them to choose the most appropriate one for SWES. These ontology combining types are ontology merging, ontology alignment, ontology integration and ontology mapping [2]. Ontology merging is the process of a new ontology creation, which is the union of the source ontologies [1]. The original ontologies have similar or overlapping domains but they are unique and not revisions of the same ontology [2].

Ontology alignment is the process of discovering similarities between two source ontologies [1]. The result of a matching operation is a specification of similarities between two ontologies [1]. That is, the task of ontology alignment is creating links between two original ontologies [2]. Ontology alignment is made when they usually have complementary domains [2]. Ontology integration is the process of generating a single ontology in one subject from two or more different ontologies in different subjects [2]. The different subjects of the different ontologies may be related [2]. An ontology mapping is a specification of the semantic overlap between two ontologies; it is the output of the mapping process [1].

In case of SWES, it is necessary to use the ontology merging because as a result we need to get such an ontology that is produced from original ontologies, which have similar or overlapping domain, which is defined by the user. Furthermore we need to get a single ontology that may be used for generating rules and may be put into an inference engine. Nowadays there are such ontology merging semiautomatic algorithms as OntoMerge or PROMPT [1]. But they are not suitable for use in SWES even because they are semiautomatic. SWES needs a fully automatic routine; otherwise the process of acquiring knowledge from SWES will take a long time. Possible fully automatic ontology merging algorithms are not suitable for use in SWES because they do not execute membership function assignment for the combined ontology elements. In addition existing semiautomatic and possible fully automatic algorithms are not aimed at further rules generation for SWES. These algorithms are created for the qualitative ontology merging generally. However it is rather costly in terms of memory and execution time. This means that it is necessary for SWES to merge the only ontology elements, which can be used for rule generation and the other elements are not necessary to be merged.

3   Knowledge Base of SWES

The concept of SWES is based on the idea that it is an expert system, which uses the Semantic Web technologies and its structure is similar to the structure of the typical expert systems [3]. Knowledge base is a key part of any expert system including SWES. It is necessary to describe the functioning of SWES, in order to develop the structure of SWES knowledge base. Operation of SWES is the following. It starts to work after receiving a request from the user. After that, SWES looks for corresponding OWL ontologies in the Web. The structure of a user's request as well as ontology search in the Web are out of the paper's scope, but these tasks will be described in future papers. Being found, ontologies are stored in SWES knowledge base. It is important that found ontologies are ready for further use that is the task of looking for more authoritative ontologies in the Web is a subproblem of the task of ontology search in the Web, and it will be discussed in the next papers, too. So, found and authorative ontologies are used to merge these found ontologies into a single ontology, and then the merged ontology is used to extract rules. Both merged ontology and extracted rules are supplied for the Jena semantic reasoner. The process of rule extraction is divided into two subprocesses. First, rules are extracted from the merged ontology and they are written into the concept map in abstract form; second, the rules from the concept map are recoded in the format of Jena rules. This is necessary to make it better for transformation to use different semantic reasoners if it would be necessary [4]. Taking all this into account, knowledge base of SWES should have:

- storage for several OWL ontologies of desired domain;
- storage for the merged ontology;
- storage for the concept map [4];
- storage for the rules in the Jena rule format.

In addition the following routines are required for SWES knowledge base:

- Rule generation routine from OWL ontology to the concept map;
- Ontology merging routine;
- Translation routine from the concept map to the Jena rule format.

Before showing the SWES knowledge base, it is necessary to notice that rule generation routine starts only when the ontology merging routine terminates and the one, merged ontology is formed. The ontology merging routine starts when OWL ontology repository is filled with ontologies of a particular subject area, where the number of ontologies in the OWL ontology repository is defined by the corresponding value and a particular subject area is defined by the user. Thus, SWES knowledge base looks like as follows (Fig. 1):

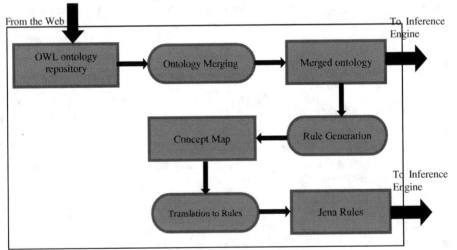

Fig. 1. The SWES Knowledge Base

It is necessary to mention that all parts of SWES knowledge base (OWL ontology repository, storage for merged ontology, concept map and storage for rules in Jena rule format) are empty at the beginning of SWES functioning. After receiving a request from the user, ontology searching function starts. The task of this function is to look for OWL ontologies in the Web, which are corresponded to a user request. Merged ontology and rules in Jena format enter the Jena semantic reasoner to infer new knowledge. Describing the function of ontology searching in the Web and the process of new knowledge inference are out of scope of this paper.

The task of rule generation from OWL ontology had already been implemented in theory and in practice. This was described in papers [5] and [4]. The task of rule transformation from coded form in the concept map to the rule form, used in Jena inference engine, is implemented in Java programming language, too. So, it is necessary to investigate ontology searching in the Web and the process of new knowledge inference to implement SWES.

4   Ontology Merging for SWES

So, ontology merging is the most appropriate type of ontology combination as is shown in Section 2. Merging of two ontologies is described here. For more qualitative work SWES needs to merge several ontologies, but not only two ontologies (although it will work with only two ontologies, too). This makes the task more complicated but at the same time it will improve the quality of future SWES work. Another question that may arise in connection with merging ontologies is redundancy of data. This question may occur while merging similar ontologies because similar ontologies have similar concepts, relations and properties. For instance, there are two relations in two different ontologies (Fig. 2):

Fig. 2. Similar relations in two different ontologies

It is clear for humans that these relations express the same meaning (Fig. 2). In terms of efficiency it would be wise to keep only one relation during ontology merging. But this redundancy may be very useful because, keeping both relations, SWES will be able to respond to two requests instead of one. Thus, it is possible to work out the following rule for merging ontologies: if concepts or relations in different ontologies are identical, then to keep only one copy of these concepts or relations in merged ontology. On the contrary if concepts or relations in different ontologies are synonymic, but not identical, then it is necessary to keep all of them in merged ontology. This is what should be done with our example in Fig. 2.

The fundamental question during the process of ontology merging is how to deal with uncertainty. Uncertainty emerges because of knowledge incompleteness in one particular ontology. It is possible to use fuzzy sets to cope with the problem of knowledge incompleteness. For this purpose membership functions assign to ontology components (concepts, relations). The principles of ontology merging and membership function assignment are as follows:

- Ontologies to be merged are considered to be defined in the same domain;
- Merging of two OWL ontologies is shown for simplification;
- Ontologies to be merged are not identical; otherwise, ontology merging is not performed;
- Assigning of membership functions occurs in the process of ontology merging;
- Membership functions are necessary only for further use in generated rules from OWL ontologies [5].

Let us describe the process of membership function assignment for ontology parts. The first case of membership function assignment in the process of ontology merging is merging of concepts with properties from different ontologies (Fig. 3):

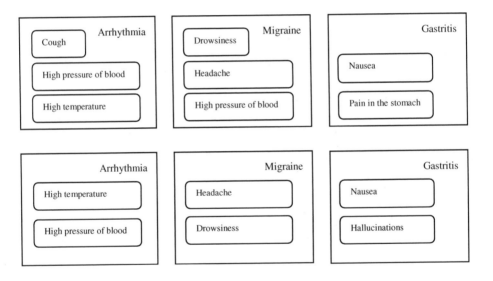

Fig. 3. Three concepts of O1 and O2 ontologies

Values of membership functions (μ) for the first case (Fig. 3) are the following:

$\mu_{Arrhythmia}$(High temperature) $= \frac{2}{2} = 1$; $\mu_{Arrhythmia}$(High pressure of blood) $= \frac{2}{2} = 1$; $\mu_{Arrhythmia}$(Cough) $= \frac{1}{2} = 0.5$;

$\mu_{Migraine}$(High pressure of blood) $= \frac{1}{2} = 0.5$; $\mu_{Migraine}$(Headache) $= \frac{2}{2} = 1$; $\mu_{Migraine}$(Drowsiness) $= \frac{2}{2} = 1$;

$\mu_{Gastritis}(\text{Nausea}) = \frac{2}{2} = 1$; $\mu_{Gastritis}(\text{Pain in stomach}) = \frac{1}{2} = 0.5$; $\mu_{Gastritis}(\text{Hallucinations})$
$= \frac{1}{2} = 0.5$;

It is possible to generate the following rules with member functions [6]:

IF High temperature ($\mu=1$) **AND** High pressure ($\mu=1$) **AND** Cough ($\mu=0.5$)
THEN Arrhythmia, $\mu_{Arrhythmia} = \text{MIN}(1,1,0.5)=0.5$

IF High pressure ($\mu=0.5$) **AND** Headache ($\mu=1$) **AND** Drowsiness ($\mu=1$) **THEN**
Migraine, $\mu_{Migraine} = \text{MIN}(0.5,1,1)=0.5$

IF Nausea ($\mu=1$) **AND** Pain in the stomach ($\mu=0.5$) **AND** Hallucinations ($\mu=0.5$)
THEN Gastritis, $\mu_{Gastritis} = \text{MIN}(1,0.5,1)=0.5$

The second case of membership function assignment in the process of ontology
merging is merging of equivalent concepts (equivalent concepts are defined by means
of two OWL axioms: equivalentClass and sameAs) from different ontologies. In Fig.
4 there are two equivalent concepts „Car" and „Automobile" in one ontology O1.
Concepts „Car" and „Automobile" of another ontology O2 are not equivalent.

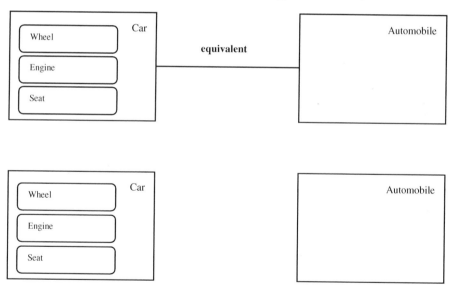

Fig. 4. Equivalent classes in O1 ontology and not equivalent classes in O2 ontology

Value of membership functions (μ) for the second case (Fig. 4) is the following:

$$\mu_{equivalent}(\text{Car, Automobile}) = \frac{1}{2} = 0.5$$

In this case the rule [5]:

IF Automobile **equivalent** Car **THEN** Wheel, Engine, Seat ∈ Automobile,

will have the following values of membership functions (μ):

$$\mu_{equivalent}(Car, Automobile) = \frac{1}{2} = 0.5, \text{ and this means:}$$

μ_{Wheel} (Automobile) = $\mu_{equivalent}$(Car, Automobile) * μ_{Wheel}(Car) = 0.5 * μ_{Wheel}(Car),

μ_{Engine}(Automobile) = $\mu_{equivalent}$(Car, Automobile) * μ_{Engine}(Car) = 0.5 * μ_{Engine}(Car),

μ_{Seat}(Automobile) = $\mu_{equivalent}$(Car, Automobile) * μ_{Seat}(Car) = 0.5 * μ_{Seat}(Car).

So, the rule looks like as follows:

IF Automobile **equivalent** Car **THEN** Wheel(μ_{Wheel}), Engine(μ_{Engine}), Seat(μ_{Seat}) ∈ Automobile.

The third case of membership function assignment in the process of ontology merging is merging of relations from two different ontologies (Fig. 5):

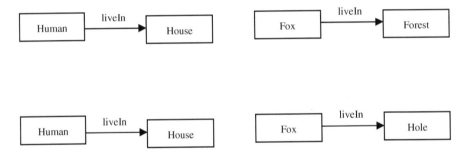

Fig. 5. Relations in O1 ontology and relations in O2 ontology

Values of membership functions (μ) for the third case (Fig. 5) are the following:

μ_{liveIn}(Human, House) = $\frac{2}{2}$ = 1; μ_{liveIn}(Fox, Forest) = $\frac{1}{2}$ = 0.5; μ_{liveIn}(Fox, Hole) = $\frac{1}{2}$ = 0.5

It is possible to generate the following rules [5] with membership functions:

IF Human **THEN** liveIn House (μ=1), that is **IF** h ∈ Human **THEN** h (liveIn House) with μ=1,

IF Fox **THEN** liveIn Forest (μ=0.5), that is **IF** f ∈ Fox **THEN** f (liveIn Forest) with μ=0.5,

IF Fox **THEN** liveIn Hole (μ=0.5), that is **IF** f ∈ Fox **THEN** f (liveIn Hole) with μ=0.5

The fourth case of membership function assignment in the process of ontology merging is merging of „part of" relations from two different ontologies (Fig. 6):

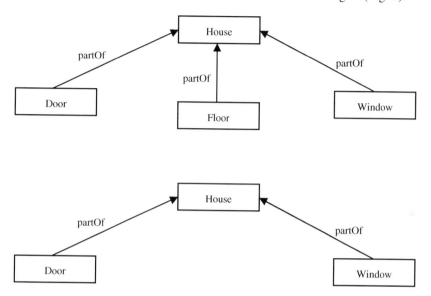

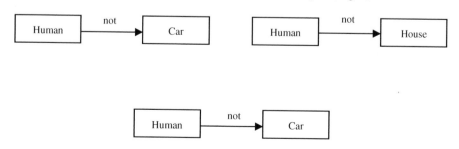

Fig. 6. "Part Of" relations in O1 and O2 ontologies

Values of membership functions (μ) for the fourth case (Fig. 6) are the following:

$\mu_{partOf}(\text{Door, House}) = \frac{2}{2} = 1$; $\mu_{partOf}(\text{Floor, House}) = \frac{1}{2} = 0.5$; $\mu_{partOf}(\text{Window, House}) = \frac{2}{2} = 1$

It is possible to generate the following rule [5] wih membership functions:

IF Door ($\mu=1$) **AND/OR** Floor ($\mu=0.5$) **AND/OR** Window ($\mu=1$) **AND** „part of" **THEN** House, $\mu_{House} = MIN(1,0.5,1)=0.5$

The fifth case of membership function assignment in the process of ontology merging is merging of negation relations from two different ontologies (Fig. 7):

Fig. 7. Negation relations in the ontologies O1 ontology and O2

Values of membership functions (μ) for the fifth case (Fig. 7) are the following:

$$\mu_{not}(\text{Human, Car}) = \frac{2}{2} = 1; \mu_{not}(\text{Human, House}) = \frac{1}{2} = 0.5$$

It is possible to generate the following rule [5] with membership functions:

IF Human **THEN** (not Car) with $\mu = 1$, that is **IF** h $\in$ Human **THEN** h (not Car) with $\mu = 1$;

IF Human **THEN** (not House) with $\mu = 0.5$, **IF** h $\in$ Human **THEN** h (not House) with $\mu = 0.5$;

The ontology merging algorithm consists of the following steps:

```
Step 1: The one OWL ontology is chosen.
Step 2: This ontology is supplemented with missing
concepts from the second ontology.
Step 3: This ontology is supplemented with missing
relations from the second ontology.
Step 4: This ontology is supplemented with missing
properties from the second ontology.
Step 5: The values of membership functions are assigned
to merged ontology elements.
```

It is necessary to mention that the task of ontology merging and membership function assignment is implemented in Java programming language using the Jena framework. However it is too early to write about experimental evaluation of this implementation, because at the realized algorithm of ontology merging values of membership functions are stored as comments (as literals in comments in terms of the Jena framework), but this situation may change. Indeed, membership functions are necessary for reasoning with fuzzy inference engine, but the Jena framework is not such a reasoner and in order to adapt it for fuzzy reasoning membership functions placed in comments may not be appropriate. This problem and its solution will be explained in the next paper.

5   Conclusions

In this paper different types of ontology combination were overviewed. Ontology merging was chosen as the most appropriate ontology combination type for SWES and was described in details. Member function assignment for the merged ontology elements was also shown. The structure of SWES knowledge base was developed, and the order of the process of ontology merging in the whole process of SWES knowledge base filling was presented.

The main result of this research is that the process of ontology merging produces a single ontology, which serves as a resource for extracting of fuzzy rules. These fuzzy rules can be used in the Jena semantic reasoner to infer new knowledge.

It is necessary to solve several tasks to implement SWES. One of these tasks is to create the function of OWL ontology search in the Web. Another task is to adapt the Jena semantic reasoner to work with fuzzy rules, because the Jena reasoner does not work with fuzzy rules by itself. One more task is to put all necessary algorithms together and then to test the whole system, that is, SWES.

References

1. Davis, J., Studer, R., Warren, P.: Semantic Web Technologies Trends and Research in Ontology-based Systems. John Wiley & Sons Ltd., Chichester (2006)
2. Choi, N., Song, I.-Y., Han, H.: A Survey on Ontology Mapping. ACM SIGMOD Record (2006)
3. Verhodubs, O., Grundspenkis, J.: Towards the Semantic Web Expert System. RTU Press, Riga (2011)
4. Verhodubs, O., Grundspenkis, J.: Algorithm of ontology transformation to rules. RTU Press, Riga (2013)
5. Verhodubs, O., Grundspenkis, J.: Evolution of Ontology Potential for Generation of Rules. In: International Conference on Web Intelligence, Mining and Semantics, Craiova (2012)
6. Bai, Y., Wang, D.: Fundamentals of Fuzzy Logic Control – Fuzzy Sets, Fuzzy Rules and Defuzzifications. Springer (2006)

Web 2.0/3.0 Technology in Lexical Ontology Development: English-Russian WordNet 2.0

Sergey Yablonsky

St. Petersburg University,
Volkhovsky Per. 3 St. Petersburg, 199004, Russia
yablonsky.serge@gmail.com, yablonsky@gsom.pu.ru

Abstract. This paper reports on the current results of the development of the English-Russian WordNet 2.0. It describes the usage of English-Russian lexical language resources and software to process English-Russian WordNet 2.0. Aspects of enhancing English-Russian WordNet 2.0 with Linked Open Data information are discussed.

Keywords: WordNet, English-Russian WordNet, Grid, LOD, Semantic Web, RDF, Web 2.0, Web 3.0.

1 Introduction

Web 1.0/2.0/3.0 networks exist and develop in the same physical space of the Internet [1- 3]. This determines the interconnection of methods and tools for extracting information and knowledge from these networks. However, we can distinguish the specificity of each option. Thus, to document network based around Web 1.0 methods to extract linguistic data from untagged text documents or HTML-documents and methods of search documents for keywords and phrases. For Web 2.0 and Web 3.0 along with known new methods of linguistic data and knowledge extraction are beginning to develop rapidly and, in fact, for the last 5-7 years, a new paradigm for extracting data from networks of Web 2.0/3.0 was formed.

Web 3.0 has created standards for semantic annotation and semantic resources connected in a network. In the Web 2.0/3.0 data, a large amount of linguistic and lexical resources in particular have been created. However, there is currently a great diversity of formats for representing these models. As such, the interchange of this data is challenging, requiring many inexact conversion programs leading to the creation of lexical "data silos".

Current work on the Semantic Web has focused on the challenge of using the Web to connect such "data silos" and allows for linking between different data sets [8-11]. The Linking Open Data (LOD) project [4] has aimed to solve these issues by publication of data on the Web using the RDF data model and, most importantly, linking data across sites. The explosion of Web 3.0 technology has led to substantial growth of web-accessible linguistic data in terms of quantity, diversity and complexity [8, 9, 11].

P. Klinov and D. Mouromtsev (Eds.): KESW 2013, CCIS 394, pp. 202–213, 2013.
© Springer-Verlag Berlin Heidelberg 2013

This paper reports about the current results of the English-Russian WordNet 2.0 development. It describes usage of LOD English-Russian lexical language resources to process English-Russian WordNet 2.0. Aspects of enhancing multilingual lexical ontology English-Russian WordNet with Linked Open Data information are discussed. In particular, we discuss how the Linked Open Data was used for creation and publication of English-Russian WordNet 2.0. We talk over in details the creation of English-Russian WordNet 2.0 from Linked Open Data resources WordNet 3.0, DBPedia and Yago2 [14]. Prototype of English-Russian WordNet 2.0 described in this paper is available at http://ru.tendrow.

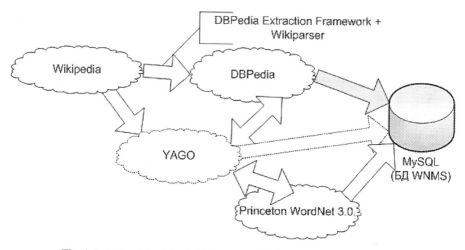

Fig. 1. Relationship of the LOD resources for integration with WordNet

2   WordNets and LOD

Web-compatible representation language framework today is usually based on lexical ontologies. Wordnets are cross-lingual lexical ontologies, including information on hypernyms, synonyms, polysemous terms, relations between terms, and sometimes multilingual equivalents [5, 6]. Wordnets are valuable resources as sources of ontological distinctions. The RDF version of Wordnet 3.0 is included in LOD and distributed by Princeton [http://semanticweb.cs.vu.nl/lod/wn30/].

WordNets provide a conceptual framework for multilingual mappings in ontologies. Linking concepts across many cross-lingual lexicons belonging to the WordNet-family started by using the Interlingual Index (ILI) [6]. Unfortunately, no version of the ILI can be considered a standard and often the various lexicons exploit different versions of WordNet as ILI. At the 3rd GWA Conference in Korea there was launched the idea to start building a WordNet grid around a Common Base Concepts expressed in terms of WordNet synsets and SUMO definitions [7]. This first version of the Grid was planned to be built around the set of 4689 Common Base Concepts. Since then only four languages with essentially various number of synsets and different WordNet (WN) versions were placed in the Grid mappings (English – 4689 synsets with WN 2.0 mapping, Spanish – 15556 synsets with WN 1.6 mapping and Catalan - 12942 synsets with WN1.6 mapping, and Japanese – 57,238 synsets with WN 3.0 mapping). So far there are just only 4 public available multilingual WN Grids in the specified format.

At the same time number of Wordnets in other languages is increasing (http://www.globalwordnet.org/gwa/wordnet_table.html). Thus integration of all these resources through Princeton Wordnet mapping and LOD is important. The current results of the English-Russian WordNet development were reported in [15, 16]. They describe usage of Russian and English-Russian lexical language resources and software to process English-Russian WordNet and English-Russian WordNet Grid (4600 synsets with WN 3.0 mapping) and design of a XML/RDF/OWL-markup of the English-Russian WordNet resources.

3   Enhancing English-Russian WordNet with Linked Open Data

There were such main steps in English-Russian WordNet 2.0 creation:

- All Russian synsets were obtained by automated processing LOD resources DBPedia and YAGO2. YAGO2 has knowledge of more than 10 million entities (like persons, organizations, cities, etc.) and contains more than 80 million facts about these entities. Unlike many other automatically assembled knowledge bases, YAGO2 As it is mentioned in http://www.mpi-inf.mpg.de/yago-naga/yago/ has a confirmed accuracy of 95%.
- For additional evaluation the resulting prototype of English-Russian WordNet 2.0 was loaded into the database editor WordNet of the WNMS project AsianWordNet [12, 13]. WNMS specifies a simplified model assuming the formation of cross-language index (inter lingual index - ILI) based on the values of English words Princeton WordNet 3.0 synsets. WNMS provides a free and public platform for building and sharing among WordNets and was adopted for Russian WordNet.

The relationship of the LOD resources for integration with WordNet is presented in Figure 1.

4   Automated Processing of LOD Resource DBPedia

From the DBPedia the following files of triplets were used:

- labels_ru.nt - as a source of WordNet concepts;
- short_abstract.nt - as a source for interpreting the meaning of the preparation.

Data processing was carried out in several stages:

1. According to the DBPedia formed Russian-English translations of articles and full database WNMS.

2. Mapping development of the English concepts of the DBPedia articles and Princeton WordNet 3.0. lemmas. In determining such conformity articles that had only pseudo- transliterations of English to Russian and articles that make up the category in Wikipedia (removal of ambiguity - homonyms) were excluded.

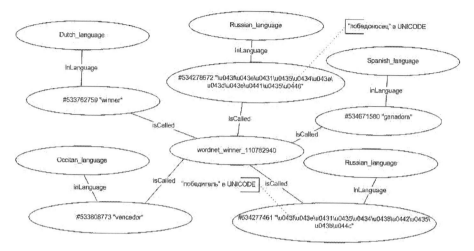

Fig. 2. Translation knowledge relations in Yago2 lexemes

5   Automated Processing of LOD Resource Yago2

The new version of the LOD resource Yago2 (Fall 2011, http://www.mpi-inf.mpg.de/yago-naga/yago/) contains more than 80 million facts about more than 10 million classes and are the result of automated processing of the Wikipedia. Resources are available at Yago2 and are presented in RDF and TSV formats.

We used a set of files in TSV - a text file with the data triplets Yago. In TSV-file format in the first position is always placed a resource identifier, the second - the subject, the third - the object, the predicate is determined by the name of TSV-file. Yago2 represented as 127 such files. Total resources in uncompressed form is over 85 GB.

For forming WordNet synsets from the Yago2 five files were extracted and uploaded in the WNMS database:

- *hasLanguageCode (~ 4 K)*. Directory of languages represented in the project Yago2. Contains the full and short name of the language and its identity;
- *inLanguage (~ 233 MB)* — defines the language of the file, which shows the specified resource in Yago2.
- *hasSynsetId (~ 3.2 MB)*. The file contains data on the compatibility of domestic designations sinseta in Yago2 sinseta identifier in the original lexical file Princeton WordNet 3.0.

- *isCalled (~ 303 MB)*. This file contains information about resources Yago2, presented in different languages. The text is written in the encoding UCS / UNICODE.
- *means (~ 368 MB)*. Contains the synonyms in the Yago2 data. Definition of synonymy is fully consistent semantics sinseta WordNet. Relationships between resources are set as presented in one language, and between the resources presented in different languages.

To determine the dependencies and build synsets 26454847 facts were uploaded.

6   English-Russian WordNet 2.0 Upload and Presentation in WNMS Editor

The opportunity to navigate through nodes and relationships defined in the Princeton WordNet in the WNMS is shown in Fig. 3. It shows an example of the DBPedia synset [St Petersburg, Leningrad, Peterburg, Petrograd, Saint Petersburg] visualization.

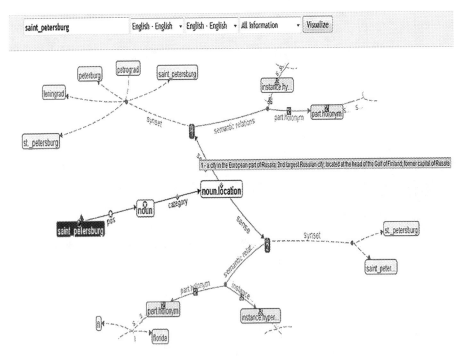

Fig. 3. Visualizing the result of translation in the editor WNMS

We use the rating system of WNMS for determining the degree of compliance. In Figure 4 for Lemma "Leningrad" this estimates - 80 (maximum for 2 options, which means that the lemma is not included in other synset), while Lemma "St. Petersburg" rating 60 (there is another synset, of which this lemma is included - there is a value that defines the city of St. Petersburg in the U.S.). A lower score indicates that the lemma is part of the more than 2 synsets.

In the first variant of translation the degree of compliance for all extracted synsets is set to 100.

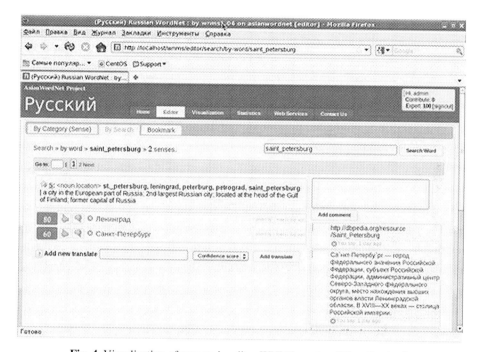

Fig. 4. Visualization of synsets in editor WNMS section "Visualization"

Figure 5 provides statistics to the WordNet part of speech and and categorizes distribution for the first variant, in Figure 6 - for the second variant. We will use in the future work the 2nd variant, as more complete.

The collaborative WNMS framework tools help our team to evaluate the result in a team with several exteral experts (Fig. 8). To assess the completeness and quality of the automated construction of English-Russian WordNet 2.0 we use a simplified synset rating scale for each translation in WNMS. The quality of each translation is assessed on a scale from 20 to 100 by the following rules:

- 100 points was the highest translation quality rate (received for personal high quality translation editing by expert). Since the Yago2 project results are declared as close to the results of the experts (according to Yago2 description - significantly more than 90%) they usually receive 90-100 points.
- 80 points (some time even 100 points after expert confirmation) was given to the unique synset translations, found in the Princeton WordNet. In fact, it refers to the situation when a word has one meaning and is presented in the form WordNet synset.

- 40-60 points was given to the translation, which corresponds to 2 and 3 synset respectively. In this case, the disambiguation requires the participation of the expert. Translation is added to each synset.
- 20 points was given to the translation, which corresponds to 4 synsets and more respectively.

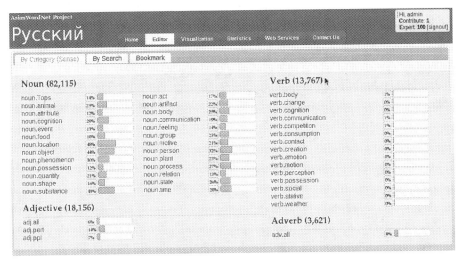

Fig. 5. Result statistics. Variant 1

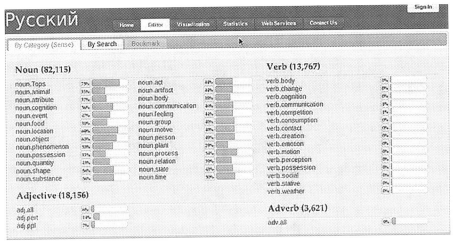

Fig. 6. Result statistics. Variant 2

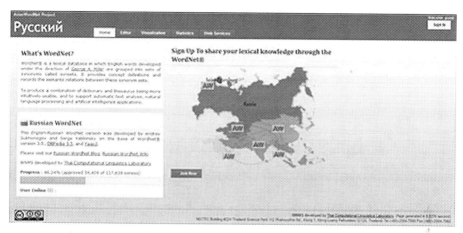

Fig. 7. Asian WordNet framework for Russian WordNet evaluation

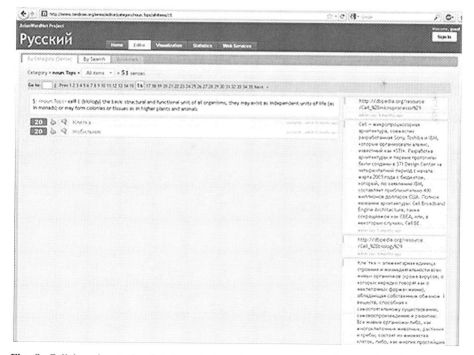

Fig. 8. Collaboration tools of Asian WordNet framework for English-Russian WordNet 2.0 evaluation (http://www.tendrow.org/)

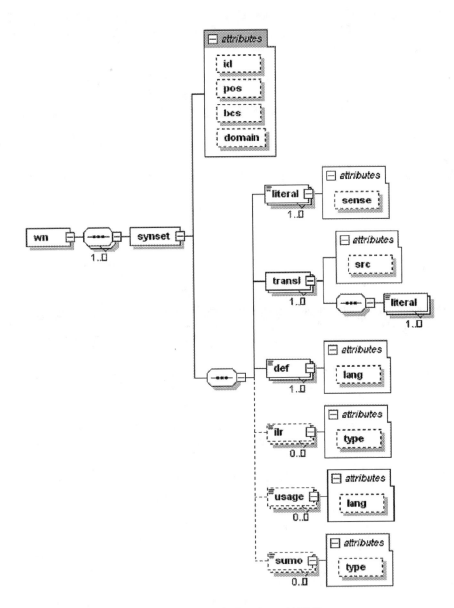

Fig. 9. Standard DTD for the Russian grid XML structure

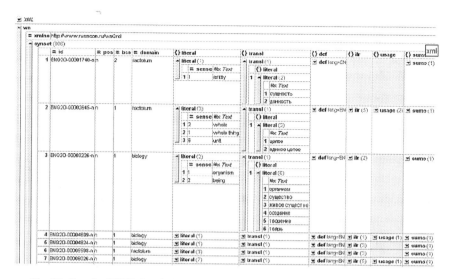

Fig. 10. Standard DTD for the Russian grid XML structure in Altova XMLSpy 2013

7 Conclusion

In this paper we have proposed a framework for usage of the English-Russian Linked Open Data (LOD) lexical language resources and software to process the English-Russian WordNet 2.0. This method allows to take advantage of web data in many languages, requiring only LOD resources. Aspects of enhancing English-Russian WordNet 2.0 with Linked Open Data information are discussed.

We have enriched English-Russian WordNet 2.0 by 30000 English-Russian translations from Open Linked Data resource YAGO2. For additional evaluation on the final stage we use Asian WordNet framework (http://www.asianwordnet.org/). AWN provides a free and public platform for building and sharing among WordNets and was adapted for Russian WordNet (Fig.7,8).

The WordNet Task Force [18] developed a new approach in WordNet RDF conversion, but the W3C WordNet project is still in the process of being completed, at the level of schema and data (http://www.w3.org/2001/sw/BestPractices/WNET/wn-conversion.html). It was used for porting of the English-Russian WordNet, wordnet 2.0 and English-Russian WordNet Grid into RDF and OWL. But still there are open issues how to support different versions of WordNet in XML/RDF/OWL and how to define the relationship between them and how to integrate WordNet with sources in other languages.

The English-Russian WordNet 2.0 was transformed into XML using the DTD for the XML structure from http://www.globalwordnet.org/gwa/gwa_grid.htm and the DTD from the Arabic Wordnet: http://www.globalwordnet.org/AWN/DataSpec.html. The English-Russian DTD and XML format for the English-Russian WordNet and English-Russian WordNet Grid are shown in Fig. 9 and 10, respectively.

Today in the English-Russian Wordnet there are two public subparts: the English-Russian Grid (4690 synsets) and the English-Russian WordNet 2.0 (http://www.tendrow.org, accessed July 25, 2013).

References

1. Tselentis, G., Galis, A., Gavras, A., Krco, S., Lotz, V., Simperl, E., Stiller, B., Zahariadis, T. (eds.): Towards the Future Internet. Emerging Trends from European Research. IOS Press (2010)
2. Breslin, J.G., Passant, A., Vrandecic, D.: Social Semantic Web. In: Domingue, J., Fensel, D., Hendler, J.A. (eds.) Handbook of Semantic Web Technologies. Springer (2011)
3. Kim, H.L., Breslin, J.G., Kim, H.G.: Representing and Sharing Tagging Data using Semantic Web. In: Handbook of Research on Social Interaction Technologies and Collaboration Software: Concepts and Trends (2009)
4. Bizer, C., Heath, T., Berners-Lee, T.: Linked data - the story so far. International. Journal on Semantic Web and Information Systems 5(3), 1–22 (2009)
5. Fellbaum, C.: WordNet: An electronic lexical database. MIT Press, Cambridge (1998)
6. Vossen, P.: EuroWordNet: A Multilingual Database with Lexical Semantic Network, Dordrecht (1998)
7. Global WordNet Grid, http://www.globalwordnet.org/gwa/gwa_grid.html
8. McCrae, J., Montiel-Ponsoda, E., Cimiano, P.: Collaborative semantic editing of linked data lexica. In: International Conference on Language Resource and Evaluation, pp. 2619–2625 (2012)
9. McCrae, J., Cimiano, P., Montiel-Ponsoda, E.: Integrating WordNet and Wiktionary with lemon. In: Chiarcos, C., Nordhoff, S., Hellmann, S. (eds.) Linked Data in Linguistics. Springer, XIV (2012)
10. McCrae, J., Aguado-de-Cea, G., Buitelaar, P., Cimiano, P., Declerck, T., Gomez-Perez, A., Gracia, J., Hollink, L., Montiel-Ponsoda, E., Spohr, D.: Interchanging lexical resources on the Semantic Web. In: Language Resources and Evaluation, pp. 2916–2925 (2012)
11. Domingue, J., Fensel, D., Hendler, J.A. (eds.): Handbook of Semantic Web Technologies, vol. 1 and 2. Springer (2011)
12. Sornlertlamvanich, V., Charoenporn, T., Isahara, H.: Language Resource Management System for Asian WordNet Collaboration and Its Web Service Application. In: Proceedings of the Seventh International Conference on Language Resources and Evaluation, pp. 514–517 (2010)
13. Robkop, K., Thoongsup, S., Charoenporn, T., Sornlertlamvanich, V., Isahara, H.: WNMS: Connecting the Distributed WordNet in the Case of Asian WordNet. In: The Global WordNet Conference (2010), http://www.cfilt.iitb.ac.in/gwc2010/pdfs/68_WNMS_WordNet__Robkop.pdf
14. Hoffart, J., Suchanek, F.M., Berberich, K., Lewis-Kelham, E., de Melo, G., Weikum, G.: YAGO2: exploring and querying world knowledge in time, space, context, and many languages. In: Srinivasan, S., Ramamritham, K., Kumar, A., Ravindra, M.P., Bertino, E., Kumar, R. (eds.) Proc. of the 20th International Conference Companion on World Wide Web, New York City, pp. 229–232 (2011)
15. Balkova, V., Suhonogov, A., Yablonsky, S.: A. Russia WordNet. From UML-notation to Internet / Intranet Database Implementation. In: the 2nd International WordNet Conference, Brno, Czech Republic, pp. 31–38 (2004)

16. Balkova, V., Suhonogov, A., Yablonsky, S.: A. Some Issues in the Construction of a Russian WordNet Grid. In: The 4th International WordNet Conference, Szeged, Hungary, pp. 44–55 (2008)
17. Suhonogov, A., Yablonsky, S.: A. Razrabotka metodov izvlechenija informacii iz veb-resursov Semantic Web dlja rasshirenija chisla perevodov anglo-russkoj versii WordNet. In: Vserossijskaja molodezhnaja konferencija. Upravlenie znanijami i teh-nologii Semantic Web, pp. 159–164 (2010) (in Russian)
18. WordNet OWL Ontology, http://www2.unine.ch/imi/page11291_en.html

Topic Crawler for Social Networks Monitoring

Andrei V. Yakushev[1], Alexander V. Boukhanovsky[1], and Peter M.A. Sloot[1,2]

[1] Saint-Petersburg National University of Information Technologies, Mechanics and Optics,
Saint-Petersburg, Russia
andrew.yakushev@yandex.ru,
avb_mail@mail.ru
[2] School of Computer Engineering (SCE), Nanyang Technological University (NTU),
Singapore
p.m.a.sloot@uva.nl

Abstract. Paper describes a focused crawler for monitoring social networks which is used for information extraction and content analysis. Crawler implements MapReduce model for distributed computations and is oriented to big text data. Focused crawler allows to look for the pages classified as relevant to the specified topic. Classifier is build using knowledge database that defines words, their classes and rules of joining words into the phrases. Based on the weights of words and phrases the text weight which indicates relevance to the topic is obtained. This system was used to detect drug community in Russian segment of Livejournal social network. Official and slang drug terminology was implemented to develop knowledge database. Different aspects of knowledge database and classifier are studied. The non-homogeneous Poisson process was used to model blogs changing since it permits to build a monitoring policy that includes blogs update frequency and day-time effect. Evaluation on real data shows 25% increase in new posts detection.

Keywords: crawling, social networks, knowledge base, document classification, monitoring, Poisson process.

1 Introduction

Social networks gained tremendous popularity during recent years and had a huge impact on the internet. They have changed the ways the information spreads in virtual and real worlds. Some social processes reflect both of these worlds and while gathering significant amount of data from the real world is complicated, data can be obtained from social networks. We can make conclusions about incidents in the real world by monitoring interest to some themes in social networks and find rapid change of interest.

This paper presents a focused crawler for social networks monitoring that tracks interest to a specified topic. Web and social networks contain a huge amount of raw data, and to be able to handle it, we've developed a distributed crawler based on the MapReduce model for distributed computations. To find some specific information in the large volumes of data, certain complex algorithms for content analysis which

P. Klinov and D. Mouromtsev (Eds.): KESW 2013, CCIS 394, pp. 214–227, 2013.
© Springer-Verlag Berlin Heidelberg 2013

should be easily embedded into the crawler are required. Crawler supports the change of crawling policies, which are the algorithms that define what information should be crawled, in what order and when.

Crawlers that mine data about specified topic are called 'focused crawlers'. To support focused crawling the system allows the embedding of the classifier that will find documents relevant to the topic. We used an approach based on the knowledge database to identify the people interested in drug theme in popular Russian social network Livejournal. With the help of the drug expert from Saint Petersburg Information and Analytical Center, the knowledge database with official and slang drugs terminology was developed. It contains keywords that describe different areas of the drug culture. The area defines a class of the word which is used for defining rules of phrases creation. Stemming and words' patterns are used to decrease a number of drug related keywords in dictionary. To indicate the strength of belonging of the word to the drug theme, the weights are used. Document relevance to the topic is determined by the weight which is calculated as the sum of the weights of its words and phrases.

Processes in social networks have dynamic nature and the state of the network changes every time. For example, the interest to the theme can change over time and may have sudden rises or falls which may indicate some processes in real world. In order to capture changes as fast as possible in the network, we have to crawl constantly the new data, e.g. perform social network monitoring. Due to the big sizes of the network, this task should be solved efficiently. We also need to find changes as quickly as possible to react fast in critical situations.

Since we do not know the exact times when new posts will appear in the blog, we have to use a model that describes blogs changing. In this model we have to take into account the features of the social networks. First feature is the strong difference in change frequencies of the blogs. There exists some blogs that are updated several times during the day and blogs that are updated only once a week. Second feature is the number of posts written per hour depends on the time of the day. During the night blogs are updated less often than during the day. We used homogeneous Poisson process to model the number of posts that are created each day in the blog. And nonhomogeneous Poisson process to model the exact time of the day when posts will be created. Under these models it is possible to predict blogs' access times that will minimize the expected value of the delay between blogs creation time and retrieval time.

2 Distributed Crawler for Social Networks

2.1 Architecture

In order to process huge amounts of data obtained from the internet and social networks we developed a distributed crawler [3]. For this we made use of MapReduce [1] and the open source framework Apache Hadoop [2] that supports parallel and distributed implementations. Hadoop was designed for managing large amounts of data and is well suited to preprocess text data from the internet and from social networks. In Apache Hadoop data is stored in a distributed file system. To limit data communication between computers, data parts are processed concurrently in locations where they are stored.

In general a crawling algorithm can be described in the following way. The crawler takes as input an URL, and then it fetches the web page referred to by that URL. After this page is parsed and the links that point to other pages are extracted, the links are analyzed and some of them can be added to the queue of all URLs, whose pages will be downloaded. Then, a new URL is taken from this queue and the process is repeated until the queue is empty or some other criterion is satisfied. This crawling process is iterative and crawlers may differ according to the number of pages processed per iteration.

We created a batch crawler that processes a fixed number of URLs per iteration. The algorithm of the crawler is almost the same as the general crawler algorithm, but several modularities are added to support extraction of structured information from social networks and to support a multi-user access mode. For each iteration the data is stored using separate files of the distributed file system Apache HDFS. This allows us to process only the most recent crawled data and reduce iteration time.

Each iteration consists of several modules, which in turn consist of several MapReduce tasks that are executed consecutively in parallel on several computes in the cluster. In order to make the crawler architecture more flexible and to simplify further development, we split a crawler into many modules that can be extended or changed.

The Crawler architecture can be divided into three subsystems: data gathering, data parsing related to the social networks under study and client crawl policies that filter data relevant to client's needs and create a list of new web pages for crawling, see Fig. 1.

The subsystem that gathers the data from the web aggregates from all clients the lists of web pages and gathers data from these pages. This subsystem consists of two modules: Frontier and Fetcher. Frontier aggregates lists of URLs from different sources, removes duplicates from them and creates one queue of URLs whose corresponding pages yet have to be fetched. The resulting queue is sorted in accordance to the page priorities and client quotas which limit number of pages downloaded for the client. The aggregation phase allows the multi-users access where each client has an individual list of pages to be crawled. This also allows us to alleviate the limitation of social networks which usually prohibit large numbers of requests to the network. The module Fetcher takes URLs from the queue and downloads the corresponding pages from the web. This module is implemented not as a MapReduce task, but as a separate application that can work on different computers concurrently. This allows us to use computers outside the Apache Hadoop cluster, within different LANs and results in more efficient web-crawling. The content of the downloaded pages is stored in separate segments of the database of raw web data. Each database segment also contains meta-information about downloaded URLs and links extracted from these pages.

The parsing data subsystem extracts entities related to social networks, like the user posts or user friends. The structured data extracted is stored in a separate database. This subsystem is represented by the module ContentParsers which can be easily extended by adding new types of parsers.

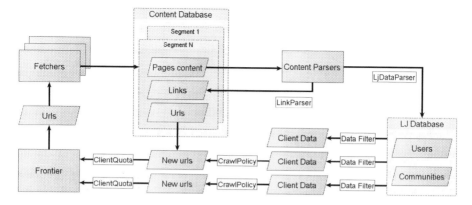

Fig. 1. Crawler architecture

For each client of the system we run a separate application which analyzes databases with social network entities, filters from it, data relevant to the client's need and copies this data to separate client's database. After this, in the module CrawlPolicy, the client's database is analyzed and lists of new URLs for fetching are created and then will be passed to the Frontier module. Each client of the system can specify a data filtering strategy and a crawling policy. This part of the crawler forms a third subsystem.

2.2   Crawl Policies

To find a data relevant to the topic in large social networks, crawlers use special algorithms to filter and rank data. These algorithms adjust to the task that crawler trying to solve and they are based on assumptions and heuristics about content and properties of the data. These algorithms are called the 'crawling policies'. For example, crawling policies can be oriented on crawling new pages to increase completeness of the database or on re-visiting pages to monitor changes and increase freshness of the database. Crawlers that are oriented on mining data about specific topic called the 'focused crawlers'. Focused crawlers can be oriented on finding home pages of the scientists or special type of content, like media content. More complex focused crawlers can be interested in content about specified topic.

Two ways of finding relevant contents can be used: querying search engine systems and direct crawling of the social network with following filtration of relevant data [6]. To use the search engine systems, the queries about required topic should be defined. For some topics it can be hard to define a strict set of queries about topic and search engines can return non-relevant data. So the following checking of obtained data with more strict data classifier should be performed. The use of direct crawling data classifier also should be defined, but this approach is more flexible because a classifier can be built without keywords or queries set. To avoid a full scan of the social network heuristics for data, the ranking are used. For example, data can be ranked based on the number of links that points to it. And again, a key component is a classifier that determines if data is relevant to the topic or not. Working with unstructured data from social network or web means that a classifier should work with raw text. Different approaches for classifier building can be used and our system allows include them flexibly in the working process. It is important note that for some themes it is impossible to use supervised learning because of the lack of training data. In this case the unsupervised methods should be used to at least identify documents that will be assessed by an expert and which will be used to train a more precise classifier.

2.3   Document Classification: Drug-Propagandists Community

This section describes an approach based on the knowledge database for unsupervised documents classification. For simplicity we will describe it on the example of finding drug-propagandists community in Russian social network Livejournal [8]. Based on the classification of blogs posts we identified people who write about different aspects of drug culture: drugs using, preparation, effects and so on. To determine if blog post contains any signs of drug terminology, we created ontology with official and informal drug related terms. The ontology[1] contains words related to the drug culture and class of words that define areas of drug culture to which a word belong. Relation between words and classes are many to many. Words can form phrases which are not an ordered set of words that appear in text consecutively, but are an unordered set of words with unlimited distance between them. The ontology contains rules for the formation of phrases that are based on the class of words. The rule that was used to construct a phrase also defines its class.

Since Russian language have a rich case system including all words forms in the dictionary, it is extremely difficult. To reduce the work of the expert who develops ontology, the ability to mention on word pattern is present. Words that are different in prefix or suffix will fall under a word pattern. We also supported words stemming which allows us to automatically reduce the inflected words to their stem (root form of the word). Stemming is based on the individual for each language heuristics. Words that describe different semantic concepts after stemming may have the same form and that's why stemming is not an absolutely accurate solution, but it has high performance which is important in handling huge text data.

Words and phrases in the ontology may be related to drug culture and to other areas of life at the same time. So, we used the weights for the classes of words and phrases that indicate the strength of belonging to drug theme. We also support ability to define a unique weight for certain entities which may be different from the weight of its class. Since a phrase is stronger indicator, its weight is higher than the sum of words it consists of. This functionality is used mainly to decrease the weight of entities frequently used in other areas. The degree of text relation to drug theme is defined by its weight. The weight of the text is calculated as the sum of its words and phrases weights. If the weight is greater than threshold, then it is classified as if it belongs to the drug theme.

---

[1]   The full drug-dictionary is freely available and can be downloaded at
http://escience.ifmo.ru/?ws=sub48

3   Livejournal Social Network Dataset

3.1   Dataset Description

We used crawler for gathering data from Russian segment of Livejournal Social Network Site (SNS). The Livejournal contains thousands of posts on different themes and is the most popular blog-platform in Russian Federation with 2.6 million Russian users. Approximately 130000 new posts are created every day by 1.7 million active users. Unlike micro-blogging sites Livejournal doesn't put limits on the size of the post which make it exceptionally suitable for text mining.

For randomly selected 100000 users that write in Russian language we collected data about their relations, interests and blogs. After the crawling was finished we have found that only 98602 blogs were downloaded successfully. Other 1398 blogs were removed by users or some network errors prevent successful downloading. From each blog we crawled 25 last posts which were used for evaluating different monitoring policies. For young or abandoned blogs we can have less than 25 posts and totally for all blogs we have 1718824 posts. For each post we know local time of its creation and so we can estimate frequency of change of the blog by analyzing time interval between posts creation.

Blogs vary greatly in the frequency of change. Fig. 2 shows the histogram of update frequencies estimated as median value of time interval between two consecutive posts. We used median value instead of average because it is insensitive to the outline values and analyzed real data contain a lot of outliners. A lot of outliners appeared in blogs that were abandoned for a long time and then were restored. Another source of outliners is "bot" blogs that creates several posts with extremely small time interval between them. During evaluation of monitoring policies we filtered out bot blogs because they distort results. To identify bot post we compared median of the time interval between posts with the specified threshold which were equal to the 5 minutes. Bot blogs have tendency to write several posts with very small time interval. And then keep silence for several days.

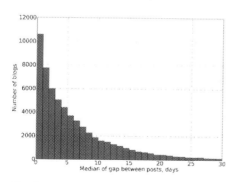

Fig. 2. Histogram of blogs update frequencies

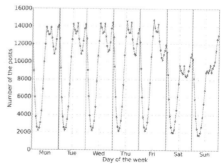

Fig. 3. Post rate during the week

Analysis of the dataset showed that blogs have strong day time effect because post rate have wide fluctuations at the time granularity of one hour. And day of the week is not so strong. Fig. 3 shows number of posts as a function of the hour of the week. Monitoring policy should consider these effects to be able effectively predict retrieve time.

3.2   Knowledge Base for Drug-Related Terminology

Knowledge base was created by drug expert from Saint Petersburg Information and Analytical Center. Database totally contains 368 words of official and slang terminology. For example official words include names of the drugs: heroin or marijuana and so on. Examples of slang terms that may refer to different concepts are snow and weed. These examples represent only names of the several drugs but dictionary also contains other classes of words: heroin, marijuana, cocaine, raw opium, pills, injections, preparation slang, syringe, needle, methamphetamine, ephedrine and general words. Examples of rules that define phrases are: "injections + drug name", "preparation slang + drug name" and so on. With the list of predefined phrases formed by mentioning concrete words dictionary contains 8359 phrases. To classify document we used its weight which is compared to the threshold. We set threshold that matches approximately 20% of blogs (not documents) to be identified as drug related. In this case document is considered as drug document if it contains at least one official term and one slang word or one phrase. We have found that small changes of the weight threshold does not change tremendously properties of the blogs classified as drug related [9]. Fig.4 shows the number of blogs identified due to each class of words.

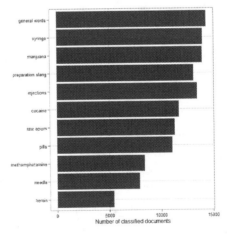

Fig. 4. Number of identified drug documents by different classes of words

4   Social Networks Monitoring

Social networks monitoring is performed for later information extraction and content analysis. Main task that our system solves is monitoring of the interest to the specified themes and detection of unexpected interest to them. In general, social networks monitoring task is defined in the following way. In the fixed N blogs for which monitoring is performed, you have to find new posts as quickly as possible. Due to the limitations of the social networks you can perform only M retrieval per day (day retrieval quota). So, you have to distribute a day retrieval quota m_i between blogs and knowing retrieval quota for the blog you have to determine the exact times of the m_i retrieval that will find new posts with minimum delay. Algorithm that solves this task we will call a 'monitoring policy'. Naïve solution is the uniform distribution of day retrieve quota and scheduling of retrieves at regular intervals. However, several features of the social networks are not taken into consideration.

One of the main features of social networks is that blogs are updated with different frequencies (see Fig. 2). There are blogs that are updated several times per day and blogs that are updated once per week. Good monitoring policy should take into account this feature and should give larger quota for blogs that are updated more often. Another feature is the diverse post intensity during the day (see Fig. 3.). During the day time a number of newly created posts is much larger than during the night time. Time of the day effect should also be considered in order to improve monitoring policy.

We solve the task of social networks monitoring by splitting it to two sub-tasks: estimation of day retrieval quota for each blog (Section 4.3.) and estimation of retrieval day times that minimizes delay (Section 4.4.). Section 4.2 describes formal definition of the retrieval delay and Section 4.4 describes evaluation of monitoring polices on the data from the Livejournal social network.

4.1   Delay and Missed Posts

We used delay metric [4] to evaluate the quality of the monitoring policy. Delay for individual post is equal to the time interval between its creation and retrieval by aggregator. More formally, if a blog produced posts at times $t_1, t_2, \ldots t_n$ and crawler retrieved them at times $a_1, a_2, \ldots a_n$ then delay for the individual post is defined as

$$D(t_i) = a_j - t_i \qquad (1)$$

where a_j is the minimum value with $t_i \leq a_j$. And total delay for the blog is the sum of posts' delays. Total delay of several blogs is the sum of delays of the blogs. Delay value is determined by the time of retrievals which are predicted by the monitoring policy. Our goal is to develop a monitoring policy capable to minimize the delay value.

We also used a number of missed posts as an evaluation of monitoring policy. Post t_i is said to be missed, if between the time of its creation and time of its retrieval a_j another post t_{i+1} was created. More formally post t_i is missed out, if $t_i < t_{i+1} \leq a_j$ where a_j is the minimum value for which $t_i \leq a_j$ holds. Both these metrics define the efficiency of the monitoring policy.

We do not use freshness or age [5, 7] as an evaluation metrics because delay suits better for the system that needs to track some events and react faster in case of emergency. Freshness considers only a number of up-to-date blogs and does not consider time between post creation and retrieval and thus does not suit for emergent systems. Age does not give any additional penalty to the missed posts and the absence of the missed posts might be also critical for emergent systems [4].

4.2 Blog Day Quota Estimation

To effectively distribute day retrieve quota between blogs we used homogeneous Poison process which models blog update frequency. Poisson process is a continuous-time counting process with properties of time-independence and stateless. Poison process models the number of events and the time that these events occurs in a given time interval. Several researches have shown that Poison process can be used to model changes of the web sites at some time granularity. Homogeneous Poisson process use assumption that events occurs with the intensity λ at any time interval. In the case of Livejournal SNS at the time granularity of one day a number of posts that are created by all blogs at each day slightly fluctuate what can be viewed as a sign to use homogeneous Poisson process. Time intervals between events in homogeneous Poisson process with intensity λ have exponential distribution with CDF $f(t, \lambda) = \lambda * e^{-\lambda t}$ and probability of observing k events in time interval t follows a Poisson distribution $P(\tau, k) = \frac{e^{-\lambda \tau}(\lambda \tau)^k}{k!}$.

Researchers showed [4] that under this model blog day quota m_i should be proportional to square root of its day post intensity λ_i multiplied by importance of the blog w_i : $m_i = k\sqrt{\lambda_i w_i}$ where k is proportionality constant that fies $\sum_{i=1}^{N} k\sqrt{\lambda_i w_i} = M$, M is the total day retrieval quota and N is number of blogs.

In general blog day quota m_i is float value and actual day retrieves number for the blog is equal to $\lfloor m_i \rfloor$. If m_i is greater than one then we perform data retrieves from blog each day, otherwise we need to determine next day to access blog. To do that we accumulate retrieve quota q_i by adding day retrieve quota m_i every day until it become greater than one. Then we perform $\lfloor q_i \rfloor$ retrieves from blog and set q_i to its fractional part $q_i = \{q_i\}$.

4.3 Prediction of Day Retrieval Time

Exact retrieval times are predicted after day retrieval quota m_i for the blog i is estimated. We do not know the exact times at which posts will be created and thus we are unable to minimize delay. However, we can minimize expected value for the delay if we will use model that describes the number of events that occurs in each hour of the day. Intensity of creating new posts at the time granularity of one hour vary greatly – during night time posts are almost not created and the peak comes to the middle of the day. To take into account this effect non-homogeneous Poisson process can be used which allows varying intensity parameter $\lambda(t)$ from the time of the day. Under this model the probability of observing k events in time interval $[a, b]$ is determined as:

$$P(k) = \frac{e^{-\lambda_{a,b}}(\lambda_{a,b})^k}{k!}, \quad \lambda_{a,b} = \int_a^b \lambda(t)\, dt. \tag{2}$$

For each blog we will use periodic non-homogeneous Poisson process with day $\lambda(t)$ estimated based on the post history. At time granularity of one hour post pattern $\lambda(t)$ will be 24-th dimensional vector and each component will tell the average number of posts created at specific hour of the day. We will call $\lambda(t)$ as post pattern. It can be shown [4] that under non-homogeneous Poisson model delay for k retrievals will be minimal, if they will be performed at time moments $t_1, \ldots, t_k$ at which

$$\lambda_{t_{i-1},t_i} = \lambda_{t_i,t_{i+1}} \tag{3}$$

holds for any $i=1\ldots k$, where $t_{k+1} = T + t_1$ and $t_0 = t_k - T$.

Retrieval time moments $t_1, \ldots, t_k$ can be found by using iterative refinement algorithm. On each iteration of the algorithm, retrieval times are looked through in increasing order and each of them is adjusted in the way that condition (3) is satisfied. Algorithm begins to work with points uniformly distributed over the day and after several iterations it converges to solution that satisfies equation (3) for each point.

We found that on real data we need to smooth $\lambda(t)$ to remove zero probabilities in order to improve quality of finding retrieval times. We got the best results in the case of using Laplace smoothing which adds 0.5 during calculation of the number of posts that fall into the time interval $[t_{i-1}, t_i]$. In this case for each $[t_{i-1}, t_i]$ we got $\lambda_{t_{i-1},t_i}(t) = \frac{n_{t_{i-1},t_i} + 0.5}{\sum_{i=1}^{k}(n_{t_{i-1},t_i} + 0.5)}$, where n_{t_{i-1},t_i} is the number of posts that were created in time interval $[t_{i-1}, t_i]$.

4.4   Monitoring Policies Evaluation

First we have checked what improvement can be obtained if time of the day effect is used in monitoring policies. Livejournal dataset described at 3.1 was used in all experiments described in this section. To check the influence of time-day effect we simulated a situation when all posts of all blogs were created at the same day. We do this simply by ignoring posts' creation date and using only posts' creation time of the day. So we have blogs with a different number of posts written at the same day and we checked how the performance of monitoring policies varies in different groups of the blogs. For each blog with n posts we perform n retrievals at times predicted by "uniform" policy and "post-pattern" policy described in section 4.3. We used Laplace smoothing during the estimation of blog post pattern. For the predicted retrieval times and actual posts creation times we calculated a delay metric and we learned that "post-pattern" policy outperforms "uniform" policy by 30%. Comparison of policies is presented at Fig. 5. The horizontal axis shows a number of posts in the blog and the vertical axis shows the average delay for blogs with a given number of posts. The figure shows that a number of posts does not influence on delay for uniform policy.

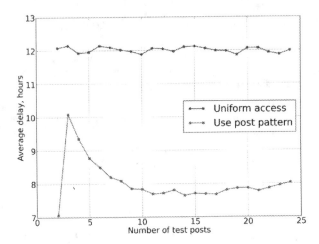

Fig. 5. Delay of monitoring policies that uses "post-pattern" and uniform policy for blogs with different number of posts written per day

Another experiment shows how the influence of total day retrieve quota on the monitoring policies performance. Based on the methods described at sections 4.2 and 4.3 we have tested 4 monitoring polices:

1. **"uniform-uniform"** – where quota is distributed equally between all blogs and doesn't take into account post pattern of the blog,
2. **"uniform-day"** – where quota is distributed equally between all blogs and post pattern of the blog is used to find retrieval time,
3. **"rate-uniform"** – where quota is distributed between blogs based on the frequency of update and post pattern is not used,
4. **"rate-day"** – where quota is distributed between blogs based on the frequency of update and post pattern is used.

To test these methods we used the posts that were created at maximum three months prior a dataset downloading time. We tested on blogs that have at least 16 posts in that period of time. Data was cleared from bots and for each blog a post pattern was estimated based on the maximum 25 last posts. In total we received 61152 blogs with 318800 posts. Results are presented at Fig. 6. The horizontal axis shows an average number of retrievals for the blogs and vertical axis shows an average delay. Results show that using post pattern improves a uniform strategy for 14%, and the use of blog update frequency gives 13% improvement. If both strategies are used, the improvement is 25%. The improvement is calculated as $1 - {D_1}/{D_2}$, where D_1 and D_2 is the sum delay for the dataset obtained by using policies 1 and 2 respectively.

The third experiment compares the monitoring polices on groups of blogs defined by the frequency of change (Fig. 7). For each blogs' group we have obtained an average delay and found out that "rate_day" and "rate_uniform" policies' delay decreases when the frequency of updates increases. This result also shows that for rarely updated blogs "uniform_*" policies gives slightly better results than "rate_*" polices.

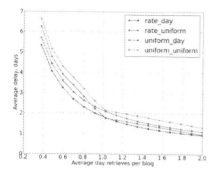

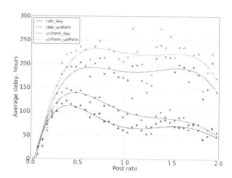

Fig. 6. Delay of different monitoring policies for different day quota values

Fig. 7. Average delay values in blogs grouped by frequency of update. Points approximated by polynomial of degree 5.

5   Related Work

A lot of crawlers exist [3, 16, 17, 18] which have different features and are adapted for different purposes. The set of properties that the crawler should have determine its architecture. And thus all systems have different properties that also have slightly different architecture. Like system in [17] we created system that is adherent to limitations of SNS but we are able to crawl different social network sites. Paper [16] describes parraler crawlers that is able to crawl social networks but they uses relational database for storing data while we uses NoSQL solutions. Our system uses MapReduce model for distributed computations and its architecture is close to the Nutch crawler [3] but is adapted for social networks crawling.

Plenty of researcher showed that ontology using can improve quality of documents classification [11, 13, 14] and clustering [12]. Also ontologies were used in tasks of information retrieval for optimization of documents relevant to the query [15]. This paper describes task of document classification without teacher which is solved by document ranking to the topic defined by the ontology. Proposed method is in fact similar to the methods described in other papers because it also uses mapping from text words to the entities defined by ontology and using ontology to correct "objective function" (that is used in classification, similarity measure in clustering or ranking). This paper will be interesting as a practical example of creating ontology-based classifier for weakly formalized and strongly noised theme.

Monitoring of the web sites [5, 6] in general or news sites particular [4] also have been studied in literature. Our research aims on the monitoring of the social networks which distinguish from the monitoring of the web sites in the way that hour of the day effect should be taken into account. And unlike news sites, blogs update much less frequent and more data is needed to estimate post-pattern of the blog. While news sites produce similar number of news per day and thus have similar frequency of update, blogs changes with very different frequencies. In this paper we propose to use smoothing to overcome lack of data. Complex monitoring strategy that will use one monitoring strategy for frequently updated blogs and another strategy for seldom updated blogs can be used to make monitoring more efficient for blogs. In this paper we assume that blogs update independently from each other but there exists models [10] that allows posts in one blog to trigger appearance of new posts in other blogs. This model can be useful in case of Twitter or Facebook SNS where reposting is very popular, however in Livejournal reposting is used seldom.

6   Conclusions

In this paper we have described architecture of the focused crawler for social networks monitoring. It is build using MapReduce model for distributed computation that allows us to handle large amounts of data. Architecture is flexible and crawler's functionality can be quite easily extended. Focused crawler is able to mine data about specified topic by providing document classifier that determines relevance to the topic. Based on knowledge database about drug culture we created a document classifier to identify blogs that write about drugs. System allows efficient monitoring of the social networks. Monitoring policy based on the Poisson processed models was used and it is demonstrated that it finds new posts much faster than naïve realization.

Acknowledgements. This work is supported by the projects "Technology of system-level design and development of inter-disciplinary applications within cloud computing environment" (agreement 14.B37.21.1870) and "Virtual testbed for complex system supercomputing simulation" (agreement 14.B37.21.0596) granted from the Ministry of Education and Science of the Russian Federation. The research is motivated by the project in frame of 220-th Degree of Russian Federation Government.

References

1. Lammel, R.: Google's MapReduce programming model — Revisted. Science of Computer Programming 70, 1–30 (2007)
2. White, T.: Hadoop: the definitive guide. O'Reilly Media, Yahoo! Press (2009)
3. Cafarella, M., Cutting, D.: Building Nutch: open source search. ACM Queue 2(2), 54–61 (2004)
4. Sia, K., Cho, J., Cho, H.: Efficient monitoring algorithm for fast news alerts. Knowledge and Data Engineering (2007)
5. Cho, J., Garcia-Molina, H.: Effective page refresh policies for Web crawlers. ACM Transactions on Database Systems 28(4), 390–426 (2003)
6. Ipeirotis, P.G., Agichtein, E., Gravano, L.: To Search or to Crawl? Towards a Query Optimizer for Text-Centric Tasks, pp. 265–276 (2006)
7. Cho, J., Garcia-Molina, H.: Synchronizing a database to Improve Freshness, 1–30 (2000)
8. Mityagin, S.A., et al.: Definition of target thresholds for drug-using indexes in respect to regional safety. Social Sciences (Obshestvennye nauki) 4, 243–251 (2012) (in Russian)

9. Mityagin, S.A, Yakushev, A.V., Boukhanovsky, A.V.: Simulation of drug-spreading in population using social network monitoring. SISP Journal 2(10), 133–151 (2012) (in Russian)

10. Simma, A., Jordan, M.: Modeling events with cascades of Poisson processes. Arxiv preprint arXiv:1203.3516 (2012)

11. Bloehdorn, S., Hotho, A.: Boosting for Text Classification with Semantic Features. In: Mobasher, B., Nasraoui, O., Liu, B., Masand, B. (eds.) WebKDD 2004. LNCS (LNAI), vol. 3932, pp. 149–166. Springer, Heidelberg (2006)

12. Hotho, A., Staab, S., Stumme, G.: Ontologies improve text document clustering. In: Third IEEE International Conference on Data Mining, ICDM 2003. IEEE (2003)

13. Bloehdorn, S., Hotho, A.: Text classification by boosting weak learners based on terms and concepts. In: Fourth IEEE International Conference on Data Mining, ICDM 2004. IEEE (2004)

14. Song, M.-H., Lim, S.-Y., Park, S.-B., Kang, D.-J., Lee, S.-J.: An automatic approach to classify web documents using a domain ontology. In: Pal, S.K., Bandyopadhyay, S., Biswas, S., et al. (eds.) PReMI 2005. LNCS, vol. 3776, pp. 666–671. Springer, Heidelberg (2005)

15. Castells, P., Fernandez, M., Vallet, D.: An Adaptation of the Vector-Space Model for Ontology-Based Information Retrieval. IEEE Transactions on Knowledge and Data Engineering (2007)

16. Chau, D.H., et al.: Parallel Crawling for Online Social Networks. In: Proceedings of the 16th International Conference on World Wide Web. ACM (2007)

17. Boanjak, M., et al.: TwitterEcho: a distributed focused crawler to support open research with twitter data. In: Proceedings of the 21st International World Wide Web Conference (2012)

18. Ravakhah, M., Kamyar, M.: Semantic Similarity Based Focused Crawling, Computational Intelligence, Communication Systems and Networks (2009)

Conceptual Framework, Models, and Methods of Knowledge Acquisition and Management for Competency Management in Various Areas

Evgeny Z. Zinder and Irina G. Yunatova

NCO "FOSTAS Foundation", R&D Group, Moscow – St. Petersburg, Russian Federation
EZinder@fostas.ru, IrinaYunatova@gmail.com

Abstract. An approach to organizing knowledge acquisition and management (KAM) and an appropriate conceptual framework for wide competency management sphere and other traditional humanities subject domains (SD) are described. The main purpose of the approach is to support possibility of SD experts work not only with the knowledge, but also with the knowledge metamodel without knowledge engineers' participation. The framework combines methods of knowledge elicitation and description well-known in humanities with formal methods for knowledge modeling. The framework includes the set of principles, a model of multidimensional space for visualization of continuing education (LifeLong Learning Space, LLLS), normalized competency metamodel (NCMM), and the process of NCMM tailoring. LLLS is used as domain-specific KAM goals model and as a tool for intuitively obvious goals visualization. Well-order and partial order relationships defined on LLLS dimensions are used for competency profiles evaluation and comparison. NCMM facilitates KAM process structuring and control. Rules for KAM process support and performance are described. The types of completed projects for more specific domains are mentioned.

Keywords: knowledge acquisition, knowledge modeling, LifeLong Learning, competencies ordering, competencies comparison, IT competencies, English language competencies

1   Introduction

Knowledge management as a set of interrelated activities has rich history. However, availability of IT for specialists from various subject domains (SD) have led to the necessity of essential changes in the ways and methods of knowledge acquisition, representation and utilizing. On the one hand, a classical goal of transforming raw information into formalized knowledge still exists. On the other hand, it is vitally important to provide opportunities for independent performing such an activity to the wide range of experts from those SDs where these experts have to perform their pragmatic professional tasks.

P. Klinov and D. Mouromtsev (Eds.): KESW 2013, CCIS 394, pp. 228–241, 2013.
© Springer-Verlag Berlin Heidelberg 2013

One of important stimuli for this research was the necessity of developing a method which could be practically applicable for knowledge acquisition and usage by experts in traditional humanities spheres. At the same time, this method should allow to present the knowledge in a way formal enough for DSS (Decision Support System) utilizing. This was a rationale for developing the method of knowledge acquisition and usage for experts from subject domains like competency management in various areas, curriculum design, English language teaching and processes management, for further using this knowledge in their business activities.

2   Competency Management and the Gap between Formal Knowledge Representation and Experts' Possibilities

Domain of competency management presents a good example of the area where traditional humanities approaches have been developed for a long time, but there exists a need in utilizing formal methods for DSS. This can be explained with the aspiration for increasing accuracy and impartiality of decision making while selecting an optimal educational trajectory for a person, relevance, validity and accuracy of selecting a performer for a specific working process, etc.

Many researches aiming at knowledge formalization have been conducted in this area [1], [2], [3]. Moreover, conceptualization of knowledge about competencies has already become an object of standardization [4] [5]. At the same time, significant national and international documents in the competency management sphere, e.g. [6], [7], are still written in a rather arbitrary and vague style. The gap existing between formal knowledge about competencies representation and possibilities of using it is admitted and discussed in [3]. However, decisions are being sought on the traditional way of collaborative work of cumbersome complex teams consisting of knowledge engineers, domain experts and other specialists. At the same time, it is admitted in [3] that changeability of the environment is one of the major problems. This changeability is also depicted in [8] where various ways of handling competency models are discussed.

It is necessary to admit that attempts to keep knowledge formalization specialists actively participating in knowledge acquisition (KA) processes do not result in essential success. Their participation is meaningful and necessary for the initial development of ontology, but only as a reference metamodel for future knowledge acquisition and representation in different forms (not only in a form of the formal upper and concrete ontologies). At the same time, SD experts have difficulties in accumulating knowledge using logical mechanisms of formalizing and subsequent applying this knowledge.

Environment changeability amplifies this effect as changes in the environment mostly entail changes in the knowledge metamodel that should be reflected by the expert himself.

3   Research Goals and the Conceptual Framework

The first specific goal of the research is to suggest the high enough level of usability of the knowledge management system with intelligible methods of knowledge acquisition and representation to SD experts. The approach is targeted at developing methods of knowledge acquisition, representation and application that could be applied by SD experts without knowledge engineers' support. This requirement is also extended to the SD expert's ability to independently expand the knowledge metamodel when professional problems change.

The second goal is to seek such a degree of formalizing and a way for formal knowledge representation that most naturally allows utilizing various classical methods of applied mathematics used for solving practical problems in each domain.

The next goal is to provide a possibility for defining and comparing different states of SD objects. To enable this possibility when dealing with objects and properties from the humanities sphere, our approach introduces special procedures for ordering "soft" properties like cognitive and affective skills and abilities of a person.

The focus of this research was forming and exploring possibilities provided by the conceptual framework for knowledge acquisition and management (KAM) combining methods of knowledge elicitation and description well-known in humanities with methods for informal description and formal modeling.

The conceptual framework includes main principles of the approach, the model of KAM goals, normalized competency metamodel (NCMM) which supports the semantics of the objects and their properties., the process and ways of NCMM tailoring, methods of «simple domains» definition for object's «soft» properties, ordered process of knowledge elicitation and structuring, rules for descriptive knowledge models transformation into formal models, and algorithms for composite indicators calculating for object's status reflecting and comparing. This paper discusses the main components of the framework.

4   Main Principles of the Approach

Main principles can be inferred from the abovementioned general goals, and they are:

- Knowledge acquisition and management (KAM) is based on the constructive domain-specific model of explicitly defined goals.
- Knowledge about objects should enable comparison of objects or different states of the objects.
- KAM metamodel represents heterogeneous characteristics of objects in a intelligible for the SD expert and compatible way.
- Both objects in general and their states changing with the lapse of time are described.
- Knowledge acquisition and modeling assumes a possibility of building various types of formal models when necessary.

- Formal knowledge model reflects changes in the course of time, can be transformed into forms comprehensible for a person and into other formal models.
- KAM metamodel developed for an extended domain is adapted for better correspondence to particular and more subject specific domains.

Mostly these principles are self-evident and don't require detailed explanation.

It is acknowledged that an intelligible form of knowledge representation is fundamentally significant. While unformalized knowledge representation might increase the percentage of inaccurate decisions, its inappropriate form most often makes doing the job absolutely impossible. For this reason, to provide an SD expert with a possibility for independent work, at the current stage of the research the tabular form similar to relational one was developed and used with requirements to retain all the necessary semantics.

The tabular form is the most natural and comprehensible for any SD expert whatever his or her qualifications or experience are. Besides, psychologically speaking, the tabular form is considered clear, concise and appropriate for easy classification and comparison [9], [10]. If elicited knowledge is stored in a well-designed normalized tabular form, it can be analyzed and processed for many purposes. In our view, the approach presented in this work also possesses the quality of "semantic stability" mentioned in [11]: "Semantic stability is a measure of how well models or queries expressed in the language retain their original intent in the face of changes to the application".

Moreover, this doesn't contradict or deny possibility of using a Gellish Model [12] or some ontology models when necessary. However, it wasn't the ultimate goal of this research to apply ontologies or Gellish language or some other known techniques for recording our findings. We concentrated our efforts on eliciting, analyzing, normalizing and ordering crucial relevant knowledge and relationships instead.

Besides, the form of stored knowledge should allow applying relevant mathematical methods and developing DSS computer tools. We will not discuss possible tools for storing knowledge as this goes beyond the scope of this paper.

The most visual and simple tabular forms of storing the knowledge together with the normalized competency metamodel (NCMM) meet the main requirements to the knowledge quality:

- necessity and sufficiency,
- integrity and semantics retaining,
- intelligibility for the subject domain expert.

It is significant that the knowledge metamodel has a tabular form too. This retains the possibility for SD expert to work with the metamodel directly.

5   Basis of the Approach for Developing the Goals Model, KAM Metamodels, and Methods

While developing the discussed approach, results of classical and current research in competency knowledge management were utilized. Analysis and development of the person's generic skills taxonomy significantly rely upon [13], [14] results; descriptive knowledge modeling is based on [15], [16] tradition; ideas of [4-5] standards for presenting competencies were used in developing tabular knowledge models. Further stages in models formalizing partly use findings of some projects utilizing competency ontological models for computer processing of this knowledge, [1], [2] in particular.

In the course of further development of [4], [1] ideas, definitions of basic concepts for extended area of "competency management" were elaborated. Our competency definition presented below was introduced in [17]:

A competency (professional) – An aggregate of interrelated knowledge of a subject domain, skills for utilizing this or arbitrary knowledge at a certain level of maturity and possibly of certain performance indicators and other conditions of utilizing this skill for successful performing of a working process or a certain type of a professional activity.

Such a definition relies on traditions of KSAO structure [15] which means "Knowledge, Skills, Abilities and Other characteristics" and suggests decomposition of a competency concept into appropriate components. Moreover, it treats a competency as applying a generic cognitive or affective skill of a certain level (e.g., "interpret", "analyze") to certain or arbitrary knowledge (e.g., "procedural knowledge of designing a database" for IT SD).

The "Other characteristics" component is the main field for reflecting the continuous changeability of the SD expert's environment by the expert himself or herself. The definition develops the idea [1],[4] stating that not only individual people can possess competencies but also objects of other kinds ("resources" in [1]) and extends the idea to related objects of various kinds thus expanding their definition in [5], [3].

The core concept is ordering levels of all the components constituting the competency in such a way that possessing a certain level G_i implies that this person already possesses all the previous levels of the same competency G_{i-1}., G_{i-2} etc. Mastering a cognitive skill of a certain level implies preliminary mastering cognitive skills of previous levels. E.g., the skill "Apply" includes "Interpret". "Apply" means to apply some knowledge factual, procedural etc; e.g., "Apply the rules of information security". The notion stems from the original [13], but is supplemented for feasibility reasons by the additional requirement for ensuring clearly and explicitly defined rules for unambiguous assigning the level (in all scales) to a specific working activity. This caused the necessity to modify existing taxonomies as, e.g., there is no consensus about ordering "high order" cognitive skills; besides in different works such scales contain different numbers of levels depending on a specific project. So, the scales and rules were developed for unambiguous assigning the level. This was achieved by explicit description of distinctions between the levels, thus making it easy for SD expert to realize that $Level_{i-1}$ is insufficient for the task while $Level_{i+1}$ is excessive. An example of using the scale "Knowledge type and volume" for competency needed for solving some imaginary problem P in ICT domain is given below.

Level 1 means having knowledge about specific professional elements, separate program functions, simple procedures. This level is insufficient for the problem P solving

Level 2 means having knowledge of level 1 + knowledge of aggregated objects en block, e.g., complex programs or equipment; criteria for selecting a certain way of problem solving

Level 3 means having knowledge of level 2 + knowledge of interrelations between components of complex objects, methods of analysis, basics of project management. This level is excessive for the problem P solving.

So, SD expert can confidently select Level 2 for competency needed for solving the problem P.

Thus, for feasibility reasons 5-level scales for generic cognitive skills , volume and type of knowledge were developed together with SD experts, using professional and educational standards ([6], [7], etc.), knowledge framework developed by [16], populated with carefully chosen examples from the specific SDs, and this enables any user to define levels of concrete working tasks, problems or functions without hesitation or mistakes. The feasibility of this was checked in several experiments with SD experts (not those who participated in developing scales). Additional mainly 3-level scales were developed for describing specific features of working conditions, restrictions or requirements, such as "The scale of typicality", "The scale of urgency" etc.

Undoubtedly, real "fieldwork" was performed for developing scales that serve as a tool of transforming fuzzy "soft" information into knowledge qualified for solving pragmatic problems. Although this approach was justified in our projects, it should be further tested in other SDs.

6 LLLS as a KAM Goals Model for the Competency Management Domain

6.1 The KAM Goals Model

An important role of knowledge goals in Knowledge management is a well-known opinion [18] which we took into consideration. As opposed to universal "domain-independent" goals models (like [19] our approach utilizes the domain-specific model based on the core concepts and processes of the modern competency management. Besides, our approach defines this model not only for defining goals of acquiring specific knowledge, but also for defining goals of the target activity in SD.

The goals model should enable representation of both end goals and intermediate goals of KAM process and Competency management processes.

In the competency management domain KAM end goals could be defined as:

- Goal 1: accurate and well-grounded planning a section of the personal lifelong learning trajectory;
- Goal 2: planning of well-grounded and optimized curricula for university professional education;
- Goal 3: optimal provision of working processes with performers having necessary and sufficient competency levels.

Each of these end goals is usually attained by performing several business tasks and achieving appropriate intermediate goals. For example, Goal 1 can be achieved by completing the following tasks:

1. Describing an actual state C_1 of a person as an object X at the moment t_1;
2. Describing a desired state C_n of an object X at the moment t_n,
3. Finding an optimal sequence of states $\{C_2, C_3, ..., C_{n-1}\}$ that forms the required educational trajectory for an object X as the trajectory for navigation from C_1 to C_n.

The state of the object X is assumed to be quite fully specified by the competency profile X, e.g., in a given academic discipline or in a sphere of professional activity.

It is assumed that for performing tasks that allow reaching Goal 2 and Goal 3 it is sufficient to operate only with competency profiles of appropriate objects similarly to Goal 1. Thereby, ultimate and intermediate KAM goals are expressed in the form of considered objects' states (of a person, an educational program etc.) in the space of possible competencies and their profiles. This assumption is valid for solving many problems, and that is why it is accepted in this version of KAM goals model.

All abovementioned enabled regarding LLLS (LifeLong Learning Space) model introduced in [20] as the main part of the KAM goals model. LLLS has a simplified three-dimensional version as well as an extended one.

For the sake of clearer visualization, a simplified three-dimensional version is presented in Fig. 1.

States C_q in LLLS are determined by triplets (a, d, g) in the following dimensions:

- dimension $\mathbf{A} = \{a_i\}$ for dates or person's age (e.g., from the moment of birth up to the end of life);
- dimension $\mathbf{D} = \{d_j\}$ for knowledge units necessary in competencies and acquired in academic and professional educational disciplines;
- dimension $\mathbf{G} = \{g_k\}$ of grades as levels of knowledge acquisition as well as skills of utilizing it.

Dimension G represents a complex composite object's characteristic. Depending on the goals scale and variants of business tasks to be solved, the set $\{g_k\}$ can comprise levels of personal abilities or represent the level of the final qualification gained as a result of knowledge and skills acquired by the object.

Dimension G can be decomposed into several more elementary dimensions P1, ..., Pm, and so an extended LLLS version is obtained by replacing the dimension G with sets of dimensions P1, ..., Pm where each of them can represent an "atomic" property of this object's competencies specified in NCMM.

One of LLLS features is existence of some order on each dimension.

Dimension A has on {a$_i$} a natural well-order for calendar time or points in the life history of an individual or another type of object.

Partial order is introduced in dimension D on {d$_j$}. For example, it is traditionally introduced in curricula by mentioning the order of studying academic disciplines {d$_j$} and educational courses.

In dimension G the grades order on {g$_k$} is related to the levels of mastering a discipline d$_j$. The order is also introduced while defining the target qualifications scale. It is also defined by levels of skills maturity in reference to the discipline d$_j$ (similar to generic skills levels [6]).

In real projects structuring LLLS does not begin from the scratch, various resources like [6], [7], professional competency standards, BoKs, etc were used.

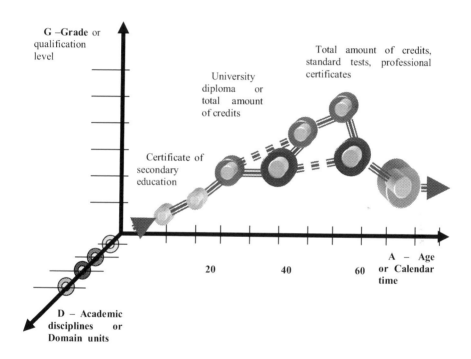

Fig. 1. LifeLong Learning Space (LLLS) by the example of a person's life history (the size of a cylindrical symbol in the position p$_{i,j,k}$ (a$_i$, d$_j$, g$_k$) roughly represents the volume of knowledge acquired on a section from a$_{i-1}$ to a$_i$)

6.2   Relation between LLLS and the Models of Knowledge about Objects

Undoubtedly, LLLS and the trajectory presented in Fig. 1 present a simplification of real processes and states. However, even a simplified three-dimensional LLLS version has meaningful features. Due to the dimension A, the most obvious one is ensuring the principle "Both objects in general and their states changing with the lapse of time are described". Ordering relationship in LLLS ensures implementation of the principle "Knowledge about objects should enable comparison of objects". For ensuring this principle the requirement of systematic defining and utilizing of ordering relationships is extended to the sets of values for all competency properties. Due to this, KAM and LLLS facilitate defining goals and performing various types of business tasks.

One classical task example is evaluating the gap between the actual competency profile and the required one.

7   Basic Version of the Competency Metamodel

7.1   Scheme of Competencies and Their Profiles in the Context of Different Types of Related Objects

The scheme of relationships between competencies sets and other types of objects was developed within this research for clarification of possible relations of competencies and their profiles to various objects from the SD. It is based on tailoring of [5] and includes the related objects "Work / working process", "Output of work process", "An individual (person or another agent)", "Role of an individual as a work performer", "Educational/training course or curriculum", "Evaluating/certifying procedure of an object". Relations of a concrete object to concrete competencies determine the set of competencies that was called *"the competency profile"* intrinsic to this object. So, not only a person or a role of the work performer, but also an educational course, competency testing procedure, and a working process itself requiring certain competencies from its performer for its successful completion, can possess the competency profile.

7.2   Competency Metamodel for the KAM Process

The developed framework includes a normalized competency metamodel (NCMM) that supports performing the process of knowledge acquisition for competencies and storing acquired knowledge in structured descriptions and logically correct formal competency models. For this purpose, NCMM inherits ideas [1], [4], [5] and some later projects, e.g. [2].   At the same time, NCMM is an original development implementing abovementioned KAM principles.

NCMM ensures normalized structure of specific competencies models (see Fig. 2). Normalization is treated here similarly to concepts [21] utilized in relational database (RDB) development. At the same time, normalization is not restricted with the requirements of [21]. In particular, descriptive and formal models structures are complemented with rules that enable retaining semantics of relationships of competencies components and their properties and relationships between components themselves.

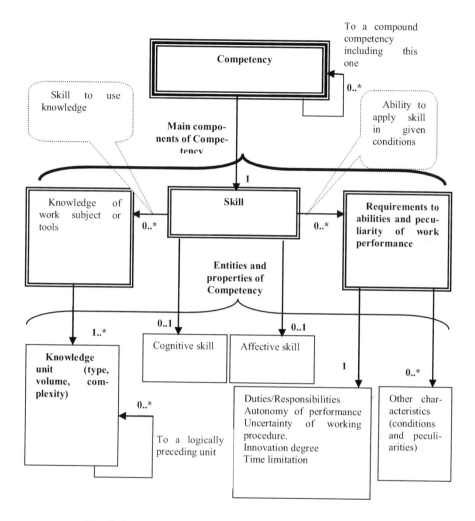

Fig. 2. Aggregated scheme of normalized competency metamodel

Utilizing NCMM for KAM process includes following the rules below:

- transition from arbitrary descriptions of competencies characteristics existing in various knowledge resources to atomic properties and their values on "simple domains" (in terms of [21], i.e., on atomic values sets obtained by decomposition of "non-simple" domains) is performed;
- structures for storing information about competencies and their components are decomposed into information entities that are sets of tuples normalized to a high degree of normalization (e.g., 5NF);

- semantics of relationships between information entities representing subject domain objects as well as semantics of relationships between entity's attributes and its identifier is fixed and supported explicitly, and this enables retaining necessary semantics for each relationship (based on a set of relationship kinds similar to [12]);
- well-order relations are introduced on "simple domains" of entity's attributes values;
- "simple domains" of properties of humanities type (cognitive and affective skills, person's abilities or requirements to them) for the NCMM basic version are adopted first of all from classical [13-14] and actual modern normative resources (e.g., [6], [7])

Utilizing two latter rules enables possibilities of implementation of the principle "KAM metamodels represent heterogeneous characteristics of objects in a compatible way". The basic version of NCMM is adapted by tailoring process to specific features of narrow domains as described below. It is essential that [21] ideas are applicable as:

- it is easier to retain semantics of relations between atomic elements of information in normalized tables,
- 5NF relations can be considered as the level of smallest but intelligible tabular forms that can be recommended for SD expert's work.

8   KAM Process Performing Support

The developed approach includes the following rules for KAM process performing:

- knowledge elicitation is well controlled by associating acquired knowledge with normalized tables supported with directories based on unambiguously defined "simple domains" of entities' attributes which represent objects' properties;
- knowledge about the object's existence and about the value of an attribute is accompanied by a corresponding mark about the time moment from a "simple domain" $\{a_i\}$ on the time axis;
- simple unambiguous transition to storing knowledge about competencies in RDB while retaining semantics is provided;
- SQL (or an equivalent in terms of logical power) can be used when storing knowledge about competencies in RDB for getting answers to many questions about competencies and related objects, i.e., for performing many business tasks;
- possibility to transform knowledge stored in an RDB form into different formal models for various methods (logical, computational) of information processing, knowledge usage and solving business problems support is provided;
- in particular, it is possible to transform knowledge into formal graph models that allow defining trajectories between different object states or objects in LLLS, determining these trajectories characteristics by using well-developed algorithms;
- besides, it is possible to transform knowledge recorded in this way into logical formal models (transformation into models like [12]is comprehensible).

A fragment of a descriptive model of knowledge about competency in IT sphere "To analyze the client's needs in the sphere of informatization" is provided in [17].

One specific feature of the presented approach is the recommendation for ordered processing of knowledge resources in the following generalized order:

- national and industrial standards of qualifications and competencies,
- standards de-jure and de-facto (e.g., international standards, Body of Knowledge, classical author's and firms' products acknowledged as standards de-facto),
- educational curricula and programs,
- managers' requests for selecting performers, instructions for completing working processes,
- business interviews with managers, production engineers, and other stakeholders.

9   Conclusion: Tailoring NCMM and Utilizing KAM for Different Goals and Domains

Suggested approach was utilized in several projects in a professional education sphere [22], in the area of managing working processes in IT sphere [23] , in the sphere of competency analysis and developing educational programs for teaching ESP (English for Specific Purposes) [24-26]. The accomplished projects demonstrated necessity and examples of NCMM tailoring in each of mentioned spheres. First of all, tailoring is required for specification of "simple domains" and specially adapted scales for values of competencies' characteristics. Other kinds of tailoring not violating the principles of the described approach are also possible.

Within the project completed for managing working processes in IT sphere, for example, tailoring resulted in the following:

- specialized sets of   levels for scales of competencies characteristics were developed, including 5-level scales for cognitive and affective skills (psychomotor skills have not been introduced in this NCMM version) and for knowledge type and volume;
- 3-level scales were developed for ordering and using additional characteristics necessary in a specific "narrow" domain in the competencies scheme (corresponds to "Other characteristics" in [3] structure);
- a specific applied algorithm performing convolution of elementary competencies' properties into composite indicators of competency and qualification level of a person taking the rules of specific subject domain into consideration was developed. This algorithm was tested experimentally.

In conclusion, we would like to highlight that utilizing the described approach, its framework and specific applied algorithms demonstrated their quite close relevance to the original purpose of this research and to KAM principles elicited and formulated in the course of conducting this research.

In particular,

- possibility of introducing ordering in domains of "soft" characteristics, where initially such relations were not used, was tested;
- possibility of SD experts to work not only with the knowledge base, but also with the knowledge metamodel without direct participation of knowledge engineers was demonstrated;
- possibilityof retaining semantics in information stored in the tabular form was shown.

References

1. Paquette, G.: AnOntology and a Software Framework for Competency Modeling and Management. Educational Technology & Society 10(3), 1–21 (2007)
2. Schuster, T., Weiß, P.: A New Approach to Competence-Based Business Partner Profiles for Collaborative Business Process Management. In: Camarinha-Matos, L.M., Boucher, X., Afsarmanesh, H. (eds.) PRO-VE 2010. IFIP AICT, vol. 336, pp. 356–363. Springer, Heidelberg (2010)
3. De Leenheer, P., Christiaens, S., Meersman, R.: Business semantics management: A case study for competency-centric HRM. Computers in Industry 61, 760–775 (2010)
4. IEEE Std 1484.20.1-2007. Data Model for Reusable Competency Definitions (2007)
5. ISO/IEC TR 24763:2011. Information technology. Learning, education and training. Con-ceptual Reference Model for Competency Information and Related Objects (2011)
6. The European Qualifications Framework for Lifelong Learning (EQF), Luxembourg (2008) ISBN 978-92-79-08474-4
7. Building the e-CF – methodology documentation. e-CF 2.0 CWA, Part III, 09/2010, pp. 1–31, Brussels (2010), http://www.ecompetences.eu
8. Bartram, D.: White-Paper-SHL-Universal-Competency-Framework.pdf, pp. 1–11 (2011), http://www.shl.com/assets/resources/White-Paper-SHL-Universal-Competency-Framework.pdf
9. Graphing Resources. Designing Tables. NC State University (2004), http://www.ncsu.edu/labwrite/res/gh/gh-tables.html
10. APA Table Guidelines. University of Washington Psychology Writing Center, WriteLab Resources, http://www.ncsu.edu/labwrite/res/gh/gh-tables.html
11. Halpin, T.: Metaschemas for ER ORM and UML data models: A comparison. Database Management 13(2), 20–30 (2002)
12. Van Renssen, A.S.H.P.: Gellish – A Generic Extensible Ontological Language. DUP Science. Delft University Press, Netherlands (2005) ISBN 90-407-2597-4
13. Bloom, B.S. (ed.): Taxonomy of educational objectives: The classification of educational goals: Handbook I, cognitive domain. Longman, New York (1984)
14. Krathwohl, D.R.: A revision of Bloom's taxonomy: an overview. Theory Into Practice 41(4), 212–218 (2002)
15. KSAO (Knowledge, Skills, Abilities, Other characteristics), Competency model of indi-vidual, http://www.humanresources.hrvinet.com/what-is-ksao/
16. Forehand, M.: Bloom's Taxonomy - Emerging Perspectives on Learning. Teaching and Technology. The University of Georgia, http://epltt.coe.uga.edu/index.php?title=Bloom%27s_Taxonomy

17. Zinder, E.Z., Yunatova, I.G.: Normalized competence meta-model focusing on continuing professional education in ICT sphere and on related objects (in Russian). OTKRYTOE OBRAZOVANIE (6), 33–45 (2011) ISSN 1818-4243 (Print)
18. Probst, G.J.B.: Practical Knowledge Management: A Model That Works. Prism 2, 1–29 (1998)
19. Schorcht, H., Nissen, V., Petsch, M.: Knowledge Goals as an Essential Component of Knowledge Management. Arbeitsbericht (Working Paper) 6 (2011), http://www.db-thueringen.de/servlets/DerivateServlet/Derivate-24560/ilm1-2011200589.pdf
20. Zinder, E.Z., Yunatova, I.G.: Prospective architectures for complex education environment (in Russian). In.: 5th International Conference The Modern Information Technology and Education in IT - 2010, Selected Works Addition Publication, pp. 25–72. MSU, Moscow (2011)
21. Codd, E.F.: A Relational Model of Data for Large Shared Data Banks. Communications of the ACM 13(6), 377–387 (1970)
22. Zinder, E.Z., Telnov, Y.F., Yunatova, I.G.: Methodology for competence model building based on proficiency standards in ICT area for further professional education curriculums creation (in Russian). VESTNIK UMO 6(2), 112–118 (2011)
23. Guzik, S.V., Zinder, E.Z., Yunatova, I.G.: New Enterprise Engineering paradigm and work process – performers' competencies alignment (in Russian). In: 16th Conference Enterprise Engineering & Knowledge Management, pp. 90–100. MESI, Moscow (2013)
24. Yunatova, I.: Educational Environment for Generation Y. In: 45th International Conference IATEFL (International Association of Teachers of English as a Foreign Language). IATEFL 2011 Brighton Conference Selections, 6.10 Symposium on Distance Language Learning, Brighton, pp. 130–133 (2011) ISBN 978-1901095388
25. Yunatova, I., Zinder, E.: Using lifelong learning space as the basis for competencies management in ELT. In: 34th SPELTA (St.Petersburg English Language Teachers Association) Conference, St.Petersburg, December 3-4 (2011)
26. Yunatova, I.: Teaching Reading Using Competency Taxonomy and Metamodel. SPELTA Newsletter (42), 4 (December 2012)

Linked Open Data Statistics:
Collection and Exploitation

Ivan Ermilov[1], Michael Martin[1], Jens Lehmann[1], and Sören Auer[2]

[1] AKSW/BIS, Universität Leipzig, Germany
lastname@informatik.uni-leipzig.de
http://aksw.org
[2] CS/EIS, Universität Bonn
auer@cs.uni-bonn.de
http://www.iai.uni-bonn.de/~auer

Abstract. This demo presents LODStats, a web application for collection and exploration of the Linked Open Data statistics. LODStats consists of two parts: *the core* collects statistics about the LOD cloud and publishes it on the LODStats web portal, a *front-end* for exploration of dataset statistics. Statistics are published both in human-readable and machine-readable formats, thus allowing consumption of the data through web front-end by the users as well as through an API by services and applications. As an example for the latter we showcase how to visualize the statistical data with the CubeViz application.

1 Introduction

For assessing the state of the Web of Data, for evaluating the quality of individual datasets as well as for tracking the progress of Web data publishing and integration, it is of paramount importance to gather comprehensive statistics on datasets describing their internal structure and external cohesion. We even deem the difficulty to obtain a clear picture of the available datasets to be a major obstacle for a wider usage of Data Web and the deployment of semantic technologies. In order to reuse, link, revise or query a dataset published on the Web, for example, it is important to know the structure, coverage and coherence of the data.

In this demo, we showcase a web application for collection and exploration of the Linked Open Data statistics. The web application is based on *LODStats* – a statement-stream-based approach for gathering comprehensive statistics from resources adhering to the Resource Description Framework (RDF) [4]. One rationale for the development of LODStats is the computation of statistics for resources from the *Comprehensive Knowledge Archive* (CKAN, "The Data Hub"[1]) on a regular basis. Data catalogs such as CKAN enable organizations to upload or link and describe data sources using comprehensive meta-data schemes. Similar to digital libraries, networks of such data catalogs can support the description,

---

[1] http://thedatahub.org

P. Klinov and D. Mouromtsev (Eds.): KESW 2013, CCIS 394, pp. 242–249, 2013.
© Springer-Verlag Berlin Heidelberg 2013

archiving and discovery of data on the Data Web. Recently, we have seen a rapid growth of data catalogs being made available on the Web. The data catalog registry *datacatalogs.org*, for example, already lists 336 data catalogs worldwide. Examples for the increasing popularity of data catalogs are Open Government Data portals (which often include data sources about energy networks, public transport, environment etc.), data portals of international organizations and NGOs, scientific data portals as well as master data catalogs in large enterprises.

Datasets from CKAN are available either serialised as a file (in RDF/XML, N-Triples and other formats) or/and via SPARQL endpoints. Serialised datasets containing more than a few million triples (i.e. data items) tend to be too large for most existing analysis approaches as the size of the dataset or its representation as a graph exceeds the available main memory, where the complete dataset is commonly stored for statistical processing. LODStats' main advantage when compared to existing approaches is that the tradeoff between performance and accuracy can be controlled, in particular it can be adjusted to the available main memory size. Furthermore, LODStats is also easily extensible with novel analytical criteria. It comes with a set of 32 different statistics, amongst others are those covering the statistical criteria defined by the *Vocabulary of Interlinked Datasets* [1] (VoID). Examples of available statistics are property usage, vocabulary usage, datatypes used and average length of string literals. LODStats implementation is written in *Python* and available as a module for integration with other projects.

This paper is organized as follows. In Section 2 we describe the architecture of the developed web platform. We give an overview on the gathered statistics in Section 3. We describe how we exposed the statistics in RDF format using the Sparqlify RDB2RDF conversion tool in Section 4. Finally, in Section 5 we show how to explore the collected statistics with the example of the CubeViz application. We conclude our work in Section 6.

2   LODStats Architecture

Figure 1 shows an overview of the general architecture of LODStats. LODStats consists of two parts: *LODStats Core* collects statistics about LOD cloud and publishes it on the LODStats web portal, the *front-end* for the data exploration.

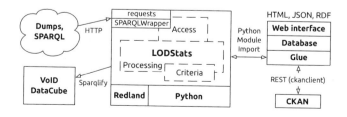

Fig. 1. Architecture of the LODStats reference implementation

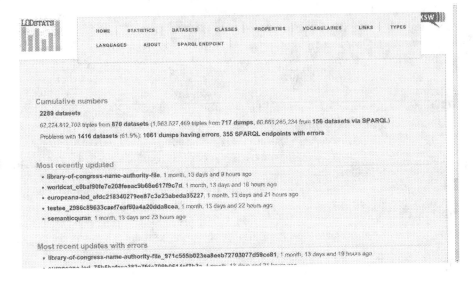

Fig. 2. LODStats front-end at `http://stats.lod2.eu`. General overview.

LODStats Core. LODStats Core is written in Python and uses the Redland library [3] and its bindings to Python [2] to parse different RDF serializations and process them statement by statement. Resources reachable via HTTP, contained in archives (e.g. zip, tar) or compressed with gzip or bzip2 are transparently handled by LODStats. *SPARQLWrapper* [5] is used for augmenting LODStats with support for SPARQL endpoints.

LODStats core has been implemented as a Python module with simple calling conventions, aiming at general reusability. It is available for integration with the Comprehensive Knowledge Archiving Network (CKAN), a widely used dataset metadata repository, either as a patch or as an external web application using CKAN's API.[2] Integration with other (non Python) projects is also possible via a command line interface and a RESTful web service.

LODStats front-end. We implemented a web interface[3] (cf. Figure 2, Figure 3), which provides continuously updated information about RDF datasets from the Data Hub (CKAN).[4] Beyond the various statistics made, the interface allows to search for common classes or properties, helping to encourage vocabulary reuse. Class and property search functionality as well as the statistics are also available via a RESTful web service for integration with other projects. The interface supports the functionality listed below.

– General LOD cloud statistics,

---

[2] `https://github.com/AKSW/LODStats`

[3] `http://stats.lod2.eu`

[4] Our implementation is open-source and is accessible at
   `https://github.com/AKSW/LODStats_WWW`

Fig. 3. LODStats front-end at `http://stats.lod2.eu`. Classes usage statistics.

- report of warnings and errors for each dataset,
- report on statistical criteria for each individual dataset,
- export as VoID and DataCube statistical metadata,
- dataset linkage explorer,
- search function for datasets, vocabularies, classes, properties, languages, datatypes,
- REST interface for the above search functions,
- Linked Data publication of statistics,
- SPARQL endpoint to query all extracted statistics,
- CubeViz installation for facet-based browsing and visualisation of the statistical metadata.

The service permanently regularly crawls data portals such as TheDataHub.org for new and updated datasets as well as (re-)computes the respective statistics.

3   LOD Statistics Overview

We evaluated every dataset available via CKAN in one of the formats LOD-Stats can handle (i.e. N-Triples, RDF/XML, Turtle, N-Quads, N3). We excluded datasets for which we know that they duplicate fractions of already analysed data such as the LOD cloud cache[5]. Results (see Table 1) show that a significant amount of datasets is solely available via SPARQL endpoints (22.3%), with 23.7% of those having errors. Problems most likely originate from either limitations set up on queries to mitigate abuse of endpoints that made gathering

---

[5] `http://lod.openlinksw.com/sparql`

Table 1. Aggregated LODStats results at different points in time

	2011-12-09	**2012-04-25**	**2013-03-01**	**2013-05-15**
Datasets	452	506	699	2289
SPARQL-only	198	215	200	511
Triples	950M	1,174M	7,4B	11B
Dumps	235M	534M	1,3B	1.5B
SPARQL	714M	640M	6,1B	9.5B
Errors	248	276	366	592
Unreachable	45	38	121	374
SPARQL issues	139	153	150	121
Parse errors	57	66	94	91
Archive issues	3	2	1	6
Warnings	2334	5029	3801	5870

statistics infeasible or from not supporting necessary extensions to SPARQL for counting triples on the endpoint side. Complete description and analysis of gathered statistics is described in [4].

4 Exposing Statistics as a Linked Data

Originally LODStats statistics are stored in a PostgreSQL relational database. In addition we publish the collected statistics as RDF data through a SPARQL endpoint[6]. In this section we describe how to establish a mapping to connect the relational database with the RDF DataCube vocabulary using the RDB2RDF mapping tool Sparqlify [6].

Mappings for Sparqlify are written using Sparqlification Mapping Language (SML). In general[7], a mapping comprises one or several views, each one consisting of *Construct*, *With* and *From* parts. *From* part specifies a SQL query for a relational database. *With* part binds Sparqlify variables to the query result. *Construct* part utilizes Sparqlify variables to build RDF triples. The RDF data is obtained row-wise.

To represent the LODStats statistics in RDF we choose the W3C RDF Data Cube Vocabulary[8]. For the data transformation from the relational database to the RDF Data Cube we define a mapping comprised of two views: `Static` and `StatResults`.

- **Static view** describes the static elements of the RDF Data Cube Model: `qb:DataSet`, `qb:DataStructureDefinition` and several `qb:component` elements. There are five `qb:component` elements in `qb:DataStructureDefinition` with one associated `qb:Dataset`. Three `qb:dimension` elements (time of measure, statistical criterion, source

---

[6] http://stats.lod2.eu/sparql

[7] Detailed description of the SML as well as the examples are located at the Sparqlify wiki http://sparqlify.org/wiki/Sparqlify_mapping_language

[8] http://www.w3.org/TR/vocab-data-cube/

dataset) explicitly identify any particular observation. Our data model includes exactly one `qb:measure` and one `qb:attribute` element.

– **StatResults view** operates on the statistical data from the relational database of LODStats application. It retrieves available statistical criteria from the LODStats database and constructs an observation for each. Observation URIs are defined as a concatenation of a *ls-qb* namespace URI with a unique hash.

An overview of the mapping process is depicted in Figure 4. The complete listing of the mapping is available at LODStats GitHub repository. [9]

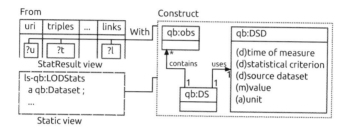

Fig. 4. Overview of an SML mapping. Abbreviations used In the figure: qb:obs - `qb:observation`, qb:DS - `qb:DataSet`, qb:DSD - `qb:DataStructureDefinition`. Inside qb:DSD: (d) stands for dimension, (m) for measure and (a) for attribute.

5   Visualizing Statistics

Well-formed RDF Data Cubes can be visualized as is by existing applications, thus providing the new insights on the data without additional effort. In this section we demonstrate the visualization of the LODStats statistics with *CubeViz*[10].

CubeViz visualizes RDF Data Cube datasets with different chart types. By defining the SPARQL endpoint inside the application, it is possible to identify the statistical data structured according to Data Cube RDF inside this endpoint. A faceted browser allows to choose from available dimensions and measures and thus select the data. The selected components and retrieved data are displayed as charts as well as plain text in the selected configuration and retrieved data tabs.

In Figure 5 we choose the LODStats SPARQL endpoint and compare the number of triples, entities, literals and links (statistical criterion dimension) in HeBIS[11], Library of Congress NAF[12] and World Bank Linked Data[13] datasets

---

[9] https://github.com/AKSW/LODStats_WWW/blob/master/LODStats-Sparqlify/lodstats.sml

[10] http://cubeviz.aksw.org/

[11] http://datahub.io/dataset/hebis-bibliographic-resources

[12] http://datahub.io/dataset/library-of-congress-name-authority-file

[13] http://datahub.io/dataset/world-bank-linked-data

(source dataset dimension) in May 2013 (time of measure dimension). The visualization is represented as a column chart. The user can easily adapt the visualization to her needs by changing visualization parameters. For instance, changing column chart to bar chart or swapping axes. The visualization parameters are configured in the configure visualization window (under a chart type icon). The online demo of this example is available at `http://cubeviz.aksw.org/example`.

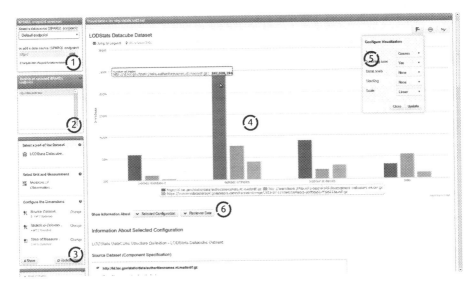

Fig. 5. Comparing the number of triples in different datasets with CubeViz. The numbers in circles refer to: 1 – SPARQL endpoint selection window, 2 – models of selected SPARQL endpoint, 3 – faceted browser for the RDF Data Cube, 4 – the visualization of the selected Data Cube, 5 – configuration for the particular chart type, 6 – area with selected configuration (i.e. dimensions) and retrieved data in plain text.

6   Conclusions

In this demo, we showcased a web application for collection and exploration of the Linked Open Data statistics. We presented LODStats – the base of the web application, an extensible and scalable approach for large-scale dataset analytics on the Web of Data. The web interface of LODStats enables the LOD statistics exploration thus allowing the users to navigate through collected statistical data. We described and performed the transformation of the collected data to RDF and showed how easily it is to visualize such a data with CubeViz.

Acknowledgment. This work was supported by grants from the EU's 7th Framework Programme provided for the projects LOD2 (GA no. 257943) and GeoKnow (GA no. 318159).

References

1. Alexander, K., Cyganiak, R., Hausenblas, M., Zhao, J.: Describing linked datasets. In: 2nd WS on Linked Data on the Web, Madrid, Spain (April 2009)
2. Beckett, D.: Redland librdf language bindings, `http://librdf.org/bindings/`
3. Beckett, D.: The design and implementation of the redland rdf application framework. In: Proc. of 10th Int. World Wide Web Conf, pp. 449–456. ACM (2001)
4. Ermilov, I., Demter, J., Martin, M., Lehmann, J., Auer, S.: LODStats – Large Scale Dataset Analytics for Linked Open Data. Under Review in ISWC (2013)
5. Herman, I., Fernández, S., Tejo, C.: SPARQL endpoint interface to python, `http://sparql-wrapper.sourceforge.net/`
6. Stadler, C., Unbehauen, J., Lehmann, J., Auer, S.: Connecting crowd-sourced spatial information to the data web with sparqlify (2013), `http://sparqlify.org/downloads/documents/2013-Sparqlify-Technical-Report.pdf`

ORG-Master: Combining Classifications, Matrices and Diagrams in the Enterprise Architecture Modeling Tool

Lev Grigoriev[1] and Dmitry Kudryavtsev[1,2]

[1] Business Engineering Group, Saint-Petersburg, Russia
griglev@gmail.com
[2] Saint-Petersburg State Polytechnic University
dmitry.ku@gmail.com

Abstract. Enterprise architecture management is the basis of systemic enterprise transformations and information technology architecture development. Nowadays enterprise architecting is almost synonymous to diagramming. Diagrams are effective for knowledge elicitation, structuring, and dissemination. But as the number of diagrams and their types grows, they overlap and evolve, it becomes hard to maintain a collection of interrelated diagrams, even with the help of a common repository. Besides the very nature of enterprise architecting requires a lot of classifications (e.g. process architecture/classification) and matrices (goals - processes, processes - organizational roles, processes - applications...). The ORG-Master tool combines classifications and matrices with traditional diagram-based technologies.

Keywords: knowledge structuring, knowledge acquisition, knowledge visualization, enterprise architecture management tool, enterprise modeling tool, matrices, classifications, diagrams, matrix method, multi-representation technology.

1 Introduction

Enterprise architecting is a proven approach for systemic organizational transformations and information technology architecture development [1]. It is supported by corresponding tools [2]. These tools document enterprise strategies, business capabilities, business processes, organizational structures, information technologies and especially their interaction and dependencies. Enterprise architecture management (EAM) tools not only capture relevant information, but also process this information, e.g. using reports, visualizations or applying analytical methods. The model development interface is the most obvious part of an EAM tool. It is the interface used to design, build, maintain and often manipulate the models that make up the architecture.

Generally, enterprise architecture (EA) models are built and maintained graphically using node-link diagrams (a type of representation scheme, that depicts elements or parameters of interest as nodes, with arrows to indicate the connections). The tool's model development interface may also use textual interfaces to allow additional information to be appended to the graphical models. Diagrams have many benefits and

P. Klinov and D. Mouromtsev (Eds.): KESW 2013, CCIS 394, pp. 250–257, 2013.
© Springer-Verlag Berlin Heidelberg 2013

are sufficient for many situations in management [3]. Diagrams work well for views, which express the EA from the perspective of specific concerns and stakeholders. They are also an essential result of any EAM initiative and are provided to different stakeholders.

Unfortunately diagrams are not so good when there is a need to develop and maintain a holistic and consistent EA model, which integrates a system of partial views, especially under the following conditions: evolving large-scale models, different and overlapping diagram types, many diagram instances. Chief architects/modelers, who support a whole system of diagrams, may benefit from matrix-based representation. There are two papers [4, 5] that compared the representation power of matrix and node-link diagrams. Ghoniem et al. [4] showed that matrices outperform node-link diagrams for large or dense graphs in several low-level reading tasks, except path finding. This difference is supported by user study experiments conducted by Keller et al., as they found that node-link diagrams offer better visual representation for small, uncomplicated entities, but they are a complex form of representation for large systems and propagation across systems [5].

2   Matrix Representation in Modern EAM Tools

Matrices are actively used in EAM. The Open Group Architecture Framework (TOGAF) recommends not only diagrams, but also matrices [6]: Actor/Role Matrix, Application/Data Matrix, Application/Function Matrix etc.

Matrix representation is supported in the majority of EAM tools:

- Matrix Editor in ARIS Design Platform [7],
- Matrix Editor in IBM System Architect [8],
- Matrix Manager in Casewise Modeler [9].

The main disadvantage of these matrix tools is that they do not support grouping on the axis / hierarchical axis. These tools display only names of the objects – instances of two user-selected types in the repository. This is a crucial limitation, since it doesn't allow working with large amount of data; long lists cannot be processed by human brain. It is especially harmful because matrices and spreadsheets are often used to deal with long lists and Excel is one of the main tools in many offices.

3   ORG-Master Multi-representation Modeling Approach

The ORG-Master modeling approach has originally been conceived in the course of the development of the business engineering toolkit in 1998 [10]. Fig. 1 represents the suggested modeling technology.

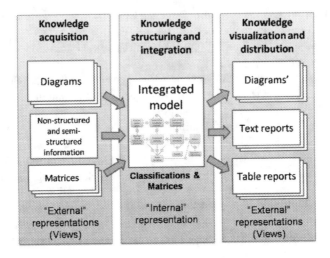

Fig. 1. ORG-Master modeling approach

The non-diagrammatic method plays the central role in this technology. The modeling process starts from knowledge acquisition. Enterprise modelers collect information about an enterprise from various sources (people's memory, documents etc.), then organize it using diagrams, classifications and matrices. Diagrams can be created in ORG-Master graphical editors, which are based on Microsoft Visio. Typically process flow diagrams, concept maps, strategy maps and organizational chart are in use during business architecture engineering. These artifacts can be discussed and agreed upon with managers (managers can also make models by themselves). This step is standard for EAM tools. Then ORG-Master integrates all the acquired knowledge using classifications (hierarchical lists) and matrices – so called "internal" representation. These integration and complex structuring is typically done by highly qualified modelers. This step helps to provide holistic big-picture and consistency in large-scale EA models. However the resultant integrated model is inappropriate for final users and enterprise stakeholders, so ORG-Master provides capabilities to specify and generate partial views from this model (diagrams, text and table reports), which will suit various concerns of various stakeholders. Consistency of the "internal" model and of the "external" views is achieved through automatic model transformations, which are based on a shared unified metamodel (enterprise ontology) and mappings (between different notations and shared metamodel). "Internal" model consistency support is described in *chapter 5*.

4   Classifications and Matrices: the ORG-Master Metamodeling Language

Classification/hierarchical list - the representation format for *objects (items), hierarchical relationships* between them and values for the properties of objects (items).

Hierarchy is the main feature of classifications, and the main relationship types are "part of", "subclass of", "be subordinated to" etc.

Matrix - the representation format for ***relationships between objects (items) from classifiers***. Example relationship types are "perform", "help achieve", etc. The major part of matrices links 2 classifiers, but n-ary matrices are also supported. Inference matrix, allows to infer implicit knowledge via the transitive property of relationships in several matrices,

Types descriptions - specify the ***object types*** *(see classes in RDFS/OWL),* ***hierarchy of types*** *(see subclass property in RDFS/OWL),* ***relationships*** *(see object properties in RDFS/OWL)* and reusable ***attributes*** *(see datatype properties in RDFS/OWL)* of metamodel, together with their taxonomies.

Fig. 2 represents an example of classification: objects (items) are listed in the window on the left, and pictograms define their types. The window on the right exhibits the taxonomy of types, which can be assigned to the objects in the current classification (see upper right property window).

Fig. 3 represents an example of matrix, which is visualized in the form of two lists. This matrix shows relationships between classifications of "Functional processes" and "Organizational roles", e.g. the selected position -"Process architecture engineering of functional system" has a responsible role "Functional system designer".

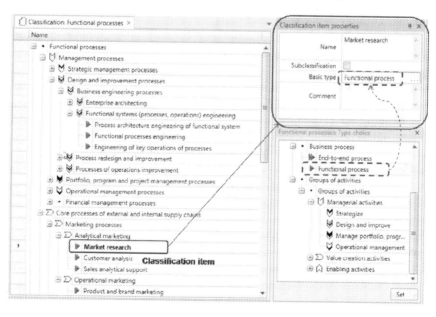

Fig. 2. Classification for storing and structuring objects/items

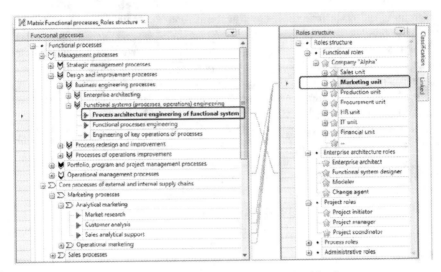

Fig. 3. Matrix allows linking two or more classifications

Fig. 4 shows the basic building blocks of ORG-Master metamodeling language.

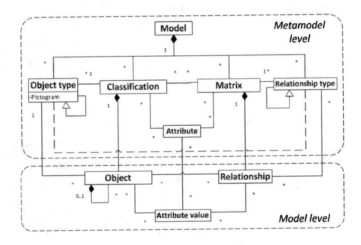

Fig. 4. Metamodeling language description

5   The ORG-Master Multi-representation Tool

The ORG-Master tool for business architecture engineering provides strong matrix-editing capabilities. ORG-Master includes the following modules: enterprise model editor, reporting and query module, diagram editor, diagram generator and meta-editor (Fig. 5).

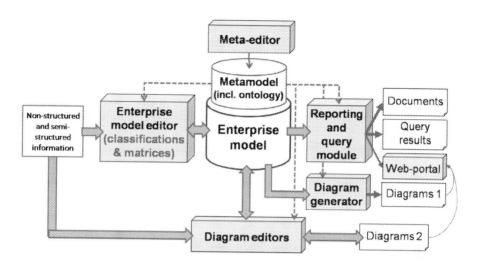

Fig. 5. The ORG-Master tool architecture

Classifications/matrices editing capabilities in the system work together with dia-gramming (graphical editor, graphical reports), which is a hybrid multi-representation technology. The main module – enterprise model editor applies classifications and matrices to knowledge acquisition (e.g. via collaboration with managers), structuring and integration. It produces large-scale enterprise models (e.g. some example 255lassifycations in real-life models include 10000-20000 elements; corresponding matrices have even more relationships). Reporting and query modules enable specification of structure and format of "external" text and table documents, then generate these doc-uments. Diagram generator produces diagrams based on model transformation. These capabilities use predefined notations and depend heavily on the metamodel – whether it is for commercial organization, or for public administration, etc. Diagram genera-tion includes automatic layout, but some complex diagrams require additional manual improvements. Besides, ORG-Master includes a MS Visio-based diagram editor, which helps to acquire knowledge using diagrams, transform it into classifica-tion/matrix form and back (works with the common base) and enables to create com-plex diagrams for final users based on the information from the integrated model.

Consistent information integration within an "internal" enterprise model is achieved manually mostly, but rests on classifications and matrices. For example, two similar actions can appear at two different process flow diagrams. When the diagrams will be transformed into an integrated "internal" enterprise model, similar actions will be at the same classification, modeling specialist will manually organize classification items and with a high probability the two similar actions will appear nearby in the actions classification (since similar elements will have structural similarity / similar place in the hierarchy). Now the modeling specialist can easily identify similarity and merge two actions in to one. Matrix mechanism will enable to link this "merged" action with two processes ("Processes – Actions" matrix).

Metamodel development and customization can be done using meta-editor – you can define object types (classes), relationship types and reusable attributes, then assign them to classifications and matrices. This module is being improved now in order to integrate principles of ontology engineering [11, 12] and Domain-Specific Modeling [13, 14]. The current version of meta-editor partially supports import from and export to Web Ontology Language (OWL). Although metamodel is fully customizable, ORG-Master methodology provides standard metamodels for certain types of organizations (commercial company, public administration, city). In order to integrate EA-related information with other enterprise information ISO 15926 can be applied. So mapping between ORG-Master metamodel and ISO 15926 is among the future plans.

A portal can be used to distribute enterprise modeling artifacts. It provides integrated hypertext and stakeholder-oriented representation of the enterprise model. The portal is an addition to modeling tool.

6   Implementation

The ORG-Master software tool together with the corresponding models and methods has had a more than 10-year long history of use in organization development and business process improvement projects. More than 30 implemented projects in Russian and CIS companies such as GOTEK Group, Kirishskaya GRES (power station), Ilim Group, Trade House PEKAR, North-Western Shipping Co., Power Machines, Irkutskenergo, Gazapparat, ASTRA, Petrovsky Trade House, OGK-1, Pit-Produkt, Eurosib, etc. All these projects were carried out by specialists of Business Engineering Group (http://bigc.ru/consulting/projects/). The GOV-Master is a version of the ORG-Master, which is targeted to the federal, regional and local authorities modeling. This tool was applied both at the federal and regional levels.

7   Conclusion

Diagramming is a predominant approach in enterprise architecting today. Although diagrams are very effective for knowledge acquisition and communication, matrix-based methods outperform them in some situations. Integration of large-scale enterprise models and support for matrix-base management methods (QFD, design structure matrix, etc.) are the examples. The paper described ORG-Master technology, which unite matrix-based representations with diagramming. ORG-Master uses classifications and matrices for "internal" knowledge representation (for professional modelers) and diagrams for "external" representation (for communication with various stakeholders). Advantages of the suggested matrix editing technology: provides big picture (context) and details simultaneously; combine model development with model exploration and analysis (e.g. gap analysis: highlighted elements without links in a matrix); compactness; large amount of information can be clearly arranged and manipulated at once. This allows the user to make a better decomposition of the problem area into subsystems.

Acknowledgement. The authors would like to thank their colleagues – Valentina Kislova, Tatiana Ouerdani, Alexey Zablotskiy, Evgenya Markelova and others – for an enormous contribution to the development of the ORG-Master technology. Special thanks go to Dmitry Koznov from SPbSU for his useful feedback about the method and the tool.

References

1. Buckl, S., Schweda, C.M.: On the State-of-the-Art in Enterprise Architecture Management Literature. Technical University of Munich (2011)
2. Scott Bittler, R.: Magic Quadrant for Enterprise Architecture Tools, ID G00234030, Gartner Inc. (2012)
3. Lengler, R., Eppler, M.: Towards a Periodic Table of Visualization Methods for Management. In: Conference on Graphics and Visualization in Engineering, pp. 1–6 (2007)
4. Ghoniem, M., Fekete, J., Castagliola, P.: On the readability of graphs using node-link and matrix-based representations: a controlled experiment and statistical analysis. Information Visualization 4(2), 114–135 (2005)
5. Keller, R., Eckert, C.M., Clarkson, P.J.: Matrices or node-link diagrams: which visual representation is better for visualising connectivity models? Information Visualization 5, 62–76 (2006)
6. TOGAF® 9.1, Part IV: Architecture Content Framework: Architectural Artifacts, http://pubs.opengroup.org/architecture/togaf9-doc/arch/chap35.html (retrieved June 20, 2013)
7. Davis, R.: ARIS Design Platform Advanced Process Modelling and Administration. Springer-Verlag London Limited, London (2008)
8. IBM Rational® System Architect v. 11.4, Information center, http://publib.boulder.ibm.com/infocenter/rsysarch/v11/topic/com.ibm.sa.help.doc/topics/c_Matrix_Editor.html (retrieved March 15, 2013)
9. Casewise Modeler, http://www.casewise.com/products/modeler (retrieved March 15, 2013)
10. Grigoriev, L., Kudryavtsev, D.: The ontology-based business architecture engineering framework. In: The 10th International Conference on Intelligent Software Methodologies, Tools and Techniques, Saint-Petersburg, Russia. Frontiers in Artificial Intelligence and Applications, pp. 233–252. IOS Press (2011)
11. Staab, S., Studer, R. (eds.): Handbook on Ontologies. Springer (2009)
12. Gavrilova, T.: Ontological engineering for practical knowledge work. In: Apolloni, B., Howlett, R.J., Jain, L. (eds.) KES 2007, Part II. LNCS (LNAI), vol. 4693, pp. 1154–1161. Springer, Heidelberg (2007)
13. France, R., Rumpe, B.: Domain specific modeling. Software and Systems Modeling 4(1), 1–3 (2005)
14. Koznov, D.: Process Model of DSM Solution Development and Evolution for Small and Medium-Sized Software Companies. In: Workshops of the 15th IEEE International Conference on Enterprise Distributed Object Computing, pp. 85–92 (2011)

User Interface for a Template Based Question Answering System

Konrad Höffner, Christina Unger, Lorenz Bühmann, Jens Lehmann,
Axel-Cyrille Ngonga Ngomo, Daniel Gerber, and Phillip Cimiano

Agile Knowledge Engineering and Semantic Web
Institute of Computer Science
Universitty of Leipzig, Germany

Abstract. As an increasing amount of RDF data is published as Linked
Data, intuitive ways of accessing this data become more and more important. Natural language question answering approaches have been proposed as a good compromise between intuitiveness and expressiveness.
We present a user interface for the template based question answering
system which covers the full question answering pipeline and answers factual questions with a list of RDF resources. Users can ask full-sentence,
English factual questions and get a list of resources which are then visualized using those properties which are expected to carry the most
important information for the user. The available knowledge bases are
(1) DBpedia for general domain question answering and (2) Oxford real
estate for housing searches. However, the system is easily extensible to
other knowledge bases.

Keywords: Question Answering, Semantic Web, Natural Language Patterns, SPARQL.

1 Introduction

As more and more RDF data is published as Linked Data, developing intuitive
ways of accessing this data becomes increasingly important. One of the main
challenges is the development of interfaces that exploit the expressiveness of the
underlying data model and query language, while hiding their complexity.

As a good compromise between intuitiveness and expressiveness, *question answering (QA)* approaches allow users to express arbitrarily[1] complex information
needs in natural language without requiring them to be aware of the underlying
schema, vocabulary or query language. Several question answering systems for
RDF data have been proposed in the past, for example, Aqualog [1,2], Power-
Aqua [3], NLP-Reduce [4] and FREyA [5]. Many of these systems map a natural
language question to a triple-based representation. For example, consider the
simple question Who wrote The Neverending Story?. PowerAqua[2] would map
this question to the triple representation

---

[1] At least as complex as can be represented in the query language.

[2] Accessed via the online demo at http://poweraqua.open.ac.uk:8080/
poweraqualinked/jsp/index.jsp

P. Klinov and D. Mouromtsev (Eds.): KESW 2013, CCIS 394, pp. 258–264, 2013.
© Springer-Verlag Berlin Heidelberg 2013

⟨[person,organization], wrote, Neverending Story⟩.

Then, by applying similarity metrics and search heuristics, it would retrieve matching subgraphs from the RDF repository. For the above query, the following triples would be retrieved from DBpedia, from which the answer "Michael Ende" can be derived:

⟨Writer, IS_A, Person⟩
⟨Writer, author, The_Neverending_Story⟩

While this approach works very well in cases where the meaning of the query can be captured easily, it has a number of drawbacks, as in many cases the original semantic structure of the question can not be faithfully captured using triples. For instance, consider the questions 1a and 2a below. PowerAqua would produce the triple representations in 1b and 2b, respectively. The goal, however, would be SPARQL queries[3] like 1c and 2c, respectively.

1. (a) Which cities have more than three universities?
   (b) ⟨[cities], more than, universities three⟩
   (c) ```
SELECT ?y WHERE {
    ?x rdf:type onto:University .
    ?x onto:city ?y .
}
HAVING (COUNT(?x) > 3)
```
2. (a) Who produced the most films?
   (b) ⟨[person,organization], produced, most films⟩
   (c) ```
SELECT ?y WHERE {
    ?x rdf:type onto:Film .
    ?x onto:producer ?y .
}
ORDER BY DESC(COUNT(?x)) OFFSET 0 LIMIT 1
```

Such SPARQL queries are difficult to construct on the basis of the above mentioned triple representations, as aggregation and filter constructs arising from the use of specific quantifiers are not faithfully captured. What would be needed instead is a representation of the information need that is much closer to the semantic structure of the original question. Thus, the TBSL approach to question answering over RDF data [6] relies on a parse of the question to produce a SPARQL template that directly mirrors the internal structure of the question and that, in a second step, is instantiated by mapping the occurring natural language expressions to the domain vocabulary. For example, a template produced for Question 2a would be:

3. ```
SELECT ?x WHERE {
    ?x ?p ?y .
    ?y rdf:type ?c .
}
ORDER BY DESC(COUNT(?y)) LIMIT 1 OFFSET 0
```

---

[3] Assuming a DBpedia namespace with onto as the prefix for <http://dbpedia.org/ontology/>.
```

In this template, c stands proxy for the URI of a class matching the input keyword films and p stands proxy for a property matching the input keyword produced. In a next step, c has to be instantiated by a matching class, in the case of using DBpedia `onto:Film`, and p has to be instantiated with a matching property, in this case `onto:producer`. For instantiation, we exploit an index as well as a pattern library that links properties with natural language predicates.

This approach is shown in [6] to be competitive and specific cases of questions that can be precisely answered with this approach but not with competing approaches are discussed there. This is done by evaluating it against the QALD benchmark, where of the 50 questions, 34 are manually determined to be solvable and 19 are answered fully correctly.

The main contribution of this paper is to provide a practical proof-of-concept of the TBSL methodology and its flexibility in adapting to different knowledge bases.

In the online demo, users can choose between two different knowledge bases: DBpedia [7] is the main information hub of the semantic web and contains factual information about several million resources and hundreds of millions of facts about them. The Oxford real estate knowledge base [8] contains relevant information for potential house-buyers in the Oxford area, such as the price, location, number of bedrooms and bathrooms as well as images and textual descriptions.

In the following section we present an overview of the system's architecture, in Section 3, we describe the online demo and finally we elaborate about future work.

2 Architecture

Figure 1 gives an overview of our approach. The input question, formulated by the user in natural language, is first processed by a POS tagger. On the basis of the POS tags, lexical entries are created using a set of heuristics. These lexical entries, together with pre-defined domain-independent lexical entries, are used for parsing, which leads to a semantic representation of the natural language query, which is then converted into a SPARQL query template. The query templates contain *slots*, which are missing elements of the query that have to be filled with URIs. In order to fill them, our approach first generates natural language expressions for possible slot fillers from the user question using WordNet expansion. In a next step, sophisticated entity identification approaches are used to obtain URIs for those natural language expressions. These approaches rely both on string similarity as well as on natural language patterns which are compiled from existing structured data in the Linked Data cloud and text documents. This yields a range of different query candidates as potential translations of the input question. It is therefore important to rank those query candidates. To do this, we combine string similarity values, prominence values and schema conformance checks into a score value. The highest ranked queries are then tested against the underlying triple store and the best answer is returned to the user. The approach is explained in more detail in the original publication [6].

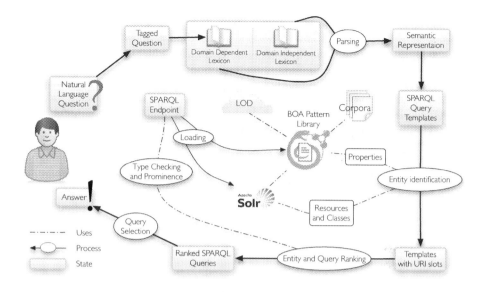

Fig. 1. Overview of the template based SPARQL query generator

3   Demo Description

The online demo can be found at `http://autosparql-tbsl.dl-learner.org/`. As the users enters a question in the search field, the list of answer resources is visualized, see Figure 2. As the answer type of our system is a list of RDF resources, only factual questions which can be answered by such a list can be answered. Examples of unanswerable queries are "How old is Stephen King?", "Why is the sky blue?" and "Is the pope catholic?".

Additional Functionality. In case the question is wrongly interpreted, expert users can choose among different interpretations, see Figure 3. When using the Oxford knowledge base, there are three additional features: (1) the resources can be sorted by criteria such as the price or number of rooms, (2) they can be shown according to their price in a bar graph and (3) they can be displayed in a map.

Identifying Relevant Information. While for Oxford houses the set of properties is fixed, in DBpedia, a RDF resource can have a big number of properties which leads to a very wide row in our table layout and makes it hard for a user to find the relevant information. To shrink the number of properties visible by default, those properties are internally sorted by their frequency in the answer set and are filtered by first applying an absolute threshold and then selecting only the k properties with the highest frequencies. Furthermore there is a manual blacklist that contains properties which relate to Wikipedia or DBpedia articles instead of the resources they represent and are typically not relevant for a user in a question answering context, such as `wikiPageUsesTemplate`. If a users wishes to add a property which is not included in the default selection, the property can always be added by selecting it in the "Show also" box.

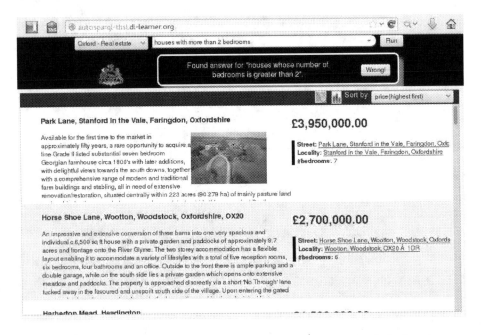

Fig. 2. The question "houses with more than 2 bedrooms" on the Oxford real estate knowledge base is answered by the with a list of houses and their properties

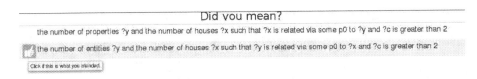

Fig. 3. Expert users can choose among different interpretations for difficult questions

Implementation. The demo is implemented in Java to make use of the rich library support for both *natural language processing* (*NLP*) and RDF. It uses the *Apache Jena*[4] framework which provides RDF and SPARQL capabilities and the Stanford JavaNLP API[5] for NLP functions such as part-of-speech tagging. The user interface is a web application[6] and is implemented in *Vaadin*[7], which is

---

[4] jena.apache.org
[5] http://www-nlp.stanford.edu/software/
[6] http://autosparql-tbsl.dl-learner.org/
[7] https://vaadin.com

a server-centric extension to the *Google Web Toolkit*[8]. The DBpedia knowledge base is accessed via the default SPARQL endpoint[9] while the much smaller Oxford housing data is loaded into a memory model from a local RDF dump. An Apache Solr[10] index is used to get resource candidates for a template slot from the DBpedia and Oxford knowledge bases. The inverted index provides an efficient lookup from template slots, like "book" in "Give me all books written by Dan Brown", to resources like `http://dbpedia.org/class/Book` which contain this word in its values for the `rdfs:label` or `rdfs:comment` property, including near matches.

4   Future Work

We are planning improvements for both the user interface and the core algorithm.

4.1   User Interface

User Feedback. We plan to increase the amount of feedback the user gets, especially regarding his search query. For time consuming queries, an estimate tells the user, that the program has not crashed but is still working and helps identify, whether the users' information needs are worth the waiting time. A detailed explanation of errors, for example that a "why-query" is generally not possible but that another one only fails, because the wanted information is not contained in the knowledge base, helps the user in formulating further queries. Furthermore, we plan to persist feedback that the program gets from the user and learn from it, like the rejection of the default interpretation and the choice of an alternative.

Use of Different Algorithms. We plan to allow using additional QA algorithms so that users can choose the algorithm that is best suited to the task at hand.

Performance and Usability Evaluation. While the quality of the TBSL algorithm has already been evaluated using the QALD benchmark (see section 1), an evaluation of user interface has yet to be done. We plan to do a quantitative study where we measure the time spent between the user entering a query and the complete displaying of the results. Furthermore we plan a qualitative study where users are asked to freely give feedback about their expectations about the interface and their experiences with it.

4.2   Algorithm

We are investigating into several qualitative and quantitative improvements of the TBSL algorithm.

---

[8] `http://www.gwtproject.org`
[9] `http://dbpedia.org/sparql`
[10] `http://lucene.apache.org/solr/`

Optimizing the URI Disambiguation. It is crucial to find the right resource for each slot because even a failure on a single one misrepresents the information need of the query and produces answers which are useless to the user. As such we strive to achieve an disambiguation rate that is as high as possible.

Multilingualism. Natural language question answering aims to remove barriers to the access of Semantic Web data by allowing lay users to query it in their own language instead of a synthetic query language like SPARQL. Adding more natural languages further increases the potential user base and facilitates querying for users who can speak English but do not have it as a native language. At first we plan to add the German language by creating German patterns and a German domain-independent dictionary.

References

1. Lopez, V., Motta, E.: Ontology-driven question answering in aquaLog. In: Meziane, F., Métais, E. (eds.) NLDB 2004. LNCS, vol. 3136, pp. 89–102. Springer, Heidelberg (2004)
2. Lopez, V., Uren, V., Pasin, E.M.,, M.: AquaLog: An ontology-driven question answering system for organizational semantic intranets. Journal of Web Semantics 5(2), 72–105 (2007)
3. Lopez, V., Uren, V., Sabou, M.R., Motta, E.: Cross ontology query answering on the semantic web: an initial evaluation. In: Proceedings of the Fifth International Conference on Knowledge Capture, pp. 17–24. ACM (2009)
4. Kaufmann, E., Bernstein, A., NLP-Reduce, L.F.: A "naive" but domain-independent natural language interface for querying ontologies. In: Proceedings of the 4th European Semantic Web Conference (ESWC 2007), Innsbruck, Austria (2007)
5. Damljanovic, D., Agatonovic, M., Cunningham, H.: Natural language interfaces to ontologies: Combining syntactic analysis and ontology-based lookup through the user interaction. In: Aroyo, L., Antoniou, G., Hyvönen, E., ten Teije, A., Stuckenschmidt, H., Cabral, L., Tudorache, T. (eds.) ESWC 2010, Part I. LNCS, vol. 6088, pp. 106–120. Springer, Heidelberg (2010)
6. Unger, C., Bühmann, L., Lehmann, J., Ngonga Ngomo, A.-C., Gerber, D., Cimiano, P.: Template-based question answering over RDF data. In: Proceedings of the 21st International Conference on World Wide Web, pp. 639–648. ACM (2012)
7. Lehmann, J., Bizer, C., Kobilarov, G., Auer, S., Becker, C., Cyganiak, R., Hellmann, S.: DBpedia – A crystallization point for the Web of Data. Journal of Web Semantics 7(3), 154–165 (2009)
8. Lehmann, J., Furche, T., Grasso, G., Ngomo, A.-C.N., Schallhart, C., Sellers, A., Unger, C., Bühmann, L., Gerber, D., Höffner, K., Liu, D., Auer, S.: Deqa: Deep web extraction for question answering. In: Cudré-Mauroux, P., Heflin, J., Sirin, E., Tudorache, T., Euzenat, J., Hauswirth, M., Parreira, J.X., Hendler, J., Schreiber, G., Bernstein, A., Blomqvist, E. (eds.) ISWC 2012, Part II. LNCS, vol. 7650, pp. 131–147. Springer, Heidelberg (2012)

TripleCheckMate: A Tool for Crowdsourcing the Quality Assessment of Linked Data

Dimitris Kontokostas[1], Amrapali Zaveri[1], Sören Auer[2], and Jens Lehmann[1]

[1] AKSW/BIS, Universitt Leipzig, Germany
{lastname}@informatik.uni-leipzig.de
http://aksw.org
[2] CS/EIS, Universität Bonn
auer@cs.uni-bonn.de
http://www.iai.uni-bonn.de/~auer

Abstract. Linked Open Data (LOD) comprises of an unprecedented volume of structured datasets on the Web. However, these datasets are of varying quality ranging from extensively curated datasets to crowdsourced and even extracted data of relatively low quality. We present a methodology for assessing the quality of linked data resources, which comprises of a manual and a semi-automatic process. In this paper we focus on the manual process where the first phase includes the detection of common quality problems and their representation in a quality problem taxonomy. The second phase comprises of the evaluation of a large number of individual resources, according to the quality problem taxonomy via crowdsourcing. This process is implemented by the tool *TripleCheck-Mate* wherein a user assesses an individual resource and evaluates each fact for correctness. This paper focuses on describing the methodology, quality taxonomy and the tools' system architecture, user perspective and extensibility.

Keywords: Data Quality, Linked Data, DBpedia.

1 Introduction

The advent of semantic web technologies, as an enabler of Linked Open Data (LOD), has provided the world with an unprecedented volume of structured data currently amounting to 50 billion facts represented as RDF triples. Although publishing large amounts of data on the Web is certainly a step in the right direction, the data is only as usable as its quality. On the Data Web, we have varying quality of information covering various domains. There are a large number of high quality datasets (in particular in the life-sciences domain), which are carefully curated over decades and recently published on the Web. There are, however, also many datasets, which were extracted from unstructured and semi-structured information or are the result of some crowdsourcing process, where large numbers of users contribute small parts. DBpedia [5,3,4] is actually an example for both - a dataset extracted from the result of a crowdsourcing process.

P. Klinov and D. Mouromtsev (Eds.): KESW 2013, CCIS 394, pp. 265–272, 2013.
© Springer-Verlag Berlin Heidelberg 2013

Hence, quality problems are inherent in DBpedia. This is not a problem per se, since quality usually means fitness for a certain use case [1]. Hence, even datasets with quality problems might be useful for certain applications, as long as the quality is in the required range.

In this paper, we first describe a data quality assessment methodology, which comprises of a manual and a semi-automatic process (section 2). However, we focus only on the manual process of quality assessment of DBpedia in this article and refer the readers to [6] for details on the semi-automatic process. The first phase includes the detection of common quality problems and their representation in a comprehensive taxonomy of potential quality problems. The second phase comprises of the evaluation of a large number of individual resources, according to the quality problem taxonomy, using *crowdsourcing* in order to evaluate the type and extent of data quality problems occurring in DBpedia. Each represented fact is evaluated for correctness by each user and, if found problematic, annotated with one of 17 pre-defined quality criteria. This process is accompanied by a tool, *TripleCheckMate* wherein a user assesses an individual resource and evaluates each fact for correctness, which is the main focus of this paper (section 3). With this study we not only aim to assess the quality of DBpedia but also to adopt a methodology to improve the quality in future versions by regularly providing feedback to the DBpedia maintainers to fix these problems.

2   Quality Assessment Methodology

In this section, we describe a generalized methodology for the manual assessment and subsequent data quality improvement of resources belonging to a dataset. This methodology consists of the following four steps: (1) Resource selection, (2) Evaluation mode selection, (3) Resource evaluation and (4) Data quality improvement. In the following, we describe these steps in more detail.

Step I: Resource selection In this first step, the resources belonging to a particular dataset are selected. This selection can be performed in three different ways:
 - *Per Class:* select resources belonging to a particular class
 - *Completely random:* a random resource from the dataset
 - *Manual:* a resource selected manually from the dataset

Choosing resources per class (e.g. animal, sport, place etc.) gives the user the flexibility to choose resources belonging to only those classes she is familiar with. However, when choosing resources from a class, the selection should be made in proportion to the number of instances of that class. Random selection, on the other hand, ensures an unbiased and uniform coverage of the underlying dataset. In the manual selection option, the user is free to select resources with problems that she has perhaps previously identified.

Step II: Evaluation mode selection The assignment of the resources, selected in Step I, to a person can be accomplished in the following three ways:

– *Manual:* the selected resources are assigned to a person (or group of individuals) who will then proceed to manually evaluate the resources individually.
– *Semi-automatic:* selected resources are assigned to a semi-automatic tool which performs data quality assessment employing some form of user feedback.
– *Automatic:* the selected resources are given as input to an automatic tool which performs the quality assessment without any user involvement.

Step III: Resource evaluation In case of manual assignment of resources, the person (or group of individuals) evaluates each resource individually to detect the potential data quality problems. In order to support this step, a quality assessment tool can be used which allows a user to evaluate each individual triple belonging to a particular resource.

Step IV: Data quality improvement After the evaluation of resources and identification of potential quality problems, the next step is to improve the data quality. There are at least two ways to perform an improvement:
– Direct: editing the triple, identified to contain the problem, with the correct value
– Indirect: using the Patch Request Ontology[1] [2] which allows gathering user feedbacks about erroneous triples.

A systematic review done in [7] identified a number of different data quality dimensions (criteria) applicable to Linked Data. After carrying out an initial data quality assessment on DBpedia (as part of the first phase of the manual assessment methodology), the problems identified were mapped to this list of identified dimensions. In particular, *Accuracy, Relevancy, Representational-consistency and Interlinking* were identified to be problems affecting a large number of DBpedia resources. Additionally, these dimensions were further divided into categories and sub-categories.

Table 1 gives an overview of these data quality dimensions along with their categories and sub-categories. Moreover, the table specifies whether the problems are specific to DBpedia (marked with a ✔) or could potentially occur in any RDF dataset. For example, the sub-category *Special template not properly recognized* is a problem that occurs only in DBpedia due to the presence of specific keywords in Wikipedia articles that do not cite any references or resources (e.g. {{Unreferenced stub—auto=yes}}). On the other hand, the problems that are not DBpedia specific can occur in any other datasets.

3   TripleCheckMate

TripleCheckMate is a tool built specifically for the purpose of the Quality Assessment Methodology (cf. section 2). The tool is released as open source[2] under

---

[1] http://141.89.225.43/patchr/ontologies/patchr.ttl#
[2] https://github.com/AKSW/TripleCheckMate

Table 1. Data quality dimensions, categories and sub-categories identified in the DB-pedia resources. The DBpedia specific column denotes whether the problem type is specific only to DBpedia (tick) or could occur in any RDF dataset.

Dimension	Category	Sub-category	DBpedia specific
Accuracy	Triple incorrectly extracted	Object value is incorrectly extracted	−
		Object value is incompletely extracted	−
		Special template not properly recognized	✔
	Datatype problems	Datatype incorrectly extracted	−
	Implicit relationship between attributes	One fact encoded in several attributes	✔
		Several facts encoded in one attribute	−
		Attribute value computed from another attribute value	✔
Relevancy	Irrelevant information extracted	Extraction of attributes containing layout information	✔
		Redundant attribute values	−
		Image related information	✔
		Other irrelevant information	−
Represensational-Consistency	Representation of number values	Inconsistency in representation of number values	−
Interlinking	External links	External websites	−
	Interlinks with other datasets	Links to Wikimedia	−
		Links to Freebase	−
		Links to Geospecies	−
		Links generated via Flickr wrapper	−

the Apache License. A successful use case of the tool can be seen in the *DBpedia Evaluation Campaign*[3] where 58 users evaluated a total of 792 resources (521 distinct) and 2928 distinct triples. A thorough description of that work can be found in [6].

In the following, we describe TripleCheckMate from a user perspective (subsection 3.1) as well as the system architecture (subsection 3.2) and extensibility of the tool (subsection 3.3).

3.1   Overview

The design of TripleCheckMate is aligned with the methodology described in section 2, in particular with Steps 1–3. To use the tool, the user is required to authenticate herself, which not only prevents spam but also helps in keeping track of her evaluations. After authenticating herself, she proceeds with the selection of a resource (Step 1). She is provided with three options: (i)*per class*, (ii)*completely random* and (iii)*manual* (as described in Step I of the assessment methodology).

After selecting a resource, the user is presented with a table showing each triple belonging to that resource on a single row. Step 2 involves the user evaluating each triple and checking whether it contains a data quality problem. The link to the original Wikipedia page for the chosen resource is provided on top of the page which facilitates the user to check against the original values. If the triple contains a problem, she checks the box "is wrong". Moreover, she is provided with a taxonomy of pre-defined data quality problems (cf. Table 1) where

---

[3] http://nl.dbpedia.org:8080/TripleCheckMate/

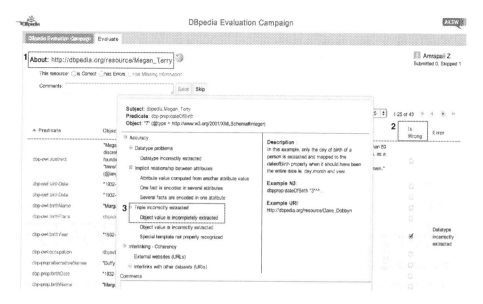

Fig. 1. Screenshot of the TripleCheckMate data quality assessment tool. First, a user chooses a resource. Second, she is displayed with all triples belonging to that resources and evaluates each triple individually to detect quality problems. Third, If she finds a problem, she marks it and associates it with a relevant problem category. A demo[4] and a screencast[5] of the tool are available.

she assigns each incorrect triple to a problem. If the detected problem does not match any of the existing types, she has the option to provide a new type and extend the taxonomy. After evaluating one resource, the user saves the evaluation and proceeds to choosing another random resource and follow the same procedure.

An important feature of the tool is to allow measuring of inter-rater agreements. This means, when a user selects a random method (*Any* or *Class*) to choose a resource, there is a 50% probability that she is presented with a resource that was already evaluated by another user. This probability as well as the number of evaluations per resource is configurable. Allowing many users evaluating a single resource not only helps to determine whether incorrect triples are recognized correctly but also to determine incorrect evaluations (e.g. incorrect classification of problem type or marking correct triples as incorrect), especially when crowdsourcing the quality assessment of resources.

3.2   Architecture

TripleCheckMate is built with *Java* using the *Google Web Toolkit*[6] (GWT) development toolkit. GWT allows one to build and optimize complex browser-based

---

[4] http://nl.dbpedia.org:8080/TripleCheckMate-Demo
[5] http://www.youtube.com/watch?feature=player_embedded&v=l-StthTvjFI
[6] https://developers.google.com/web-toolkit/

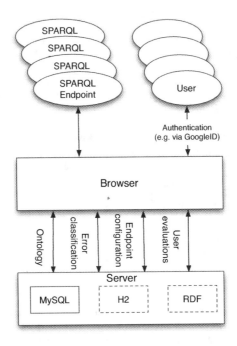

Fig. 2. Architecture of the TripleCheckMate tool

applications as it provides a static typed programming interface (Java) and compiles the output to native cross-browser HTML+Javascript. A Java Web Server (Apache Tomcat or Jetty) is used as a backend along with a MySQL database engine.

Figure 2 depicts the general TripleCheckMate architecture. In order to minimize the dependencies and make TripleCheckMate as portable as possible, all the application logic is built on the frontend. The applications' backend is used only to store and retrieve evaluation related data. The database schema of the backend is depicted in Figure 3.

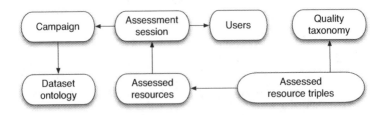

Fig. 3. The backend database schema where the arrows depict the foreign key constrains relations between the tables

When the user enters the application, the available campaign and all the relevant configuration is loaded. In the future we plan to support multiple simultaneous campaigns. The user authentication is performed through the *Google OAuth 2.0*[7] protocol. If the user enters the application for the first time, her entry is transparently stored in the users table. A new session is created every time a user enters the application and all the evaluations in that session are associated. In order to speed-up the *per class* resource selection option, the class hierarchy is cached in the *Dataset ontology* table.

Finally, our data model separates the general resource evaluation (*Assessed resources*) from the detailed triple evaluation (*Assessed resource triples*). The rationale for this are cases where the user wants to mark a resource as completely correct or comment on missing information. In *Assessed resource triples* we store detailed evaluations at the triple level and assign errors to triples based on the *Quality taxonomy*.

Technically, after every complete resource evaluation, the evaluation results are submitted to the server and the user statistics are re-aggregated for an up-to-date contributor ranking. The communication to the server is performed with RPC requests facilitated by the GWT developer toolkit. Finally, for the SPARQL Endpoint communication we implemented a very lightweight client-side SPARQL framework where we encode SPARQL queries in *GET* requests and parse results in the JSON-LD format.

3.3   Extensibility

Although TripleCheckMate was initially built for the purpose of the *DBpedia Evaluation Campaign*, it can meanwhile be easily customized to support any arbitrary (open or closed) dataset with a SPARQL endpoint.

Most of the configurations lie in the database. The SPARQL endpoint configuration is stored in the *campaign* table. The Dataset ontology and *Quality Taxonomy* hold the respective data as tree structures and, thus, can be easily changed to any ontology or taxonomy. The database connection configuration is stored in property files. Finally, visual end-user changes can be performed directly into the HTML and GWT Layout files.

As a data store backend, we support MySQL at the moment, although any JDBC compatible database can be used. The embedded in-memory H2 database is also supported as it provides a JDBC interface. We plan to ship TripleCheckMate with a preconfigured H2 database, as a standalone evaluation tool. Finally, RDF as data store is also a feature our community base expressed interest to implement. [8]

---

[7] https://developers.google.com/accounts/docs/OAuth2

[8] https://groups.google.com/d/topic/dbpedia-data-quality/rkXfR1BR4uY/discussion

4   Conclusions and Future Work

In this paper, we described *TripleCheckMate*, a tool for crowdsourcing the assessment of Linked Data. We discussed the architecture, usability and extensibility of the tool. Additionally, we described a data quality assessment methodology which included a quality problem taxonomy. The methodology and taxonomy are integral parts of the tool. The tool has already been successfully tested in assessing the quality of DBpedia and can be easily configured to work with any dataset that provides a SPARQL endpoint.

In future versions of the tool, we will include further support for the methodology outlined in section 2 by directly integrating semi-automatic methods, which can then filter those triples of a resource, which are most likely to cause problems. We will investigate whether this can improve the efficiency of the quality assessment. Moreover, we also plan to include support for the patch ontology [2] as an output format.

Acknowledgment. This work was supported by grants from the EU's 7th Framework Programme provided for the projects LOD2 (GA no. 257943), DIACHRON (GA no. 601043) and GeoKnow (GA no. 318159).

References

1. Juran, J.: The Quality Control Handbook. McGraw-Hill, New York (1974)
2. Knuth, M., Hercher, J., Sack, H.: Collaboratively patching linked data. CoRR (2012)
3. Lehmann, J., Bizer, C., Kobilarov, G., Auer, S., Becker, C., Cyganiak, R., Hellmann, S.: DBpedia - a crystallization point for the web of data. Journal of Web Semantics 7(3), 154–165 (2009)
4. Lehmann, J., Isele, R., Jakob, M., Jentzsch, A., Kontokostas, D., Mendes, P.N., Hellmann, S., Morsey, M., van Kleef, P., Auer, S., Bizer, C.: Dbpedia - a large-scale, multilingual knowledge base extracted from wikipedia. Semantic Web Journal (under review, 2013)
5. Morsey, M., Lehmann, J., Auer, S., Stadler, C., Hellmann, S.: DBpedia and the Live Extraction of Structured Data from Wikipedia. Program: Electronic Library and Information Systems 46, 27 (2012)
6. Zaveri, A., Kontokostas, D., Sherif, M.A., Bühmann, L., Morsey, M., Auer, S., Lehmann, J.: User-driven quality evaluation of dbpedia. To Appear in Proceedings of 9th International Conference on Semantic Systems, I-SEMANTICS 2013, Graz, Austria, September 4-6. ACM (2013)
7. Zaveri, A., Rula, A., Maurino, A., Pietrobon, R., Lehmann, J., Auer, S.: Quality assessment methodologies for linked open data (under review), http://www.semantic-web-journal.net/content/quality-assessment-methodologies-linked-open-data

Development of an Ontology-Based E-Learning System

Dmitry Mouromtsev, Fedor Kozlov, Olga Parkhimovich, and Maria Zelenina

National Research University of Information Technologies, Mechanics and Optics
St Petersburg, Russia

Abstract. The paper describes the experience on using ontologies and other semantic technologies in e-learning and distant education. The main goal of the project is development of an ontology-based e-learning system to rectify a range of problems which currently exist in the Russian education, including the weak structuring of educational resources and the lack of connections between their individual components. The paper presents the ontology-based model and the platform called *Information Workbench* which are used in the system.

Keywords: e-learning, education, online learning, Semantic Web in education, ontological models of educational programs.

1   Introduction

One of the problems currently existing in the Russian education is the weak structuring of educational resources, or the lack of connection between individual components. Nowadays the ontological approach is used for organization of content of all types, including educational content [1]. This ensures uniformity, consistency and scientific nature in the structuring of data and sources. Another important advantage of the described approach is the ability to use special software for intelligent searching and information processing. It is generally sufficient to apply semantic tagging to existing resources, which generally does not require significant investments to upgrade the entire infrastructure. The so-called triplets – structures in the form of an "object-predicate-subject" model – are usually used in frames of the described approach to formalize different kinds of relation, properties and limitations. The simple model makes it possible to create graphs of concepts, which represent the model of the subject area, which, in turn, enables integration of educational resources into a unified semantic network.

1.1   Examples of Using Semantic Technologies in the Context of Educational Resources

Semantic technologies are being widely implemented in education resources in most developed countries. The most famous projects in the area of educational Linked Data are probably the Linked Universities initiative – an alliance of European universities engaged into exposing their public data as Linked Data [2] and the Open University – a distance learning and research university with over 240.000 students [3].

P. Klinov and D. Mouromtsev (Eds.): KESW 2013, CCIS 394, pp. 273–280, 2013.
© Springer-Verlag Berlin Heidelberg 2013

Some further examples of implementing semantic web technologies in education are outlined below:

1.2   SemUnit

The SemUnit project was initiated by French higher education institutions. This project aims at taking advantages of Semantic Web and Linked Data to improve e-learning services for a wide set of French higher education institutions. In frames of the project, there was developed an OWL ontology taking into account the semantics of LOM elements, as well as the architecture [4].

1.3   LOD.CS.UNIPA – Linked Open Data at the University of Palermo

The main goal of the project is the transformation process of data already available on the web site of the Computer Science curricula web site at the University of Palermo into data ready to be connected to the LOD [5].

1.4   LODUM - Linked Open Data University of Münster

The Linked Open Data University of Münster (LODUM) project establishes a university-wide infrastructure to publish university data as Linked Open Data. The main goals are to increase visibility and accessibility of data produced and collected at the university, and to facilitate effective reuse of these data [6].

1.5   mEducator 3.0

mEducator 3.0 is a content sharing approach for medical education, based on Linked Data principles. Through standardization, it enables sharing and discovery of medical information [7].

It is noticeable that in the latest time, since the 2010th, there is a growth in publications published by Russian scientists, which ascertain usefulness and practicability of the use of semantic web technologies in education [8]. Attempts are made to build prototype systems, but at the moment there are known no fully workable educational environment based on semantic technologies, created on the basis of a Russian university.

The reasons listed above determine the relevance of the project. The ontology-based model and the Information Workbench platform are described below.

2   The Ontology-Based Model

For the presentation and storage of knowledge and data, which are necessary for the functioning of the system, the following series of ontologies were developed:

— Curriculum ontologies that define a set of basic concepts and structure of distant learning courses;
— Test ontologies that provide validation and comparison of tests, which are offered by course tutors to test students' knowledge as well as relevance of the curriculum structure
— Library ontologies, which are used for saving and storage of information about requires and/or suggested readings.

Since the basic ontology of the system is the curriculum ontology, the latter will be presented in detail. For the development of this ontology was used a top-level Academic Institution Internal Structure Ontology (AIISO) [9] hat represents classes and properties of the internal structure of the university. The AIISO ontology contains the following classes: Center, College, Course, Department, Division, Faculty, Institute, Institution, Knowledge Grouping, Module, Programme, Research Group, School, Subject, and Organizational Unit. The main aim of the developed ontology is presenting of a course structuring and providing an automated matching of course modules by defining semantic relations between course topics and terms. In order to fulfill the described tasks and to define concepts which had been not covered by the top-level ontology, the following classes were added: Format, Lesson (5 subclasses), Resource, SubjectArea (1 subclass), Testing Knowledge (6 subclasses). The class Knowledge Grouping was extended. The main classes of the developed ontology are shown in Fig. 1 (the added classes and subclasses are in bold).

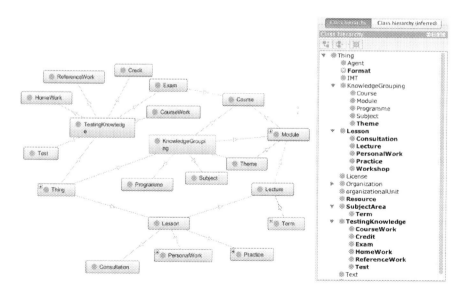

Fig. 1. Main classes of the curriculum ontology

The class "KnowledgeGrouping" is contained in the AIISO ontology and is a set of resources, learning objectives, schedules and other materials. Subclasses of this class are: "Program", "Subject", "Course" and 'Module". It the developed ontology we use subclasses "Course" and "Module". The "Course" subclass contains information about the exam format and about Modules that form the distant course. The 'Module" subclass describes logical (thematic) topics the course can be divided into and about lessons it can contain.

The class "TestingKnowledge" was added for assessment of the knowledge level of students who take the distant course. Subclasses of this class are methods of knowledge assessment and evaluation that are used in the given curriculum, for example, "homework", "individual task", "test", "exam", "term paper" etc.

The class "Lesson" is used for storage information about individual activities – parts of each module. The class contains existing formats of classwork, for example, lectures, practical work, independent work, consultations of the teacher. For example, the 'Lecture" subclass contains information about the topic and the length of each lesson, basic terms that are used in the lesson and necessary materials (lecture notes, video lectures, books).

The ontology also has classes to store data about individual multimedia used in the educational process, the types of activities than ensure successful completion of the course, the order of lectures, classes and assessments etc. These classes expand and complete the developed ontology with the necessary elements of the distant course and also ensure compliance with the SCORM standard [10].

3   The Repository of Educational Ontologies

Deployment of the e-learning system and implementation of the developed ontologies requires a platform (such as a repository) for collecting, storing, editing, reporting, and analysis of educational materials and descriptions of educational processes. It should provide open access to learning materials. Educational materials are stored in the format of structured data (triplets) and are open for external access, in accordance with the principles of Linked Data. The basic platform requirements are:

— Capturing of teaching materials from outside sources and their transformation into the structured format;
— Providing the data to users in a variety of formats (text, graphics, multimedia);
— Providing data to third-party Linked Data (SPARQL-endpoint);
— The ability to edit and create new educational materials and to make alterations to the educational process;
— Linking educational materials with external sources (digital libraries, multimedia resources, social networks);
— Analysis of the relevance of the training materials and courses (update of data obtained from external sources);
— Analysis of the quality of the teaching materials (correspondence of tests and modules, the rating quality system for evaluation of offered materials);
— Search for educational materials;
— Different access rights for different groups of users.

3.1   Reasoning of the Platform Choice

We decided to choose a ready-to-use platform for processing of structured data. We compared the following systems:

Semantic Media Wiki

The Semantic Media Wiki system is the most popular platform for presenting and editing of Open Linked Data. The platform enables representing Linked Data in the form of Wiki-pages and their dynamic generation using the installed templates [11].

OntoWiki

In addition to knowledge representation in form of Wiki-pages the OntoWiki platform has a powerful functionality for creating and editing Linked Data. The platform allows the user to input forms-based data, has an ontology editor and a system of interaction between the data providers (authors) [12].

For development and operation of the portal we used the "Information Workbench" platform (IWB).

The difference of the system from its analogues is the presence of additional functionality beyond the simple representation and editing of structured data. The system has the following features:

— A wide selection of ready to use mechanisms for the collection of structured and unstructured data from external and local sources;
— The possibility of extending the functionality of the platform through the integration of new "widgets", providers and services;
— Support of user access based on group policies
— Maintenance of change log;
— Availability of different ways of structured data representation: Wiki-pages, tables, graphs etc.
— SPARQL-endpoints.

The IWB platforms has functionality of its analogues (Semantic media Wiki, OntoWiki), but provides a wider functionality of collecting Linked Data as well as non-structured data from external resources [13, 14].

3.2   The Following Steps Are Accomplished

Deployment and configuring of a server with Information Workbench system on the basis of NRU ITMO; implementation of the first test learning ontology; loading of test course data (modules, lectures, terms etc) into the system, their visualization in form of Wiki-pages with the use of test, graphics and multimedia data.

Some screenshots of the working platform are given below (Fig. 2-3).

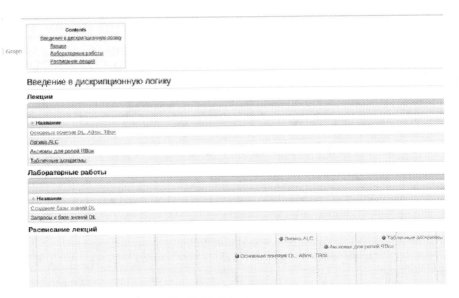

Fig. 2. Module structure

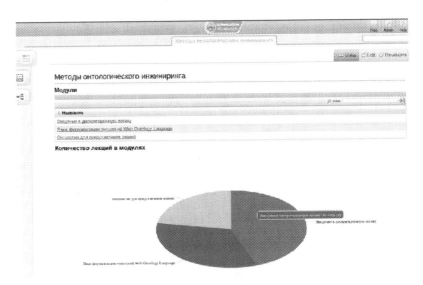

Fig. 3. Course structure

The prototype of the system can be found at http://linkedlearning.tk/.

4   Conclusion and Future Expectations

The goals of the presented project are not limited by creating an ontological e-learning system. Within the frames of the project, NRU ITMO aims at solving a range of strategic problems, such as:

— To implement a Knowledge Management system into the educational process, with ontological knowledge bases as its core elements;
— To encourage students to participate in organization of the educational process and therefore to attract young people to work at the university;
— To conduct PR in the area of creation the newest educational technologies;
— To stimulate the academic student mobility by distant education and joint educational programs;
— Development of educational resources for use not only in NRU ITMO but also with perspective of "transferring" them to other interested educational institutions.

We expect that the project will achieve the following results in the future:

— Understanding of the existing situation and trends on the international level. Projection of the world experience to the Russian environment.
— Forming the vector of development of educational technologies tailored to specific areas of training.
— Demonstration of the functionality of the latest semantic technologies in terms of deploying a prototype of the ontological educational platform for the integration of existing electronic educational resources and adding new ones.
— Illustration of alternative interactive and gaming formats of presenting the educational content.

References

1. Anderson, T., Whitelock, D.: The Educational Semantic Web: Visioning and Practicing the Future of Education. Journal of Interactive Media in Education, Special Issue on the Educational Semantic Web, 1–15 (2004)
2. Linked Universities, http://linkeduniversities.org/lu/
3. The Open University, http://www.open.ac.uk/
4. Isaac, Y., Bourda, Y., Grandbastien, M.: SemUNIT – French UNT and Linked Data. In: The 2nd International Workshop on Learning and Education with the Web of Data at the World Wide Web Conference, Lyon, France (2012)
5. Taibi, D., Panasci, G., Leziti, B.: LOD.CS.UNIPA Project: An experience of LOD at the University of Palermo. In: The 2nd International Workshop on Learning and Education with the Web of Data at the World Wide Web Conference, Lyon, France (2012)
6. Kessler, C., Kauppinen, T.: Linked Open Data University of Muenster - Infrastructure and Applications. In: Demos of the 9th Extended Semantic Web Conference, Heraklion, Greece (2012)
7. Hendrix, M., Protopsaltis, A., Dunwell, I., de Freitas, S., Petridis, P., Arnab, S., Dovrolis, N., Kaldoudi, E., Taibi, D., Dietze, S., Mitsopoulou, E., Spachos, D., Bamidis, P.: Technical Evaluation of The mEducator 3.0 Linked Data-based Environment for Sharing Medical Educational Resources. In: The 2nd International Workshop on Learning and Education with the Web of Data at the World Wide Web Conference, Lyon, France (2012)
8. Hladky, D.: LOD Russia – Enabling Russian National Knowledge with Scientific Open Data. In: Workshop "Web of Linked Entities" at the 11th International Semantic Web Conference, Boston MA (2012)

 9. Academic Institution Internal Structure Ontology (AIISO),
    `http://vocab.org/aiiso/schema`
10. Sharable Content Object Reference Model (SCORM), `http://scorm.com/`
11. Krötzsch, M., Vrandečić, D., Völkel, M.: Semantic mediaWiki. In: Cruz, I., Decker, S.,
    Allemang, D., Preist, C., Schwabe, D., Mika, P., Uschold, M., Aroyo, L.M. (eds.) ISWC
    2006. LNCS, vol. 4273, pp. 935–942. Springer, Heidelberg (2006)
12. Auer, S., Dietzold, S., Riechert, T.: OntoWiki – A tool for social, semantic collaboration.
    In: Cruz, I., Decker, S., Allemang, D., Preist, C., Schwabe, D., Mika, P., Uschold, M.,
    Aroyo, L.M. (eds.) ISWC 2006. LNCS, vol. 4273, pp. 736–749. Springer, Heidelberg
    (2006)
13. Haase, P., Schmidt, M., Schwarte, A.: The Information Workbench as a Self-Service Plat-
    form for Linked Data Applications. In: The 2nd International Workshop on Consuming
    Linked Data, Bonn (2011)
14. Haase, P., et al.: The Information Workbench - Interacting with the Web of Data. Technical
    report, fluid Operations & AIFB Karlsruhe (2009)

Sci-Search: Academic Search and Analysis System Based on Keyphrases

Svetlana Popova[1,2], Ivan Khodyrev[3,4], Artem Egorov[2], Stepan Logvin[2],
Sergey Gulyaev[2], Maria Karpova[2], and Dmitry Mouromtsev[5]

[1] Saint-Petersburg State University, Saint-Petersburg Russia
svp@list.ru
[2] Saint-Petersburg State Polytechnic University, Saint-Petersburg Russia
ARTEGO@fuit.spbstu.ru
[3] Saint-Petersburg State Electrotechnical University, Saint-Petersburg Russia
[4] VISmart, Saint-Petersburg Russia
kivan.mih@gmail.com
[5] Saint Petersburg National Research University of Information Technologies,
Mechanics and Optics, Saint-Petersburg Russia
d.muromtsev@gmail.com

Abstract. Structured data representation allows saving much time during relevant information search and gives a useful view on a domain. It allows researchers to find relevant publications faster and getting insights about tendencies and dynamics of a particular scientific domain as well as finding emerging topics. Sorted lists of search results provided by the popular search engines are not suitable for such a task. In this paper we demonstrate a demo version of a search engine working with abstracts of scientific articles and providing structured representation of information to the user. Keyphrases are used as the basis for processing algorithms and representation. Some algorithm details are described in the paper. A number of test requests and their results are discussed.

Keywords: Representing search results, academic search engine, keyphrase extraction, clustering, indexing, informational retrieval.

1   Introduction

Internet could be considered as a dynamic source of information, which is constantly updating. Possibility to gather and process new data could be used to obtain new knowledge. In the field of science it is especially important. To work efficiently researcher needs to have an overview of the current state of the art in his field, which allows him to choose the strategy of research and save time. However to achieve this goal to have a good searching methods of relevant documents is not enough. In addition, it is important to represent search results in a suitable form for the researcher's needs. In times when the number of online scientific articles grows very fast and a search query usually results in a dozens of relevant documents, the structured presentation of results comes into first plane. In this paper we present an academic search

P. Klinov and D. Mouromtsev (Eds.): KESW 2013, CCIS 394, pp. 281–288, 2013.
© Springer-Verlag Berlin Heidelberg 2013

system (`http://sci-search.uni.me`), which helps in searching scientific articles and presenting the state of a scientific domain.

2   Related Work

Today there exists a number of search engines related to databases of scientific publications: Microsoft Academic Search[1], Scirus[2], CiteSeerX[3], Google Scholar[4] and others. Traditionally, a result of searching requests in these systems is presented as a list of documents. These systems also usually allow facet search. Most of the systems use relevant keyphrases, by clicking on which ones can obtain quite a long list of documents. However, such a list doesn't reflect dynamics of a particular domain and doesn't allow skipping a group of thematically close documents, which currently have no interest. Another problem is a small number of documents for some specific domains making it hard to find information. In this case a list representation would shuffle relevant documents with irrelevant which further confuses researcher. The main goal for our system is to avoid mentioned problems.

Sci-Search search engine is based on active usage of keyphrases. Comparing to lists of words, keyphrases allow not only extract important words, but also reflect the context of their usage. In [1] a search interface using keyphrases for document representation is proposed. Authors show that such presentation is more convenient for end-users. In a search engine Keyphind (Phind) [2] keyphrases were used for indexing. Search results are represents as a list of keyphrases and each keyphrase is associated with a group of documents and other phrases. In [3 - 5] a problem of the searching results clustering is addressed, without focusing on academic search. These approaches use ranked query result lists from search engines like Google and they build keyphrases using only titles and snippets.

In Sci-Search system we integrate keyphrase-based clustering of obtained search results with keyphrase annotations of clusters and documents. To generate keyphrases we use titles of publications and abstracts, based on assumption that abstracts reflect main theme of an article. We extract keywords that are popular in each year and for the whole period for each query. For the most popular keywords, we depict dynamics of their popularity for a given period. We assume that such presentation of search results could help scientists in domain analysis and in search of interesting papers.

3   System Description

The user interface (Fig. 1) contains a number of tabs containing different points of view on the search query results. A list of related keyphrases is shown for every retrieved document. We present results from the "Analytic info" and "Diagrams" tabs,

---

[1] `http://academic.research.microsoft.com`

[2] `http://www.scirus.com`

[3] `http://citeseer.ist.psu.edu/index`

[4] `http://scholar.google.ru`

because they contain demonstrative representation of a query and help user in domain analysis. The "Diagrams" tab illustrates popularity dynamics of twenty most significant keyphrases in documents obtained by request. The "Analytic info" tab returns useful information for analysis of domain area, such information is grouped by year and includes most popular keywords and a set of clusters, annotated with keyphrases. Annotation to each cluster contains two types of keyphrases: phrases occurred in most documents of a cluster and phrases which mostly characterize current cluster and not other clusters. First type helps in identification of thematically interesting groups of documents. Second one allows not to miss more rare but still significant themes. As information is grouped by year, it allows estimation of general dynamics in the domain of search query.

In Sci-Search system all the data, gathered by crawler, is automatically annotated with keyphrases, which are then used in indexing. Clustering algorithm is used on a stage of query results processing.

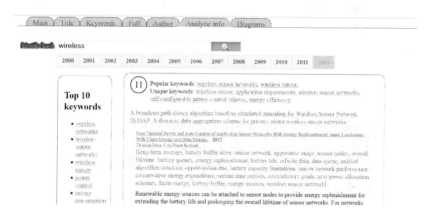

Fig. 1. User interface Sci-Search System

3.1   Extraction of Keyphrases

Nouns and adjectives are the most useful parts of speech to solve a keyphrase extraction problem [6-10]. Additionally we have noticed that in abstracts of scientific articles most multiword sequences of nouns and objectives are strongly related to the general theme of an article. In our research [11] we proposed the simple approach for keyphrase extraction from abstracts of scientific articles having relatively high results comparing to the state of the art. We discuss it in this part. Our approach is based on empiric observation, that among possible keyphrase sequences of nouns and adjectives consisted from only one word, the number of correct keyphrases is much less than in multiword keyphrase. In the same time, the number of one word sequences usually greatly exceeds the number of multiword sequences. Thus, cutting one word sequences allows improving the quality of keyphrases extraction and our experiments proves it. We reduced keyphrase extraction task to the extraction of sequences of nouns and adjectives with length from 2 to 5. Phrases are extracted during the process of consecutive word reading from a document. When a noun or an adjective occurs, the phrase building begins. It finishes with the occurrence of a word being not noun or adjective, or a punctuation mark, or when phrase length reaches 5 words. In any of these cases the built phrase is added to the list of keyphrases (if the phrase has the length of at least 2 words) and a parser waits for a next occurrence of noun or adjective. For part-of-speech tagging we used Stanford POS tagging tool[5]. All our experiments in [11] were conducted on Inspec dataset [6], [7], [10] containing scientific abstracts and a golden standard of keyphrases for each document (keyphrases extracted by experts). We compared results of our algorithm with the golden standard. F-measure to evaluate the quality of our results was used [6]. For proposed algorithm F-measure=0.40 improves results from [6, 7] and is computationally more simple. Our approach also doesn't need a machine learning as, for example, Kea used in [2]. Table 1 contains examples of abstracts and automatically extracted keyphrases.

Table 1. Examples of automatic extracted keyphrases

Abstracts	Keyphrases
A frequency-tunable and switched beam antenna is proposed. Variable capacitances are loaded to monopole antenna elements and switch the radiation beam as well as the frequency band. Numerical results of the frequency band and beam pattern of the proposed antenna are shown with varying the value of variable capacitances.	*beam antenna, radiation beam, frequency band, antenna elements, beam pattern, variable capacitances, disaster-resilient wireless*
In recent ten years, wireless sensor network technology has a rapid development. After a brief introduction of the wireless sensor network, some main research results of energy conservation and node deployment is provided. Then the applications of WSN in the medical health, environment and agriculture, intelligent home furnishing and building, military, space and marine exploration are outlined. In addition, we analyze the advantage of WSN in these areas. Finally, we summarize the main factors that affect the applications of wireless sensor network	*wireless sensor network technology, wireless sensor, brief introduction, medical health, node deployment, energy conservation, marine exploration, intelligent home furnishing, main research results, rapid development, main factors, wireless sensor network*

In Sci-Search system we are using additional list of stop-phrases, such as: «previous approaches», «other hand», «last works», etc. It was built by an expert using frequency statistics of most used phrases in scientific abstracts. We didn't make a difference between phrases being identical after stemming or containing different word order in a phrase. For stemming we divided phrases into single words and used a Porter stemmer[6].

3.2   Clustering

For clustering we used an algorithm based on k-means variation. Each document was represented as a set of keyphrases. On first stage, the cluster centroids were built.

---

[5] http://nlp.stanford.edu/software/tagger.shtml
[6] http://tartarus.org/martin/PorterStemmer

Each centroid is a set of keyphrases. At first algorithm runs through all documents and if a set of keyphrases doesn't have an intersection with other centroids with more than one phrase, then this set of keyphrases becomes centroid itself. When the first generation of centroids is built, similar of each document to each centroid are calculated and documents are distributed among centroids according to the most similarity. We have used Jaccard index for similarity calculation:

$$\text{Jaccard} = \frac{A \cap D}{A \cup D}, \tag{1}$$

where A — is a set of keyphrases in a centroid, D — set of keyphrases which represent document. After documents are distributed among clusters, centroid recalculation takes place. New centroids are built as sets of keyphrases, which occurred not less than in 2/3 documents of a cluster. If centroid contains less than 2 keyphrases, it is deleted. When new centroids are built, documents are distributed among clusters with new centroids. Such process is repeated 5 times. Clusters obtained on last iteration are considered as a result.

3.3   Annotation of Clusters with Keyphrases

We used two types of annotations for clusters, which are separately shown to a user. First type ("Popular keywords") reflects main theme of a cluster. To form it, from all keyphrases not more than five most frequent phrases are selected. Each of selected phrases had to occur in more than a half of the documents of a cluster. If a cluster is rather small and there are no phrases fully occured in other documents, then the cluster is represented by a zero number of keyphrases. Second type of annotations ("Unique keywords") should allow finding unique documents characterizing current cluster but not any others. Phrases were selected by weight calculated using formula: N/R where N is a number of documents with that phrase in a cluster and R is a number of documents with that phrase in other clusters.

4   System Demonstration

To obtain data for a test demonstration, the crawler was written gathering data for the theme "the theory of automatic control". The source of data is DBLP[7]. Abstracts of publications were taken from sites of electronic libraries, if a link on DBLP page were provided for a particular paper. For the system demonstration more than 13,000 articles were extracted and processed. We show examples of searching results on tabs "Analytic info" and "Diagrams". Two queries were processed and the results are depicted in Table 2 and Fig. 2 for queries "wireless" and "robot". In Table 2 data about clusters with two types of keywords is presented. First type is called "Popular keywords" and it reflects frequent keyphrases in a cluster, second type, "Unique

---

[7] http://www.dblp.org

keywords", reflects keywords, which are frequent for this particular cluster and rare for other clusters. Top 10 keyphrases in 2012 year for queries: "wireless" (wireless networks, wireless sensor networks, wireless sensor, power control, energy consumption, interference model, topology control, link scheduling, optimal control, topology control algorithm) and "robot" (mobile robot, humanoid robot, robotic systems, robot manipulators, multi-robot system, robot arm, real robot, real time, robot hand, energy consumption). Fig. 2 depict examples from "Diagram" tab containing usage dynamics of 20 the most popular keywords, related to the query depending on a year and a percentage of documents where they are used among other documents. Fig. 3 represents documents from two clusters for query "wireless" in 2012 year.

Table 2. Clusters and cluster's keyphrases for queries "wireless" and "robot" in 2012 year

Query: "wirelss"	Query: "robot"
Cluster size and cluster's keyphrases	*Cluster's keyphrases*
Cluster size: 11 **Popular keywords**: wireless sensor networks, wireless sensor. **Unique keywords**: wireless sensor, energy efficiency, wireless sensor networks, self-configurable power control scheme, application requirements.	Cluster size: 10 **Popular keywords**: mobile robot. **Unique keywords**: fuse different directional identification results, directional information, mobile robot, bandwidth allocation, results identification.
Cluster size: 4 **Popular keywords**: interference model, link scheduling, individual nodes, wireless networks, important goals. **Unique keywords**: stochastic arrival processes, maximum feasible traffic, interference model, overall network topology, important goals.	Cluster size: 5 **Popular keywords**: robotic systems. **Unique keywords**: power plants, scientific knowledge, hierarchical fashion, promising applications, new actions.
Cluster size: 3 **Popular keywords**: energy consumption, network lifetime. **Unique keywords**: local information, multi-hop communication, low-delay route, initial topology, interference reduction.	Cluster size: 5 **Popular keywords**: humanoid robot. **Unique keywords**: compensatory head/eye movements, modular framework, low throughput, brain-computer interfaces, simple form.
Cluster size: 3 **Popular keywords**: wireless networks, power control, link rates. **Unique keywords**: link rates, weighted max-min rate fairness problem, profit maximization, rate max-min fairness, piecewise linear link rate.	Cluster size: 4 **Popular keywords**: energy consumption. **Unique keywords**: energy consumption, stochastic force fields, average power consumption, energy consumption model, angular velocity.

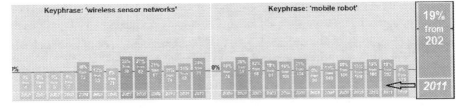

Fig. 2. Dynamics of keyphrases "wireless sensor networks" and "mobile robot" for queries "wireless" and "robot" since 2000 in "Diagrams" tab. Each column contains information about the percentage of documents which contain the phrase to the number of found documents for a particular year.

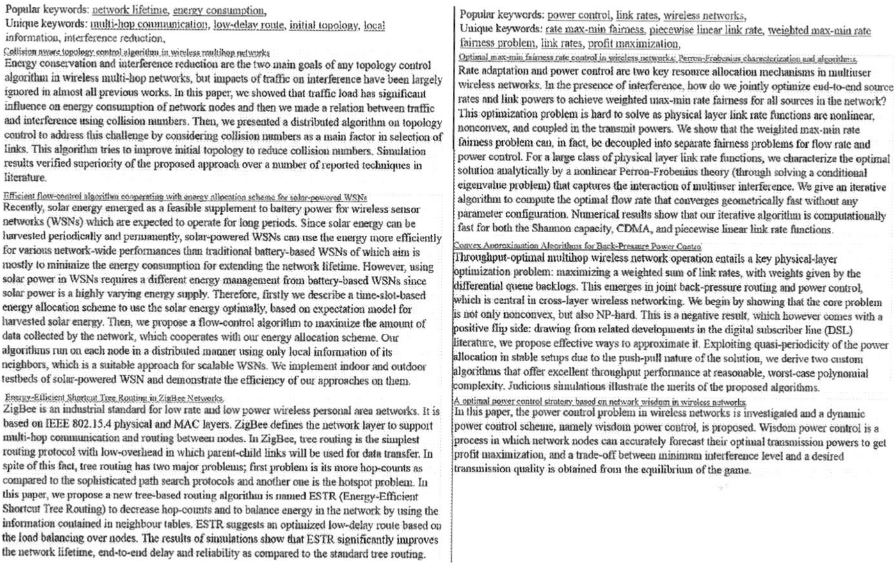

Popular keywords: network lifetime, energy consumption,
Unique keywords: multi-hop communication, low-delay route, initial topology, local information, interference reduction,

Collision aware topology control algorithm in wireless multihop networks

Energy conservation and interference reduction are the two main goals of any topology control algorithm in wireless multi-hop networks, but impacts of traffic on interference have been largely ignored in almost all previous works. In this paper, we showed that traffic load has significant influence on energy consumption of network nodes and then we made a relation between traffic and interference using collision numbers. Then, we presented a distributed algorithm on topology control to address this challenge by considering collision numbers as a main factor in selection of links. This algorithm tries to improve initial topology to reduce collision numbers. Simulation results verified superiority of the proposed approach over a number of reported techniques in literature.

Efficient flow-control algorithm cooperating with energy allocation scheme for solar-powered WSNs

Recently, solar energy emerged as a feasible supplement to battery power for wireless sensor networks (WSNs) which are expected to operate for long periods. Since solar energy can be harvested periodically and permanently, solar-powered WSNs can use the energy more efficiently for various network-wide performances than traditional battery-based WSNs of which aim is mostly to minimize the energy consumption for extending the network lifetime. However, using solar power in WSNs requires a different energy management from battery-based WSNs since solar power is a highly varying energy supply. Therefore, firstly we describe a time-slot-based energy allocation scheme to use the solar energy optimally, based on expectation model for harvested solar energy. Then, we propose a flow-control algorithm to maximize the amount of data collected by the network, which cooperates with our energy allocation scheme. Our algorithms run on each node in a distributed manner using only local information of its neighbors, which is a suitable approach for scalable WSNs. We implement indoor and outdoor testbeds of solar-powered WSN and demonstrate the efficiency of our approaches on them.

Energy-Efficient Shortcut Tree Routing in ZigBee Networks

ZigBee is an industrial standard for low rate and low power wireless personal area networks. It is based on IEEE 802.15.4 physical and MAC layers. ZigBee defines the network layer to support multi-hop communication and routing between nodes. In ZigBee, tree routing is the simplest routing protocol with low-overhead in which parent-child links will be used for data transfer. In spite of this fact, tree routing has two major problems; first problem is its more hop-counts as compared to the sophisticated path search protocols and another one is the hotspot problem. In this paper, we propose a new tree-based routing algorithm is named ESTR (Energy-Efficient Shortcut Tree Routing) to decrease hop-counts and to balance energy in the network by using the information contained in neighbour tables. ESTR suggests an optimized low-delay route based on the load balancing over nodes. The results of simulations show that ESTR significantly improves the network lifetime, end-to-end delay and reliability as compared to the standard tree routing.

Popular keywords: power control, link rates, wireless networks,
Unique keywords: rate max-min fairness, piecewise linear link rate, weighted max-min rate fairness problem, link rates, profit maximization,

Optimal max-min fairness rate control in wireless networks: Perron-Frobenius characterization and algorithms

Rate adaptation and power control are two key resource allocation mechanisms in multiuser wireless networks. In the presence of interference, how do we jointly optimize end-to-end source rates and link powers to achieve weighted max-min rate fairness for all sources in the network? This optimization problem is hard to solve as physical layer rate functions are nonlinear, nonconvex, and coupled in the transmit powers. We show that the weighted max-min rate fairness problem can, in fact, be decoupled into separate fairness problems for flow rate and power control. For a large class of physical layer link rate functions, we characterize the optimal solution analytically by a nonlinear Perron-Frobenius theory (through solving a conditional eigenvalue problem) that captures the interaction of multiuser interference. We give an iterative algorithm to compute the optimal flow rate that converges geometrically fast without any parameter configuration. Numerical results show that our iterative algorithm is computationally fast for both the Shannon capacity, CDMA, and piecewise linear link rate functions.

Convex Approximation Algorithms for Back-Pressure Power Control

Throughput-optimal multihop wireless network operation entails a key physical-layer optimization problem: maximizing a weighted sum of link rates, with weights given by the differential queue backlogs. This emerges in joint back-pressure routing and power control, which is central in cross-layer wireless networking. We begin by showing that the core problem is not only nonconvex, but also NP-hard. This is a negative result, which however comes with a positive flip side: drawing from related developments in the digital subscriber line (DSL) literature, we propose effective ways to approximate it. Exploiting quasi-periodicity of the power allocation in stable setups due to the push-pull nature of the solution, we derive two custom algorithms that offer excellent throughput performance at reasonable, worst-case polynomial complexity. Judicious simulations illustrate the merits of the proposed algorithms.

A optimal power control strategy based on network wisdom in wireless networks

In this paper, the power control problem in wireless networks is investigated and a dynamic power control scheme, namely wisdom power control, is proposed. Wisdom power control is a process in which network nodes can accurately forecast their optimal transmission powers to get profit maximization, and a trade-off between minimum interference level and a desired transmission quality is obtained from the equilibrium of the game.

Fig. 3. Contents of two clusters for the query "wireless" in 2012 year (size of each cluster is 3 documents)

5   Discussion and Conclusion

Data collected and processed in the system gives an insight on what happened in a particular scientific domain during some period. Such information could be useful in educational and academic purposes when somebody wants to understand state of the art in a particular area and its dynamics. Formed clusters, described in tables, allow to group thematically close documents reducing a task o scientific domain search task to the search of useful cluster. Cluster annotations allow evaluating related specific themes. Main themes of a search query domain could be extracted using 10 most popular keywords, built for a particular year. Diagrams allow identifying frequently used keyphrases, depending on a year and a percentage of documents where it is used.

Now there are some limitations of the system demo-version: Sci-Search contains information about 13000 papers taken from DBLP and related to the "theory of automatic control" domain. We are planning to increase paper coverage greatly. Now such a small size of a database is a reason of a small number of documents resulted in a query. Cluster forming algorithm dealing with a small number of documents could lead to a poor quality of clustering. However, Pic. 3 and a manual look through the list of clusters in system shows their adequacy, and we assume that it shows perceptiveness of the proposed approach.

Another limitation of our approach is that it is more suitable for professionals in a particular domain rather than for newcomers. For the last category of researchers it is more important to find main articles from a domain to get insights on what does the particular keyphrase mean, because they could mean different things such as simply co-occurring terms, sub-fields of a particular domain or different approaches, which just occur together frequently in documents. We assume that some kind of a visualization technique could improve a novice user experience and we are planning to work on it in later releases.

Another challenge for Sci-Search system is filtering of commonly used phrases, such as "important goals", "application requirements", "promising applications" etc. Such filtering could be done using stop-phrases list, however now it contains not much phrases and will be updated in the future. In addition, we are planning to implement an algorithm detecting such phrases automatically and filtering them. We assume that it will increase clustering and annotating quality as well single document annotations with keyphrases.

Acknowledgments. This work is supported by the federal target program "Kadry". The program Research project 16.740.11.0751. Code of competition 2011-1.2.1-302-031. Code of application 2011-1.2.1-302-031/5.

References

1. Li, Q., Bot, R.S., Chen, X.: Incorporating Document Keyphrases. In: The 10th Americas Conference on Information Systems, New York (2004)
2. Gutwina, C., Paynterb, G., Wittenb, I., Nevill-Manningc, C., Frankb, E.: Improving browsing in digital libraries with keyphrase indexes. Journal of Decision Support Systems 27(1-2), 81–104 (1999)
3. Bernardini, A., Carpineto, C.: Full-Subtopic Retrieval with Keyphrase-Based Search Results Clustering. In: Web Intelligence and Intelligent Agent Technologies (2009)
4. Zhang, D., Dong, Y.: Semantic, hierarchical, online clustering of web search results. In: Yu, J.X., Lin, X., Lu, H., Zhang, Y. (eds.) APWeb 2004. LNCS, vol. 3007, pp. 69–78. Springer, Heidelberg (2004)
5. Zeng, H.J., He, Q.C., Chen, Z., Ma, W.Y., Ma, J.: Learning to cluster web search results. In: The 27th Annual International ACM SIGIR Conference on Research and Development in Information Retrieval, pp. 210–217 (2004)
6. Hulth, A.: Improved automatic keyword extraction given more linguistic knowledge. In: Conference on Empirical Methods in Natural Language Processing, pp. 216–223 (2003)
7. Mihalcea, R., Tarau, P.: TextRank: Bringing order into texts. In: Conference on Empirical Methods in Natural Language Processing, pp. 404–411 (2004)
8. Kim, S.N., Medelyan, O., Yen, M.: Automatic keyphrase extraction from scientific articles. Language Resources and Evaluation, Springer Kan & Timothy Baldwin (2012)
9. Xiaojun, W., Xiao, J.: Exploiting Neighborhood Knowledge for Single Document Summarization and Keyphrase Extraction ACM Transactions on Information Systems 28(2), Article 8 (2010)
10. Zesch, T., Gurevych, I.: Approximate Matching for Evaluating Keyphrase Extraction. In: International Conference RANLP 2009, Borovets, Bulgaria, pp. 484–489 (2009)
11. Popova, S., Khodyrev, I.: Ranking in keyphrase extraction problem: is it useful to use statistics of words occurrences? Proceedings of the Kazan University Journal (2013)

Semantically-Enabled Environmental Data Discovery and Integration: Demonstration Using the Iceland Volcano Use Case*

Tatiana Tarasova[1], Massimo Argenti[2], and Maarten Marx[1]

[1] ISLA, University of Amsterdam, Science Park 904, 1098 XH Amsterdam
{t.tarasova,maartenmarx}@uva.nl
[2] ESA, European Space Agency, ViaGalileo Galilei, 00044 Frascati, Rome

Abstract. We present a framework for semantically-enabled data discovery and integration across multiple Earth science disciplines. We leverage well-known vocabularies and ontologies to build semantic models for both metadata and data harmonization. Built upon standard guidelines, our metadata model extends them with richer semantics. To harmonize data, we implement an observation-centric data model based on the RDF Data Cube vocabulary. Previous works define the Data Cube extensions which are relevant to certain Earth science disciplines. To provide a generic and domain independent solution, we propose an upper level vocabulary that allows us to express domain specific information at a higher level of abstraction.

From a human viewpoint we provide an interactive Web based user interface for data discovery and integration across multiple research infrastructures. We will demonstrate the system on a use case of the Iceland Volcano's eruption on April 10, 2010.

Keywords: Earth Science, data integration, ontology, RDF Data Cube vocabulary.

1 Introduction

Environmental data is provided and consumed by different Earth science communities. To find relevant data and combine it into a single data product for further analysis, one needs to solve multiple issues arising from different types of data heterogeneity. The most difficult integration problems are caused by semantic data heterogeneity [1] which comes from the mismatch in terminology. In order to be able to discover relevant data and further integrate it with other data, one has to be aware and understand the meaning of specific terms used in different scientific disciplines for data description. This task becomes very challenging in the interdisciplinary setting of environmental research, where scientists work with data that spans multiple disciplines, including the disciplines

* This work was supported by the EU-FP7 (FP7/2007-2013) project ENVRI (grant number 283465).

© Springer-Verlag Berlin Heidelberg 2013

in which they are not very well trained. Indeed, a geologist is unlikely to be aware of what specific instruments were used to measure the ocean temperature, or what are the units of measure used in the atmospheric domain.

In the context of the European project, Common Operations of Environmental Research Infrastructures (ENVRI)[1], we are developing a system for environmental data discovery and integration across multiple disciplines. We performed the metadata and data harmonization tasks, and our contributions relate to both tasks. The result of the metadata harmonization process is the Geospatial metadata model in RDF[2]. The harmonization of data was based on two components: (i) the RDF Data Cube vocabulary [12] and (ii) the ENVRI vocabulary, the upper level vocabulary to align domain semantics. Data Cube provides an observation-centric model that allows one to represent and interlink observations as single entities, instead of operating with whole files or databases that contain these observations. On top of such granular representation, one can construct queries to retrieve and combine single observations from various data sources. The use of the RDF Data Cube vocabulary for environmental data representation was already considered in previous works. However, they were limited to specific Earth science domains. Instead, in our work we define an upper level vocabulary that provides generic terms to describe environmental observations. We use this vocabulary to plug in various existing domain ontologies and vocabularies to provide domain specific information.

In the rest of the paper, we overview the related work in Section 2. Section 3 describes our system. In Section 4 we explain how we will present the system through a live demonstration, and conclude with a discussion of the challenging components of the system and the future work in Section 5.

2   Related Work

In our work we employ the ontology-based approach to resolve semantic heterogeneity of data coming from multiple Earth science disciplines. The application of ontologies to align semantics of environmental data is considered in a number of previous works such as [8,5,2,3,4]. What makes our work different from these efforts is a modelling approach. We model environmental observations as separate entities, whereas, the mentioned works consider collections of observations as they were grouped by data providers, e.g., data files, databases, etc. As a result, we provide more granular representation of environmental data and more flexible ways of querying and integrating the data. Our modelling approach was inspired by the RDF Data Cube vocabulary [12]. Data Cube was designed as a generic framework to publish multi-dimensional data in RDF. In the following we overview the existing efforts on modelling environmental data using the RDF Data Cube vocabulary.

---

[1] http://envri.eu/
[2] RDF stands for the Resource Description Framework
   http://www.w3.org/TR/rdf-concepts/

The Linked Environmental Data (LED) initiative[3] was established to contribute to the publication and integration of environmental data sets as Linked Data[4]. The result of this work was the publication of the Environmental Specimen Bank (ESB)[5] as Linked Data [7]. To provide semantic interoperability of the data, they use the RDF Data Cube vocabulary as a global framework that captures structural semantics of environmental data. They adopt a set of domain ontologies to encode information of various application domains. These ontologies are plugged into the global ontology through a set of predefined properties proposed in [9]. We implement a similar ontological framework based on Data Cube and a set of domain ontologies. While the LED initiative defines properties specific for publication of the ESB data, such as *specimen* and *substance*, we define a set of generic properties, which can be used to describe any kind of environmental data.

Other examples of the environmental Linked Data integration come from the UK government[6] which released the measurements of bathing water quality as Linked Data. Data Cube was also used to structure these measurements, but for the specific information about bathing-waters, e.g., zones of influence and sampling points, custom vocabularies were developed. The bathing-waters measurements were linked to the UK Ordnance Survey data published earlier as Linked Data[7]. This demonstrates how other Linked Data sets can be used in order to enrich environmental data. The interlinked data sets were used to build a map visualization of the water measurements[8].

3   Description of the System

Our system allows environmental scientists to discover and integrate heterogeneous data coming from different environmental infrastructures. The entry point for users is the ENVRI portal http://portal.envri.eu/. There are two paths for data discovery: (i) syntactic search using time windows, bounding box and free text search, and (ii) semantic search using a tree view to select terms from the existing Earth Science ontologies and vocabularies. The results of the user's queries are shown in the portal listing the data series and all the data sets contained in each data series. The user can proceed to access the proper data set or request data integration. Next, we discuss two components of our system: (1) Open Search and Semantics (OSS) (in Section 3.1) and Linked Data Integration (LID) (in Section 3.2).

---

[3] https://github.com/innoq/iqvoc/wiki/Linked-Environment-Data

[4] The term of Linked Data refers to a set of principles introduced by T. Berners-Lee in http://www.w3.org/DesignIssues/LinkedData.html

[5] http://www.innoq.com/de/referenzen/upbweb

[6] http://data.gov.uk/linked-data

[7] http://data.ordnancesurvey.co.uk/

[8] The map is available at http://environment.data.gov.uk/bwq/explorer/

3.1 Open Search and Semantics (OSS)

The OSS architecture is illustrated in Fig.1. There are two main services implemented by the OSS component: data discovery and semantic tagging.

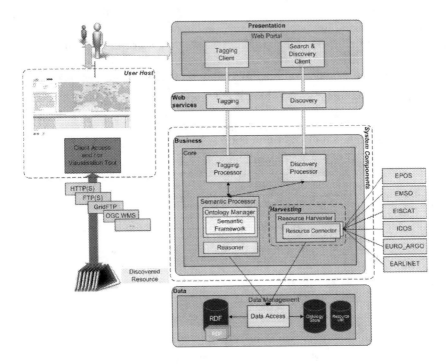

Fig. 1. The Open Search and Semanitcs subsystem

Data Discovery. Data discovery is performed by users through syntactic or
semantic search. Semantic search is enabled by the ENVRI metadata catalogue
which was the result of the metadata harmonization process. During the metadata harmonization, we developed the Geospatial metadata model[9]. We followed
the guidelines suggested by the Infrastructure for Spatial Information in the
European Community (INSPIRE) [11]. Our model extends the guidelines with
richer semantics by re-using classes and properties from well-known ontologies,
such as the DCLite4G vocabulary[10] and the Friend of a Friend vocabulary[11].

Semantic Tagging. Semantic tagging is the supporting activity to enable semantic data discovery. The following Earth science ontologies and vocabularies
were integrated into the Geospatial metadata model:

---

[9] The model is described at http://portal.genesi-dec.eu/news/?id=117

[10] http://dclite4g.xmlns.com/

[11] http://xmlns.com/foaf/spec/

- The Global Change Master Directory (GCMD)[12]
- The GEneral Multilingual Environmental Thesaurus (GEMET)[13]
- The Societal Benefit Area vocabularies (SBA)[14]

This tagging is performed automatically during the harvesting phase to start the knowledge base population. Manual tagging is also available to extend the automatically generated knowledge base. For instance, automatic tagging during harvesting identifies series of vegetation data within the *Agriculture* subcategory of the SBA vocabulary. Additional tagging of this data can be performed depending on the underlying use case. Consider, for example, scientists who investigate the impact of a volcano eruption. They might be interested in studying the changes in vegetation in the region of the Volcano. Thus, they can proceed with manual tagging using terms from the vocabulary which is more familiar for them, e.g., the SBA *Disasters* subcategory or the GCMD *Human Dimensions/Environmental impacts* category.

Implementation. The data is discovered through the OpenSearch standard protocol[15]. The semantic infrastructure is based on SESAME[16] where the repository of the registered data catalogues is located. In total, the repository contains 288.971 triples generated for 1350 data series from several research infrastructures, including the Integrated Carbon Observation System (ICOS)[17], Euro-Argo[18] and others indicated in Fig. 1.

3.2   Linked Data Integration (LDI)

The architecture of the LDI subsystem is illustrated by Fig. 2. The main goal of LDI is to provide a unified view of the structure and semantics of heterogeneous environmental data. The core LDI components are the RDF Data Cube vocabulary and the ENVRI vocabulary which were the results of the data harmonization process.

During the data harmonization process we built a model that captures structural and domain semantics of environmental data. We considered two standards: the RDF Data Cube vocabulary[19] [12], and the Observation and Measurement (O&M) model[20] [10].

Data Cube defines concepts that express structural semantics of environmental data, such as observation, metadata property and data set, but it does not

---

[12] http://gcmd.nasa.gov/

[13] http://www.eionet.europa.eu/gemet/

[14] http://www.earthobservations.org/

[15] http://www.opensearch.org/

[16] http://www.openrdf.org/

[17] https://icos-atc-demo.lsce.ipsl.fr/homepage

[18] http://www.argodatamgt.org/

[19] The vocabulary is currently a W3C candidate recommendation.

[20] The O&M model is a joint Open Geospatial Consortium (OGC) and ISO standard 19156.

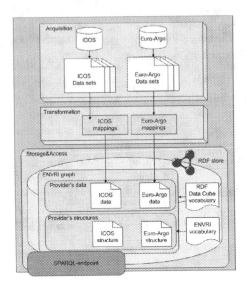

Fig. 2. LDI architecture

provide domain specific terms. To define a source of common domain specific terms, we identify basic terms that are used to describe environmental observations, e.g., feature of interest, procedure and unit of measure. For this, we refer to the O&M model. The terms were used to construct the ENVRI vocabulary[21] which serves as an upper-level vocabulary for semantic alignment between various domain ontologies and vocabularies that we re-use. For example, the generic class *Unit of Measure* was populated with instances *Degree Celsius* and *Parts Per Million*, which are (respectively) units of measure of the ocean temperature and the CO2 concentration in the atmosphere. Among other resources, that we re-used to encode domain specific information, are the W3C Time Ontology in OWL[22] to represent temporal information, and the GeoSPARQL vocabulary[23], the OGC standard to represent and query geographic information.

Implementation. For the demonstration we acquired data from two environmental research infrastructures: ICOS and Euro-Argo (cf. the data acquisition in Fig. 2). ICOS provides measurements of the CO2 concentration in the air. Euro-Argo provides observations of the ocean temperature. In total, 35 data collections were obtained with 10520 observations which resulted in 136556 RDF triples. The RDF representation was generated from the original text files using the terms of the vocabularies and ontologies which we discussed above. The generation was done in a semi-automatic manner using the RDF Data Cube

---

[21] The ENVRI vocabulary is published at `http://data.politicalmashup.nl/RDF/vocabularies/envri`

[22] `http://www.w3.org/TR/owl-time/`

[23] `http://www.opengeospatial.org/standards/geosparql`

plug-in for Google Refine[24]. The Virtuoso native RDF store[25] was used to store the RDF representation of the data and expose it through the public SPARQL-endpoint available at `http://data.politicalmashup.nl/sparql/`. More detailed description of the data transformations can be found at `http://staff.science.uva.nl/~ttaraso1/html/envri.html`

4   Demonstration Overview

The demonstration will be based on the "Iceland Volcano" use case: "An environmental scientist wants to discover the specific event of the Eyjafjallajokull Volcano outburst in April 10, 2010 in various data sets and see if correlations are relevant".

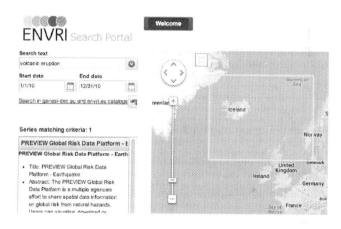

Fig. 3. The ENVRI portal

We will divide our demonstration into two parts. In the first part we will show how data can be searched on our portal using both syntactic and semantic searches:

1. We will show how to construct a search query using the graphical user interface[26] illustrated in Fig. 3 and interact with the ENVRI portal to adjust the search query. We will use three search areas: time windows, bounding box and free text search to construct a search query that retrieves data from year 2010 that was collected in the area near the Iceland Volcano and that was automatically tagged with the term *volcanic eruption*.
2. We will demonstrate how to perform manual tagging on our portal. For this, we will tag with *volcanic eruption* the ocean temperature data that was not tagged automatically. We will then show how the data can be discovered

---

[24] `http://refine.deri.ie/qbExport`

[25] `http://virtuoso.openlinksw.com/dataspace/doc/dav/wiki/Main/`

[26] Due to the space restriction, we include only one screenshot from the ENVRI portal.

using the semantic search functionality of the ENVRI portal by browsing through the available Earth science vocabularies.

In the second part of our demonstration we will show how the data from various data sets can be integrated into a single data product. We will demonstrate execution of a number of queries across the data sources registered at the ENVRI portal, e.g., *"Retrieve all the observations for the days of the Volcano eruption (from 20 March to 23 June, 2010)."*. We will present the underlying SPARQL queries and discuss the usage of the RDF Data Cube vocabulary and the ENVRI vocabulary in the integration process.

5 Conclusions and Future Work

We presented the ENVRI portal for semantically-enabled Earth science data discovery and integration. Our main contributions are (i) the metadata harmonization model which was defined as an extension to the INSPIRE guidelines, and (ii) the data harmonization model which is built on top of the RDF Data Cube approach and the ENVRI vocabulary. We believe that Data Cube brings interesting possibilities for data integration. For example, in the Iceland Volcano use case, the scientist was interested in data provided by several institutes *during specific time period*. The ICOS data is organized by atmospheric stations which perform measurements. In order to retrieve all relevant ICOS data, each data collection has to be examined. Similar situation was with the Euro-Argo observations that were provided in separate collections grouped according to the float that performed measurements. With Data Cube, we were able to automatically perform the task of retrieving and integrating measurements from all these ICOS and Euro-Argo data collections.

The works underlying the metadata and data harmonization processes were carried out separately. The challenging task for us now is to align two harmonization models. We observe that the ENVRI vocabulary contains top level abstract concepts, such as *monitoring facility*, whereas the metadata harmonization model contains more specific instances of this concept, e.g., *platform* and *instrument*. We will further investigate the possibility of plugging in the ENVRI vocabulary to the metadata catalogue.

One of the drawback of the observation-centric representation is the amount of RDF triples it generates. This becomes impractical in the Earth science domain where data volume amounts to terabytes or petabytes of data. To the best of our knowledge, there is no work related to the adoption of the RDF Data Cube vocabulary for such big amounts of data. We plan to address this issue in our work by reducing the amount of data to be transformed to Data Cube at the step of data discovery.

References

1. Ziegler, P., Dittrich, K.R.: Three Decades of Data Integration - All Problems Solved? In: 18th IFIP World Computer Congress, WCC 2004 (2004)

2. McGuinness, D., Fox, P., Cinquini, L., West, P., Garcia, J., Benedict, J., Middleton, D.: The virtual solar-terrestrial observatory: A deployed semantic web application case study for scientific research. In: Proceedings of the 19th National Conference on Innovative Applications of Artificial Intelligence (2007)
3. Rezgui, A., Malik, Z., Sihna, A.K.: DIA Engine: Semantic Discovery, Integration, and Analysis of Earth Science Data. In: Proceedings of the Geoinformatics Conference (2007)
4. Sinha, A.K., Malik, Z., Rezgui, A., Dalton, A.: Developing the ontologic framework and tools for the discovery and integration of Earth science data. Cyberinfrastructure Research at Virginia Tech (2006)
5. Raskin, R., Pan, M.: Semantic Web for Earth and Environmental Terminology (SWEET). In: Proc. of the Workshop on Semantic Web Technologies for Searching and Retrieving Scientific Data (2003)
6. Bizer, C., Heath, T., Idehen, K., Berners-Lee, T.: Linked Data: Evolving the Web into a Global Data Space, vol. 1. ACM Press (2008), http://linkeddatabook.com/editions/1.0/
7. Rüther, M., Fock, J., Hubener, J.: Linked Environmental Data. In: 24th International Conference on Informatics for Environmental Protection (2010)
8. Pundt, H., Bishr, Y.: Domain ontologies for data sharing - an example from environmental monitoring using field GIS. Journal on Computers & Geoscience 1(28), 95–102 (2002)
9. Rüther, M., Bandholtz, T., Schulte-Coerne, T.: Linked Environment Data: SCOVO-fying the Environment Specimen Bank. In: ESWC (2009)
10. Geographic Information: Observations and Measurements. OGC Abstract Specification, http://www.opengeospatial.org/standards/om
11. State of progress in the development of guidelines to express elements of the INSPIRE metadata implementing rules using ISO 15836 (Dublin Core). European Commission (2008), http://inspire.jrc.ec.europa.eu/reports/ImplementingRules/metadata/MD_IR_and_DC_state
12. The Data Cube vocabulary, http://www.w3.org/TR/2013/WD-vocab-data-cube-20130312/

Author Index